JOHN STUART MILL, SOCIALIST

JOHN STUART MILL

Socialist

Helen McCabe

McGill-Queen's University Press
Montreal & Kingston · London · Chicago

© McGill-Queen's University Press 2021

ISBN 978-0-2280-0573-5 (cloth)
ISBN 978-0-2280-0574-2 (paper)
ISBN 978-0-2280-0593-3 (ePDF)
ISBN 978-0-2280-0594-0 (ePUB)

Legal deposit first quarter 2021
Bibliothèque nationale du Québec

Printed in Canada on acid-free paper that is 100% ancient forest free
(100% post-consumer recycled), processed chlorine free

LIBRARY AND ARCHIVES CANADA CATALOGUING
IN PUBLICATION

Title: John Stuart Mill, socialist / Helen McCabe.
Names: McCabe, Helen, 1984– author.
Description: Includes bibliographical references and index.
Identifiers: Canadiana (print) 20200327577 | Canadiana (ebook)
    20200327682 | ISBN 9780228005735 (cloth) | ISBN 9780228005742
    (paper) | ISBN 9780228005933 (ePDF) | ISBN 9780228005940 (ePUB)
Subjects: LCSH: Mill, John Stuart, 1806–1873. | LCSH: Socialism.
Classification: LCC HX243 .M38 2021 | DDC 335/.1—dc23

Set in 11/15 Adobe Caslon Pro
Book design & typesetting by Garet Markvoort, zijn digital

JOHN STUART MILL, SOCIALIST

CONTENTS

Acknowledgments
vii

Introduction
3

CHAPTER ONE

Socialism as the Means to Maximizing Happiness:
Mill's Crisis of Faith and the Expansion of the
Horizons of Human Society
19

CHAPTER TWO

Criticisms of Capitalism and Mill's Idea of a
"Perfected" System of Private Property
43

CHAPTER THREE

Mill's Assessment of Contemporary Socialism(s):
Community, Cooperation, and Revolution
93

CHAPTER FOUR

Mill's Socialist Principles
137

CHAPTER FIVE

Mill's Socialist "Utopia"
197

Conclusion
239

Notes
271

Bibliography
331

Index
347

ACKNOWLEDGMENTS

This book has had a very long gestation, being the outcome of a project that began life as my undergraduate thesis and became the focus of all my post-graduate, and most of my post-doctoral, research. Many thanks, then, are owed to a great many people for the support, guidance, and constructive criticism they gave along the way. I do not mention everyone here by name, for fear of this running the well-known dangers of an Oscar acceptance speech.

Thanks, then, to Michael Freeden, Marc Stears, Alan Ryan, and Eugenio Biagini (as well as two anonymous referees) for suggesting this topic, supervising my undergraduate thesis, commenting on my M.Phil., and examining my doctorate. To Pauline Adams and Anne Manuel, librarians of Somerville College during my time there, for access to the Mill Collection. But most of all to David Leopold for being my D.Phil. supervisor (and for his ongoing support) and for his good-humoured and patient help, insightful criticism, and generous sharing of a great fund of knowledge.

Over the years I have benefited a great deal from conversations with a number of Mill scholars, many of whom I am proud, now, to call friends. Thanks in particular must go to Piers Norris Turner, Christopher MacLeod, Dale E. Miller, Joseph Persky, Wendy Donner, and Jonathan Riley, as well as the organizers of many conferences, workshops, and symposia; and to everyone who has attended a panel where I have spoken on this topic, especially at MANCEPT (2007); the Utopian Studies conferences in Limerick (2008) and New Harmony (2014); Sciences Po (2010); Oxford (2011); a one-day workshop on Forgotten British Socialists (Warwick, 2015); ISUS (Lille, 2016); Southampton (2017); the Sorbonne (2018); York (2018); the PPE Conference (New Orleans) 2019; and the organisers and participants of the Frankfurt workshop on Market Socialism in February 2020.

Similarly, I am very grateful to the members of CELPA at the University of Warwick, particularly Matthew Clayton and Adam Swift, for many stimulating conversations that honed my analytical skills for relevant parts of this book. I am also very grateful to members of CONCEPT at the University of Nottingham, and especially to David Stevens and Christopher Woodard for hosting a workshop on an early version of this manuscript, and for all the useful comments I received.

I am glad, also, to get the chance to express my deep gratitude to friends and family who have kindly tolerated, and even encouraged, my enthusiasm for this topic – and particularly those who sustained a somewhat flickering hope when I began to lose faith that this book would ever see the light of day. A particular mention must go to Cath Jones and, of course, my parents Karen and Paul McCabe.

Finally, many thanks to the two anonymous reviewers of this manuscript for their helpful comments; to other anonymous reviewers, whose comments have much improved related work; to the editors who published it; and to Richard Baggaley, Kathleen Fraser, and Matthew Kudelka for shepherding me through this publication process.

INTRODUCTION

[O]ur ideal of ultimate improvement went far beyond Democracy, and would class us decidedly under the general designation of Socialists. While we repudiated with the greatest energy that tyranny of society over the individual which most Socialistic systems are supposed to involve, we yet looked forward to a time when society will no longer be divided into the idle and the industrious; when the rule that they who do not work shall not eat, will be applied ... impartially to all; when the division of the produce of labour, instead of depending ... on the accident of birth, will be made by concert, on an acknowledged principle of justice; and when it will no longer either be, or be thought to be, impossible for human beings to exert themselves strenuously in procuring benefits which are not to be exclusively their own, but to be shared with the society they belong to.[1]

If one knows anything about John Stuart Mill, it is probably that he is revered as one of the "founding fathers" of liberalism – a "paradigmatic liberal"[2] whose defence of free speech remains unparalleled and whose *On Liberty* is still a touchstone for liberals everywhere. He championed the rights of women and minorities; stood as a Liberal candidate in Parliament; and was vehemently anti-paternalist. Though modern liberals have had concerns about his utilitarianism (preferring a more Kantian foundation for fundamental rights, rather than consequentialism), and Mill's perfectionism is criticized by "political" liberals as lacking proper neutrality between reasonable conceptions of the good, Mill is viewed by most modern liberals as one of the "giants" upon whose shoulders they – as intellectuals and ideologues – stand.

This is a view with a long history. But it is only part of the story. This book seeks to tell the other side.

By the mid-1840s, Mill viewed himself as a socialist. He did not endorse any particular contemporary form of socialism: he was not a Marxist, or an Owenite, or even a Fourierist or Saint-Simonian. Instead, he put himself "under the general designation of Socialist,"[3] developing his own unique and nuanced view. His form of socialism was decentralized, cooperative, and voluntarist. It was rooted in worker cooperatives, complemented by some state provision (preferably at a local level). He celebrated individuality, eccentricity, independence, autonomy, and difference – but he also vehemently supported relations of equality and fraternity; a commitment to the common good; and an end to selfishness and the willingness to "get ahead" at the expense of others. He hoped we would not merely tolerate, but cherish, difference; he also hoped we would feel as badly about not living "in unity" with others as we currently do about murdering or stealing from them. He looked forward to an end to the "aristocracies of birth" – not just those of race, religion, and sex, but also of class and talent. He supported collective ownership of property, with the product of common labour being distributed according to democratic decisions; he also thought we should achieve that through democratic, individual-led processes rather than the revolutionary seizure of private assets. His evolutionary view of justice would have allowed several possible distributive principles to be expedient at various points in history, but he called the idea of "from each according to their capacities; to each according to their needs" a "still higher" principle than any other.[4] He was undoubtedly a champion of liberty, but he was also fundamentally committed to utility, progress, security, equality, and fraternity.

It is likely that much of this is a surprise. If you have studied politics, you probably know Mill the liberal. If you have studied philosophy, you probably also know Mill the utilitarian. Debate has raged over whether Mill's liberalism is consistent with his consequentialism. Indeed, some advocate a "two Mills" view, whereby Mill is seen as an inconsistent thinker, trammelled by his utilitarian upbringing and ultimately advocating two entirely separate and incompatible views.[5] Much work has been done by "revisionists" (starting with the incomparable work of

Alan Ryan) to show that Mill's huge body of work is in fact consistent. My argument follows in this train. But instead of trying to show that Mill could consistently be a liberal *and* a utilitarian, I am interested in showing how Mill built all six of his core principles into a consistent, nuanced, and socialist whole. This avoids some of the disputes about whether a utilitarian can *really* be a liberal. It also transcends those debates, as many simply do not arise when we see Mill as a socialist.

One might, however, think that Mill is inconsistent in a different way. For Mill is the author of *On Liberty* and not *On Socialism*. Indeed, his *Chapters on Socialism* are a critical engagement with contemporary forms of socialism, not a rallying cry to the cause. How could Mill write so many texts advocating "liberal" positions and still think of himself as a socialist? Indeed, some have felt this so strongly that they advance a different "two Mills" thesis: there is John Stuart Mill the liberal, and there is Harriet Taylor Mill the socialist, and somehow she managed to force her liberal lover into advocating positions that were far removed from his "authentic" views.[6] This argument relies on taking Mill's word regarding Taylor's authoring parts of *Principles of Political Economy*, but not taking his word regarding her co-authoring all of *On Liberty*.[7] It also requires us to ignore a wide range of texts beyond *Principles* where Mill's socialist ideas are evident. Rather than seek to blame Taylor for Mill's socialism, I start from a position of assuming that Mill might have been neither deluded nor inconsistent, and looking to map how his various commitments make a coherent (and – as it transpires – socialist) whole.

A different answer to the claim that Mill is inconsistent in advocating "liberal" reforms while calling himself a socialist lies in the fact that Mill saw himself as engaged both in immediate political action and in theorizing about the future. He saw these two practices as inherently connected: he believed we needed a North Star by which to navigate in politics as much as in exploration.[8] But one might be both – to extend the metaphor – sea captain and astronomer. Mill thought many things were good about the contemporary regime of individual property and that much improvement could be made without fundamentally changing the system. He wholeheartedly believed that the utilitarian-radical reforms championed by his father and Jeremy Bentham (or something very similar) needed to be implemented to rid Britain of the last vestiges of feudalism, and he spent much of his life fighting for these reforms (having been trained as a campaigner literally from birth). It is neither inconsistent nor hypocritical, however, to think that the reforms one currently champions are not the last word in social reform, but only necessary steps toward something better. Mill championed broadly "liberal" reforms and principles in public debate for most of his life, but he changed his mind as to whether these would result in the best possible society, or merely a greatly improved society that would transition into something much better.[9] My argument in this book is that this much better future society, which Mill thought we ought to consider as the "North Star" even in navigating contemporary political reform, was socialist.

Similarly, although Mill does sometimes use the word "utopia," and the idea of a "North Star," he was wary of being overly prescriptive. Thus, we do not find a detailed blueprint for future societies in Mill, of the kind beloved by many of his socialist contemporaries. He thought organic trial-and-error would allow the best institutions to evolve over time, as education, knowledge, and the human capacity for sympathy improved, so long as this process was allowed to proceed in its natural way without unfair and illegitimate action on the part of elites, whose power would, by this process, by eroded and eventually eradicated.[10] In an age of increasing combination of labour, the spread of democratic institutions, and the widening of suffrage, the world belonged to the workers, and they would shape their own futures with, he ardently hoped, guidance from those with knowledge and expertise – not just academic economists, public philosophers, or elected politicians, but also those who had already made progressive experiments in practical economics, from profit-sharing to cooperation, and from whose mistakes, as well as successes, others could usefully learn.[11]

Just as he came to see the Benthamite program of reform for which he had been raised as standard-bearer as no longer the *dernier mot* of "fundamental improvement in social arrangements," so Mill also saw that his utopian vision might not be the last word, or the "ideal of ultimate improvement."[12] But he thought this vision would be a very good start and that it approximated the best we could currently imagine to be feasible.[13]

One aim of this book is to reconstruct Mill's utopia, bringing together the disparate passages from his extensive collected works that shed light on his view of the "ideal." That is, I aim to lay out in as much detail as possible the content of Mill's socialism. This involves using the tools of both the history of political thought and analytical political theory. I have tried hard not to fill in any potential gaps "for" Mill; I seek only to uncover what is there. I have also approached the project without expectations: I have not, that is, made a list of what "a socialist" needs to believe, and tried to find it in Mill.[14]

Instead, I have traced the development of his ideas and sought to understood what Mill himself meant when he called himself a "socialist" – in terms of both his own political philosophy and what he understood "socialism" to mean. When we *do* see what Mill meant, it looks like socialism. But this ascription has come after the investigation, not before. Indeed, when I first heard that Mill called himself a socialist, I was bewildered (as I am sure many others have been): I was pretty sure I knew what socialism was, and I hadn't seen any in Mill, even when I went away and read *Chapters*. In part, this is because I was brought up within an understanding of "socialism" as Marxist and/or social democratic as practised in northern Europe and still preached (by and large) by the British Labour Party. But I was also brought up with knowledge of the history of cooperation, and once I had delved into *Principles*, Mill's claim to a "qualified socialism"[15] appeared much more plausible. The more I have researched, the more plausible it seems.

This plausibility is not widely accepted. Although the question of whether Mill was correct in his self-identification has been called "well-worn,"[16] there is no consensus about Mill's socialism. Indeed, most works on Mill do not mention this element of his thinking, even where it might be appropriate.[17] There have, however, been several articles[18] and chapters[19] on the topic, and engagements to a greater and lesser degree in books on Mill.[20] That said, Mill's socialism has not spawned as much debate as his feminism, or the question of how to understand his utilitarianism; and nowhere near as much ink has been spilled over it as over his harm principle. Moreover, as Wendy Sarvasy rightly notes, "Mill's socialism is rarely taken to pose a serious threat to his stature as a theorist of liberal-capitalism."[21] That is, Mill's socialism is almost never seen as something that could undermine the specific pedestal later generations have put him upon, or change the place in which he has been set in the canon. Yet it does.

Surveying the then extant literature (in 1985), Sarvsay writes that "to account for his confession of socialist leanings" scholars either emphasise Mill's "romantic weakness for the downtrodden" or "his moral repugnance for existing industrial conditions," or they blame Taylor.[22] These views persist today, with some additional rationales, none of which allow Mill's socialism to seriously undermine the view that, in the end, he endorsed liberal-capitalism. Several scholars highlight what they see as fundamental commitments in Mill's philosophy that make it impossible for him to be a socialist, including to private property;[23] competition;[24] Malthusianism;[25] the need for education;[26] and non-revolutionary methods of reform.[27] Relatedly, much of the exploration of Mill's socialism treats it as an entirely economic question, and one where – ultimately – Mill's commitment to individuality led him to reject socialism in favour of *laissez-faire*.[28] Others argue Mill was a Romantic, not a socialist.[29]

Some go so far as to argue that his interest in, and apparent commitment to, socialism was just a sign of his liberal tolerance and his desire to get even the "wrong" side of a debate a fair hearing (perhaps merely to prevent the "truth" of liberal-capitalism from becoming a "dead dogma").[30] Others conclude that Mill was not a socialist for long, and certainly not when he wrote *On Liberty*, which is seen as more "authentic" to the "mature" Mill than his brief "flirtation" with socialism.[31] In a similar vein, although Jonathan Riley seeks to show that those who entirely deny Mill's socialist sympathies are mistaken, he also seeks to emphasize that Mill left the future "open" between socialism and a reformed form of individual property.[32] Similarly, Dale Miller asserts that the voluntarist, anti-statist nature of Mill's "socialism" is compatible with libertarianism and that Mill's "socialist" future would feature a hybrid system of cooperatives and private ownership.[33] Neither stance challenges Mill's standing as a liberal-capitalist or a theorist of negative liberty, nor asks us to critically reflect on the assumption that Mill's account of individual liberty entailed a future of private-property relations.

Sarvasy writes that "the main weakness of this approach is that it ignores or undervalues Mill's historical sensibility and preoccupation with the dynamics of change,"[34] and that is certainly *one* problem with this view. It encourages people to mistake institutions Mill championed *for now*, in his own transitional age, as his view of the best institutions humanity *could ever have*. In turn, this encourages people to read Mill's endorsement of socialism as "the ultimate end" of humanity as him putting off socialism into an unreachable future, thereby dismissing it from serious political discussion and endeavour.

But Mill meant almost the opposite. As Joseph Persky points out, Mill adopted the view that *all* institutions and their underlying principles were "transitional" and that they were "good" (or "bad") relative to their specific historical context.[35] In the 1830s he called Saint-Simonism "the true ideal of a perfect human society ... which, like any other model of unattainable perfection, everybody is the better for aspiring to, although it be impossible to reach it."[36] Though his ideas regarding the precise *form* of socialism that represented this "North Star" changed over time, nevertheless the "ultimate end" was a standard and guide, not something so far distant it could safely be ignored.[37] Thus, the approach criticized by Sarvasy leads to confusion between Mill's predictions as to what *will* happen regarding socialist reforms and his opinions regarding what *should* happen. Lastly, it leads to misunderstandings regarding the nuances of Mill's approach to socialism and communism; and the rationale underpinning his endorsement of various forms of socialism arising from considerations of whether they were (ultimately) desirable, feasible, and "available as a present resource."[38]

Similarly, Sarvasy rightly notes that Mill's view of history is central to the development of his socialism, key to understanding much of his writing on the subject, and vital for understanding his proposed methods of reform. But Mill's concept of "transitional" and "organic" ages alone does not fully explain the extent of his socialist commitments, nor the extent of their impact on our understanding of Mill's concepts of liberty, equality, fraternity, security, happiness, and progress.

Moreover, that it misses this contextual element of Mill's position is not the only problem with this view. Many of these accounts approach Mill expecting to find a liberal defending capitalism, and then anything which does not fit this picture is dismissed as not the "authentic" or "mature" Mill. Quentin Skinner has pointed out some of the flaws with this approach to the history of political thought.[39] Although I do not entirely embrace a Skinnerian attitude to studying Mill, this is certainly a problem with some previous commentary on Mill's socialism. A similar problem has beset commentators who think that because they can find little that looks like Marxism in Mill, he cannot have been a socialist.[40] But this, of course, ignores the wide and disparate range of political ideas known as socialism before Karl Marx ever published a word or even put pen to paper. Perhaps one might argue that only Marxism is "really" socialism: but this seems an unwarrantedly narrow view of what a "real socialist" might mean.

Another problem is that the general approach sees Mill's socialism as something "extra" to his "real" political theory (i.e., the ideas in *On Liberty*). But his socialism was not peripheral to his political thought, and we see Mill wrestling with the questions of how to balance the competing claims of liberty, equality, and fraternity in various texts that help contextualize the discussion in *On Liberty* and are interesting in their own right.[41] Even this response, of course, privileges *On Liberty*. Perhaps it *is* the text, of all of Mill's *oeuvre*, that has best stood the test of time, the one to which we still most frequently turn as a source of ideas and defences of key freedoms (as, indeed, Mill predicted[42]). But in terms of understanding Mill's own thought, on his own terms, it is not clear that *On Liberty* ought to have this privileged status as *the* place in which he expounds *all* – or at least the key tenets – of his political philosophy. "Liberty" is only one of six key principles of Mill's political philosophy, the others being happiness, progress, security, equality, and fraternity, and these elements get lost, or at least are seen out of focus, when we magnify *On Liberty* as *the* text in Mill's opus.

Bruce Baum has a different criticism of existing approaches, which is that we should not be debating "whether Mill, despite his socialist self-designation, should be counted as a socialist." "Whether Mill's ultimate political economic ideal is indisputably a form of socialism is less important," Baum argues, "than the extent to which he provides support for the democratic socialist goal of extending democracy and the freedom of self-government beyond the state and into modern economies."[43] That is, instead of arguing about how we should label Mill's political philosophy, we should be applying his insights, or at least seeing that we could recruit him for a modern-day battle over freedom and the economy.

Of course, this relies on a particular methodological view of the purpose of studying historical thinkers, and not everyone would agree. I concur, though, that fighting over how to *label* Mill can distract us from understanding what he actually had to say. (And on that topic, it is certainly worth highlighting Baum's attempts to take Mill's socialist commitments seriously, and trace the consistency of his views regarding liberty and cooperative socialism.) Like Baum, I think we should move on from the question of *whether* Mill was a socialist, and also – to some extent – from the question of *what kind*, in part because Mill's socialism, like so much of his political thought, was unique (or, rather, like much of *their* thought, Mill and Taylor's socialism was unique). On the other hand, this position is far from mainstream in Mill scholarship, or in understandings of political philosophy more widely. So the argument for Mill's socialism – however apparently "well-worn" – still needs making. Also, laying out in detail, and at some length, the development of Mill's socialism, its content, and its historical context helps us better to understand his view, and his critiques of contemporary capitalism, as well as what there might be in both that is of use to reformers today.

As with Baum's work connecting Mill's commitment to liberty with his socialism, Gregory Claeys connects Mill's anti-paternalism to his socialism – again, showing that these two elements of Mill's political philosophy, so often seen as being in tension with each other, are actually closely linked.[44] Sarvasy embraces Mill's socialism and uses it to explain his writings on democracy and, in particular, how *Considerations on Representative Government* reveals a theory of democracy for a transition between capitalism and socialism.[45]

Concerning the egalitarian element of Mill's socialism, John Rawls sought to position Mill as a "property-owning democrat" rather than a "liberal socialist."[46] As Baum rightly notes, Rawls – and Rawlsians – "offer some support for liberal socialism, but chiefly to achieve distributive justice rather than as a way to maximise freedom."[47] Indeed, the two principles of justice deal separately with maximal liberty and fair distribution.[48] Baum sees Mill as "advanc[ing] a form of liberal democratic socialism for the enlargment of freedom as well as to realise social and distributive justice."[49] I agree that Mill does see socialism as maximizing freedom *and* achieving social and distributive justice. He *also* sees it as securing fraternity (alongside security, progress, and – ultimately – happiness), and this has been underexplored in the existing literature.

Separately to writing on Mill's socialism, there is increasing interest in his concept of distributive justice,[50] and his ideas regarding equality.[51] In particular, recently Persky has linked what he sees as Mill's luck-egalitarianism to his socialism, while Piers Norris Turner has emphasized Mill's "democratic egalitarianism," a position that better encapsulates Mill's view of justice under socialism.[52] These questions are intimately linked to his socialism – a topic too often dominated by the question of Mill's commitment to liberty.

In moving scholarship and understanding forward, then, from what has already been written on Mill's socialism, this book seeks to encapsulate the entirety of Mill's view of socialism: to see Mill as a *socialist* and to understand what that means. This work grows naturally out of existing interest in Mill's socialism; in his account of economic freedom; in his egalitarianism; and in his concept of distributive justice.

As such, one audience at whom this book is aimed is fellow Mill scholars. In true Millian fashion, of course, this is the case whether you find egalitarianism and fraternity – indeed, whether you find socialism – attractive or not. To the extent that you find new truths here, Mill would think it all to the good. To the extent that you find mere falsehood, which strengthens your existing reading of Mill, then that is all to the good, too. I hope this book will spark fruitful debate on Mill's socialism, his ideas of fraternity, and his egalitarianism, and perhaps respark some old debates regarding his consistency as a thinker, the role of Taylor in his work, and precisely what kind of liberty he was defending.

I hope, too, that there is something here for the "calmer and more disinterested bystander,"[53] who is less concerned with what *Mill* had to say than in exploring what might be useful ideas for contemporary society, whoever said them. That is, one audience at whom the book is aimed is other political philosophers, and also politically concerned citizens, in the hope that it might contribute to wider debates around what "socialism" and "liberalism" might look like, as well as the institutional arrangements that are compatible (or not) with core Millian principles.

It is true that Mill wrote during a stage of capitalism very different to our own. An age of Empire and, in most countries, of monarchy. One in which communication relied on the handwritten or press-printed word; lighting relied on gas or candle wax; railways, steamboats, and sailing vessels were the fastest forms of transport; and roads were dominated by foot traffic and horse-drawn carts. Where computing was still a dream in the minds of Ada Lovelace and Charles Babbage; currency was still tied to its value in actual quantities of precious metals;

and financial transfers involved physical cash, coin, and bullion. Where the factory system was still in its infancy; and where the proletariat was still an emerging and far from universal class. Similarly, he was writing in a stage of socialism very different to our own. Mill counted himself as "under the general designation of Socialist" before 1848, long before the emergence of Marxism-Leninism, Maoism, or social democracy – before, even, Marx and Engels penned *The Communist Manifesto*.[54]

Thus, one might think Mill's socialist ideas could only be of interest to the historian:[55] our economies have changed, and socialism has both benefited from the insights of Marx and been burdened by the legacy of twentieth-century communism. "Socialism," indeed, is in itself often seen as a dirty word, an insult, marking someone out as dangerous.

One the other hand, though I do not think that finding such contemporary relevance is the *main* task of the history of political thought, Mill's ideas often speak to contemporary concerns. For instance, there is increasing acknowledgment that GDP is not a good measure of a country's "success"; that we need to take environmental concerns seriously, which will involve radically changing our relationship to production, consumption, and "nature"; and that in "developed" countries, many people are working ever longer hours, on stagnant wages, with an ever widening gap between rich and poor. All of this echoes Mill's critiques of capitalism. Similarly, there is an increasing interest in solving some of the world's current problems by "rewriting the rules" of contemporary capitalism, adopting forms of "property-owning democracy" and "community wealth building" that might involve profit-sharing or cooperation and the kinds of restrictions on inheritance that Mill advocated as "first steps" toward progressive social reform; or via other ideas we see in his work such as (re-)nationalization of key services and universal basic income.[56]

To put my own cards on the table: if I didn't find Mill's vision appealing, I would probably not have spent so many years researching this same topic. (That said, my main motivation has been to understand a puzzle in Mill: investigating one line in his *Autobiography* has led down a remarkably deep rabbit hole!) Though it is not a blueprint for reform, I think there is much to be admired in Mill's socialist vision and in his organic, peaceful, piecemeal, incremental, grassroots-oriented, authentic approach to social change, and his willingness to engage with the processes of actually enacting radical policy via existing economic, social, and political institutions. True, this view will probably never appeal to certain Marxists, but we need to start recognizing that there is much more to socialism than traditional, "revolutionary" Marxism. (Where "we" here refers both to academics and to active citizens.) Similarly, we need to see that there may be much more to liberalism than what is often imagined, and that libertarianism does not have a monopoly on what it means to be "liberal," and to take seriously the idea conjured by Rawls of a "liberal socialism," without necessarily needing to adopt a Rawlsian normative or epistemological framework.

But I also think it is important to read history, and historical figures, accurately. There may be many ways of reading *On Liberty*, and the rest of Mill's corpus, which accord with certain specific political ideologies. Conscripting Mill for a specific political campaign, however, is not the same as understanding Mill or explaining his position. Mill scholars are at risk of deeply misunderstanding Mill if we see him as a "classical," *laissez-faire* liberal and not as a socialist. This has broader implications: Mill's arguments for freedom of thought, conscience, speech, and action are still (arguably) the best that have been written; and they are very prominent in political discourse, judicial rulings, and social understandings of what it means to be "free." But generations of political philosophers – often with their own political motivations born out of an ardent desire to oppose totalitarianism – have read Mill's theory of freedom as wholly "negative" (in Isaiah Berlin's terminology[57]), and his economics as a corollary of that, verging on the libertarian, defending *laissez-faire*, limited government, and low taxation. This is in part the outcome of seeing Mill solely as the author of *On Liberty*, or of seeing *On Liberty* as the work that embodies his entire political philosophy.

This is not to say that Mill was not centrally concerned with liberty. But he felt that *On Liberty* would "survive" longer than, say, *Principles*, *Considerations*, *Utilitarianism*, or *The Subjection of Women* not because it was the text with the most normative weight, but because it would become increasingly politically salient. This is a practical, political rationale, though based on a firm belief in the normative significance of the message of *On Liberty* regarding "the importance, to man and society, of a large variety in types of character, and of giving full freedom to human nature to expand itself in innumerable and conflicting directions."[58] But Mill *also* had normative commitments to equality and fraternity that are equally central to his philosophy, along with progress, security, and happiness.

When we only see Mill as the author of *On Liberty*, then, we risk misunderstanding his entire corpus by looking on that text as the one to to which all his others led, or the one superior to all his others. We also risk misunderstanding Mill's concept of liberty itself – as expressed in the passage from the *Autobiography* just quoted, for instance, it is evidently not as "negative" as is usually believed.

This is important for liberals, and possibly also important for libertarians who would like to claim Mill as one of their own. It is also important for people who would see themselves somewhere to the left of "liberalism." Traditional Marxists may dismiss Mill's concern with individual liberty and "the free development of individuality" as "bourgeois individualism," trapped by contemporary, capitalist ideology. But Mill's commitment to liberty *and* equality – to trying hard not only to imagine what both together would look like, but also to actually make that vision a reality – shows he does not privilege "bourgeois" freedoms, such as of trade, at the expense of others, such as flourishing. Indeed, the idea that freedom "is the creative manifestation of life arising from the free development of all abilities of the whole [person]" could come from Mill – though, in actual fact, it comes from Marx.[59] Similarly, Mill's idea aligns well with the claim that in a socialist future, "in the place of old bourgeois society, with its classes and class antagonism, we shall have an association, in which the free development of each is the condition for the free development of all."[60]

Of course, Marx (and Engels) and Mill (and Taylor) had different ideas about what "socialism" might look like, and – perhaps even more importantly – the process and speed by which modern society might be steered toward an improved, socialist future. The purpose of this book is not to persuade Marxists that there might be more similarities between Mill and Marx than Marx himself acknowledged (as have later writers): though I do think we are still waiting for the definitive book on this relationship, this book has no pretences to be it. Instead, the purpose of the book is to bring to the world something previously unseen – Mill the socialist.

The book proceeds as follows. In Chapter 1, I tackle head-on some of the reasons we might consider the very idea of Mill's socialism to be implausible: between his Benthamite upbringing and his writing of *On Liberty*, where is there space for Mill's ideas to have expanded to include socialism, and why would have he been looking for something "beyond" classical liberalism? In this chapter, I explore why Mill stopped seeing the philosophic-radical commitments of his youth as being the last word in social progress.

In Chapter 2, I consider Mill's criticisms of *laissez-faire* capitalism, which, in the main, he had been brought up to champion and see as the final stage of human progress. I then chart the criticisms Mill felt would have bite even against "the régime of individual property ... as it might be made" in the "old" world and a "new" one.[61] In Chapter 3 I explain what it was Mill found desirable in socialism; what forms of socialism (both among those being suggested by contemporaries, and his own formulation) he thought humanity might one day be able to institute; and whether or not he thought that institution would be desirable. I then consider what changes Mill proposed for people living in contemporary Britain and France (with which he was most interested) to start a gradual, peaceful, piecemeal, voluntary, grassroots led movement toward the realization of his preferred form of socialism.

In Chapter 4 I explore Mill's core principles (not just "utility," but those secondary principles adherence to which allows us to maximize utility – security, progress, liberty, equality and fraternity). Understanding Mill's commitments helps us see his reasons for preferring socialist institutions, and why, at a really fundamental level, he saw himself as "under the general designation of Socialist." For Mill, it is socialism that will achieve the greatest happiness of the greatest number.

In Chapter 5, I map Mill's "utopia." I look at what Mill thought society could achieve in terms of change almost immediately, and how this would form a "path" toward further developments of socialism, some of which he was willing to sketch, though he was opposed to looking too far into the future, leaving such decisions for the people of that time to make.

In Chapter 6, I conclude by tracing some of the implications of this reinterpretation of Mill for our wider understanding of his thought, and dealing with some arguments regarding the longevity or authenticity of Mill's socialism. In particular, I show how understanding him as a socialist might help aid our understanding of what Mill meant by "the permanent interests of man as a progressive being," which the harm principle is supposed to protect.[62] I also highlight that this exploration reveals a number of paths not taken regarding the improvement and transformation of capitalism – paths suggested and endorsed by someone who is often seen as contemporary capitalism's great champion. This ought to change our understanding not just of Mill, but of socialism and the possibilities of social(ist) change that do not demand a wholescale, immediate, violent revolution, but instead could be brought about in a piecemeal, peaceful and organic manner. Mill provides a sophisticated vision of cooperation, egalitarianism, human flourishing and social harmony in a decentralized, diverse, free, friendly, and "green" society characterized by mutual concern for one another's well-being: it is time we paid due attention to his ideas.

CHAPTER ONE

Socialism as the Means to Maximizing Happiness: Mill's Crisis of Faith and the Expansion of the Horizons of Human Society

> The only actual revolution which has ever taken place in my modes of thinking, was already complete. My new tendencies had to be confirmed in some respects, moderated in others: but the only substantial changes of opinion that were yet to come, related to politics, and consisted ... so far as regards the ultimate prospects of humanity, to a qualified Socialism.[1]

When trying to understand, or even comprehend the idea of, John Stuart Mill's socialism, it can sometimes seem hard to see where there is intellectual, political, or imaginative space for him to develop into a socialist. Mill was brought up championing such core classical liberal concepts as representative government, free trade, and limited government, and for guides and teachers he had such great figures as Adam Smith, David Ricardo and, of course, Jeremy Bentham and James Mill.[2] In later life he not only wrote *On Liberty*, one of *the* classic liberal texts, but also continued to support representative government and universal suffrage;[3] favoured female equality;[4] stood for the Liberal Party in Parliament; sought to bring Governor Eyre to justice for rights abuses in Jamaica;[5] and was constantly concerned about the oppressive and enervating effects of state power, leading him to favour limited government, *laisser-faire*,[6] and a raft of political, economic, and social freedoms. True, his last work was titled *Chapters on Socialism*, but this was a critical evaluation of the claims of current socialists, not a rallying cry to their cause in the way of *The Communist Manifesto*. When, then, could Mill have become a socialist? He appears to have been a liberal from cradle to grave. And *why* should Mill have found any element of socialism desirable? He appears to have been completely committed to a comprehensive liberal program of reform. This chapter addresses these questions as a means of clearing the ground before the book moves on to a more analytical exploration and assessment of the substantive content of Mill's socialism.

In brief, the answer to these questions lies in the specific changes to Mill's philosophy that arose from the "crisis in my mental history"[7] that he underwent in the winter of 1826–27, which left him looking for new answers to old questions just at the time he came into contact with Saint-Simonian ideas. In particular, the idea of history progressing between "critical" and "organic" ages led him to him realize that philosophic-radical reforms were *also* transitional and not the "last word" in the historical development of human social institutions. Moreover, the idea that economic "laws" of distribution were mutable by human endeavour opened up a new landscape of possibilities for economic – and thus social and political – organization. Mill found the Saint-Simonian aims of collective ownership of property, the requirement that every individual do his or her fair share of labour, and remuneration being based on a more socialist principle of justice to be "desirable and rational," and he thought the "proclamation of such an ideal of human society could not but tend to give a beneficial direction to the efforts of others to bring society ... nearer to some ideal standard."[8] This "ideal standard" was something other than the "ideal" of philosophic-radicalism and was the start of the development of Mill's "qualified socialism."[9]

MILL'S EARLY "PHILOSOPHIC-RADICALISM"

Mill's earliest political philosophy, in which he was inculcated from birth as part of the infamous educational experiment that constituted his childhood, was a species of radicalism.[10] Like radicalism more generally, it had as its central tenets commitments to representative government (including equal electoral districts, the secret ballot, and universal suffrage[11]); free trade; pursuit of peace as the road to international trade; freedom of the press; liberty of speech, action, exchange, ownership of property, and religion (including decriminalization of atheism); eradication of the power of the aristocracy and the established church; and reforms of education, the legal system, and the penal code.[12] This "radical" political philosophy could be broadly described as "liberal," particularly in its emphasis on formal, legal reform; toleration; free trade; and securing equal constitutional rights and liberties for all.

Mill's early political theory was based on the utilitarian (ethical, legal and political) theory of Bentham and James Mill;[13] the associationist psychology of David Hartley and James Mill; the political economy of Smith, Ricardo and (again) James Mill; and the population theory of Thomas Malthus.[14] He recalls his youthful heroes were the Girondins and the *philosophes* of the French Revolution, and that he dreamed "of figuring, successful or unsuccessful, as a Girondist in an English Convention."[15]

Mill also says that "from the very earliest period when I had formed any opinions at all on social or political matters" he was committed to "a principle of perfect equality" between the sexes, "admitting no power or privilege on the one side, nor disability on the other."[16] As Maria Morales rightly notes, this was a more substantive egalitarian commitment than is often assumed, and than was shared by other contemporary radicals.[17] It is evidently a reason why Mill was drawn to the feminist ideas of the utilitarian socialist William Thompson;[18] however, Mill – at this point in time – did not extend this substantive egalitarianism beyond gender relations. Although a proponent of representative government elected by universal suffrage, for instance, he thought (with James Mill) that reform would put the aristocracy on their mettle, not abolish them, and felt that "a leisured class ... is an essential constituent of the best form of society."[19] Even so, his early substantive egalitarianism is a point worth bearing in mind as we look for "space" in Mill's political philosophy for him to grow into a "qualified" socialism.

Mill had contact with socialism from as early as he had contact with radicalism, through his father and Bentham's links to Robert Owen.[20] (James Mill met Owen through a mutual friend, the Quaker philanthropist William Allen, in London in 1803, and introduced him to Bentham, who invested in Owen's experiments at New Lanark, though these were more exercises in paternalism than in the socialism Owen would later develop.[21])

In 1825, Mill (and a group of friends) debated with Owenites in London,[22] where Mill showed both knowledge of and admiration for Thompson's work and Owen's socialism, and professed this "friendly debate" was between two groups who had "in view the same great end, the improvement of the human race."[23] Mill was not, he says, "an enemy to Mr. Owen's system" because he was "an enemy to no system which has for its object the amelioration of mankind." That said, he had several concerns about the Owenite scheme, and he certainly did not endorse it. The "Cooperative system" Mill wrote, "might ... facilitate the attainment of good education, of good laws, and of good government ... but yet, the Cooperative system is not the same thing with good government, good education, good laws."

Owenism, Mill feared, was unworkable, particularly because Mill could not see how people would be brought to work when their subsistence was already (at it would be under this scheme) secured whether they worked or not.[24] It was inefficient, particularly as the start-up costs of an intentional community would be very high. This money would be better spent directly on reforms. Indeed, Mill said that two-thirds of the population would have starved by the time Owen's Parallelograms were up and running.[25] If the money was instead spent directly on education and "working upon the press" (particularly regarding family planning), in twenty years many of the problems of poverty could be solved. Cooperation was not necessary, as self-interest could be harnessed in a reformed system of competition to make people as happy as they would be under cooperation. Lastly, cooperation was too restrictive of liberty, being "in its very nature ... a system of universal regulation," and it being "delightful to man to be an independent being," there was "pleasure in enjoying perfect freedom of action" such that "to be controlled, even if it be for our own good, is in itself far from pleasant." Thus "other things being alike, it is infinitely better to attain a given end by leaving people to themselves than to attain the same end by controlling them."

Mill, then, up to 1825, certainly knew of the main contemporary form of socialism, and professed himself in sympathy with its aims (particularly regarding feminism), but he preferred philosophic-radical means to effect those ends. However, his own viewpoint was broadly "liberal" in terms of goals and the means to achieve them (legal, political, and economic reform in favour of *laissez-faire*, and formal equality of opportunity). The egalitarian impulse was already there in his feminism, alongside his liberal commitment to "independence," anti-paternalism, and widespread personal liberty, and in his genuine concern with the contemporary suffering of the poor. This he blamed, in the main, on poor education and bad public morality regarding family planning; on bad economic policies aimed at benefiting rich landowners; and on bad governmental institutions that had been designed to respond to the interests of an established elite rather than to maximize the general happiness. However, Mill was by no means a socialist at this point, and his belief in the efficacy and sufficiency of the philosophic-radical project meant there was not really the "space," opportunity, or impetus for his views to develop towards socialism.

MILL'S MENTAL "CRISIS" AND REACTION AGAINST PHILOSOPHIC-RADICALISM

The creation of this "space," opportunity, and impetus came in the winter of 1826–27 when Mill suffered his famous "crisis in my mental history."[26] Up to this point, Mill had believed that a life spent bringing about utilitarian reforms would ensure not just the greatest happiness of the greatest number, but his own personal maximal happiness as well. During the winter of 1826–27, however, this zeal was lost when he asked himself this simple question: "If everything I am fighting for was achieved, would I myself be happy?" The answer, he realized, was "No." Indeed, Mill considered himself incapable of feeling happiness.

He lost faith in the principles for which he had been fighting, which no longer seemed inspiring or worthwhile; in the educative system that had created, in him, a being greatly lacking in emotional capacity, and that had poisoned the very wellspring of his motivations; and in the program of political reform for which he had been groomed to be the standard-bearer. This threw him into a deep depression: "my heart sank within me: the whole foundation on which my life was constructed fell down."

Much has been made of this "crisis," and different ways of interpreting it have been offered.[27] I want to emphasize that Mill saw it as a seminal moment, one that, particularly with hindsight, he recognized as marking a break with his Benthamite past and the beginnings of his adoption of a new political philosophy of his own making – what he calls "the only actual revolution which has ever taken place in my modes of thinking."[28]

Attention has previously been paid to how the "crisis" affected Mill's understanding of utility and led him to favour the indirect pursuit of happiness through the direct pursuit of the development of one's own individuality (including the active pursuit of a variety of projects one reflectively found fulfilling, rewarding, or otherwise important).[29] There has also been some scholarly focus on how Mill's reassessment of associationist psychology's "doctrine of Philosophical Necessity" after his "crisis" led to his adoption of the idea that we had cohesive, "active" selves that were at least part-authors of our own actions.[30] I want to focus on two oft-overlooked elements of Mill's "crisis" that led to important changes in his political philosophy specifically regarding the possibility and desirability of socialism: first, changes to his philosophy of history, particularly regarding "stages" of human social progress and the status of his current age; and second, changes to his political economy, particularly regarding the nature of the laws of distribution.

Neither of these changes was a direct outcome of Mill's asking himself the fateful question regarding the possibility of his own future happiness. But they *are* the outcome of the general re-evaluation of, and dissatisfaction with, philosophic-radicalism and, in particular, the views of his father which stemmed from his negative answer to that question. Both changes are due, in some part, to his engagement with Saint-Simonism, the second form of socialism with which Mill had real contact, and which had a good deal of influence over him, though the root causes of the change in his opinion lie even earlier.

MILL AND SAINT-SIMONISM

Mill met Henri Saint-Simon in 1820 (while he was staying in Paris with Jean-Baptiste Say), but, as Mill notes, this was before Saint-Simon was known "either as the founder of a philosophy or a religion."[31] Mill's first real encounter with Saint-Simon*ism* was in 1828 when he met Gustave d'Eichthal, a young Saint-Simonian visiting England to study the effects of industrialization.[32] This was the beginning of a lifelong correspondence and friendship.[33] D'Eichthal gave Mill several editions of the Saint-Simonian journal *Le Producteur* and a copy of Auguste Comte's *Traité de Politique Positive*,[34] and these, coupled with their extensive correspondence and friendship, were "a great influence" on Mill's life.[35]

When Mill first made contact with the Saint-Simonians, their ideas were not fully formed. However, he recalled in later life that the scheme they "gradually unfolded,"

> under which the labour and capital of society would be managed for the general account of the community, every individual being required to take a share of labour, either as thinker, teacher, artist, or producer, all being classed according to their capacity, and remunerated according to their works, appeared to me a far superior description of Socialism to Owen's. Their aim seemed to me desirable and rational, however their means might be inefficacious.[36]

Though he was never convinced about "the practicability, nor … the beneficial operation of their social machinery," he thought "the proclamation of such an ideal ... could not but tend to give a beneficial direction" to other "efforts ... to bring society ... nearer to some ideal standard." He particularly admired their treatment of "the family" and their proclamation of "the perfect equality of men and women, and an entirely new order of things in regard to their relations with one another."

Mill's sketch gives a good overview of the content of the Saint-Simonians' socialism, highlighting their commitment to collective property, communal organization of production and distribution, understanding of distributive justice, egalitarianism (particularly regarding women), and emphasis on a duty to contribute. There are many echoes with Mill's own views, even though he never fully endorsed Saint-Simonism. However, rather than the content of their socialism, and whether Mill adopted any of it, in this chapter I am interested in two other vital elements of their thought – their understanding of history, and their view of the "laws" of production and distribution.

The Progress of History

One area in which the Saint-Simonians greatly influenced Mill was in his philosophy of history.[37] Mill's reaction to the dispute between Thomas Macaulay and James Mill regarding the perceived ahistoricism of the latter's *Essay on Government* revealed to him a fundamental difference of opinion with his father. Macaulay charged James Mill with writing about politics in such a way that one might think people had never previously formed states or made political institutions: James Mill's reply revealed that he did not think history was apposite in questions of political theory. Mill was disappointed by his father's response.[38] Although he thought our reasoning about politics ought to be deductive (and not just inductive, as Macaulay would have it),[39] he felt that a part of the answer to the question "What are the best political institutions?" had to encompass specific questions about what society, and at what point of time or progress, these political institutions were being designed for. Representative government might be "the best," and also "best for" late Georgian Britain: but that did not mean it was "best" for Norman Britain, or for all contemporary countries.[40]

Mill first revealed these changes in his view in *The Spirit of the Age*, and they raised outcry from his philosophic-radical friends: Francis Place said Mill had turned into some kind of German mystic[41] (Thomas Carlyle said the same, but he meant it as a compliment[42]). Mill was "greatly struck" by Saint-Simonian ideas about a "natural order of human progress"[43] (for Comte, a tripartite scheme),[44] and especially the "division of all history into organic periods and critical periods."[45]

The Saint-Simonians believed that humanity was constantly improving, with people creating institutions that suited their current stage of progress in one age, then throwing them off as they became unsuitable. Periods of social stability in which the institutions of society were universally supported, and there was a prevailing ideology that adequately explained the world, were "organic" ages, and those in which institutions were being thrown off were "critical" or "transitional" ages. They were critical because the people within them criticized everything about the preceding age, and transitional in that not only was the previous age destroyed during them, but the institutions of the new, organic, age were built.

As examples of organic ages, Mill followed the Saint-Simonians and offered the periods in Greek and Roman history when the pantheon of gods was really believed in, and the mediaeval period when the spiritual and temporal power of the Catholic Church was universally acknowledged. For critical periods he suggested Athens in the time of Sophocles, Plato, and Aristotle, and the Reformation, which, Mill argued, ushered in a critical period that "has lasted ever since, still lasts, and cannot altogether cease until a new organic period has been inaugurated."[46]

Mill thought "the distinction between the ... critical, & the organical [*sic*], epochs" was "one of the most valuable parts of the Saint-Simon philosophy."[47] That said, he did not wholly adopt the optimism of the Saint-Simonian idea of progression: though Mill viewed humanity as infinitely perfectible, and saw history as the story of the (non-linear) progress of humanity toward perfection, it is not clear he thought we would ever achieve it.[48] Perfection was an ever-receding horizon toward which humanity was inexorably moving, but it could never arrive there, and its progress was best represented by a jagged rather than straight line. That said, it is worth emphasizing not only that Mill believed human nature was perfectible, but also that it was a test of good government if it aimed at improving the people it governed and allowed them to progress.[49]

There are several important outcomes of Mill's adoption of this Saint-Simonian view of history, the first one to point out being that it opened up the space for an age of future improvement beyond Mill's contemporary age. This he now saw as being (in Europe and America) a "critical" age, beginning with the Reformation and ongoing through several revolutions. But within every critical age were the seeds of the future organic age, and this critical age, too, would end in a new organic period. The reforms and institutions preferred by his father and Bentham might well be the best "critical" institutions – tearing down the last vestiges of feudal privilege, hierarchy and structures, and providing people with the tools to critically assess their previous age and free themselves from its trammels – but they were not necessarily best-suited to the organic age to come. Indeed, they could not be best suited to such an age, being inherently "critical," whereas an organic age would need new, organic, institutions to create, govern and reproduce it. It is this new organic age that had the potential to be socialist.[50]

Here, then, is one way in which, in the aftermath of his "crisis," a space opened up for Mill in which socialism became possible: *something* would come after the philosophic-radical institutions he had previously championed as the *dernier mot* of reform and human improvement; his father's ideas would not be the last word, after all. There is a second way in which this space opened up and socialism became more possible, which also had to do with changes in Mill's ideas triggered by the Saint-Simonians (though, in this case, Mill says, they were cemented by his relationship with Harriet Taylor).[51] This concerns the very possibility of important economic institutional change.

The Laws of Production and Distribution

Mill had been, almost from birth, deeply involved in the growth of the relatively new subject of political economy.[52] His economics changed during his crisis because of his exposure to Saint-Simonians' thought, especially his acceptance of their arguments that private property was not necessarily fundamental to securing utility; and that although the laws of production are fixed by nature, the laws of distribution are man-made. As Mill puts it in the *Autobiography*, his "eyes were opened to the very limited and temporary value of the old political economy, which assumes private property and inheritance as indefeasible facts, and freedom of production and exchange as the *dernier mot* of social improvement." The Saint-Simonians had brought home to him "a new mode" of thinking.[53]

This "new mode" "consisted chiefly in making the proper distinctions between the laws of the Production of Wealth ... and the modes of its Distribution."[54] "The common run of political economists," Mill wrote, "confuse ... together, under the designation of economic laws, which they deem incapable of being defeated or modified by human effort," the "laws" of production and distribution.[55] However, he now saw them as distinct.

The laws of production, Mill continued to believe, are "dependent on the property of objects" and thus cannot be changed, bent, or transgressed (think, for instance, of the adage that the world cannot be fed from a single plant pot). But the modes of distribution, "subject to certain conditions, depend on human will," and thus distributive outcomes can be "modified by human effort" and are liable to be evaluated on the grounds not just of efficiency but of justice as well. As Mill explained, "[classical] political economists confuse these together, under the designation of economic laws ... ascribing the same necessity to things dependent on the unchangeable conditions of our earthly existence, and to those which, being but necessary consequences of particular social arrangements are merely coextensive with these." This leads them to assume that "the shares which fall, in the division of the produce, to labourers, capitalists, and landlords" are "an inherent necessity, against which no human means can avail."

Mill now thought this was mistaken. Although there were certain "necessary consequences of particular social arrangements" that *were* "coextensive" with them, these social arrangements themselves were a matter of human choice and construction and thus capable of change by human endeavour. That is, capitalism necessitates a certain division of the means of production and the product of labour among labourers, capitalists, and landlords. Similarly, feudalism necessitates a particular division among landowners, freemen, and serfs. However, these two divisions are very different, arising from the differences in the systems themselves. Moreover, *both* systems are human constructions and change as a result of human endeavour. Thus, capitalism as it currently existed was not "fixed" but capable of being improved. Indeed, so committed was Mill to this new truth that he criticized Harriet Martineau (and classical, *laissez-faire* economists like her) for not seeing it, but rather assuming that the current economic model was "as little under human control as the division of day and night."[56]

This view has been much criticized, but Mill's distinction is both plausible and consistent.[57] Within any society, however it determines distribution, the laws of production are dependent on physical laws. Similarly, "given certain institutions and customs, wages, profits, and rent will be determined by certain causes," which are also predictable and determined.[58] But these causes are themselves the outcome of social arrangements ("certain institutions and customs"), and social arrangements are human constructions and can be changed by human effort.[59] Mill can appear to imply that laws of production are completely immutable, and that laws of distribution are entirely malleable, but this was not his actual position. Rather, he was positing that the *laws* of production (though not necessarily how production is carried out) are immutable because they are "dependent on the properties of objects," for instance, on the fixed fecundity of a piece of land (which, no matter what improvements in technology, working practices, and fertilization we employ on it does have a maximal limit). The laws of distribution are *also* predictable and "fixed" in the sense that a certain set of social arrangements will necessarily lead to a certain set of "co-extensive" distributions – but the set of social arrangements *itself* is changeable. We might have, for instance, a slave-owning society; or a feudal society; or a system with particular rights over landownership giving rise to rent; or a system of communal property in not only land but all the instruments of production. Each of these will give rise to a certain set of "coextensive" distributions, but *which* of these we have is a matter of human choice and endeavour.

Of course, in this way, the laws of production and distribution are interrelated: our "modes of production" (to borrow Marx's term) are in some sense dependent on previous distributions (e.g., of ownership rights over, and profits arising from, land, capital, and labour), and the social system we have that "gives" our current laws of distribution depends on what was produced in the past, and how.[60] But what Mill wanted to emphasize was that distributive outcomes are, to some extent at least, dependent on human choice, because the social systems with which they are "coextensive" are a matter of human construction and *can* be changed through conscious human action.

That is, it might be true that a field of a certain size, worked on by the maximally efficient labour force with the best technology and knowledge, will produce a determinable amount of produce – but how the landowner, farmer, technology owner, and day labourers divide up that product is not fixed in the same way this fecundity is fixed. Human choices have led to a social structure that divides up ownership of land, capital, and labour in a certain way – and human choices also determine how we apportion the shares to each. It might, of course, be true that human psychology is such that if we were to apportion the shares differently, we would jeopardize the efficiency of production itself (perhaps capitalists simply would not invest in new technology if they were not certain they would receive a larger share of the product than labourers). That said, human psychology *itself* is, to a great degree (according to Mill), the product of social institutions and structures that are, themselves, human constructions. Improvement in education (understood in a very broad sense) can change what people are psychologically capable of.[61] Distributive outcomes are not outside human control or influence in the same way as planetary orbits. In fact, distributive outcomes are the product of a particular stage of human progress. A feudal society is bound by the same basic fecundity of land as a modern society (even though modern society might well exploit it much more effectively than feudal society had the technology and knowledge to do); *how* a given society distributes the resources gained from that same land must vary as greatly as its political organization does.[62]

This opens up another "space" in which socialism became not only possible but probable. Mill believed that how the resources of society are parcelled out is a political decision, and the more people are allowed to be a part of that decision-making, the less likely they will be to accept that they should sustain an elite in idleness; this is what leads them to embrace socialist ideas. Moreover, this at least opens up the possibility of other distributions being feasible and possible – something that the "modern" school of political economy denied. The malleability of the laws of distribution, then, offered the potential for something "beyond" classical, *laissez-faire* economics, something that was more open to questions of justice in distributions and more amenable to the demands of the workers. In these two ways, the writings of the Saint-Simonians opened up a space for Mill beyond contemporary society and the philosophic-radical reforms he had previously championed as the "last word" in human improvement.

However, Mill could have believed *this* without thinking that what would come *after* the reforms he had previously championed could, would, or should be socialist. I will address this point in more detail in the next chapter, but it is worth noting here that in the 1830s, we see an important change in Mill's ideas regarding at the very least what *might* come after the existing age, and a strong expression that this would be desirable. He writes that the Saint-Simonian scheme is

> impracticable indeed – but differing from Owenism, and from every other Utopia we ever read of, in this, that the impracticability is only in degree, not in kind; and that while most other visionary projects for reforming society are not only impossible, but if possible, would be bad, this plan, if it could be realised, would be good. It is the true ideal of a perfect human society; the spirit of which will more and more pervade even the existing social institutions, as human beings become wiser and better; and which, like any other model of unattainable perfection, everybody is the better for aspiring to, although it be impossible to reach it. We may never get to the north star, but there is much use in turning our faces towards it if we are journeying northward.[63]

I do not wish to argue that Mill's socialism was Saint-Simonian – it changed over time and was never wholly Saint-Simonian even in the 1830s. But statements like this show more than an ambivalent view as to what *would be good*, even if Mill remained unwilling to commit himself as to *what would actually happen*.[64]

One task in this chapter has been to show how the space opened up for Mill to see the possibilities of reform, and a type of society beyond what was imagined by his father and Bentham. Another is to try to explain why something beyond Benthamite reform might have seemed attractive to Mill. These quotes go some way toward showing that something beyond Benthamism *was* attractive. I have already mentioned Mill's commitment to progress and perfectionism – if there was *room* for more progress beyond this critical age, then we might assume Mill would think that would be good, given his general commitment to progress. And his realization that there could be improvements in the division of the product of labour, if human will was harnessed to achieving that, allowed him to entertain more radical ideas regarding alleviating the plight of the poor and undoing what he saw as injustices in current systems of distribution beyond what was imagined possible by his fellow Benthamites and classical economists. Another answer, however, arises from his adoption of the idea of critical and organic ages, and in particular from his assessment that there was much to be desired about organic ages, especially regarding social harmony, unanimity of interests, and social cohesion.[65]

THE "ORGANIC" NATURE OF AN ORGANIC AGE

Mill was persuaded by the Saint-Simonians that history was split into "organic" and "critical" ages. "Critical" ages were characterized by widespread skepticism about all past institutions; they were a time when the social fabric as well as the political, social, and religious institutions of the previous age were ripped up and reformulated. Mill valued much that characterized a "critical" age, but says that he learned in this period not to take "the peculiarities of an age of transition in opinion … for the normal attributes of humanity."[66] He also disliked much that characterized a critical "age of unbelief"; he preferred, in the long run, the Saint-Simonian critique to the conservative "bitterness" of Carlyle:

> I looked forward, through the present age of loud disputes but generally weak convictions, to a future which shall unite the best qualities of the critical with the best qualities of the organic periods: unchecked liberty of thought, unbounded freedom of individual action in all modes not hurtful to others; but also, convictions as to what is right and wrong, useful and pernicious, deeply engraven on the feelings by early education and general unanimity of sentiment, and so firmly grounded in reason and in the true exigencies of life, that they shall not, like all former and present creeds, religious, ethical, and political, require to be periodically thrown off and replaced by others.[67]

It was this that attracted him to the tripartite view of history proposed by Comte, who predicted that we were approaching a "positivist" organic age that held out the promise of this "general unanimity of sentiment ... firmly grounded in reason and in the true exigencies of life," which would, therefore, "not ... require to be ... thrown off" ever again.

Mill's desire for "unchecked liberty of thought" and for "unbounded freedom of individual action in all modes not hurtful to others" is familiar from his famous arguments in *On Liberty*. But his idea that it would be desirable that "convictions as to what is right and wrong, useful and pernicious" be "deeply engraven on the feelings by early education" is more surprising, given his apparent desire in *On Liberty* that we all be open to changing our opinions, even – perhaps especially – about such fundamental things as these, where it transpires that our opinions are either wholly or partly faulty. It is important to emphasize the desire Mill expresses for these convictions to be rooted in "general unanimity of sentiment," as well as his interest in a core element of an organic age – that people's fundamentals concerning ethics, political organization, and social structures be shared and fixed, giving them a real sense of shared interests and a meaningful "common" good, rather than what he elsewhere calls the "irritating sense of contrariety of interest"[68] that marked contemporary society.

In the immediate aftermath of his "crisis," Mill – though on the one hand mourning the sense of comradeship he had once shared with his fellow philosophic-radicals[69] – became concerned that "sectarianism" and "the spirit of argumentation" were not helping the current critical age grow into a new, organic age, but merely unduly extending it.[70] Mill was concerned to "strengthen the sympathies" not only with those who agreed with him, but also with "those who differ,"[71] and he disliked the antagonism that, he felt, characterized his contemporary critical age.

This desire to "strengthen the sympathies" was an important element of Mill's utilitarianism, as Jonathan Riley has rightly argued, emphasizing Mill's claim that we all have a desire to live in unity with our fellows.[72] Thus, Riley argues, when it comes to actions that can rightfully be called right or wrong, Mill thought there ought to be harmony between our actions and feelings and the feelings and aims of others.[73] Thus, Riley includes social harmony as one of the "permanent interests of man as a progressive being," which is how Mill parsed what he meant by "utility in its largest sense."[74] Social harmony in this way becomes not merely *conducive* to happiness but a part of it. That is, Mill thought we are happier when we are in sympathy with others and not in conflict with them, and when there is social stability of the kind that characterises an "organic" age. Similarly, he thought that "free institutions are next to impossible … among a people without fellow-feeling" because "the united public opinion, necessary to the working of representative government, cannot [then] exist."[75] This desire for social harmony, unanimity of sentiment, and "fellow-feeling" as core elements of happiness, and as necessities for good government, stemmed from his mental "crisis" and was quite different from the Benthamite utilitarianism that he previously endorsed. It is most evident in his analysis of, and discomfort with, class struggle and antipathy.

We see this critique as early as 1831, when Mill criticized the "*laissez-faire* spirit of the prevailing philosophy," which, he said, is "the idea by which, either consciously or unconsciously, nine-tenths of the men who can read and write, are at present possessed."[76] This view led men to believe "that every person, however uneducated or ill-educated, is the best judge of what is most for his own advantage, better even than the man whom he would delegate to make laws for him." The result of this "is to make mankind retrograde, for a certain space, towards the state of nature, by limiting the ends and functions of the social union, as strictly as possible, to those of a mere police." "The idea," he added, "that political society is a combination among mankind for the purpose of helping one another in every way in which help can be advantageous, is yet a stranger to the immense majority of understandings." Evidently, this view is the one Mill preferred.

Indeed, in a letter to Carlyle, Mill directly linked the idea of *laissez-faire* (as an economic principle but also as a broader principle of social philosophy) with the work of the "critical" age.[77] It was a "negative" principle that "has work to do yet, work, namely, of a destroying kind, & I am glad to think it has strength left to finish that, after which it must soon expire: peace be with its ashes when it does expire, for I doubt much if it will reach the resurrection." "I wish you could see something I have written lately about Bentham & Benthamism," he added, "but you can't." We, however, can. And in it we see criticism of Bentham for having a philosophy that, though it had many advantages for application to legislation, was "apt to fail in the consideration of the greater social questions – the theory of organic institutions and general forms of polity."[78] These questions, Mill said, relate not merely to the consequences of individual actions, and how best to create legislation that will harness even the individual least in tune with the general interest to act in accordance with the general happiness by making the commission of crime too costly; but also to "the great instruments of forming the national character; of carrying forward the members of the community towards perfection, or preserving them from degeneracy." As Mill noted, these were not things with which Bentham was concerned. But, Mill said, "this signal omission is one of the greatest deficiencies" of Bentham's "speculations on the theory of government."

Here, then, we get a sign of Mill's concern with "organic institutions" and, indeed, with a theory of how to bring them about. We also see signs of his perfectionism, and a notion that, while individuals are each individually perfectible, they are also members of a community that itself is capable of perfection, and that this community can have, or can at least impart to people, a "character" that differs from community to community. It is this "character" that would embody the common, communal "common sense" or shared knowledge of right and wrong and the other important attitudes sketched above.

Mill furthered this line in *Coleridge*. Here, he said, "the third essential condition of stability in political society, is a strong and active principle of cohesion among the members of the same community or state."[79] This "strong and active principle of cohesion," he immediately went on to say, is not what is vulgarly thought of as "nationalism." That is, it is not based on "senseless antipathy to foreigners," "indifference to the general welfare of the human race," "or unjust preference for the supposed interests of our own country." Instead, Mill meant "a principle of sympathy, not of hostility; of union, not of separation"; "a feeling of common interest among those who live under the same government, and are contained within the same natural or historical boundaries"; "that one part of the community do not consider themselves as foreigners with regard to another part; that they set a value on their connection; feel that they are one people, that their lot is cast together, that evil to any of their fellow-countrymen is evil to themselves; and do not desire selfishly to free themselves from their share of any common inconvenience by severing the connection."

He cited as good examples of states that have enjoyed this "community of interests," "those ancient commonwealths" such as Rome, which "succeeded in establishing the feeling of a common country amoung [sic] the provinces of her vast and divided empire." It is striking that ancient Rome is one of his examples of an "organic age." Mill went on to criticize "the French philosophers of the eighteenth century," who were among his childhood heroes, for "overlook[ing]" "these essential requisites of civil society" and "disregard[ing] the elementary principles of the social union." Conservatives rightly noted the need for these "elementary principles," but these "critical" thinkers preoccupied themselves with weakening government and thus destroying the bad institutions and "unsettling everything which was still considered settled, making men doubtful of the few things of which they still felt certain; and in uprooting what little remained in the people's minds of reverence for anything above them, of respect to any of the limits which custom and prescription had set to the indulgence of each man's fancies or inclinations, or of attachment to any of the things which belonged to them as a nation, and which made them feel their unity as such."

Thus, though Mill admitted that "when society requires to be rebuilt, there is no use in attempting to rebuild it on the old plan," he feared the French revolutionaries "threw away the shell without preserving the kernel; and attempt[ed] to new-model society without the binding forces which hold society together."

Here, then, we see Mill's new-found realization that there are such "binding forces," and a new-found commitment to the importance of a certain kind of social unity, based on "a principle of sympathy" and "union"; on "a feeling of common interest"; on a sense that our "lot is cast together" as a community that entails a willingness to shoulder burdens arising from this connection; and on a valuing of this connection and "community of interests" in its own right. This is echoed in his criticism of the "laissez-faire" that "[c]ivilisation … calls tolerance," which, though it no longer puts a "moral hero" to death for heresy, ensures he will "be everywhere ill spoken of, and … fail in all his worldly concerns; and if he be unusually fortunate he may, perhaps, be so well treated by the rest of mankind, as to be allowed to be honest in peace."[80] Mill here was evidently concerned that contemporary "toleration," though devoid of violence, was also devoid of "sympathy" with one's fellow-men, whom we would happily see "fail in all his worldly concerns" because we disliked their moral views.

It was because of this lack of sympathy that in 1839 Mill expressed his hope to see a new "Reform Party" that would build a coalition between the middle and working classes, which would breed "goodwill" between the classes. He hoped especially that the middle classes would do as they should, and support working-class efforts to set up workers' cooperatives to "carry on the great operations of industry independently of individual capitalists, independently of inequality of wealth and the irritating sense of contrariety of interest" that characterized contemporary society.[81] It is not that Mill was convinced that these socialist experiments would work. If they did, he wrote, it would be good. But if they did not, it would *still* be good, in that they would provide a useful "instruction … in political economy" to workers that these "utopian" schemes were *not* the route to their improvement, and that, instead, they should pin their hopes on philosophic-radical reforms to existing capitalism. That is, they should look to "correction of the abuses of government; the improvement of their own habits, and a due proportioning of their numbers to the field of employment" either through colonization or "forbearing to call them into existence" (i.e., family-planning) to improve their lot.

Mill still put his faith, then, in philosophic-radical reforms as the most useful immediate course of action to improve society and, in particular, the position of the poor. But he was evidently worried about "the irritating contrariety of interests" that marked contemporary society. He called for the working classes – and particularly the Chartists campaigning for universal suffrage – to cast their desire for reform not in terms of "predominance" but rather in terms of "equal justice"; and for the middle classes to give a fair hearing and response to the rightful demands of the workers for this "equal justice." "If ever democratic institutions are to be obtained quietly," he wrote – that is, without a violent revolution – "a great change in the sentiments of the two great classes towards each other must precede the concession" of power.

This critique of contemporary society as "critical" (i.e., "not organic") in the sense of there being this "irritating contrariety of interests," instead of the kind of harmony of interests based on shared understandings of right and wrong; sympathy with our fellow-men; and a sense of "community of interests" that we not only recognize but value, is something that developed in Mill's thought as he came to critique his initial philosophic-radicalism in the aftermath of his mental "crisis." It is a further indication of his opening to the realization that his father's preferred reforms were not the "last word" in maximizing human happiness, and improving society, as he had previously thought them to be. And, although evidently Mill discovered this thought through not only the socialist Saint-Simonians, but also conservatives such as Carlyle and Samuel Taylor Coleridge, it is an important element of what attracted him to socialism (which coined this new word because of its emphasis on the "social") and opened up the conceptual "space" for his own form of socialism to develop. That is, it was another area in which he found his early political philosophy wanting, and it was something that continued to inform the development of his "mature" political philosophy as he searched for the best way to build not only *a* new organic age, but perhaps the *final* one (a task that would include, of course, finding the best kind of architectural blue-print to try and follow).

Even though we might expect Mill (from *On Liberty*, at least) to favour the characteristics of a "critical" age, he found key elements of *both* ages to be not only desirable but vital for maximizing human happiness. Besides supporting freedom of speech, thought, and action, he admired the "organic" elements of harmonization of interests and, indeed, core views regarding the "fitness" of social, religious, and political institutions for society and individual life/happiness being shared by everyone in society to such an extent that they were almost not even recognized as such, but seen as "natural" (a useful at least partial synonym for "organic").

One might, of course, think this was just an aberrant reaction to his "most extreme Benthamism,"[82] and that a later move away from writers such as Carlyle and Coleridge might evidence a move back toward endorsing "critical" rather than "organic" societies. This is not the case. These same ideas are visible in Mill's concern regarding class warfare from the 1840s onwards;[83] in his writing about good government in the 1860s;[84] in *Utilitarianism*;[85] and in his *Autobiography*.[86] Instead, this was a concern that grew on Mill as he critically reflected on contemporary political, social, and economic institutions and read the works of the Saint-Simonians, Carlyle, and Coleridge, finding in them something that was lacking in Benthamism. It would remain a central concern throughout his life.

CONCLUSION

When trying to understand the idea of Mill's socialism, it can seem hard to see where there is intellectual, political, or imaginative space for Mill to have developed into a socialist. Knowing his upbringing, the arguments of *On Liberty*, and his commitment to "*laisser-faire* the general rule" in *Principles of Political Economy*, it can seem as though he found "classical" liberalism sufficient from cradle to grave. However, Mill's mental "crisis" in the winter of 1826–27 opened up conceptual space in at least three ways, which made him reassess, and ultimately find wanting, his original philosophic-radicalism.

The future scope of human society opened up to a greater distance with Mill's realization that he lived, not in an "end of history," but merely in a "critical age" that would eventually be replaced by an "organic" one. The institutions championed by his father, Bentham, and his fellow philosophic-radicals were sufficient and indeed ideally suited for the contempory age, but not for a future age. This must involve further political reform, including the building of a new social cohesion and harmony. It would also necessitate further economic reform: the modes of distribution that were championed by his father and other political economists were only attendant on *those* institutions – they were not necessarily the "best" for all time. Indeed, given the relationship between the laws of distribution and social institutions (which were a human construction), as humanity built *new* institutions, modes of distribution would also have to change – preferably into something (even) more just than what his father championed. This, and the new sense of social solidarity, would greatly improve human happiness in ways that Bentham, for instance, had missed in his analysis of utility. In this way, then, Mill's "crisis," and the means by which he sought to recover from it – and in particular his engagement with Saint-Simonian thought – led him to "a qualified socialism," the content and development of which the rest of this book will explore.

CHAPTER TWO

Criticisms of Capitalism and Mill's Idea of a "Perfected" System of Private Property

> I had seen little further than the old school of political economists into the possibilities of fundamental improvement in social arrangements ... The notion that it was possible to go further ... in removing the injustice – for injustice it is whether admitting of a complete remedy or not – involved in the fact that some are born to riches and the vast majority to poverty, I then reckoned chimerical ... In short, I was a democrat, but not the least of a Socialist.[1]

John Stuart Mill records that his mental "crisis" brought about the only "revolution" that ever occurred in his thinking – but that still to come were substantial changes to his views regarding "political economy," changes that, particularly through the 1840s and early 1850s, led him away from his initial views toward something "under the general designation of Socialist."[2] The previous chapter explored how his reaction to his "crisis" carved out the necessary "space" for a possible socialist future.

In that chapter, I noted that Mill referred to Saint-Simonism as the "North Star" by which we should navigate social reform. He did not think the Saint-Simonians' scheme practicable, but he did think that, if it was, it would be desirable. But at least in the 1830s, Mill was not sanguine about the world changing to such an extent that their scheme would soon be practicable. Moreover, as in the 1820s, he thought that a great deal of progress could be achieved within the framework of individual property, so long as it was substantially reformed. Given that this aim was more "available as a present resource"[3] than any type of socialism, he felt this should be the focus for contemporary reform, though guided by the "ultimate" of human progress as represented by the Saint-Simonian "North Star."

Mill describes this reformed system of individual property in *Principles* as "the régime of individual property, not as it is, but as it might be made."[4] In the 1830s and early 1840s, his ideas as to what this might look like were developing beyond the traditional Benthamite reforms to those of primogeniture and entails he had used to champion.

Importantly, this "régime" would not look precisely like "laissez-faire" capitalism – at least not as Mill (and his contemporaries) understood it, or as we generally understand the term.[5] This is worth emphasizing, because Mill is generally seen as a proponent of *laissez-faire*, and this, in turn, is used as a reason for thinking it impossible he could ever "really" be a socialist.[6] Mill's concerns with *laissez-faire* have their roots in his mental "crisis," and it may be that he was trying to maintain a distinction between classical views of *laissez-faire* and his own position in *Principles*, where he uses the esoteric spelling "laisser-faire."[7] Certainly what he says there should be "the general rule" is not what is usually understood by the term, though it fits within the general sense of "leaving alone."

Moreover, Mill had concerns about the contemporary concept of *laissez-faire* capitalism; indeed, he had concerns about the existing regime of individual property, and about such regimes more broadly. These might, in a final determination by the people of the future, turn out to be lesser evils than those inherent in socialism (and particularly communism), but it is worth flagging the fact that Mill *did* have these concerns and did not simply or wholeheartedly endorse regimes of individual property (be they *laissez-faire*, *laisser-faire*, or some other variety). This is important, in part because it weakens the prevailing view of Mill as a supporter of not only *laissez-faire* but also capitalism more widely (perhaps as an inherent part of his liberalism), and in part because it helps us see what Mill found attractive in certain kinds of socialism.

In this chapter I first sketch Mill's criticisms of the contemporary usage of "laissez-faire" and show what he meant by his term "laisser-faire." I then consider the other criticisms of capitalism he mounts, some of which may only be criticisms of contemporary capitalist practices (and thus not necessarily flaws with capitalism *per se*), but some of which confront more fundamental problems that would apply to any system of private property. These are criticisms made on the grounds of justice and equality; freedom and individuality; the social ethos; proto-environmentalism; and efficiency. Not all of them can be overcome even in a much-reformed system of individual property, which *always* leads to inequality. In understanding Mill's critique of even ideal regimes of individual property, we will be able to see what led him to socialism.

MILL'S CRITIQUE OF "LAISSEZ-FAIRE"

Bruce Baum is right to note that one ought not to confuse Mill's commitment to individual liberty with *laissez-faire*.[8] What Mill defends in *On Liberty* is complete individual freedom in a self-regarding sphere; and he explicitly says that "trade is a social act" – that is, it is not a self-regarding action[9] – though "laisser-faire" ought to be "the general rule."[10] That Mill did not mean by this the same thing as his contemporary supporters of *laissez-faire* had in mind, however, is clear from his early critiques of the term,[11] critiques he develops more fully in *Principles*.

According to Mill, the doctrine of *laissez-faire* sets out to limit government to as little as is necessary for enforcing promises and protecting people from force and fraud.[12] Mill makes several criticisms of this principle, but the main thrust of his argument is that this doctrine does not properly define the legitimate functions and limits of government.[13] That is, it does not encompass some legitimate functions of the state (e.g., the state managing property on the behalf of "incompetent" heirs, and, more fundamentally, the necessarily *social* determination of property rights themselves). Moreover, it allows for some illegitimate functions (e.g., wrongly enforcing the promise to be a slave). It ought not, then, to be the guiding principle of our economic policy.

That said, he thought there was merit in some arguments put forward by proponents of *laissez-faire*. He disagreed with the argument that the government would become overburdened if it did more than protect people from force and fraud, and enforce their promises, pointing out that no one expects one single government department to deal with every governmental interference/action.[14] However, he did agree that there should be an inviolable "circle" around people, interference with which by the government should be opposed.[15] He also thought we ought to be wary of *any* extension of government power, for this could lead to the tyranny of the majority and a decline in individuality – though, of course, this entailed *caution*, not an outright ban.[16] He also agreed that government provision can often be inefficient, especially as individuals are generally better judges of their own interests than civil servants. Lastly, he concurred with proponents of *laissez-faire* in their belief that the habit of relying on the government for things to be done for one breeds the wrong kind of character in a nation, leading to a people incapable of doing things on their own collective agency and initiative.

However, Mill fundamentally disagreed with the premise upon which *laissez-faire*, as an economic *and* a social doctrine, was predicated. This viewed society as a conglomeration of individuals, held together as minimally as possible by a government (the classic "nightwatchman" view of the state). On this view, government – and indeed society – are necessary evils, which allow everyone to safely pursue their own interests. Mill did not endorse this idea of society, writing, rather, that society could be a "combination among mankind for the purpose of helping one another in every way in which help can be advantageous."[17] In a similar vein he extolled Comte's idea regarding labour. This, he said, "has great beauty and grandeur in it," and realization of it "would be a cultivation of the social feelings on a most essential point."[18] Comte's idea was "that every person who lives by any useful work, should be habituated to regard himself as not an individual working for his private benefit, but as a public functionary; and his wages, of whatever sort, not as the remuneration or purchase-money of his labour, which should be given freely, but as the provision made by society to enable him to carry it on, and to replace the materials and products which have been consumed in the process."

Comte noted that "in modern industry everyone in fact works much more for others than for himself" because "his productions are to be consumed by others, and it is only necessary that his thought and imagination should adapt themselves to the real state of the fact." Mill expressed a concern that things were not quite so simple, for "a strong sense that he is working for others may lead to nothing better than feeling himself necessary to them." This feeling, instead of prompting us to "freely giv[e] ... his commodity, may only encourage him to put a high price on it":

> What M. Comte really means is that we should regard working for the benefit of others as a good in itself; that we should desire it for its own sake, and not for the sake of remuneration, which cannot justify doing what we like: that the proper return for a service to society is the gratitude of society: and that the moral claim of any one in regard to the provision for his personal wants, is not a question of quid pro quo in respect to his co-operation, but of how much the circumstances of society permit to be assigned to him, consistently with the just claims of others. To this opinion we entirely subscribe.[19]

Setting wages via the market may, Mill acknowledged, "represent a practical necessity," but, he insisted, it did not "represent ... a moral ideal." Civilization may – as yet – not be able to organize things any better "that this first rude approach to an equitable distribution ... But ... the true moral and social idea of labour is in no way affected" by that.

This passage shows how different Mill's view was to traditional *laisser-faire* and explains that even when he says "*laisser-faire* the general rule" he means both "for now" and also that this is a compromise with the current state of human nature and reality, not a normative ideal. Mill's "ideal" view of society, and of work, is fundamentally opposite to libertarianism and to the atomistic view of society that underpins the moral case for *laissez-faire*.

Among other things, this view gave Mill a fundamentally different outlook on what society, and government, was *for* to supporters of *laissez-faire*. This led to Mill allowing a broader scope for both coercive ("authoritative") and what he saw as non-coercive ("non-authoritative") governmental actions than traditional supporters of *laissez-faire* would have allowed.[20]

According to Mill, authoritative governmental actions impact on individual liberty in inhibiting, regulatory, or coercive ways. They are not necessarily bad in themselves – the authoritative prohibition of murder is, for instance, both necessary and good. What *is* bad is too many authoritative actions, especially those that extend into "self-regarding" areas. As Mill put it, "the authoritative form of government intervention has a much more limited sphere of legitimate action" than non-authoritative actions, and "there are large departments of human life from which it must be unreservedly and imperiously excluded." Non-authoritative actions are not coercive: instead, they help individuals achieve their aims, often through the provision of services. These are not coercive, for the government has no monopoly on the services and does not mandate their use.

Mill set out guidelines as to what authoritative and non-authoritative actions are justified, and preferable, in *Principles*. They do not fit under the heading of "enforcing promises, and prevention of force and fraud" favoured by proponents of *laissez-faire*. Regarding authoritative interferences, Mill declared that where people cannot look after their own interests, the government has to step in and look after them for them (an obvious example being children – Mill insisted that the government should appoint either family members or its own officials to look after them if their own parents are dead, or not doing their duty).[21] The government should interfere authoritatively with contract-making in order to ensure that no one can sign away their future irrevocably – this edict stretches from voluntary slavery (banned entirely) through marriage (which should only be allowed if it is dissolvable) to employment contracts (where people should be prevented from agreeing to either pay or conditions without the contract being negotiable at regular and frequent intervals).[22] Mill also argued that the government can authoritatively decree that all its citizens must be educated.[23] Furthermore, the government should interfere authoritatively to enforce acts that are already generally willed but that cannot be enacted without executive action (i.e., to solve coordination problems): his prime example is legislation limiting working hours.[24] Lastly, Mill argued that the government should be charged with street cleaning and lighting and other aspects of public health.[25]

Mill also endorsed several non-authoritative interferences. One of these was a monopoly on the coining of money.[26] Another was municipal ownership, and provision, of utilities such as gas and water; yet another was state ownership/provision of means of communication such as canals, roads, and railways.[27] Regarding the efficiency and utility of government management of such things, Mill pointed out that the same arguments arose against their provision by the joint-stock companies that at the time were responsible for their provision.[28] Moreover, though there was ostensible competition between providers, these joint-stock companies were monopolies in all but name. That being the case, the public might as well benefit from the monopoly profits rather any private individuals – indeed, Mill seems to have thought there was a greater claim of utility, perhaps even justice, in the government maintaining these monopoly profits, for there would be injustice in allowing an individual to reap the profits of import levies.

Mill also supported, as a non-authoritative interference, government provision of education.[29] Education in government schools would not necessarily be free; rather, it would be means-tested. However, *all* children were to be assured of an education, even if their parents did not have the means to pay for it.[30] He also approved the provision of a poor law, at least at a basic level of subsistence and in "less-eligible" conditions, in order to prevent anyone from dying because they were destitute,[31] and he supported the orchestration of acts of public benefit that it would be difficult to organize privately, such as geographical exploration and research in both science and the arts, including "endowments" for "the learned class."[32]

In brief, Mill supported a number of government interferences that could not be justified under the principles of *laissez-faire* but that *could* be justified by Mill's assertion that society should be a combination of individuals seeking to help one another and by his idea that a real political community is one in which "one part of the community do not consider themselves foreigners with regard to another part," but "set a value on their connection" and "feel ... that their lot is cast together" and therefore will pay, or do, "their share of any common inconvenience," including helping shoulder common burdens even where this might involve provision of services they themselves may never need nor desire.[33]

Moreover, contrary to most definitions of *laissez-faire*, Mill embraced not only governmental interference in the market but also trade union action.[34] Indeed, he went so far as to say that any market without trade unions (or similar) would not really be free, because only when working people can associate to protect their interests as labourers can they "higgle," and thus ensure that the real market wage is being offered, not the one that employers can impose as they see fit because they hold more power.[35] This is a very different picture than is usually offered by adherents of *laissez-faire*, and shows that what Mill felt was a "positive good" that could be secured by governmental interference was of a far wider scope than many would assume.

Mill's view of "laisser-faire," then, is not usually what is understood as "*laissez-faire* capitalism." When Mill says "*laisser-faire* the general rule," what he has in mind is the right "general rule" for "the present stage of human improvement," as the passage from *Auguste Comte* suggests. That is, this whole long section of *Principles* has for its subject what Mill said "the political economist, for a considerable time to come, will chiefly be concerned with," which is, "the conditions of existence and progress belonging to a society founded on private property and individual competition," where, he thought, "the object [which] ought to be principally aimed at ... is not the subversion of the system of individual property, but the improvement of it, and the full participation of every member of the community in its benefits."[36] But this means "*laisser-faire*" is *only* "the general rule" within a system of individual property. It does not mean this system had moral priority for Mill, in and of itself. And it does not mean he was endorsing even his own version of *laisser-faire* as the "*dernier mot* of legislation."[37] Indeed, we can see that Mill really saw it as the expedient response to actual contemporary conditions – conditions he sought to change.

Moreover, not only was Mill not a supporter of "*laissez-faire*" as either we, or his contemporaries might understand it, but the very fact that he thought "the system of individual property" was capable of "improvement" shows he was not an uncritical supporter of contemporary capitalism. I now consider Mill's critiques of contemporary capitalism more broadly – that is, beyond, his concerns regarding the doctrine of *laissez-faire* – before going on to consider which of these criticisms might remain unmet even by "the system of individual property" that had been "improved" such that "the full participation of every member of the community in its benefits" had been secured. That is, even by the "régime of individual property, not as it is, but as it might be made."[38]

MILL'S CRITICISMS OF CONTEMPORARY CAPITALISM

Evidently, Mill much preferred the current system of individual property to feudalism – it was more productive and efficient, offering a chance to eradicate poverty, and it went hand-in-hand with important advances in knowledge and with political and social reforms such as representative government, civil liberties, and the destruction of inherited and established privilege. When faced with paternalist theorists,

Mill clearly argued against what was being hailed as a "return" to feudal relations of dependence and protection as inappropriate, unsuitable, and outdated, as well as arguing that such relationships never really existed as anything other than exploitation, conquest, and use of force.[39]

However, Mill was not an uncritical supporter of capitalism, offering five grounds for criticizing contemporary institutions.[40] First – inefficiency and waste. Capitalist production was often inefficient and wasteful, for three reasons. One, because the worker had no interest in anything other than working as little as possible for his or her wage and only worked diligently when directly under their master's eye.[41] Two, because it devoted "the greater part" of society's "unproductive labour"[42] to "objects" of "little worth."[43] Three, because it involved so many "mere distributors" taking an "enormous portion of the produce of industry."[44]

Second – liberty and individuality. So strongly did Mill feel this that he wrote, "the restraints of Communism" (of which he lists several) "would be freedom in comparison with the present condition of the majority of the human race." Most contemporary labourers had little or no choice of occupation or freedom of movement, and were "practically as dependent" on "fixed rules" and "the will of others" as they could be, short of slavery. Moreover, half the world's population (women) lived in "entire domestic subjection."[45] Lastly, *On Liberty* critiques the lack of opportunity for the "free development of individuality," and limited civil liberties enjoyed, in a society with individual property (though the critiques do not *only* apply to such a society).

Third – equality and justice. Capitalist distribution was so illegitimately *unequal*, wrote Mill, that "attempts … to defend private property, on the ground of justice, must inevitably fail" because "the distinction between rich and poor, so slightly connected as it with merit and demerit, or even with exertion and want of exertion in the individual, is obviously unjust."[46] He thought it was unjust that "some are born to riches and the vast majority to poverty";[47] that some people, who were perfectly *capable* of labouring, "were exempt from bearing their share of the necessary labours of human life" without having "fairly earned rest by previous toil";[48] and that remuneration was so unequally "apportioned ... almost in an inverse ratio to labour," with "the largest portions" going "to those who have never worked at all, the next largest to those whose work is almost nominal, and so in a descending scale."[49] These injustices compounded a further injustice, the "prodigious inequality" with which the "benefits" of unproductive labour were distributed, with a "large share ... fall[ing] to the lot of persons who render no equivalent service in return."[50]

One injustice, then, is that there is a class of people who, through mere accident of birth, do not labour yet benefit most by the labour done by others. Another is that remuneration *ought* to be proportioned to effort or exertion, yet in contemporary capitalism almost the opposite occurs, such that those who do the least receive the most, and "remuneration" tends to "dwindle" as "work grows harder and more disagreeable."[51] Mill's criticism that "the most fatiguing and exhausting bodily labour cannot count with certainty on being able to earn even the necessaries of life" is connected to this problem of an "inverse ratio" between effort and remuneration, but it is also speaking to a separate point – that those who *were* willing (as well as able) to work under contemporary capitalism, and, indeed, who worked the hardest, were still not guaranteed subsistence, still less the full fruits of their labour.

This is connected to another problem regarding subsistence and capitalism's inability – or, at least, unwillingness – to secure it for everyone. Mill characterized contemporary capitalism as akin to a race commanded by an infamously cruel Roman emperor in which "those who came hindermost" would be put to death. "It would not be any diminution of the injustice," Mill insisted, "that the strongest or nimblest would ... be certain to escape. The misery and the crime would be that any were put to death at all."[52]

Similarly, Mill thought that if there was to be a "race" in life, people ought to "start fair" in it and have what we might now think of as fair equality of opportunity to make the most of their natural talents, industry, and abstinence.[53] He criticized existing capitalist institutions that "have not held the balance fairly between human beings, but have heaped impediments upon some, to give advantage to others; they have purposely fostered inequalities, and prevented all from starting fair in the race."[54]

Lastly, concerning equality and justice, Mill criticized contemporary capitalism for not even achieving the kind of justice it was designed to produce: the laws of private property, under contemporary capitalism, did not guarantee the labourer the fruits of his labour, but instead "have made property of things which never ought to be property, and absolute property where only a qualified property ought to exist."[55] That is, contemporary capitalism allowed people to unfairly benefit from the labour and abstinence of others, and to also benefit from property in, for instance, land, which is not the product of anyone's labour, while not securing for many labourers the fruit of their own efforts.

Overall, then, contemporary capitalism was open to a number of criticisms on the grounds of justice and inequality. Indeed, Mill went so far as to say that even the problems of the least optimal kind of communism were "as dust in the balance" compared to the injustices of contemporary capitalism.[56]

Fourth, Mill criticized capitalism's obsession with the relentless pursuit of growth. This critique has two strands. One is proto-environmentalist.[57] Mill wrote passionately and eloquently about the paucity of a world with "nothing left to the spontaneous activity of nature; with every rood of land brought into cultivation, which is capable of growing food for human beings; every flowery waste or natural pasture ploughed up, all quadrupeds or birds which are not domesticated for man's use exterminated as his rivals for food, every hedgerow or superfluous tree rooted out, and scarcely a place left where a wild shrub or flower could grow without being eradicated as a weed in the name of improved agriculture."[58] He saw contemporary capitalism, with its relentless pursuit of growth, as inexorably leading to this.

The second element is also linked to his final ground for criticizing capitalism: the social ethos that the pursuit of growth both is motivated by and engenders:[59] the "struggling to get on" by the "trampling, crushing, elbowing and treading on each other's heels which form the existing type of our social life." If we *are* going to relentlessly pursue riches, he said, it would be better if everyone had an equal opportunity to do it. However, it would be better still if, "while no one is poor, no one desires to be richer, nor has any reasons to fear being thrust back, by the efforts of others to push themselves forward."[60] Or "that society at large should not be overworked, nor over-anxious about the means of subsistence."[61] Or, again, where there will be "a well-paid and affluent body of labourers; no enormous fortunes ... but a much larger body of persons than at present, not only exempt from the coarser toils, but with sufficient leisure, both physical and mental, from mechanical details, to cultivate freely the graces of life, and afford examples of them to the classes less favourably circumstanced for their growth."

Moreover, Mill criticized the very metric of success against which capitalist societies (and the people within them) measure themselves: "I know not why it should be a matter of congratulation that persons who are already richer than any one needs to be, should have doubled their means of consuming things which give little or no pleasure except as representative of wealth: or that numbers of individuals should pass over, every year, from the middle classes into a richer class, or from the class of the occupied rich to that of the unoccupied."[62] Indeed, he insisted we need, not "increased production," but "a better distribution," and to use technology to lighten people's labour, rather than increasing the amount of stuff we produce.

Lastly, Mill criticized the quality of relationships in contemporary capitalism: "the need of greater fellow-feeling and community of interest between the mass of the people and those who are by courtesy considered to guide and govern them," he said, "does not require the aid of exaggeration." "We yield to no one," he continued, "in our wish that 'cash payment' should no longer be the universal nexus between man and man."[63] His hope was that "the employers and employed should have the feelings of friendly allies, not of hostile rivals whose gain is each other's loss" and that they will be bound by "real attachment." Where "subordination" is legitimate, this will not be, as it generally is now, "either hypocrisy or servility" but "the result of personal qualities" "equally" on *both* sides. There will not be the "concealed enmity" toward the "whole class of employers, in the whole class of the employed" nor the ensuing "deep-seated alienation of feeling."[64] That is, the very quality of relationships between people needed to change in order to overcome contemporary class antagonisms and achieve meaningful social harmony.

Contemporary capitalism, then, was focused on the wrong things (increasing material wealth for a very few, exemplified in being able to cease labouring altogether); and fostered the wrong kind of relationships among people – instead of real community of interests, or a sense of "sympathy" and "union," there was class warfare, the "irritating contrariety of interests," and a general willingness to "elbow" another out of the way for personal gain, often to that other's destruction.

Mill was not, then, an uncritical supporter of contemporary capitalism either in theory or in practice. On the other hand, he clearly thought contemporary capitalism preferable to feudalism, and he made plain in *Principles* that what we ought to consider – particularly in comparison to socialism – was not *contemporary* capitalism, but "the régime of individual property ... as it might be made."[65] This would be a regime that had overcome, or at least mitigated, the problems Mill had raised against contemporary capitalism as much as possible, and it is to the question of what this would look like that I now turn.

"The Régime of Individual Property ... as It Might be Made"

There are two ways of interpreting what Mill meant by "the régime of individual property ... as it might be made." On the one hand, we might parse this as "the existing régime of individual property as, by feasible and attainable improvements, it might be made by workers, capitalists, voters, politicians, economists, civil servants etc. over time." On the other hand, there is "the régime of individual property as it might be created from scratch in a world without existing property relations."[66] Mill briefly mentioned the latter in *Principles*, but spent more time considering the former. It is worth exploring the more "ideal" version, because this view of what private property might look like if it did not start from existing non-ideal circumstances gives us a better view of Mill's perspective on what made individual property defensible and, indeed, desirable; it also helps us navigate toward a clearer view of what Mill thought might be achieved through gradual improvement even in countries with existing property regimes.

"The régime of individual property ... as it might be made" by "colonists, occupying ... an uninhabited country"

Mill invited us to consider "a body of colonists, occupying for the first time an uninhabited country; bringing nothing with them but what belonged to them in common, and having a clear field for the adoption of the institutions and policy which they judged most expedient." If they adopted private property, it would not be accompanied by "the initial inequalities and injustices which obstruct the beneficial operation of the principle" in existing "old" societies:

> Every full grown man or woman, we must suppose, would be secured in the unfettered use and disposal of his or her bodily and mental faculties; and the instruments of production, the land and tools, would be divided equally among them, so that all might start, in respect to outward appliances, on equal terms ... [C]ompensation might be made for the injuries of nature, and the balance redressed by assigning to the less robust members of the community advantages in the distribution, sufficient to put them on a par with the rest. But the division, once made, would not again be interfered with; individuals would be left to their own exertions and to the ordinary chances for making an advantageous use of what was assigned to them.[67]

For the modern reader, the idea of "colonists," and whether they could actually find an "uninhabited country," is problematic. Mill might have had in mind places such as Australia, New Zealand, Canada, and parts of what is now the United States. We, however, can imagine these "colonists" as landing on the Moon, or Mars. The point is to make a thought experiment – *if* people arrived in a country without existing property arrangements (neither existing there already, nor brought with them), what would they do – institute individual property, or a form of communal property?[68] *If* they picked individual property, they could institute the "best" form of it, for they would not have to compromise with existing non-ideal circumstances that might mean that, in the real world, the "ideal" could never be attained.

Mill's sketch of an "ideal" regime of individual property speaks directly to some of his concerns about contemporary capitalism and more obliquely to others. Most obviously, this "ideal" regime is deliberately designed to expunge "the initial inequalities and injustices which obstruct the beneficial operation of the principle [of private property] in the old societies."[69]

Concerning freedom and individuality, no adult would be "fettered" in the "use and disposal of his or her bodily and mental faculties." That is, no occupations would be barred to (or reserved for) people on the grounds of class, religion, familial relationships, or gender. Even if this did not end, it would evidently help mitigate against, some of the problems Mill identified with regard to freedom and individuality in contemporary capitalism – particularly, but not solely, the problem of female domestic subjection.[70]

Similarly, the equal endowment might allow all colonists to work for themselves, either as subsistence farmers or as self-employed artisans and professionals (such as doctors). This would alleviate many of the criticisms Mill made of the contemporary system on the grounds of freedom and inequality, although such people might not enjoy very much freedom of choice regarding their occupation, or much ability to change it (subsistence farmers, for instance, being strongly tied to their work, hours, and land, with little opportunity for pursuing other employment options). If the colonists somehow managed to institute working for wages, then all of the concerns Mill had about lack of freedom in a wage system would apply just as much as they do to contemporary capitalism, unless the colonists adopted profit-sharing, which is less liable to this concern. Similarly, if the colonists adopted worker cooperatives, the concerns about liberty and independence would be assuaged – but then they would not have a regime of individual property anymore. Lastly, if the colonists worked entirely independently, they would risk forgoing what Mill evidently saw as the great advantages of "combined" labour, and the regime would be less efficient than it might be (notwithstanding Mill's concern about overproduction).[71] In terms of freedom and individuality, then, this regime would be a vast improvement on contemporary capitalism, but it would not be perfect.

Let us turn now to the question of justice and equality. "The instruments of production" – that is, land and tools – "would be divided equally" among the initial colonists. (It is not clear whether Mill envisaged *only* "full grown" colonists, or whether, if he was imagining that the colonists might arrive with children, he *also* thought these children would get an initial share.) This would prevent many of the injustices Mill identified in contemporary capitalism regarding people's unequal "start in the race" – no one would begin with an unfair advantage in terms of their ownership of capital. Indeed, Mill went even further in trying to make the race "fair," suggesting that the initial division would *not* be equal, but rather would involve "compensation ... for the injuries of nature" and "redress" the "balance" between the weaker and stronger members of the community. This would also mitigate somewhat a further concern Mill had regarding distributive justice – that unequal remuneration stemming not from choice but from natural "strength or capacity" unfairly "giv[es] to those who have; assigning most to those who are already favoured by nature"[72] – by at least initially giving more to those who "by nature" have least (or less). Evidently, the colonists' regime would be more just than contemporary capitalism.

The last element of Mill's sketch seems to be ruling out redistributive policies. However, Mill argued that even in current, non-ideal conditions, it was proven that "society can and therefore ought to insure every individual belonging to it against the extreme of want; that the condition even of those who are unable to find their own support, needs not be one of physical suffering, or the dread of it," and that "the fate of no member of the community needs to be abandoned to chance" so long as this "relief" was administered in conditions of "restricted indulgence, and enforced rigidity of discipline."[73] For him, this realization was "a step to something beyond": perhaps in a more "ideal" world, "relief" might be generous regarding "indulgences" (as well as "ample in respect to necessaries"), or might not have to be "accompanied by conditions which" those receiving it "disliked." It is hard to see why society would not still have this duty in a more ideal world, in cases where people had initially been provided with the means to "find their own support" but had become unable to do so, unless Mill thought this initial distribution would mean no one would ever be unable to support themselves. Note that Mill was deliberately arguing against the suggestion that people who bring their indigence on themselves somehow "deserve" to be left in conditions of want and need, a concept of justice that would presumably still hold in the "ideal" colony (unless conditions were so extreme there that society *could not* support such people). I suggest, therefore, that the restriction on redistribution did not rule out the provision of some sort of safety net for Mill's colonists, and that this would make it more just than contemporary capitalism. (Or at least *as just* as contemporary capitalism, if Mill felt that the Poor Law reforms had indeed provided this basic safety net to everyone.)

Mill allowed for the equal apportioning of "land" as well as "tools." It is worth our interrogating that proviso as well, because Mill noted elsewhere that though individual property in the *product* of land ought to belong to the labourer,[74] "the earth itself, its forests and waters, and all other natural riches, above and below the surface ... are the inheritance of the human race".[75] "If the land derived its productive power wholly from nature, and not at all from industry ... it not only would not be necessary, but it would be the height of injustice, to let the gift of nature be engrossed by individuals." It is, however, true that the land *does* derive "its productive power" at least in part from "industry" and that the promise of individual benefit motivates people to improve land.[76] Even this, though, does not necessitate individual *ownership* of land; it simply secures exclusive use and profit. Mill left open in *Principles* the question of whether land ought to be individually owned, "occupied for one season only," "be periodically re-divided as population increased," or owned jointly, or whether "the State might be the universal landlord, and the cultivators tenants under it."[77] Elsewhere he defended only the owner's "full enjoyment of whatever value he adds to the land by his own exertions and expenditure" rather than full "ownership" rights over land as those are usually understood.[78]

Given what Mill said about landownership, then, it is not clear whether "equal apportionment" of land to all the "colonists" would be "ideal." That is, there would be problems with it, even if these were not exacerbated through inheritance. Perhaps, as Mill was providing a very thumbnail sketch of an "ideal" form of individual property before going on to discuss the possibilities of "common ownership" in more detail, he did not want to get bogged down in details regarding the best form of landownership in this passage, given his detailed discussion of it elsewhere. Perhaps the limits on inheritance (to which I turn next) would solve the problems inherent in *existing* rules concerning landownership. Or perhaps Mill thought the colonists would implement the kind of tax and limited proprietary rights he himself favoured, but felt there was no need to go into that level of detail of their arrangements at this stage of *Principles*.

Perhaps, too, we see here a tension between a thought experiment and reality. Perhaps Mill really did think that equal portions was the best plan for new colonies – that this view, though not "just" in an abstract sense of the word, was the most expedient option for the real world. Certainly, he supported private ownership of land in some *actual* colonies such as Australia and New Zealand (though he could hardly have seen them as "uninhabited" – perhaps he thought *areas* of them were).[79] He was particularly in favour of Wakefield's scheme for using the profits from land sales to fund further colonization.[80] But even then, with this "ideal" sketch he would have had one eye on realities – perhaps on the funding of further colonization, and certainly on the harnessing of an individual profit motive to ensure that land use was maximized. *That*, of course, would involve the kind of social ethos that Mill was not particularly fond of (one centred around growth and personal gain) and might lead to the kind of environmental problems he was concerned about in contemporary capitalism. But perhaps Mill thought these were bridges this "colonist" society could cross as they became more pertinent. Evidently, it is not wholly possible to separate the reality from the ideal, even in Mill's thought experiment. Still, this question of landownership shows that even "the régime of individual property ... as it might be made" by "colonists occupying ... an uninhabited country" could not entirely escape some of the criticisms of contemporary capitalism that Mill made on the grounds of justice.

I have mentioned the potential impact of "inheritance" several times now, so it is time to think about it in more detail. Evidently, in the initial sketch Mill gave, he had in mind only the *first* generation. If contemporary laws of inheritance were permitted, then very quickly people would cease to start "on a par with the rest" in this society. Indeed, individuals' ability to pass on their wealth intergenerationally was one of the elements of the contemporary regime of individual property that Mill linked with "the initial inequalities and injustices which obstruct the beneficial operation of the principle in the old societies."[81]

Elsewhere, Mill advocated a limit on inheritance:[82] it should be no more than sufficient for a "comfortable"[83] or "moderate independence."[84] His goal was to "restrict ... what anyone should be permitted to acquire ... by the mere favour of others, without any exercise of his faculties," and to ensure that "if he desires any further accession of fortune, he shall work for it."[85] He did not give any more detail as to what this "independence" would look like.

Discussions in the scholarly literature are concerned with the "non-ideal" world – more specifically, with how contemporary capitalism might be reformed through, for instance, inheritance taxes.[86] This seems to be a separate question from the one that asks which laws of inheritance might be instantiated in a brand-new country that is "unhampered by previous possession" (the idea of being "unhampered" is illuminating), where the founders brought "nothing with them but what belonged to them in common" and where they had "a clear field for the adoption of the institutions and policy which they judged most expedient."[87] From what Mill said elsewhere, we can surmise that this "moderate" or "comfortable" independence would be sufficient to train someone for their preferred occupation (if there was enough capital to be left to them for that) and perhaps to buy them any necessary tools and licences and so on, in order that they had a fair chance at pursuing that occupation and making as much of a success of it as their own talents and efforts would allow. But it would not be enough to allow anyone to live *without* labouring for their entire life.[88]

Of course, this position allows for a certain relativity in terms of what a "comfortable" or "moderate" independence would mean, even if we allow that the other elements of "the regime of individual property ... as it might be made" by "colonists occupying ... an uninhabited country" would have far fewer, or far less great, differences in wealth. And this, in turn, undermines some of Mill's more egalitarian claims regarding the inherent unfairness of people not starting equally "in the race" by mere accident of birth: as he noted, such equality is not really compatible with any system of private property.[89] Again, then, even this "ideal" form of individual property cannot be made immune from *all* of Mill's criticisms.

Turning to the other grounds on which Mill criticized contemporary capitalism, there is little in this sketch to help us determine whether this regime would be more efficient than contemporary capitalism. There is a risk that the colonists would not enjoy the efficiency gains of combined labour, but merely all work independently; on the other hand, a smaller population might, at least initially, overcome the problem of "middlemen." Similarly, there is not really enough evidence to hazard a guess as to the impact on the "worth" of the products of unproductive labour (Should there even *be* any such products in a society just, as it were, "starting out" in a new world?), or the equity of their distribution. All things considered, then, this regime would be in some respects more efficient, and in some respects probably less efficient, than contemporary capitalism.

Lastly, there is the question of the social ethos of this regime compared to that of contemporary capitalism. There might well be an improvement in class relations, because initial parity might ensure there *were* no classes of employers and employed. Even if some people did end up employed by others, it is not clear that class antagonism would arise, given the initial division of resources, which would likely make the colony's workers more independent than contemporary proletarians. Much of this might depend on whether future generations cemented these classes through inheritance, giving rise to two classes in perpetuity.

Perhaps the emphasis on at least initial "parity" (to which, of course, all the colonists would have to agree) is a sign that the colony would not be marred by the "elbowing, crushing and trampling" that characterized contemporary society. Yet the idea is that there is "parity" at the start of a *race* – and without the safety net I argued we ought to imagine is included, this would be pretty akin to the "race" Mill disparaged in *Chapters* (where the "crime" would be that "any are put to death at all" for coming "hindermost" in it). (Though perhaps there would be this safety net in the colony.) Similarly, if there is still an emphasis on personal gain, on being "one up" on one's neighbours, and on relentlessly pursuing growth, there will be the same environmental problems down the line. Even the regime of individual property as it might be established by "unhampered" colonists, then, would be liable to some criticisms on the grounds of its social ethos.[90]

To sum up: the "regime of individual property ... as it might be made" by "colonists occupying ... an uninhabited country" would be much better than contemporary capitalism in a variety of ways. Its people would be more free and independent, though not entirely so, being potentially very much bound to their jobs or suffering from the same problems of wage labour as contemporary workers. It would be much fairer, with a more just division of initial assets going beyond strict equality to try and "compensate" for differences in strength and talent so that everyone would "start on a par." I have presumed, too, that it would try to preserve this "parity" in subsequent generations through limits on inheritance, though, as Mill noted, *no* system of individual property could allow everyone to start *completely* equal (a problem exacerbated even by his idea of a "moderate independence"). Thus, it would still be open to some criticisms of the grounds of justice and equality. On other important grounds, however (efficiency and the social ethos), it is not clear that there would *necessarily* be an improvement over contemporary capitalism, though a lack of class antagonism would be an important gain (so long as this lasted for more than the initial generation).

"The régime of individual property ... as it might be made" in *"the old societies"*

Mill did not give a detailed account of what the "régime of individual property ... as it might be made" in "the old societies" might look like, but we can piece together a pretty clear idea from what he says in *Principles*, *The Claims of Labour*, and *Chapters on Socialism*. The key elements were designed to ensure more equitable divisions of wealth and the products of labour; more efficient working and distributing practices; a better social ethos; and greater scope for liberty and individuality. His preferred reforms included limitations on the right of bequest and inheritance; transforming wage relations into "partnerships" through profit-sharing; the right forms of authoritative and non-authoritative state interventions in the market (including provision of some goods and services); and changes to the social ethos. Mill took as his starting point the very non-ideal realities of existing capitalism (built, as he reminded his readers, not on any acknowledged principle of justice to do with individual property, but on a history of conquest exacerbated by the self-interested machinations of vested class interests[91]). We should not be surprised, then, if this "régime" – even at its best – is not immune from criticism.

Taxation and Inheritance

Mill envisaged a society in which there were still individual owners of capital but very few individual owners of vast fortunes. In particular, his reformed version of individual property would have a very different system of taxation and inheritance.

Mill opposed a graduated income tax. Such a tax was first introduced in England during the Napoleonic Wars and then reintroduced in 1842 by Sir Robert Peel to address a growing budget deficit. When Mill wrote about it, then, it was in the context of this being a new fiscal strategy, and one that people were beginning to argue could be used to redistributive, egalitarian effect. "I am as desirous as anyone that means should be taken to diminish those inequalities [of wealth]," Mill said, "but not so as to relieve the prodigal at the expense of the prudent."[92] Claeys argues that Mill believed "the state has as one basic aim[,] rectifying social and economic inequality,"[93] but it was a specific *form* of inequality he had in mind, at least when writing about taxation in contemporary capitalism – the inequalities generated by inheritance. "It is not the fortunes which are earned, but those which are unearned, that it is for the public good to place under limitation," Mill said.[94] Again, he referred to the idea of the government ensuring that "all start fair" in the race, and he described graduated income taxes as "hanging a weight upon the swift to diminish the distance between them and the slow."[95] He added that "[m]any, indeed, fail with greater efforts than those with which others succeed, not from any difference of merits, but difference of opportunities: but if all were done which it would be in the power of a good government to do, by instruction and legislation, to diminish this inequality of opportunities, the difference of fortune arising from people's own earnings could not justly give umbrage."

Good government, then, should tax earned income equally (if it needs to tax income at all), leaving a portion sufficient for the necessities of life untaxed. By "equally," though, Mill means that people should make an equal sacrifice, not that everyone should pay the same amount in tax.[96] (In modern terms, he supported a proportional – or "flat" – income tax, with some income being below a taxation threshold.) Preferably, government should turn most of its attention to taxing unearned increments on land,[97] and to the taxation of inheritance. Dependents left without support should be provided for if they would otherwise be a burden on the state (notwithstanding the testator's wishes); intestate estates (apart from this proviso) should escheat to the state.[98] Apart from some special exemptions, Mill otherwise believed that all anyone should be able to inherit was a "comfortable" or "moderate independence."

Other commentators have estimated this to be quite a large amount.[99] However, Claeys rightly notes that these phrases of Mill's (and another, "a limited amount," which is to be found in a manuscript taken to be Taylor's work, but which is in Mill's handwriting[100]) remain uninterrogated by most Mill scholars, and undefined in Mill's own writing.

In considering the claims of children, Mill wrote: "The parent owes to society to endeavour to make the child a good and valuable member of it, and owes to the children to provide, so far as depends on him, such education, and such appliances and means, as will enable them to start with a fair chance of achieving by their own exertions a successful life. To this, every child has a claim; and I cannot admit, that as a child he has a claim to more."[101]

Everyone acknowledges that people owe to illegitimate children "the amount of provision for his welfare which will enable him to make his life on the whole a desirable one," Mill said. "I hold that to no child, merely as such, anything more is due." Mill went on to criticize the parenting of many "possessors of terminable incomes" who raise their children "in habits of luxury which they will not have the means if indulging in after-life." Some argued that rich parents ought to (i.e., have a duty to) leave to their children "greater provision ... than would suffice for children otherwise brought up" because of the habits and expectations they will have formed. But Mill felt "this ... is a claim which is particularly liable to be stretched further than its reasons warrant."

The case, he felt, was the same as for those younger sons whose eldest brother inherited all under a system of primogeniture. Such men "are brought up in the same habits of luxury as the future heir, and they receive as a younger brother's portion ... enough to support, in the habits of life to which they are accustomed, themselves, but not a wife or children." Mill added: "It really is no grievance to any man, that for the means of marrying and of supporting a family, he has to depend on his own exertions. A provision, then, such as is admitted to be reasonable in the case of illegitimate children, for younger children, wherever in short the justice of the case, and the real interests of the individuals and of society are the only things considered, is, I conceive, all that parents owe to their children, and all, therefore, which the State owes to the children of those who die intestate."

Here, though, Mill seems to have been sketching two different things. First, there is the idea that children, while still children, are owed by their parents (or by the state, if the parents die intestate) an education and training sufficient to set them up for a decent chance in life. Second, there is a more generous view that children – or at least the children of wealthy parents, who have been brought up not to have to work – even as adults are entitled to inherit enough money to keep them from working *so long as they are single* but not if they want to marry and have children.

This second view allows for quite some leeway in interpreting "moderate" and "comfortable": what is "comfortable" for the children of Bill and Melinda Gates is not the same as what is "comfortable" for me, or even for the children of Barack and Michelle Obama. In a later letter, Mill wrote that people should be allowed to inherit enough to "aid, but not ... supersede personal exertion."[102]

Claeys reads this as a radical break from *Principles* – even from the 1871 edition of *Principles* that was published slightly earlier in the same year.[103] Some care needs to be taken, however. In his letter, Mill was explaining why he did not support immediate land nationalization, but rather the less radical approach of the Land Tenure Reform Association.[104] An immediate nationalization would, he thought, prove very difficult to administer in the current state "of our political morality & of our administrative habits," as – he held – had proved to be the case even in democratic New York. Moreover, Mill believed that if the state was going to nationalize land it should compensate the landowners. He was not sure that under the plan proposed by his correspondent, the costs of compensation would be met by the gains of nationalization. Moreover, he felt that the costs of a "great alteration" such as nationalizing land "ought to be fairly shared by the whole community who are to benefit by the reform." In this context, he wrote: "I have very radical notions as to what *is* the fair mode of sharing any burthen among the whole community." He would "throw a very large proportion of it upon property ... which has been inherited, & forms the patrimony of an idle class." But there was no justice in making this fall more heavily on those who had inherited land rather than money. He concluded: "I would lay a heavy graduated succession duty on all inheritances exceeding that moderate amount, which is sufficient to aid but not to supersede personal exertion." He further suggested using the funds thus raised to compensate landowners when their land was nationalized, as then "the land-holders themselves would bear ... quite fairly, a large share of the burthen."

It is not, then, immediately clear whether Mill was suggesting this form of taxation *only* if it went hand-in-hand with land nationalization, or whether this had a wider application. That is, was this delineation of "that moderate amount, which is sufficient to aid but not to supersede personal exertion" something Mill would tax up to as part of a fair scheme for compensating landowners for nationalization of land? Or was it actually parsing what he said in *Principles* about "a moderate independence" (which is about *all* kinds of wealth inheritance, not just land)?

In *Principles* Mill left open the question of landownership: he explained that he did not think it could be justified by the means used to justify other kinds of private property, but he also said that different systems of landownership were expedient at different points in history. His letter may be suggesting that at a future date, when it was expedient that land be nationalized, when it was also feasible, and when it was practically possible to institute nationalization, then this should go hand-in-hand with an even more radical tax on inheritance. Given that this was *not yet* expedient, however, we cannot say that Mill *would* have endorsed this form of taxation. Indeed, one reason why Mill did not spell out precisely what he meant by "a moderate independence" or "a comfortable independence" in *Principles* is that that book was meant to address *general* principles and to offer advice regarding what was *currently* achievable. By which I mean it is not clear that Mill changed his mind between the final edition of *Principles* and writing this letter in October 1871. Instead, we see Mill putting forward a general principle in *Principles* that would have different precise meanings in terms of policy at different times, as people, and our institutions and capacities, changed. What Mill believed expedient for contemporary society did indeed change from the first edition of *Principles* to the last – as did his view of what kinds of radical reform might *ever* be expedient. But we cannot say with certainty say that Mill definitely changed his mind *on this* during a few months in 1871.

What we *can* say is that Mill thought a reformed system of private property *might* be reformed so as to involve not just reforms to land tenure, but also so extreme a tax on inheritance that we could only inherit what would "aid" a life supported by our own labour. Certainly, it would involve limits to inheritance, guided by expediency, which means that people could not support a family (perhaps could not even support themselves) in a life of idleness solely on what they had inherited. "Aid" still needs some interpretation, which Mill did not provide: it might "aid" us, for instance, to inherit enough to pay off our mortgage outright (or never need one) – it might only "aid" us in affording regular tickets to a favoured form of entertainment, and a nice holiday each year. Either interpretation, of course, is in line with Mill's position that no society is "salutary" where there is any "class" of people who do not labour, save those who have earned rest by previous toil.[105] This makes plain that this "previous toil" would have to be their *own*, not that of someone else. Claeys calls the view expressed in the 1871 letter "by Mill's standards, egalitarianism with a vengeance," and the position in *Principles* a form of "radical meritocracy."[106] He is correct that in Mill's view a reformed system of individual property would be a radical meritocracy. As we will see, though, Mill entertained even more radically egalitarian ideas than this – though not concerning a reformed system of individual property.

Still, what parents left their children would vary with their economic position.[107] At least in the current state of affairs, this would entail relatively significant inequalities of starting position for children. Even in a more radically meritocratic future society (one in which land nationalization was expedient), there would still presumably be some people who had been left an inheritance sufficient to "aid" their working lives, and others who had not been. Indeed, as Mill continued to note, a situation of *everyone* "starting fair" was impossible to secure under any system of individual property.[108] Thus, although "the régime of individual property ... as it might be made" in "the old societies" would be much *more* just than existing capitalism, it would still be liable to criticism on the grounds of inequality and injustice.

Property in Land

Aligned to Mill's desire to prevent the inheritance of large amounts of capital, thereby reinforcing existing class inequalities and the injustice of people benefiting by something other than their personal exertion, Mill recommended several changes in the regulation of property in land. As "the earth itself, its forests and waters, and all other natural riches, above and below the surface ... are the inheritance of the human race,"[109] property in land cannot be justified by the principal that otherwise justifies property – securing for the labourer the fruit of their own labours[110] – and there is no justification for allowing "sinecurist[s] quartered on it" from benefiting from their ownership when they do nothing to cultivate or improve land.[111] At the same time, the promise of individual benefit motivates people to improve land.[112] For this reason, it is good to secure to people certain proprietary rights over land (e.g., exclusive claim on the product of one's labour on that land), though this does not imply that these rights are absolute,[113] or that land can be inherited, or that one necessarily has a right to precious resources found under land one has cultivated. Even so, the land might be owned communally, or privately,[114] and it could be "periodically re-divided," or "the State might be the universal landlord, and the cultivators tenants under it."[115]

Regarding ways to address the injustice of landownership in contemporary capitalism, Mill proposed a "peculiar taxation" on the "Future Unearned Increase of the Rent of Land" so far as that could be ascertained.[116] This taxation would not be retrospective, and any landowner wishing to relinquish his land would be paid a market rate for it.

> In this manner that increase of wealth which now flows into the coffers of private persons from the mere progress of society, and not from their own merits of sacrifices, will be gradually, and in an increasing proportion, diverted from them to the nation as a whole, from whose collective exertions and sacrifices it really proceeds. The State will receive the entire rent of the lands voluntarily sold to it by their possessors, together with a tax on the future increase of rent on those properties whose owners have sufficient confidence in the justice and moderation of the State to prefer retaining them.

This is reminiscent of the story Mill told in *Principles* of the "organic" process by which individually held capital would become the property of worker cooperatives.[117] Here, the state would "organically" come to own land; but Mill was not saying that the state would come to own *all* land. When coupled with his recommendations for reform to inheritance, though, it is clear that what any individual could own would be only a very small amount of property in land, and that owning land would not provide the kind of advantage it currently does (for most landowners), for the "unearned increment" of increasing land values would be taxed. That is, people could inherit the land their forefathers had farmed, or the land upon which stood the factory they had inherited; but Mill's view of inheritance was directly aimed at breaking up large landed estates (particularly those on which the landowners themselves did little or no work). Indeed, Mill thought his plans would "pull down all large fortunes in two generations."[118]

Mill also argued for state ownership of sites of "historic, scientific, or artistic interest"; and for state ownership of wilderness for the purpose of preservation; and for the state to make better use of existing public land (the wishes of its original endower notwithstanding) – for example, for "sanitary works, improved dwellings, public gardens, co-operative buildings, co-operative agricultures, [and] useful public institutions of every kind."[119] He also supported "home colonisation" – giving public land to "small proprietors,"[120] or allowing them to rent it, or allowing cooperative farms to cultivate it.[121]

STATE PROVISION OF GOODS AND SERVICES

It was not only land (and the uses of it noted above) for which Mill favoured state ownership at the national or municipal level. For instance, he advocated state ownership of railways and roads, and municipal ownership (and provision) of utilities such as gas and water.[122] He also at least suggested it would be permissible for the government to provide public hospitals; national banks; a postal service; "manufactories"; and a corps of civil engineers, so long as the government did not maintain a monopoly on these professions or services.[123] This seems to speak to some of his concerns regarding efficiency as well as justice.

Whether or not one inherited wealth, people would all be educated to as high a level as they either desired or were fit for.[124] If one had parents who could pay for, or contribute to, one's schooling, they would pay. If not, the state would pay.

Mill advocated that everyone work save (perhaps) those who had been left the "moderate independence" mentioned above; those who were unable to work (for instance, because of severe disability); or those who had "fairly earned rest through previous toil."[125] Probably he had in mind here people who had saved capital and invested it in their old(er) age, allowing them to retire from the labour market. But he might have had in mind something like an old age pension.

PRODUCTION AND PROFIT-SHARING

Moving from ownership of the means of production to production itself, in the regime of individual property as it might be made in the "old" societies of the world, most of this would be done through firms that Mill described as "association[s] of labourers with capitalists"[126] – that is, through profit-sharing. (I say "most," because Mill did not rule out some single-person owner/worker businesses.) As Mill described it (at some length, in *Principles*), profit-sharing is where some (or all) of the profits of the firm are shared among the labourers in a way determined by the employer.[127] It is, therefore, rather different from modern models of "profit-sharing" that involve paying staff a proportion of their wages as shares. The price of shares is not directly dependent on the hard work and effort of workers, but on the trading value of those shares on the stock market (based on a wide variety of factors, of which the perceived efficiency and the work ethic of employees are not highly salient). It is also not like the contemporary practice of workers' pensions being invested, by funds, in other companies. It is also not identical to the John Lewis model of worker co-ownership in the UK (where the company is owned by a trust on behalf of the employees, and all workers receive the same percentage of their salary as an annual bonus arising from the profits). On Mill's model, shares are not necessarily the same, but may depend on performance, in an attempt to tie incentives to work even more closely to the share of profits received.

Some production would be done (as noted above) by the state, though presumably it, too, could utilize profit-sharing or some other form of worker participation. Lastly, some scientists, artists, poets, explorers, and so on would be paid on government salaries ("pensions") – as, of course, would the necessary bureaucrats at the state and municipal levels.[128]

These profit-sharing firms would compete in markets. Initially, there might be trade unions to ensure fair working of the wage market, but Mill evidently thought that profit-sharing would eventually end the need for unions to "higgle" over wages (i.e., it would balance out owners' monopoly power with their monopsony power), as profit-sharing would stop the labourers and capitalists being pitted against each other, each seeking to exploit the other as much as possible, and make them partners in production.

These, then, were the basic economic mechanisms and institutions of this regime. Mill seems to have imagined that this regime might reach – or come into being within – a "stationary state": that is, one in which there was no further increase in production, profits, or total amount of wealth, or advances in technology or extensions of international trade that could increase these things.[129] He did not think this needed to be the parlous state his fellow economists feared, particularly if people ceased to pursue growth at all costs, with individual economic gain vis-à-vis their compatriots the only hallmark of success. He said: "Most fitting, indeed, is it, that while riches are power, and to grow as rich as possible the universal object of ambition, the path to its attainment should be open to all, without favour or partiality. But the best state for human nature is that in which, while no one is poor, no one desires to be richer, nor has any reason to fear being thrust back, by the efforts of others to push themselves forward."[130]

That is, in the current state of human nature and institutions, equality of opportunity in the "race" is what should be aimed for. But this is not, in itself, an ideal goal, nor is it the best we can either achieve or desire. In a stationary state, we might achieve a world that, though not entirely egalitarian, is marked by a very different social ethos and focus for human endeavour.

This reformed system of individual property "as it might be made" in the "old societies," then, would mitigate and even overcome a number of Mill's criticisms of contemporary capitalism. It is evidently far removed from that system, and equally far removed from our own (and from most libertarian utopias). There would be great gains for justice, equality, efficiency, freedom, individuality, the social ethos, and the environment. But there would also still be problems on these scores.

Regarding justice and equality, this society would still be unjust and unequal (though far less unequal than contemporary society), though the fact that everyone was working would be an important gain for both. To some extent, the injustice and inequality would arise from this society's gestation in less than ideal circumstances – for example, the pre-existence of different social "classes" with more, or less, to leave to their children. But it would also be because "meritocracy" would allow those who were more talented, or more able to work longer and harder, to gain the most and then (even under Mill's most radical view) pass at least some of this on to their children. Yet "meritocracy" itself, on Mill's view, is imperfectly just, for to the extent that remuneration is due to "natural difference of strength or capacity," it is merely "assigning most to those who are already most favoured by nature."[131] Moreover, it is not clear that meritocracy, even when we try to limit inequalities of outcome to one generation, based on individual efforts and talent rather than inheritance, can necessarily overcome the other injustices Mill highlighted in contemporary capitalism regarding unjust remuneration.

Mill wrote: "To judge of the final destination of the institution of property, we must suppose everything rectified, which causes the institution to work in a manner opposed to that equitable principle, of proportion between remuneration and exertion, on which in every vindication of it that will bear the light, it is assumed to be grounded."[132]

As already noted, this regime would prevent the injustice Mill saw in there being a "class" of people who did labour, but who benefited the most from the productive and unproductive labour of their society through unfair distributions. It seems plausible to think that under this regime, too, there would be a better "ratio" between work done and remuneration received (in contrast to the "inverse ratio" characterizing contemporary capitalism).

Profit-sharing might guarantee that "the most fatiguing and exhausting bodily labour" could "count with certainty on being able to earn ... the necessaries of life."[133] If not, there would need to be a minimum "living wage" and good labour protections in the workplace (and proper regulation and monitoring), coupled with a safety net for the unemployed. Mill did not mention these, though he was open to the idea of legislation passed democratically such as would limit working hours; meanwhile, the state would use its authoritative capacity to address coordination problems and realize the desires of the majority (in line with the general good), which no individual worker could realize alone.[134] Similarly, the state could step in to address concerns about workers' health and safety.[135]

In addition, this reformed system of individual property (especially proposed reforms to inheritance and landownership) would help ensure that "the largest portions" of the produce of labour would no longer go "to those who have never worked at all" and that "the next largest [would go] to those whose work is purely nominal."[136] But it is not clear that these reforms – or, indeed, *any* reforms – could prevent "remuneration dwindling as the work grows harder and more disagreeable," for there would still be a market for wages, and much hard and disagreeable work is low-skilled and therefore low-paid (because lots of people *could* do it, and the products it produces are low in value). That is, under a system of wage labour and individual property, clockmakers are *always* going to command higher wages than rock-breakers, and teachers more than cockle-pickers. Thus, even the most reformed system of individual property will be liable to some criticisms on the grounds of justice and inequality.

There would still be some inequalities regarding how people "start" in the race, and in this regime there would be no apparent means of mitigating against the injustice of rewarding those who already have most with even more. *Some* elements of that inequality might be mitigated against – for example, by the state paying for the education of those whose parents could not afford to pay for it themselves.

What is more, Mill endorsed as "higher" principles of justice both "equal shares" and "from each according to his capacities, to each according to his wants."[137] Neither of these seems achievable in a system of individual property. Perhaps profit-sharing schemes could adopt one of these principles – but then it is not wholly clear that they would work. That is, would the incentive structure that is supposedly built into profit-sharing, making it successful, exist (or exist in the same way) if one of these principles was adopted? Equal shares might harness workers' interests to their employers in some respects – the harder they worked, the bigger the "pie" from which they would get an equal slice (though, as Mill discussed with socialist schemes employing this principle, there would be a free-rider problem, and it would not be negated by a new social ethos, for the regime of private property "as it might be made" is still essentially individualistic – it is an *individual* desire for *personal* gain that is harnessed through profit-sharing). The same cannot be said for "from each according to his capacities, to each according to his wants," which seems to be in direct opposition to the incentive structure that makes profit-sharing work.[138] Yet these principles are "higher" (i.e., better) principles of justice – and this adds to the justice-based grounds on which it would be possible to criticize even this regime of individual property.

Turning to efficiency, almost all businesses that engage in profit-sharing would enjoy a great gain in efficiency (by harnessing the workers' interests more firmly to the success of the firm). That said, it is not clear that this regime could overcome all of Mill's concerns regarding the inefficiency of middlemen, nor whether it would increase the "worth" of the products of "unproductive labour," even if it did distribute them more fairly. On this point, however, Mill's idea that a society in a "stationary state" could devote some public funds to art and would learn to focus not on growth and "the art of getting on" but on "the Art of Living" might mean improvements in "worth" and fair distribution.[139]

Concerning freedom and independence, there would be many gains inherent in meaningful equality of opportunity, with the attendant focus on education being based on merit, not means, and (at least we presume from Mill's other writing) with the professions being opened up to all genders, races, and social classes. State funding for railways and roads might make moving from place to place, and thus from job to job, easier for people, aiding their freedom of movement and employment. Wider distribution of property would also aid people's freedom in that it would potentially provide them with more time for leisure and the development of their individuality. Similarly, it seems plausible to think Mill believed that "the régime of individual property … as it might be made" could emancipate women from "entire domestic subjugation," thereby addressing one of his criticisms of contemporary capitalism.[140]

That said, it is clear from Mill's descriptions of profit-sharing businesses in *Principles* that as regards being under the will and command of their employers, workers in profit-sharing companies were not obviously much freer than their contemporaries in non-sharing organizations.[141] Moreover, Mill was not sanguine that increasing equality led to increasing toleration, as his comments on Alexis de Tocqueville's *Democracy in America* show.[142]

Concerning Mill's proto-environmentalist concerns, state protection of wilderness, and of sites of historic, artistic, and scientific interest – even with increased enclosure of common land for farming – would mitigate at least some of these. So would a change in the social ethos as we approached the stationary state and abandoned our relentless pursuit of growth in favour of something better (so long as we did, in fact, do this).

This brings me, lastly, to the social ethos itself. Mill continued to speak of a "race" in which we try to make the running fair (particularly regarding starting positions). But unlike in contemporary capitalism, this "race" would not be for mere survival. I briefly mentioned earlier Mill's defence of at least a "less-eligible" Poor Law, and he evidently foresaw this as something that would be included in the regime of private property as it might be made in the old societies.[143] Indeed, it might involve whatever he meant by "something beyond"[144] this, if there were ever sufficient improvement in people's character and the general social ethos. Only in the stationary state might we overcome the feeling that life is a "race" at all, which – Mill felt – would be a vast improvement.

Similarly, Mill wrote that his "Utopia" was to "heal ... the widening breach between those who toil and those who live on the produce of former toil," and he saw profit-sharing as the means to do this, through "raising the labourer from a receiver of hire – a mere bought instrument in the work of production, having no residuary interest in the work itself – to the position of being, in some sort, a partner in it."[145] This would help improve the social ethos, in terms of both healing class antagonisms and replacing the "cash-nexus" as the only medium by which employers and employees interacted (though it would remain important, as employers would still pay their employees wages). Profit-sharing might result in each class having less of a desire to exploit the other, and seeing the other as a human and not just an object (either of hire, or of payment). Still, class differences exist, and workers and employers are not *equal* partners (in remuneration, or in production): one side still owns the means of production, and the other (only) their labour. Moreover, the fact that workers need to be incentivized by payments to improve their performance shows that such a regime, even at its most radically reformed, would still represent a "compromise with the selfish type of character formed by the present standard of morality."[146]

Overall, then, Mill's idea of "the régime of individual property, not as it is, but as it might be made" in "the old societies" and by "colonists" arriving in an "uninhabited country" was free of many of the problems he identified with contemporary capitalism (and the *laisser-faire* government it involved would be very different from our usual understanding of *laissez-faire*). But it could not solve *all* of the problems Mill identified concerning liberty and independence; justice and equality; efficiency; proto-environmentalism; and the social ethos, or a sense of community and the common good. Yet these were key elements, for Mill, in any "good" or "ideal" society – core elements, that is, of utility and therefore of a society that could maximize it. It is these concerns, which took Mill beyond even "the régime of individual property ... as it might be made" in terms of the "ideal" or "ultimate form of human society," to being "under the general designation of Socialist."[147] Because it is generally assumed this "régime of individual property" was what Mill *really* preferred, in the next section I briefly explain why this received view ought to be challenged.

BEYOND INDIVIDUAL PROPERTY

In Chapter 1 I sketched how Mill's changing views of history and the laws of economics opened up "space" for a transition to something "beyond" existing property relations. One might suppose that by this he meant more reform than he had previously thought possible to individual property, but without abandoning that system altogether. His self-designation as a socialist should cast doubt on that, and so too should an exploration of the problems Mill saw with capitalism. He apparently realized that many of those problems would remain even in an "ideal" version of individual property, and certainly within the kind of individual property regime we could achieve in the "old" societies of the world (starting, as we would, hampered by the facts of how property relations came to be as they are). Thus, Mill's adoption of Saint-Simonian ideas regarding history and economics opened up space "beyond" contemporary society that *might* be socialist; indeed, his concerns regarding even a reformed version of individual property opened up the possibility that society *should be* socialist.[148] Persky argues that Mill's economics meant he thought it *would be* socialist: I would pull back a little from that and say it meant he thought it *was likely to be* socialist. Here, my reading is more similar to that of Claeys, who writes that the *Autobiography* and "the famous change in the third edition of ... *Principles*" "appear to show that after the revolutions of 1848 Mill ... came to see socialism as a more civilised stage of society towards which modern conditions were tending and in which a superior ideal of human nature might eventually be realised."[149]

In *Principles*, Mill wrote that political economists, for the foreseeable future, would be concerned with systems of individual property, and that "the object to be principally aimed at in the present stage of human improvement, is not the subversion of the system of individual property, but the improvement of it, and the full participation of every member of the community in its benefits."[150] Jonathan Riley notes that many people have mistrusted Mill's self-designation as a "socialist,"[151] and counters them with these words: "against those who conclude [Mill] affirmed the moral superiority of capitalism over socialism ... I argue that he consistently affirmed the reverse, and left open the possibility that a decentralised socialism would eventually become established."

Mill certainly did affirm the moral superiority of socialism over capitalism (his concerns regarding individuality notwithstanding). In this chapter, I have focused on the *problems* with capitalism, which should show that Mill did not (at least) affirm its morality *simpliciter*: later chapters will show in more detail how and why he thought socialism was morally superior.

However, Mill did more than "le[ave] open the possibility that a decentralised socialism would become established," though I acknowledge that he "consistently focused on gradual reform of private property arrangements and left open the possibility that socialism would never arrive" (that said, *contra* Riley, "if society approached intellectual and moral perfection," for Mill, it would have to be socialist). Like Riley, I do not see Mill's statement in *Principles* that the choice between communism and a perfect regime of individual property is not clear-cut, and will depend on questions of what best preserves individuality, as implying that Mill, *really*, thought capitalism was preferable. Also, we ought not to read Mill as ambivalent over the two. Instead, he expressed a strong commitment to the arrival of socialism (by peaceful means) — for him, it was *desirable* and what *should* happen.

Riley emphasizes what he sees as Mill's ambivalence between socialism and a reformed version of individual property. Dale Miller writes that "for Mill the question of whether a given form of socialism should be adopted is equivalent to that of whether enlightened workers in a reformed capitalism would eventually adopt it."[152] Mill often does express ambivalence about what *will* happen in *Principles*, though even there he calls the peaceful transition to a cooperative future "the nearest approach to social justice ... which it is possible at present to foresee."[153] And in his *Autobiography* he shies away from predicting a socialist future, though he certainly endorses the normative value of one:

> [O]ur ideal of future improvement was such as would class us decidedly under the general designation of Socialists ... [W]e ... looked forward to a time when society should no longer be divided into the idle and the industrious ... when the division of the produce of labour, instead of being dependent as in so great a degree it is, on the accident of birth, should be made by concert, on an acknowledged principle of justice, and when it should no longer either be, or be thought to be, impossible for human beings to exert themselves strenuously for benefits which were not to be exclusively their own, but shared with the society they belong to.[154]

That is to say, Mill thought that *if* the choice was between current capitalism and communism, then communism would win, but that it wasn't our current choice at all, because we could reform current capitalism (and should do so). Moreover, *if* the choice came down to one between communism and a reformed system of individual property, then the people of the future would be better able than we are to decide whether to implement communism or a reformed system of private property (or something else, of course), as we do not have the necessary knowledge.

But that is not the same as him having no opinion as to what he *hoped* people would choose in the future. (Not least, because he saw communism and socialism as distinct.) Mill was both political scientist and political philosopher, and if in the former role he was wary of making *predictions*, that does not mean he had no normative *preferences* in the latter. This passage, at least, does not show that Mill was ambivalent toward socialism or opposed to it; rather, he did not want to *prescribe* what people of the future ought to do. And we can see why Mill would not want to do that – the right "organic" institutions for a forthcoming organic age would best be built by those living in that age (or on the cusp of it). Though Mill did not have precisely Marx's concerns about writing "recipes ... for the cookshops of the future"[155] (indeed, he liked the amount of detail often presented by "utopian" socialists, seeing it as marking an effort to work out feasibility), he did think there would be necessary knowledge only available to the people of the future regarding the best forms of institutions – knowledge that, in part, would be derived from further "experiments in living" by socialists.

Evidently, Mill thought that individuality would, and should, be a deciding factor for the people of the future. That is, it was worth trading some inequality, and even some "comfort and affluence," for independence, individuality, and freedom.[156] It is generally assumed that this evidently gave the prize to individual property – but the textual evidence is not so clear-cut. For one thing, even the *best* form of individual property might pose some problems for independence, liberty, and individuality. For another, Mill said that criticisms of communism on these grounds was "no doubt ... vastly exaggerated." Lastly, what Mill was comparing with "the régime of individual property ... as it might be made" here was communism (small, self-sufficient communities of about a thousand people, with joint ownership of both the means of production and articles of consumption, and an equal division of the produce of labour, or one based on need), but this was not the *only* available form of *socialism*. Thus, even if Mill *did* think that in a choice between *communism* as it might be, and individual property "as it might be made," the latter ought to triumph, this does not tell us much regarding his own commitment to socialism.

Similarly, we ought not to underplay the importance of "social justice" to Mill. Individuality is certainly a key part of utility, but so is justice. Mill would clearly prefer a "just" society to an "unjust" one with equal protections for individuality, if both were available. As we have seen, even the "régime of individuality property ... as it might be made" was not fully just. Of course, perhaps "full" justice would not be attainable – or perhaps only at such a cost to other important elements of utility (e.g., individuality, but also, potentially, security) that it would not be worth the cost. But we ought not to assume that Mill did not think both could be achieved together.

Moreover, to refer back to Riley's specific thought – it is not clear that Mill's willingness to leave open the possibility that socialism would never arrive undermined his own "commitment" to socialism. The fact that Mill was not a historical determinist about socialism's arrival does not undermine his *normative* commitment to it. One does not have to be an historical determinist to be a socialist.

It is also the case that the "ambivalence" of this particular passage in *Principles* is undermined not only by Mill's clear normative preference for "decentralised socialism" as "the nearest approach to social justice" later in *Principles*, but also by his reference to "the brilliant future reserved to the principle of cooperation" in the same text, and by his heralding, in an 1864 speech, of "the new millennium" of cooperation that would be extended to all workers.[157] Indeed, Mill made very plain in *Principles* that "the poor have come out of leading-strings, and cannot any longer be governed or treated like children," and that they would soon demand more and more independence, equality, and political power.[158] He wrote those words in the context of his discussion of profit-sharing and "associations of the workers among themselves," and though he did not predict an "organic" transition from contemporary capitalism to "decentralised socialism," it seems plausible that he thought it likely and welcomed it.[159] For Mill, in this sense, history was in the hands of the working classes – in an age of representative government and declining respect for their supposed "betters" (i.e., landed aristocrats, clergymen and capitalist employers), *their* political, economic, and social demands would have to be listened to and accommodated; it was *they* who would comprise the "majority" in whose interests, at least if unchecked by concern for the common good, modern democracy would wield its power. They would be the people of "futurity" who decide. This does not mean Mill had no preference regarding which option they chose, or that he thought they would be choosing wrongly if they chose socialism.

Moreover, from very early on, Mill expressed a belief that we ought to guide our choices as regards immediate political reforms by the "ideal." Here, he uses the metaphor of the North Star in navigation. "Though we may only be sailing from the port of London to that of Hull," he said – that is, making relatively incremental reforms – "let us guide our navigation by the North Star."[160] Mill consistently identified socialism with "the ultimate prospect of human society,"[161] "an ideal ... even ... a prophecy of ultimate possibilities,"[162] and the "ideal of ultimate improvement,"[163] and he saw socialist principles of justice as a "higher ideal" than the ones underpinning private property. This gives weight to the idea that Mill looked to something "beyond" individual property. And though it might not be possible for society ever to "arrive" at the "ideal," just as it is not possible to "arrive" at the North Star, it is important to see that Mill *did* think the "ideal" was socialist – and this is one of the reasons he put himself "under the general designation of Socialist." His was a *normative* commitment, not a *predictive* one, but this does not somehow undermine his claim.

That said, I also think Mill's view is more predictive than Riley, Miller, and others allow. Mill did not say socialism definitely *would* come to pass, but he certainly made it plain that he thought it very likely. I have just sketched some more normative reasons (regarding worker independence, and so on) why he thought this was the case. Persky convincingly argues that Mill's understanding of economics meant that he thought socialism *was* likely, and perhaps even *would* come to pass, though without Mill saying as much in as many words.[164]

First, workers are *attracted* to socialism in a normative sense (as fairer than capitalism, and as allowing more dignity and independence to workers) and are moving toward cooperation because this is what efficient production demands. That is, Persky argues, Mill makes empirical observations about trends in production toward "the economies of scale of modern technologies," which workers will not abandon, though they will demand a greater share of the benefits of these. This will lead to "the workers eventually choosing democratic co-operatives for a fundamental restructuring of production ... This is the direction progress is moving."

Second, Persky adds that "like most classical economists Mill was reasonably sure that as an empirical matter the rate of return on capital would fall, indeed fall toward zero," resulting in "the stationary state." He writes: "This piece of empiricism played an almost quaint role in [Mill's] hopes for co-operatives. Mill looks forward to the capitalists retiring from the scene, leaving a good deal of their capital in the hands of worker associations. While Mill worries that cooperatives won't be as adventurous with respect to technology as individual owners, he is sure that the combination of rising wages, falling profit rates, and the attractiveness of working in the expanding co-operatives will leave capitalists on the side-lines."

That is, wages will rise as cooperatives expand, because the return to workers in cooperatives will be higher than to those who continue to work for wages: this means employers will have to offer higher wages in order to attract workers as they compete for an ever-decreasing pool of wage labour. Higher wages in themselves affect profits, but so do the other pressures on capitalism, including the increasing amount of capital competing for a return as capitalists continue to save; further pressure on wages as population rates decrease (as a result of increases in worker education and female emancipation); and falling efficiency within capitalist firms as only the least good workers remain working for employers rather than joining, or forming, cooperatives. Mill accepted that "the free importation of relatively cheap wage-goods" would delay the fall of the rate of profit to zero.[165] If there has been no control of the population rate (and, therefore, wages remain at Malthusian subsistence level), then these cheap imports must have the effect of lowering agricultural rents, which, combined with low wages, increases the surplus for capitalists (profit being what remains to capitalists when they have paid wages, rents, the costs of primary resources, and the costs of capital depletion, i.e., to replace broken machinery). If, on the other hand, the workers have succeeded in lowering the population rate, then cheap imports means wage values rise (though not wages), but there is no impact on rent and the inexorable decline in the rate of profits continues unaffected.

Similarly, technological change may delay the stationary state. Technology (at least as employed by capitalists not in a stationary state) improves the productivity of the workforce. This increases the surplus available to capitalists as profit. If there is no limit to the population rate, this will delay the arrival of the stationary state. But if there has been a fall in the population rate (such that the workers, in having children, only *replace* their own labour overall rather than increasing the available amount of labour, and thus lowering wages), then eventually this expansion of fixed capital (in technology) will contribute to higher wages.

Thus, Persky reads Mill as thinking that the stationary state was an economic certainty. He also reads Mill as seeing it arriving fairly soon, for Mill consistently noted that the rate of profit "is habitually within ... a hand's breadth of the minimum, and the country therefore on the very verge of the stationary state."[166] Though he notes that Mill is "a bit vague" on how strong the counter-tendencies "are likely to be."[167]

Importantly, if we achieve the high-wage, low-population rate type of stationary state, this will provide (on Persky's plausible reading) the *economic* underpinning for his idea that capitalists might first, invest in cooperatives, and second, exchange their capital for an annuity provided by cooperatives, with the result that cooperatives will organically subsume privately owned capital, thereby transforming a system of individual property into one of communal property. Capitalists would do the former because cooperatives would offer a "fair" rate on loaned capital that would at least equal, and perhaps better, the rate that could be expected from investing in (less efficient, as sketched above) privately owned firms in an era of declining profits. They would do the latter because a zero rate of profit means there is no point in saving (i.e., investing) for one's old age: an annuity from a cooperative will suddenly appear to be the best bet. So socialism could emerge from capitalism without either violence on the part of the workers or altruism on the part of capitalists.

Here, though, we ought to note that Mill was not certain which kind of stationary state would in fact emerge. Persky is right to note that Mill saw many tendencies that encouraged him to think it might be the high-wage/low-population-rate version. But Mill was not completely sure, and a lot of steps would have to be taken before this could happen (including some very tough ones, such as overcoming the entrenched power of established religion over people's beliefs about how many children they ought to have). So we should be cautious about thinking that Mill was *certain* that the "good" kind of stationary state would emerge. (On the other hand, Mill thought we could experiment with socialism before we reached the stationary state, so this does not undermine his conviction that workers were likely to *try* to implement socialist reforms to the economy – indeed, he witnessed them doing so in his own lifetime, and encouraged them to do so.)

Persky further argues that "Mill's vision of the socialism to come is based on something like a materialist conception of history." "Mill clearly identifies the transition from capitalism to co-operatives as an organic process brought on by the very success of the capitalists in accumulating savings and driving down profits." Persky does not develop this argument in much detail, but he sees Mill's political economy of progress as predicting a move toward socialism as the "natural" and unavoidable outcome of existing property relations, class tensions, and worker ambitions for a better future.

I am not convinced that Mill really did have a solely materialist conception of history, though I acknowledge that his theory and Marx's have similarities arising from their common roots in Saint-Simonian and German Idealist theory.[168] (I explored the Saint-Simonian elements of Mill's view in detail above, but it is worth noting that he recalled that these views were "the general property of Europe, or at least of Germany and France" at the time, only "they had never, to my knowledge [in the 1830s], been so completely systematised as by these writers, nor the distinguishing characteristics of a critical period so powerfully set forth."[169]) I agree, though, that he thought economic forces were propelling both economic and social change and that it would be impossible to reverse these changes (whatever paternalist employers desired, we could not return to feudalism). Even so, Mill left open the possibility of a transformation that was not "total" and that would result in the sort of "patchwork" economy sketched by Miller (in which there would be some privately owned firms/property, and a market economy occupied mainly by cooperatives).[170]

Thus, there are three reasons to be cautious concerning whether Mill thought socialism *would* arrive. First, as just noted, it is not clear how long he thought it really would be before the stationary state arrived, nor how strong the countervailing tendencies would prove to be (i.e., imports from expanding markets, and technological change). Although, as noted above, we could make experiments in socialism *before* the arrival of the stationary state, if the economic conditions of that state were *necessary* for the complete transformation of the economy (socialism, on this view, being ultimately dependent on a zero rate of profit), then Mill left open the possibility of avoiding the stationary state, perhaps not forever, but certainly for a very long time. Second, and more importantly, Mill was much more cautious than Persky reads him regarding the *nature* of the stationary state if and when it did arrive – that is, it might not be the "good" form, and it was only the "good" form that would spontaneously transform itself into socialism. Third, we have no warrant to read Mill as having a materialist concept of history that makes the arrival of socialism *inevitable*. But I do agree with Persky that serious consideration of Mill's economics (and not just his political philosophy) shows that Mill really did think that the arrival of socialism was very likely and that according to his economic account, the future was less "open" than Riley (and others) read it as being.

CONCLUSION

In this chapter I have shown that Mill was not a "*laissez-faire*" liberal; nor was he an uncritical supporter of either contemporary capitalism or even "the régime of individual property as it might be made" in either the "old" world or the "new." He criticized contemporary capitalism on the grounds of justice and equality, freedom and individuality, the social ethos, proto-environmentalist concerns, and efficiency. Not all of these concerns could be overcome by reforms to the regime of individual property. Individual property *always* leads to inequalities: wage labour *always* leads to a lack of freedom for workers, even under profit-sharing.

In his review of Mill's assessment of "capitalism versus socialism," Riley rightly notes that in *Principles*, after arguing "that existing laws and customs of private property ought to be reformed to promote a far more egalitarian form of capitalism than hitherto observed anywhere," Mill "went on to suggest that such an ideal capitalism might evolve spontaneously into a decentralised socialism involving a market system of competing worker cooperatives."[171] It is this that, as Riley also notes, Mill calls "the nearest approach to social justice ... which it is possible at present to foresee."[172] I explore this in Chapter 4. Already, we can see from his criticisms of capitalism, and how many of these are still pertinent regarding a reformed regime of individual property, how Mill could have been looking for something even better in a new, organic, age.

As noted in Chapter 1, some commentators have taken Mill's warm words regarding the possibilities of reforming the system of individual property, his leaving open the question of whether communism would be chosen by the people of the future over this reformed system of individual property, and his general unwillingness to *predict* socialism's triumph or even arrival, as a sign that he did not *really* want reform to go beyond the reforms to individual property I have sketched above. (Indeed, so radical is *that* program that many earlier commentators tried to deny that Mill went even this far.) The preceding section shows why this view is mistaken: Mill normatively endorsed socialism and also thought it was very likely to emerge in the near future.

Furthermore, some commentators see in Mill's criticisms of contemporary forms of socialism a sign that he was not "really" a socialist. For this reason, in the next chapter I consider in detail Mill's attitude toward contemporary socialism, to show exactly where he differed and (ultimately) why this did not affect his own self-identification, but rather sheds useful light on the content of his own socialism.

CHAPTER THREE

Mill's Assessment of Contemporary Socialism(s): Community, Cooperation, and Revolution

It is the true ideal of a perfect human society; the spirit of which will more and more pervade even the existing social institutions, as human beings become wiser and better; and which, like any other model of unattainable perfection, everybody is the better for aspiring to, although it be impossible to reach it. We may never get to the north star, but there is much use in turning our faces towards it if we are journeying northward.[1]

Several scholars writing about Mill's socialism have taken elements of his various assessments of socialism as evidence that he was never "really" a socialist, or that his "flirtation" with socialism was short-lived. However, these interpretations misread the context, and extent, of Mill's negative assessments of different forms of socialism. Certainly, he was not a socialist when he debated against the Owenites in the 1820s,[2] but Mill does not claim he was – his political philosophy developed into something "under the general designation of Socialist" in the mid-to-late 1840s.[3] In that time Mill changed his mind about a number of elements of Owenism that he had previously viewed negatively (including its "practicability,"[4] its desirability, and the costs associated with implementing it) and came to see that there was much more to "socialism" than Owenism. Similarly, he was certainly not a supporter of "revolutionary socialism," as the *Chapters on Socialism* make plain: he thought it was dangerous, but evidently tempting to the frustrated working classes.[5] However, there is much more to socialism (both historically and conceptually) than Marxist "revolutionary socialism," and Mill endorsed an evolutionary albeit still radical form of socialism in *Principles of Political Economy*, which he was re-editing and republishing at the same time he was writing *Chapters*.[6]

Other scholars have linked Mill to "utopian socialism" – that is, the ideas of Robert Owen, Henri Saint-Simon (and his followers, the Saint-Simonians), Charles Fourier (and his Fourierist followers, particularly Victor Considerant); Etienne Cabet (father of "Icarian" socialism); and Louis Blanc.[7] It is certainly true that these were the forms of socialism with which Mill engaged over the longest period of time, and the ones that influenced the change in his own philosophy. It is also true that what Mill sketched as his "Utopia" was plausibly socialist.[8] But Mill never produced the kind of detailed blueprint for the ideal society (what Marx dismissively characterized as "recipes for the cook-shops of the future"[9]) that usefully defines "utopian socialists" and that links them much more strongly and clearly than any similarities between their different ideas.[10] Unless we follow Marx and Engels and think there is *only* Marxist socialism or "utopian" socialism – itself not a helpful dichotomy – we ought not to see Mill's "socialism" as "utopian."

Indeed, Mill was not an uncritical advocate of any of the forms of socialism extant in his day. In this chapter I explore his assessment of contemporary socialism(s), in order to see what he found attractive and unattractive about the idea. This will make it easier to explore Mill's *own* form of socialism.

MILL'S DEFINITION OF SOCIALISM

We ought to start by ascertaining what Mill meant by socialism. This has two dimensions: which socialisms did Mill know and have in mind when discussing socialism? And what did he take the term, conceptually, to cover? An answer to the first question was briefly given above but is worth exploring in more detail.

The Forms of Socialism with which Mill was Familiar

Mill knew of the ideas of Owen and several leading Owenites as early as the 1810s and 1820s. He was familiar with works by Owen himself; with William Thompson's *An Inquiry into the Distribution of Wealth Most Conducive to Human Happiness* and *Appeal of One Half the Human Race, Women, Against the Pretensions of the Other Half, Men, to Retain Them in Political, and thence in Civil and Domestic, Slavery* (co-authored with Anna Wheeler); and with the ideas of early Owenites such as John "Gale" Jones and Connop Thirlwall.[11] From much the same time he was also familiar with the ideas of the Christian Socialists Frederick Maurice[12] and Edward Vansittart Neale.[13] Later, he came to know the English co-operator George Jacob Holyoake,[14] through whose books (which Mill praises in *Principles*) he would also have had knowledge of a number of other Owenite communities.[15]

Turning to French forms of socialism, Mill met Saint-Simon himself in 1820[16] and had a lifelong friendship with Gustave d'Eichthal, who became one of the twelve highest-ranked Saint-Simonians.[17] He also met the "chiefs" of Saint-Simonism, Barthélemy Prosper Enfantin and Amand Bazard, in Paris in 1830 (when Mill went to witness the revolution happening there),[18] as well as another Saint-Simonian missionary to England, Charles Duvreyier,[19] and he knew of the missionaries Gregorio Fontana-Rava and Giacchino Prati.[20] While the Saint-Simonian school was still in existence, Mill read every edition of the *Globe* (its main mouthpiece) and even contributed an article to it.[21] Although Mill was clear that he was "not a St. Simonist [*sic*] nor at all likely to become one,"[22] and also declared that it was "only *one* among a variety of interesting and important features of the time we live in,"[23] he regularly defended them in print against both persecution by political authorities in Paris[24] and pillory by the press in England.[25] Moreover, he did what he thought useful to help the Saint-Simonians in their quest to convert England, though he thought them unlikely to succeed.[26] Indeed, he wrote that their scheme, though currently "impracticable," ought to be the "North Star" by which Britons navigated social reform.[27]

Mill first became aware of Fourier in 1832, when some of the Saint-Simonians, including Jules Lechavalier and Abel Transon, joined his sect[28] (which was some time after Fourier's main works were first published[29]). Mill's initial attitude was by no means sympathetic. He described Fourier as "a sort of ... Owen who is to accomplish all things by means of cooperation & of rendering *labour agreeable*, & under whose system man is to acquire absolute power over the laws of physical nature; among other happy results, the sea is to be changed into lemonade."[30] (Fourier actually only said that the sea, because of changing mineral content due to the melting of the polar icecaps, would *taste* of – pink – lemonade.[31])

Mill first took Fourier seriously after reading his ideas as transmitted by Considerant, in 1849,[32] and introduced the scheme into *Principles* that same year.[33] By the time he came to write *Chapters*, Mill was also familiar with Fourier's *Theory of the Four Movements*, and owned (though this does not guarantee read!) an 1851 translation of Fourier's work titled *The Passions of the Human Soul*.[34] He quoted extensively from Considerant's *La Destinée Sociale* (first published 1834–38) in *Chapters* – presumably using his own translations, as he cited the French edition – though it is not clear how early Mill read this; and he had evidently read other works, including Considerant's *Le Socialisme devant le vieux monde, ou le vivant devant les morts*.[35]

Mill did not discuss Cabet's Icarianism[36] at any length. But he did mention it very briefly in *Principles*;[37] and he defended Cabet in the English press both in the 1830s (when Cabet was prosecuted for libel against the French king[38]) and fifteen years later (when he was tried, *in absentia*, for conning people into investing in his Icarian emigration scheme: Cabet later returned with proofs that he had not misappropriated the funds, but had been buying land – as promised – for the founding of an Icarian community in America).[39]

Blanc was one of the socialists whom Mill personally knew best. They became friends when Blanc was living in exile in London after

1848, and Blanc was one of the few people Mill ever invited to his home.[40] "His very devoted" Blanc presented Mill with a copy of his *History of the French Revolution* (Paris, 1847).[41] Mill also knew of the ideas of other French cooperative socialists, having certainly read the work of Buchez, and having long-standing links to the French republican movement of the 1830s, out of which much French producer cooperation grew.[42] It was their schemes for "National Workshops," and the ideas of other socialists such as Considerant, who were part of the Provisional Government formed after the February 1848 revolution, whom Mill was referring to when he wrote that it was "wretched to see the cause of *legitimate* Socialism thrown back" by violence in June 1848 and its aftermath.[43]

Lastly, Mill and Marxism. It may seem incredible to the modern reader, given Marx's fame in the intervening 150 years, and given that Marxism is often seen as synonymous with socialism and indeed a complete definition of it, that it is very likely that Mill never in his life heard of Marx.[44] Actually, Marx remained relatively unknown throughout Mill's lifetime. His fame really began with the publication of *Capital*. Volume 1 was published, in German, in 1867;[45] fascicules circulated in French from 1872 to 1875;[46] English copies were available in 1887; Mill died in 1873.

It has been said that "it cannot be too strongly emphasised that Mill knew nothing of Marx or of Marxism,"[47] but this is a little too categorical. Mill makes reference to a work that we now know was written by Marx ("Workingmen and the War"), which Mill came across through his contacts with British members of the International Working Men's Association (IWA),[48] and as *Chapters* shows,[49] he was exposed to some ideas we would now call "Marxist,"[50] having been sent a copy of the program of the IWA by the members of the Nottingham branch,[51] along with an "able" pamphlet by Thomas Smith titled "Letters on the [Paris] Commune," in 1872.[52] That said, Mill would have had no particular reason to attach any importance to Marx's name,[53] and some of what he read that was penned by Marx is not all that distinctively "Marxist."[54] However, Mill does seem to have had knowledge of more clearly "Marxist" ideas, and he may therefore have read more than we know penned by Marx – for example, all the points that in *The Communist Manifesto* Marx says will be "pretty generally applicable" to all countries could be summed up in the phrase Mill used to describe the goals of "the revolutionary Socialists": "the management of the whole productive resources of the country by one central authority, the general government. And with this view some of them avow as their purpose that the working classes, or somebody in their behalf, should take possession of all the property of the country, and administer it for the general benefit."[55]

Mill's Conceptual Account of Socialism

Mill treats these various schemes both under the general heading of "socialism" and under the subheadings of "communism" and "socialism." This can lead to some confusion in understanding his views, which reflects linguistic change in Mill's own lifetime, with "socialism" being adopted in England by thinkers (like Owen) whom Mill would later call "communists."[56]

As Mill understood it, all forms of socialism were opposed to "the régime of individual property" as currently constituted and indeed to private property itself (and therefore to any "régime of individual property ... as it might be made"). In his time, then, socialism viewed private property, especially individual ownership of capital, as the root of contemporary social evils. It followed that socialism involved communal ownership of property understood broadly speaking as capital or "the instruments and means of production" (to a more or less exclusive degree – Fourier, for instance, allows some individual ownership of capital, which can be invested in communally owned associations in order to generate an interest payment).[57] Socialists did not bar individual ownership "of articles of consumption." That is, an individual might retain "the exclusive right ... to his or her share of the produce when received, either to enjoy, to give, or to exchange it," although the land might belong to the "community ... and ... be cultivated on their joint account," and "the dwelling assigned to each individual or family as part of their remuneration might be as exclusively theirs ... as any one's house now is," as might "any ornamental ground which the circumstances of the association allowed to be attached to the house for purposes of enjoyment." "The distinctive feature of Socialism," Mill insisted, "is not that all things are in common, but that production is only carried on upon the common account, and that the instruments of production are held as common property."

Another "distinctive feature" of socialism in Mill's time was that the "division of the produce" of labour was done in "public" and in accordance with "rules laid down by the community" based on principles of justice rather than by chance.[58] If there were inequalities, these were justified – or at least justifiable to, and by, the principles of justice endorsed by people living in the same community.

Mill drew four distinctions between various "types" of socialism related to how the "physical means of life and enjoyment" (i.e., articles of consumption) are distributed; the "scale" of the association envisaged (from the whole state, to small "village"-sized communes, or even smaller "associations"); the means advocated for implanting these schemes (from incremental, organic, voluntarist change to the violent and complete overthrow of every element of the existing system); and the extent to which these systems are supposed to be self-sufficient and self-contained, or allow for (or rely on) a *some* interactions among different, mutually-dependent associations.

Under the first heading came his main distinguishing difference between "communists" and other socialists. "Communists" proposed "absolute equality in the distribution of the physical means of life and enjoyment."[59] "Socialists" "admit inequality, but grounded on some principle, or supposed principle, of justice or general expediency." On this division, Mill counted Owen and Cabet as "communists," along with Blanc (though Mill noted that Blanc endorsed complete equality only "as a transition to a still higher standard of justice, that all should work according to their capacity, and receive according to their wants." Blanc's idea of "higher" justice might be a form of "socialism," not "communism," though – like communist principles of justice – it presupposed the ability to divorce remuneration from effort).

Both "communists" and "socialists" proposed a variety of scales: Owen advocated small-scale "villages"; Cabet, whole-state communism.[60] Saint-Simon advocated whole-state socialism; Fourier, small-scale socialist associations. Similarly, some communists and socialists advocated gradual change through the "multiplication" of associations, all founded by volunteers who had been persuaded of the superiority of socialism.[61] On the other hand, the "revolutionary Socialists" wanted an immediate overthrow of the regime of private property and its immediate replacement by something entirely new.[62]

Socialism could also involve self-sufficient communities of different scales (who might or might not interact) – for example, in the ideas of Owen, Thompson, Cabet, and Saint-Simon. Or communities might not be intended to be self-sufficient, but to trade with one another even for necessities within a broader political community comprised of many "associations" – for example, Blanc and other "cooperative socialists" including Holyoake, Neale, Buchez, and the Rochdale Pioneers, and also, to some extent, Fourier. Put briefly, socialism could either be "communist" or "non-communist"; state-scale or small-scale; "evolutionary" or "revolutionary"[63]; and, for want of a better differentiation, "self-sufficient" or "interactive."

In Table 3.1, I categorize the kinds of socialism that Mill knew and engaged with.[64]

Mill was only ever in favour of small-scale, evolutionary schemes. In *Chapters* he made very plain the disaster he thought awaited the violent, immediate overthrow of an entire existing society, particularly by people who not only did not have, but prided themselves on not having, a plan for reconstruction.[65] It would, he said, be a Hobbesian state of nature, out of which must only come centuries more of oppression and tyranny, if any survived it at all. Mill was also never convinced about either the desirability or the feasibility of state-scale socialism.[66]

Mill was not a complete advocate of *any* extant form of socialism, though there were some he much preferred to others. In the rest of

TABLE 3.1

Owenism (e.g. as advocated by Owen and Thompson[1])	Communist; small-scale; evolutionary; self-sufficient (with some interaction with other communities, particularly in Thompson's schemes).
Saint-Simonism	Socialist; state-scale; evolutionary; self-sufficient.
Fourierism	Socialist; small-scale; evolutionary; self-sufficient, but interacting in a "World Congress of Phalanxes."
Icarianism	Communist; state-scale; evolutionary; self-sufficient.
Blancianism	Communist (perhaps transitioning to socialism); small-scale; evolutionary; interactive.
Revolutionary Socialism	Unclear whether "communist" or "socialist";[2] state-scale; revolutionary; self-sufficient.
Cooperation ("association of labourers among themselves"[3] either as producer or consumers)	"Socialist" in the main, though could choose "communist" principles of distribution; small-scale; evolutionary; interactive.

1   Owen, *Book of the New Moral World*, xiii–xix; Thompson, *Inquiry*, 168–7; 256–7; and 274–80.
2   Mill did not mention what he took the distributive preferences of "revolutionary Socialism" to be in Chapters, which reflects the unwillingness he denigrates on their part to make concrete plans for "after the revolution."
3   Mill, *Principles*, 775.

this chapter I look at the problems he identified even with extant forms of socialism, leaving aside, for the most part, revolutionary socialism, having just flagged its main problems. Then I consider what it was Mill found attractive in socialism broadly conceived, in order to turn, in the following chapter, to a reconstruction of his own "qualified socialism."[67]

We can already see, however, generally what it was Mill had in mind when he spoke of "socialism." By that word he meant schemes that involved communal ownership of "the means of production" and in which production was done solely "on the common account," as well as a public just (at least supposedly) distribution of "articles of consumption" whereby individual "ownership" (entailing certain exclusive rights over use and disposal) was granted over these items. This is opposed to the contemporary "régime of individual property," under which goods were produced on the individual capital owner's account, with surpluses being produced with an eye to personal gain through advantageous trade; the means of production as well as articles of consumption were privately owned, and people had unjustified rights regarding inheritance of both kinds of property; and the division of the product was a private affair based in part on personal exertion but a great deal more "on accident alone."[68] Also, Mill's socialism was distinct from the "régime of individual property … as it might be made" both in a "new" world and the "old" one, where, again, production would be on the private account; the means of production and articles of consumption would be privately owned (excepting, perhaps, land), though inheritance rights would be much more constrained than at present; and the distribution would be private and the result of personal exertion (in itself, somewhat "accidental"), although it might be better founded on principles of justice (e.g., securing the labourer the fruits of his or her labours) and less on "accident" (and a history of force) than under contemporary capitalism.

MILL'S CRITICISMS OF SOCIALISM AND SOCIALISTS

Over time, Mill's attitude toward socialism, and specific socialists, changed. But the grounds of his critiques remained stable, even when he altered his assessment of whether particular socialist schemes were merited such criticism. These criticisms encompassed the following: queries regarding whether all the criticisms that socialists levelled at capitalism were founded on a good understanding of economics;

questions of feasibility (i.e., would the proposed scheme work and be self-sustaining once up and running?); doubts regarding the justice of the specific principles of distribution endorsed by different schemes; worries regarding the survival of individuality; concerns regarding the possibility, and the potential costs, of immediate implementation; and considerations of whether a scheme could *ever* be implemented by people in the current, very imperfect state of humanity, and whether there was an available means of improving humanity to the point that they *could* implement such schemes. In this section, I explore each of these concerns in more detail.

Socialist Critiques of Capitalism

Mill agreed with a number of socialist critiques of capitalism, particularly on the grounds of capitalism's inefficiency; its unjustifiable inequalities; its social ethos; and the dire poverty faced by a large part (if not the majority) of the working classes.[69] I will return to these issues later, in the section about the elements of socialism that Mill found attractive. For now ... Mill did not agree with *all* of the socialist critiques of capitalism, and this (among other things) prevented him from being identified with any specific version of contemporary socialism. (That said, the differences between Mill and his socialist contemporaries have been exaggerated, and that he was not a member of any contemporary socialist sect did not preclude him from being "under the general designation of Socialist."[70])

Mill engaged most directly, and at most length, with socialist critiques of capitalism in *Chapters*, taking Blanc, Owen and Considerant as exemplars. The criticisms he lists regard the evils associated with competition; inefficiency; and a wrong social morality, particularly regarding social inter-relations, how people viewed work, and fraudulent trading practices.[71] The assessment of competition, as others have noted,[72] appeared to create the widest breach between him and contemporary socialists: in *Principles*, he defended the idea of competition against socialist critiques,[73] arguing against many of Blanc's critiques of it and finding him guilty of the "exaggeration" that "is not wanting in the representations of the ablest and most candid of Socialists."[74]

Blanc declared that competition "is for the people a system of extermination."[75] Poor people were left with no option but to work for wages (i.e., they could not cultivate land, or hunt and fish on it, as it had all been taken into private ownership and "vagabondage" and begging were illegal), but competition between them drove those wages down in a "continual fall." This was exacerbated by the problem of high birth rates among the poor. Blanc rejected the classical political economist's argument that competition is beneficial as it leads to lower prices for commodities: this, he said, might happen in the short run, but in the long run competition advantages large producers and monopolists over small manufacturers and shopkeepers, so low prices are "maintained only so long as there is a struggle; no sooner have the rich competitors driven out their poorer rivals than prices rise." He thought that competition led to inefficiency and oversupply because there was no coordination of industry and because speculators were encouraged to "gamble" for the chance of great profits rather than produce what was actually needed. Lastly, he felt that competition made people "venal" and "invades even the domain of thought" by creating "a vast confusion calculated to arouse jealously, mistrust, and hatred, and to stifle, little by little, all generous aspirations, all fair self-sacrifice, and poetry."

Mill rejected Blanc's claim that wages were falling – wages might fluctuate over time, but overall, they were increasing.[76] Moreover, he rejected the idea that only socialism could prevent overpopulation. Competition, he believed, led to higher wages in the long run. He also rejected Blanc's argument that competition leads eventually (and inexorably) to higher prices, with the caveat that prices might rise in those few industries that tend toward monopoly and that are run, in capitalism, by "great joint-stock companies" (e.g., railways).[77] This was why, as he argued in *Principles*, the state ought to "reserve" such industry "to itself," or ensure that it is "carried on under conditions prescribed, and, from time to time, varied by" it, thus guaranteeing the public a cheaper supply than would come from private industry. Overall, however, competition led to high wages and low prices: "the present system is not, as many Socialists believe, hurrying us into a state of general indigence and slavery from which only Socialism can save us."[78]

On the other hand, Mill agreed with the socialists that competition does not guarantee quality: indeed, the profit motive encouraged distributors to try to sell inferior-quality goods, and the proliferation of distributors could make it difficult for consumers to discern who had higher-quality goods for sale before those people were driven out of the market.[79] This links to Mill's assessment of the socialists' assertion that capitalism is inefficient.[80] He advocated the expansion of consumer cooperatives as a cure.[81]

Mill also agreed with Blanc, Owen, and Considerant regarding the bad social morality or ethos that permeated, and was encouraged by, contemporary capitalism, criticizing the "greed" that exploited "cupidity" at the consumer's expense.[82] Indeed, he argued that "the moral objection to competition, as arming one human being against another, making the good of each depend on evil to others, making all who have anything to gain or lose, live as in the midst of enemies, by no means deserves the disdain with which it is treated by some of the adversaries of socialism ... Socialism, as long as it attacks the existing individualism, is easily triumphant."[83]

He reiterated Blanc's language regarding how "as wealth increases and greater prizes seem to be within reach, more and more of a gambling spirit is introduced into commerce; and where this prevails not only are the simplest maxims of prudence disregarded, but all, even the most perilous, forms of pecuniary improbity receive a terrible stimulus," and how this leads to "the morality of the trading classes" being "more and more deteriorated."[84] "On this point, therefore," Mill wrote, "Socialists have really made out the existence not only of a great evil, but of one which grows and tends to grow with the growth of population and wealth." (In the modern context, we might consider the kinds of incentives for "pecuniary improbity" and "perilous" investments offered by the massive gains available to, and desired by investors in, global financial markets.) However, Mill thought society as it then existed could do a good deal more to protect against this evil, through existing laws against fraud and through the creation of cooperative stores, particularly ones that sourced their goods from cooperative wholesalers.

Thus, there were two main differences between Mill and the socialists whose criticisms he cited: first, he denied that competition, except in some specific cases, was lowering wages; and second, he thought that competition between producers led to lower prices (which was good for consumers and thus for workers, as workers are also consumers). However, two things are worth noting. First, Mill advocated some solutions to these problems – most obviously, consumer cooperation – that were "partly grounded on socialistic principles."[85] Second, though his belief that competition led in the long run to high, not low, wages, and to low, not high, prices, separated him from socialists such as Blanc, it did not separate him from *all* contemporary socialists. In fact, the idea that competition between producers – particularly producer-cooperatives – would happen and would benefit consumers can be found in the ideas of a number of co-operators, for instance Neale,[86] Holyoake,[87] Michel Goudchaux, Alexandre Marie, Hipployte Carnot, Louis Garnier-Pages, and Armand Marrast, as well as Buchez and his followers in *L'Atelier*.[88] Thompson (in what has been called his "second-best" utopia[89]) also envisaged competition between mainly self-sufficient "villages" for goods and services, though not in the labour market.[90] Fourier imagined competition between "phalanxes" and between "series" of workers within phalanxes, which would harness people's "cabalistic passion" and motivate them through a competitive sort of "emulation."[91] These ideas have a strong echo in Mill's use of the word "emulation." He contended that "a contest, who can do most for the common good, is not the kind of competition which Socialists repudiate";[92] he entertained the notion of competition between cooperative associations in the spirit of "a friendly rivalry in the pursuit of a good common to all."[93]

Mill denied that competition led to reduced wages, but this does not mean he advocated competition in the labour market. Instead, he thought that the poor were increasingly unwilling (and rightly so) to work for wages but would want a fairer share of the product of their labour as well as a greater amount of input into their work and working conditions.[94] He predicted that eventually, and much sooner than many people currently imagined, no one would be willing to work for wages and instead would insist on cooperative associations – an outcome he said "would be the nearest approach to social justice, and the most beneficial ordering of industrial affairs for the universal good, which it is possible at present to foresee."[95] His disagreement regarding competition in the labour market, then, was over what he saw as economic facts: the effects of competition on wages were not what socialists said they were, and therefore we ought not to believe we were headed for "general indigence and slavery from which only Socialism can save us."[96] But this empirical observation did not undermine the *normative* force of socialism's other critiques of competition in the labour market, many of which Mill agreed with (regarding the social ethos, people's "morality," and the quality of interpersonal relationships). Nor did this empirical observation undermine Mill's *other* empirical observation, that working people *were* increasingly unwilling to work for wages and to be regarded merely as a "receiver of hire" rather than as a partner in production.[97]

To sum up this subsection: Mill agreed with several socialist critiques of contemporary capitalism, though he also thought several of the problems they identified could be cured within a regime of individual property, in part through the adoption of ideas founded on socialist principles (which, of course, would already make this regime something of a hybrid). He disagreed with the antipathy toward competition in all forms displayed by some socialists, and he sought to straighten out both what he saw as their muddled or erroneous economic thinking and what *was* in their ideas (a more normative critique) that had bite against capitalism, or any regime of individual property. This difference between Mill and contemporary socialists regarding competition *is* a difference, and it may be what Mill had in mind when he called his ideas "a qualified socialism" and "under the general designation of Socialist."[98] But it was not enough to completely prevent him from being a socialist at all.

Having considered Mill's assessment of the socialist critiques of capitalism, I now explore some of the other assessments he made of contemporary socialist schemes, beginning with the core question of their very feasibility.

Socialism's Feasibility

Mill wrote that "the *practicability* then of Socialism, on the scale of Mr. Owen's or M. Fourier's villages, admits of no dispute."[99] However, "the attempt to manage the whole production of a nation by one central organization is a totally different matter." He called "the idea of conducting the whole industry of a country by direction from a single centre ... obviously chimerical."[100] Evidently, Mill did not think that *any* state management or ownership of the means of production, or provision of goods and services, was "impracticable" or "obviously chimerical," given that he supported a number of such state activities as part of his conception of "the régime of individual property ... as it might be made." However, his warnings regarding the potential problems of government ownership and provision (in his chapter on *laisser-faire*) give us some clue as to why he doubted the practicability of state-wide management of the *entire* economy.

Specifically regarding Saint-Simonian state socialism (which he often labelled "impracticable"[101]), Mill had two main concerns. First, whether it would be in the capacity of any individuals actually to (as the Saint-Simonian scheme demands) apportion work according to capacity, and reward according to how well people performed their functions. Second, whether "any use which they could make of this power would give general satisfaction, or would be submitted to without the aid of force," which he called "a supposition almost too chimerical to be reasoned against."[102]

Concerning the feasibility of small-scale socialism, which Mill considered in much more detail, he thought most forms of it were "practicable" but raised a variety of concerns regarding how well it would work, particularly in its communist forms. He also dismissed some common critiques, which he himself had to some extent shared in the 1820s. It is worth noting that Mill said that, "not believing in universal selfishness, I have no difficulty in admitting that Communism would even now be practicable among the *elite* of mankind, and may become so among the rest."[103]

In his earliest speeches against Owenites, Mill declared that Owenism would prove itself unstable (thus, unfeasible) unless private property was completely outlawed.[104] Moreover, if private property *was* so outlawed, the scheme would still be inefficient, for neither workers nor managers would have any motivation to work effectively.[105] Furthermore, there would be a strong likelihood (as Thomas Malthus had argued[106]) that the community would soon starve as there would be nothing to check the population rate, which would soon outstrip production.

By the time he came to write *Principles*, however, he judged Owenism to be not "impracticable"[107] so long as the population was kept under control[108] – something that he now thought the power of public opinion in communist associations would encourage to such a degree that "the Communistic scheme, instead of being peculiarly open to the objection drawn from the danger of over-population, has the recommendation of tending in an especial degree to the prevention of that evil."[109] Such schemes "could ... permanently subsist ... without positive discomfort," he said in earlier editions of *Principles*;[110] members could produce "sufficient to maintain them in comfort," he averred in later ones.[111] They would not be rendered infeasible by the problem of people lacking a motive to work: communism would be able to motivate people through threat of penalties ("positive repro[of]") and by harnessing both their "public spirit" and "power of emulation,"[112] the ability of which to excite "the most strenuous exertions for the sake of the approbation and admiration of others" had been "borne witness to by experience in every situation in which human beings publicly compete with one another, even if it be in things frivolous."[113] The "eye" of "the whole community" would be on each worker, and this would be enough to keep them at their tasks, just as "the eye ... of one master" already was under contemporary capitalism.[114] At the very least, "Communistic labour ... would ... probably be more energetic than that of a labourer for hire,"[115] especially as Mill also thought that the more educated the worker, the more likely he would be to work hard without surveillance – and all communist schemes insist that all workers will be educated.[116]

In his early speeches against Owenism, Mill highlighted some concerns regarding the efficient management of communist communities. Though these concerns are not raised in *Principles*, he addresses them in some depth in *Chapters*.[117] Communism provided no incentive for the best leaders to put themselves forward (taking on more work and responsibility for no increase in reward), and the necessarily committee-like nature of decision-making might make innovation difficult to implement (though Mill thought innovators would still innovate, because they enjoyed doing it and would find it hard not to).[118]

Another recurring concern regarding the feasibility of communism is whether it is possible to fairly apportion work equally.[119] As Mill said, "there are many kinds of work, and by what standard are they to be measured one against another? Who is to judge how much cotton spinning, or distributing goods from the stores, or bricklaying, or chimney sweeping, is equivalent to so much ploughing?" That is, how can we determine that work is equally burdensome when different types of work are so qualitatively different? Working equal hours is not the answer because some work is much harder than other kinds. Mill rejected the general communist answer to this problem, which was to make people work all jobs by turn, because by "putting an end to the division of employments," this "would sacrifice so much of the advantage of co-operative production as greatly to diminish the productiveness of labour." Moreover, "even in the same kind of work, nominal equality of labour would be so great an inequality, that the feeling of justice would revolt against its being enforced." "All persons are not equally fit for all labour; and the same quantity of labour is an unequal burthen on the weak and the strong, the hardy and the delicate, the quick and the slow, the dull and the intelligent."[120] This is a claim about feasibility as well as equality: if "the feeling of justice would revolt," then people will not agree to this work-regime, and the community will collapse.

After 1852, in *Principles*, Mill revealed a change in his position on this question:

> [T]hese difficulties, though real, are not necessarily insuperable. The apportionment of work to the strength and capacities of individuals, the mitigation of a general rule to provide for cases in which it would operate harshly, are not problems to which human intelligence, guided by a sense of justice, would be inadequate. And the worst and most unjust arrangement which could be made ... under a system aiming at equality, would be so far short of the inequality and injustice with which labour (not to speak of remuneration) is now apportioned, as to be scarcely worth counting in the comparison.[121]

In *Chapters* Mill suggested that "there should be a dispensing power, an authority competent to grant exemptions from the ordinary amount of work, and to proportion tasks in some measure to capabilities."[122] This, he noted, might be abused by free-riders, and "[t]he squabbles and ill-blood which could not fail to be engendered by the distribution of work whenever such persons have to be dealt with, would be a great abatement from the harmony and unanimity which Communists hope would be found among the members of their association."[123] However, it is a sign that, again, he thought the problems of equality when apportioning labour were not "necessarily insuperable," though he did not use this phrase in *Chapters*.

Mill did not have similar concerns regarding the feasibility of small-scale socialism, particularly of the kind advocated by Fourier.[124] He consistently argued that Fourierism "does no violence to any of the general laws by which human action ... is influenced." Everyone would have the opportunity to gain an individual advantage from every degree of labour, abstinence, and talent they possessed, for Fourierism did not withdraw the motives to effort that were present in current society, and that were lacking in communism. Although he was not wholly convinced by Fourier's explanation of how labour would be made "attractive" (thinking the "attractiveness" of "disagreeable" labour currently voluntarily undertaken might be due, in a great part, to its voluntary nature, which would disappear under Fourierism), he was more persuaded that such work might be *made* attractive if it were linked to higher honour and remuneration. He also spoke approvingly of the Fourierist idea that the necessary labour would get done because no one need do it excessively, particularly as there would be many more people to take a share of the necessary labour, since everyone would be working, and there would be much less labour wasted on unnecessary things (as in contemporary capitalism). Though admitting some reservations, he concluded that such concerns flagged "difficulties, not impossibilities," which did not detract from the overall "practicability" of Fourierism, which "admits of no dispute,"[125] for Fourierism had "the greatest foresight of objections, of all the forms of Socialism":[126] "[t]here is scarcely an objection or a difficulty which Fourier did not foresee, and against which he did not make provision beforehand by self-acting contrivances."[127]

Similarly, Mill thought that small-scale cooperative socialism of both producer and consumer kinds was eminently feasible – indeed, he wrote many pages for *Principles* detailing how such schemes worked.[128] He predicted that they would be the form of association that was "likely to predominate,"[129] asserting that these associations were perfectly capable of competing successfully with capitalist firms.[130] Mill was evidently concerned, in 1852, that the associations – though in themselves feasible – would not survive the "ruin" of "everything free, popular, or tending to improvement" brought about by the actions of "[t]he unprincipled adventurer who has for the present succeeded in reducing France to the political condition of Russia" (i.e., Napoleon III), but noted in later editions that reports of their death were greatly exaggerated, and that associations were feasible even under conditions of political repression.[131] Indeed, he concluded that "the prosperity attained by some of them even while passing through this difficult period … must be conclusive to all minds as to the brilliant future reserved for the principle of co-operation."

These cooperative associations pooled the capital (which was often incredibly small) of the members; worked under managers elected by the workers themselves and according to rules they themselves drew up (which were often much stricter, even, than those in capitalist firms); and distributed the product of their labour according to principles of justice to which all members agreed.[132] Mill thought that "associations" that implemented equal shares, and Blanc's "higher" principle of justice, were both feasible, though not at the current time. (They were, he said, "adapted to a much higher moral condition of human nature" than "the selfish type of character formed by the present standard of morality, and fostered by the existing social institutions," adding that "an attempt at a higher ideal, until education shall have been entirely regenerated," was unlikely "to prove immediately successful."[133]) As he noted in his description of these schemes, those which had started out distributing according to equal shares had swiftly changed to something more like piece-work.[134]

This was a principle of distribution that Mill supported (even adding a footnote in its defence to *Principles* after 1857[135]) as most perfectly respecting the fundamental principle of individual property, "the guarantee to individuals of the fruits of their own labour and abstinence."[136] It also encapsulated "contract," which was "the system, of all others, in the present state of society and degree of civilisation, most favourable to the worker; though most unfavourable to the non-worker who wishes to be paid for being idle."[137] However, we should note the caveats "in the present state of society and degree of civilisation": piecework represented "justice" and "fairness" in *contemporary* society, and support for it represented good character (rather than a desire to free-ride on the labour of others), but like all principles of justice associated with private property, it was a transitional principle, currently just because expedient, and representing a compromise between selfishness (even though not as bad as idle free-riding) and the ideal notion of labour and reward as identified by Comte.[138]

Mill thought that socialist "social transformation" would be "practicable" only after "an equivalent change of character" had "take[n] place both in the uncultivated herd who now compose the labouring masses, and in the immense majority of their employers," who must "learn by practice to labour ... for generous ... and not as hitherto solely self-interested" purposes.[139] He also "looked forward to a time when ... the rule that they who do not work shall not eat, will be applied not to paupers only, but impartially to all," and a basic step toward achieving that was that people did indeed work if they wanted to eat. He wanted to encourage independence and pride among workers, for these would lead to them contributing according to their capacities (as socialists would put it), rather than – as he currently saw it – doing their best to contribute as little as possible for the highest possible wages. This is a key reason why he called for stronger measures to encourage workers to identify their interests with those of their employers, for instance through measures based on encouraging the "elite" to undertake a process of "self-help," profit-sharing,[140] and ultimately cooperation; but piecework would also foster this (similarly, profit-sharing, as detailed in *Principles*, would allow for unequal apportioning of the profits shared, according to contribution, talent, or industry.)[141] Associations that implemented piecework, or other systems of remuneration that justified inequalities in terms of talent, industry, or effort, "by the very process of their success, are a course of education in those moral and active qualities by which alone success can be either deserved or attained," and might lead to the feasibility of "higher" principles of justice.

Overall, then, small-scale socialism was much more feasible than state-scale socialism. Moreover, those versions of socialism that factored in the potential problems of motivating people as they currently were to work without the driver of individual interest that capitalism tried to harness, as well as the potential limitations of human knowledge (and our own unwillingness to accord omniscience to others), were more feasible – at least in the short term – than types that did not. One reason why Mill called for experimentation in different forms of small-scale socialism (both communist and non-communist forms) was in order to see, through experiment, whether these forms of socialism really *were* feasible and what changes might need to be made to the workings of the schemes in order to ensure their feasibility.[142]

The "Availability" of Socialism

That some kinds of socialism were more *immediately* feasible than others draws us neatly toward the question of whether different forms of socialism were, as Mill said, "available as a present resource" to society.[143] Could some of those forms be implemented immediately, rather than far into the future? Mill advocated the immediate implementation – by those who wanted to try them – of some forms of small-scale socialism (most obviously, from the 1830s onwards, cooperative associations, and after 1849, Fourierist associations).

He seems to have thought that Saint-Simonism would never be "available as a present resource" – even in the 1830s, when he seemed to imply that continual change in humanity might make that form "practicable," he then immediately likened it to the North Star, which we would never reach but nonetheless ought to use as a navigational guide.[144] In *Principles* he noted that something similar to Saint-Simonism had been achieved by Jesuit priests in their colonization of Paraguay but that the scheme "would not be borne" in modern times "unless from persons believed to be more than men, and backed by supernatural terrors," which was not very likely.[145] Even so, Mill concluded his section on Saint-Simonism and Fourierism with a plea that socialists be allowed to conduct their experiments, so perhaps he did think it was "available as a present resource" to some – or perhaps this was more meant to include those kinds he *did* think immediately available (such as Fourierism and cooperative socialism).[146]

Mill had some similar concerns regarding communism, at least in the late 1840s, when he argued that, though it could well be true that a set of communist teachers could educate children to be communists, and thus achieve communism within a generation, it was not clear where such teachers were to be found or who would teach *them*.[147] These concerns did not make their way directly into *Principles* or *Chapters*, both of which portray communism as a regime that might conceivably be available to people in the distant future (i.e., to those who might choose it, or choose a reformed form of individual property); and both of which include communism as a socialist scheme meriting a fair trial.[148] That said, in *Chapters* and *Considerations on Representative Government* it is clear (and in *Principles* it is at least implied) that communism is not for everyone – at least right now – and that "to be successful, [it] requires a high standard of both moral and intellectual education in all members of the community" – though this education, in itself, is feasible.[149] Indeed, Mill forthrightly declared: "I reject altogether the notion that it is impossible for education and cultivation such as is implied in these things to be made the inheritance of every person in the nation; but I am convinced that it is very difficult, and that the passage to it from our present condition can only be slow."[150]

Given the "demoralising" effect of "the present state of society," it might be true that "only a Communist association can effectually train mankind for Communism," and that this was all the more reason to try out communism, and try to prove "by practical experiment, its power of giving this training" and ability to "give to the next generation … the education necessary to keep up" the necessary "high level" of "moral education" "permanently." Even so, Mill was at pains to make clear that he "d[id] not seek to draw an inference against the possibility that Communistic production is capable of being at some future time the form of society best adapted to the wants and circumstances of mankind," though this would "long" be "an open question," only provable through "trial of the Communistic principle under favourable circumstances."[151]

He put the "arrival" of communism somewhat sooner (for some) in *Considerations*: "whenever it ceases to be true that mankind, as a rule, prefer themselves to others, and those nearest to them to those more remote, from that moment Communism is not only practicable, but the only defensible form of society; and will, when that time arrives be assuredly carried into effect. For my own part, not believing in universal selfishness, I have no difficulty in admitting that Communism would even now by practicable among the *elite* of mankind, and may become so among the rest."[152]

In sum, Fourierism, cooperative socialism, and possibly also small-scale communism were "available as a present resource," at least to what Mill called "the élite of mankind" (including, of course, those working people in England and France who were already attempting socialism).[153] State-scale socialism, however, was not available as a present resource. Small-scale socialism was more available than small-scale communism because it demanded less of the "moral education" of its members. These are, of course, all evolutionary forms, whose very success can pave the way for further successes.[154] Mill may also have believed that at least the revolutionary part of revolutionary socialism was immediately available (i.e., we could immediately have a revolution). But he did not think that a socialist reconstruction in the chaos on the other side of a revolution was plausible, and therefore the *goals* of these socialists were not immediately available, or at least not through the means they advocated.

THE "COST" OF IMPLEMENTING SOCIALISM

This takes us nicely to the question of the "cost" of implementing socialism. Evidently, revolutionary socialism was much too costly.[155] Those forms that Mill saw as "available as a present resource," however, he was at pains to show were not very costly, and what burdens they did impose would fall only on those who had volunteered to bear them.[156]

In the 1820s, he certainly viewed Owenism as much too costly to be attempted[157] – indeed, he posited that two thirds of the population would have starved by the time Owen's Parallelograms were up and running.[158] He may have continued to think Owenism too costly to be worth the risks, at least in the current state of the world, and certainly, it was not Owenite forms of socialism for which he loudly claimed the right to, and importance of, a trial. One might expect him to have also considered Icarianism too costly (it being a state-wide form of communism); yet Mill defended Cabet in the press when he was tried *in absentia* for fraud after going to the United States with his followers' funds to purchase land for their schemes. So perhaps Mill thought Icarianism was also not too costly for those who were willing to undertake the burdens.[159]

This, probably, becomes the heart of the matter, at least in Mill's later assessments of socialism: if people are willing to conduct socialist "experiments in living," they ought to be able to do so, and the costs to them cannot be considered too high. It is when they try to force those experiments on unwilling others that the moral costs begin to mount. There must also be, though, a consideration concerning the necessary capital outlay, and this, of course, is easier to muster for small-scale forms of socialism.

The Risks to Individuality Posed by Socialism

I turn now to a different concern Mill had with socialism, one that has led many to argue that he could not really have been a socialist.[160] Certainly, intuitively at least, Mill's commitment to "the free development of individuality" shown so strongly in *On Liberty* appears to be a sticking point for the plausibility of his being a socialist.[161] It is clear that Mill did have individuality-based concerns regarding socialism, but we ought to look carefully at precisely what these were, for when we do, it is less evident that Mill could not have been a socialist.

Mill's concern about socialism's negative impact on individuality and "independence" hearkens all the way back to his first debates against the Owenites. Owenism was, Mill said, "in its very nature ... a system of universal regulation," and though he was "not one of those, who set up liberty as an idol to be worshipped," and was willing to embrace "regulation and control" "when there is special advantage to be obtained" by it, he believed "there is a pleasure in enjoying perfect freedom of action ... to be controlled, even if it be for our own good, is in itself far from pleasant, and ... other things being alike, it is infinitely better to attain a given end by leaving people to themselves than to attain the same end by controlling them ... It is delightful to a man to be an independent being."[162]

Later, in *Principles*, he reiterated his concern that communist forms of socialism would leave no room for individuality.[163] In every edition, Mill worried that life under communism would be "monotonous"[164] and whether it would

> be consistent with[165] that multiform development of human nature, those manifold unlikenesses, that diversity of tastes and talents, and variety of intellectual points of view, which not only form a great part of the interest of human life, but by bringing intellects into stimulating collision, and by presenting to each innumerable notions that he would not have conceived of himself, are the mainspring of mental and moral progression.[166]

What changed more significantly is, that though Mill gave even more weight to the thought that people ought not to trade equality for individuality,[167] he said from 1852 onwards that "no doubt, this, like all the other objections to the Socialists['] schemes, is vastly exaggerated."[168]

In communist schemes, people's non-working lives could be free from anti-individualist pressure: they need not always live together; nor need what they do in their spare time be anything other than their choice; nor need what they choose to do with their share of the produce be dictated by anyone other than themselves. Moreover, people need not be chained either to a locality or to a particular occupation. Mill went so far as to argue that if communist societies only made what was actually of use, then the people living in them would have a great deal more leisure time than people in current society, and such unconstrained leisure time would surely be of benefit to individuality and freedom.

In the earliest editions of *Principles* Mill also worried that "each would be the slave of all"[169] under communism, but this was dropped from later editions.[170] Those later editions also spent more time emphasizing the relative freedom for workers under communism, even though continuing to emphasize the drawbacks of a society that did not permit "the free development of individuality."[171] Indeed, by the time of the 1852 edition, Mill said these concerns would be "as dust in the balance" if the choice was solely between communism with all its "difficulties, great or small,"[172] and the contemporary system, for, among other things, "the restraints of Communism would be freedom in comparison with the present condition of the majority of the human race."[173] This statement remains in all subsequent editions.

His position was not as forthright in *Chapters*, in which he reiterated his concern regarding the possible negative impact of communism on individuality, particularly the worrying possibility of "a delusive unanimity produced by the prostration of all individual opinions and wishes before the decree of the majority," but did not say that this charge was "vastly exaggerated."[174] This might suggest that when he wrote *Chapters*, he thought this was a greater danger than when he first wrote those words in *Principles*. On the other hand, *Chapters* was begun in 1869 and left unfinished, and in the final edition of *Principles*, published in 1871, this passage remains intact, which suggests more that Mill phrased things differently in *Chapters* than that he had really changed his mind. Still, it is clear that Mill was worried about the impact of communism on individuality throughout his life, and that to the extent it did negatively affect individuality, communism was less desirable than a system that would preserve it. This concern can be overplayed, however, and it is important to note – as Sarvasy rightly does – that at least from the time of writing the *Principles*, Mill only said there was a *danger* of repression of individuality under communism – he did not say it was an *inevitable* outcome of communism.[175] *This* idea might be what the modern reader, with more knowledge of the consequences of Soviet-style state communism than Mill had, reads into his text, but it is not what Mill himself wrote. Moreover, Mill did not rule out the possibility that future generations would work out a way to combine communism with individuality in an acceptable way; he was only saying that he could not see exactly how to do it.[176]

It also ought to be emphasized that these concerns applied *only* to communism and that Mill did not think that all forms of socialism were "communist." That said, he had some concerns in the 1830s regarding an overreliance on the state that might be engendered by Saint-Simonism,[177] and we can see that these – and similar concerns he raised in his discussion of *laissez-faire* – would have applied to any state-wide conception of socialism (communist or not). However, in *Principles*, Mill insisted that under Saint-Simonism, "society would wear as diversified a face as it does now; [and] would be still fuller of interest and excitement," thus implying that it posed less of a problem for individuality than communism did (and perhaps would be better for individuality than contemporary capitalism).[178]

Mill certainly did not think that Fourierism was open to the same concerns regarding individuality as communism.[179] He expressed admiration for the way in which something approximating equality would "practically result" from Fourierism's arrangements of labour and distribution, "not, (as in Communism) from the compression, but on the contrary, from the largest possible development, of the various natural superiorities residing in each individual."[180] As noted in the previous chapter, Mill did not think contemporary capitalism was particularly conducive to individuality, freedom, or independence: nor was it certain that "the régime of individual property ... as it might be made" would be a complete improvement because of the lack of freedom inherent in wage relations. Indeed, as others rightly argue, it was Mill's commitment to *everyone's* individuality and independence that led him to endorse cooperative socialism.[181] As Mill himself put it, he felt this position had been "promulgated ... less clearly and fully in the first edition [1848], rather more so in the second [1849], and quite unequivocally in the third [1852]" edition of *Principles*.[182] Mill was certainly deeply concerned about the survival of individuality, and he had some concerns regarding the dangers posed to this by state-wide forms of socialism (both communist and non-communist) – but these concerns were not raised by small-scale forms of (non-communist) socialism.

The Justness of Different Forms of Socialism

I noted earlier some of Mill's critiques of capitalism on the grounds of distributive justice. Socialism is not based on the same claims of justice as those which Mill calls the only grounds supporting individual property that will "bear the light" – those of securing for the labourer the full fruit of his or her labour and abstinence.[183] These grounds could legitimate private holdings of capital (though not land), and socialism advocates communal ownership of the means of production. The defensible principle of justice underpinning individual property also links remuneration with effort, which Mill thought was, ultimately, unjust. On the other hand, much of the socialist critique of capitalism centres on how *little* of the fruit of his or her labour the labourer actually receives (most of it being taken by the employer or going to non-labouring landowners). In part, this is a consequence of the view that value arises from labour. Thus, even if socialists do not want people to benefit from their abstinence through the ensuing generation of capital, they are interested in what they see as a more just distribution of the product of labour to labourers (as well as fairer apportionment of labour itself, such that there is no "idle," propertied class).

Mill engaged with several socialist principles of justice, and he had some concerns about all of them that it is worth exploring. But it is important first to emphasize that the fact that these principles were not capitalist principles was not what made Mill criticize them – indeed, he referred to them as "higher" than the principles ostensibly underpinning capitalism (and really underpinning his vision of "the régime of individual property … as it might be made"). He saw these "capitalist" principles as a "compromise" with the ideal, but a necessary compromise, given the current imperfect state of humanity. That is, they were currently expedient.

Persky has usefully explored Mill's "progressive" view of justice, explaining how he differentiated between what might "ideally" be just – "the egalitarian commitment of utilitarianism" – and what we might achieve given the current state of human character and our economic, social, and political institutions.[184] This insight is extremely helpful in exploring, and explaining, Mill's views on justice and also in explaining the flaw in some misreadings of Mill, which do not take his view of the changing nature of the expedient into account.

Mill considered socialist principles in terms of both "justice" and "expediency." He helpfully summed up some of the socialist claims of justice as follows: "Some Communists consider it unjust that the produce of the labour of the community should be shared on any other principle than that of exact equality; others think it just that those should receive most whose needs are greatest; while others hold that those who work harder, or who produce more, or whose services are more valuable to the community, may justly claim a larger quota in the division of the produce."[185]

These ideas correspond to Owenism; Blancianism; and a mix of Saint-Simonism, Fourierism, and the principles implemented by cooperative socialists respectively. Mill wrote that "the sense of natural justice may be plausibly appealed to in behalf of every one of these opinions." It is not their intuitive justice, at least, that Mill had concerns about. (That is, he did not dismiss any of these principles as inherently *unjust*, even though – evidently – they are not related to the principle of justice that underpins individual property.) He did not consider many of them to be currently expedient, but this is a different matter than that of their inherent justness.

Mill did, though, have some deeper concerns about the justice of certain socialist principles. First, he had some concerns that applied only in current non-ideal circumstances. He criticized contemporary union tactics of using a "moral police, which occasionally becomes a physical one," against the introduction of measures like piecework; and workers' insistence that wages ought to be the same for all – or, as Mill puts it, that "bad workmen ought to receive the same wages as good."[186] He felt something "similar" would happen if there was an immediate widespread "diffusion" of socialist principles, particularly the idea of equal shares. This was part of a wider concern that where "the public" interferes "with purely personal conduct," "it interferes wrongly, and in the wrong place."[187] But it also speaks to Mill's concern that people were all too willing to free-ride on others (be they employers, or fellow workers), thus violating what he saw as important principles of justice.

Mill thought that socialist "social transformation" would be "practicable" only after "an equivalent change of character" had "take[n] place both in the uncultivated herd who now compose the labouring masses, and in the immense majority of their employers," who must "learn by practice to labour ... for generous ... and not as hitherto solely self-interested" purposes.[188] Rightly or wrongly, he identified the demand for equal pay for equal hours worked (not equal output or effort) as being self-interested, and as retarding progress – even though that progress might lead to the adoption of "higher" principles of justice, which might include equal shares. The difference seems to have related to the rationale for the claim. On Mill's reading, one is self-interested, and the other more impartially recognizes principles of justice. Self-interest leads to worse outcomes than impartiality (at least when it comes to justice). Mill, therefore, had concerns about the immediate implementation of "socialist" principles in contemporary society, but these were concerns about expediency. He also had concerns about the justice of some socialist claims, which casts greater light on his criticisms of capitalist principles of justice *qua* justice.

Mill was concerned that inequality of remuneration, when it was based not on choice but on some natural aptitude or strength, was not "really just," for it gave most to those who already had most by nature.[189] Indeed, he thought that maintaining the link between remuneration and effort was an expedient "compromise" between a "higher" ideal and the facts of current reality – something more just was not feasible (i.e., was not expedient), but that did not undermine the fact that the compromise was less than fully just. Thus, schemes such as Fourier's, which skilfully combined securing sufficiency with rewarding talent, effort, and abstinence (thereby boosting returns on invested capital), were improvements on the justice of existing capitalism, but not fully just. Fourierism might not have fallen afoul of the problem of unjust inequalities arising from strength, in that what work one did was a matter of choice under Fourier's scheme: but to the extent that labour and particularly talent were rewarded, his scheme was less than fully just. The same might go for the Saint-Simonian conception of justice, expressed by Mill as "every individual being required to take a share of labour, either as thinker, teacher, artist, or producer, all being classed according to their capacity, and remunerated according to their works,"[190] or, more pithily, by Robert Southey as "[t]o everyone, according to his capacity; to every capacity according to its works,"[191] as this also involved remuneration according to "capacity," which is something accorded by "nature," not by choice (particularly given that under the Saint-Simonian scheme, one's work is accorded by one's capacities, which are judged by the ruling authority rather than being the outcome of choice).[192]

Mill viewed equal shares as reflecting a "higher" principle of justice than those endorsed by capitalism, Saint-Simon, or Fourier, or those of other socialist schemes that allowed unequal remuneration (save Blanc's) – though such equality was also not without its problems. Some of those problems had to do with feasibility: in the current imperfect state of humanity, Mill thought (and, indeed, believed that experiments in France in 1848 had shown) that people were simply incapable of working under a principle of equal shares.[193] Knowing that they would get the same as everyone else whether they worked or not, they chose not to work at all. This issue had to do with expediency, not justice.

Mill's second problem with equal shares had more to do with justice than with expediency. In the 1840s he wrote that equal shares involved "an abuse of the principle of equality" because it "demand[ed] that no individual be permitted to be better off than the rest, when his being so makes none of the others worse off than they otherwise would be."[194] Interestingly, he would not repeat this concern in later editions of *Principles*. Instead, in *Chapters*, Mill writes that "it is a simple rule, and under certain aspects a just one, to give equal payment to all who share in the work." This indicates that he had changed his mind somewhat since the earliest editions of *Principles*.[195] It is also worth remembering here Mill's concern with equal *labour* (and whether it was either possible to achieve or really just).

Such considerations lead us naturally to the question of what Mill found "attractive" in various kinds of socialism, a topic with which the next section is concerned. To summarize this subsection: Mill thought that socialist principles of justice were in many respects "better" than the ones underpinning individual property, though he was not sure whether it was feasible to currently employ them (that is, they were not currently expedient). He had concerns about the injustice that might still arise under socialist systems such as those advocated by Fourier and Saint-Simon, and about the communist idea of equal shares (and taking an equal share in working). He clearly preferred some sort of inequality based on both need and the capacity to work. He did not think that the problems he raised with socialist and communist principles of justice were insurmountable, or that they ruled out socialism, though their inexpediency did mean that few forms of socialism were "available as a present resource." He clearly believed that we ought to work to improve ourselves, and humanity more generally, and that the "reality" of human imperfection did not rule out the eventual feasibility of something "higher," nor did it let us off the hook for trying to improve society in order to make such principles expedient. And this, in itself, offers some clue as to why Mill saw himself as "under the general designation of socialist," even if he did not completely endorse the immediate, universal adoption of any of these principles.

Conclusions Regarding Mill's Criticisms of Socialism and Socialists

Clearly, Mill did not wholeheartedly support any extant form of socialism. He raised concerns about the different forms with which he engaged on six grounds. First, regarding their opposition to competition, which he thought misplaced to the extent that competition between producers guaranteed cheapness to consumers. Second, regarding the feasibility of various socialist schemes – he found small-scale, evolutionary forms of non-communist socialism much more feasible than other kinds. Third, regarding the "availability" of types of socialism "as a present resource" for society. Again, small-scale, evolutionary forms were much more "available" than others. Fourth, regarding the cost of implementing socialist reforms. Similarly, evolutionary forms that could be implemented by volunteers, whether in "state-wide" forms such as Icarianism, or small-scale versions such as cooperative socialism, were least costly, whereas revolutionary socialism was so costly we should not consider attempting it. Fifth, regarding the risks different schemes posed to individuality, with communism posing more of a risk than non-communist socialism, and cooperative socialism, in particular, strengthening individuality. Finally, regarding the justness of different forms, with non-communist socialism being the *least* just.

These assessments provide a helpful clue to understanding what was "qualified" about Mill's socialism and why he said his ideas were "under the general designation of Socialist," given that there were evidently differences between his own ideas and those of his socialist contemporaries. But it should also be clear that none of Mill's assessments – at least from the 1840s onward – actually prevented him from being *some* sort of socialist. Indeed, contemporary socialism was not monolithic, and Mill had no more serious differences with contemporary socialists than they had with one another. I will look at the content of Mill's own socialism in more detail in the next chapter. Before that, it is worth detailing what it was that Mill found "attractive" about various socialist schemes, to balance the criticisms just explored and to help prepare the canvas for a more detailed picture of Mill's own socialism.

MILL'S ACCOUNT OF WHAT WAS "ATTRACTIVE" ABOUT SOCIALISM

Mill was never a paid-up member of any socialist sect, but he consistently maintained that socialism would be the "ultimate end" of humanity, and this links to his earlier likening of the "ideal standard"[196] of a socialist utopia to the "North Star" by which social reformers ought to navigate.[197] His identification of socialism with the "ideal standard" and with the "ultimate end" of human society indicates that he thought socialism normatively attractive, not that he thought it was so far distant an option as not to be worth serious study or political attention.

The socialisms with which Mill engaged were less vulnerable to the criticisms he levelled against not just contemporary capitalism but also the "régime of individuality property ... as it might be made" in the "old" world and a "new" one. Their solutions to these problems informed what Mill found "attractive" about socialism. In this section, I will briefly take each in turn.

Efficiency

Mill harboured several concerns regarding the efficiency of communist production, particularly with regard to the ability of communist associations to recruit the most able managers. However, he thought that even communist production (which he thought the least efficient "socialist" form of production) would be no more inefficient than contemporary capitalist production, and that other forms of socialism would be more efficient.[198]

Cooperative socialism, which of necessity involves cooperative wholesalers, would be an improvement regarding distributive efficiency, for it would get rid of wasteful "middle-men."[199] These distributors would of necessity also be missing from self-contained forms of socialism, such as self-sufficient communist associations: and even if these traded with one another (as Thompson suggested, for instance), this would be done more along the lines of cooperatives rather than the profit-seeking distributive mechanisms of contemporary capitalism.

Socialism would also presumably involve a "better distribution" of the benefits of unproductive labour, given that everything would be distributed more fairly. Additionally, at least some forms of socialism advocated supporting artists, which might improve the "worth" of the products of unproductive labour.

Overall, then, there were definite advantages regarding the efficiency of socialism, and it was not liable to the same critiques on this ground that capitalism was (though Mill had other efficiency-related concerns regarding socialism, not the least of which was how to recruit the best managers). Mill thought that maintaining some element of competition would ensure this efficiency (in terms of cheapness of consumables, and innovation), and he saw this as a matter on which he disagreed with a number of leading socialists. Still, the increased efficiency in many respects of socialism made it attractive.

Freedom and the Emancipation of Women

Mill thought that at least some forms of socialism could have a positive impact on individuality (indeed, cooperative socialism best encapsulated his concept of liberty, extending it into the workplace), and thought even communism was more "free" than contemporary capitalism. He linked his criticisms of the unfreedom experienced by workers in capitalism with the "domestic subjection" of women, and it is worth mentioning here that Mill found the feminism of many socialists very attractive.

Socialists were not the *only* people to be feminists in the nineteenth century. Even so, it is striking how abhorrent even Mill's fellow radicals at *The Examiner* found the Saint-Simonian idea of "community of women."[200] Setting aside his various disagreements with them, Mill admired the feminism of many Owenites, most obviously Thompson. Mill's own early writings on feminism echo the tone of Thompson and Wheeler's *Appeal*, particularly in his, and their, likening of women's position to that of slaves.[201] Mill argued for some of the same positive solutions to women's position, including the franchise; equality between men and women, and marriage as a partnership of equals; greater independence of women (not seeing marriage as their only respectable choice or praiseworthy goal in life); greater availability of divorce;[202] and different ideas regarding the very meaning of "chastity" and "promiscuity."[203]

Although Saint-Simon himself said relatively little about women, his followers increasingly focused on women's emancipation, and "by 1831 it had become their central concern."[204] In language similar to that of the Owenites (and Mill) the Saint-Simonians talked of women's initial "slavery" and her current "subordination," believing that this would be "successively weakened and shall at last disappear," women's current position being "incompatible with the social state of the future which we foresee."[205] In words that foreshadow Mill's much later arguments in *Subjection of Women*, Enfantin argued that it was the mission of the Saint-Simonians to rescue women from men. Mill translated his words as follows: "I know not that there exists so much as one woman from whom man does not think himself entitled to exact fidelity, devotion, obedience, in exchange for the insulting guardianship which his haughty reason and his brute strength deign to grant to the being whom he regards as a child destitute of strength and destitute of reason."[206]

Like the Saint-Simonians, Mill supported the "dissolubility" of marriage[207] and he agreed with many of their criticisms of that institution.[208] At least some Saint-Simonians thought that in some ways men and women had inherently different natures, with men being more "rational" and women more "sentimental,"[209] though this did not mean that they ought not to be equals or that women could not perform "rational" tasks.[210] This is reflected in some of the sentiments Mill expressed in *On Marriage*, for which several feminists have criticized him, as is the Saint-Simonian desire that, in the future, people of either sex would display the "best characteristics of both."[211]

Mill continued to praise the feminism of other socialists[212] (though he distanced himself in public from Fourier's "peculiar opinions" regarding marriage[213]), and he called cooperative socialism "the nearest approach to social justice" only on the understanding that women would play an equal part in the activities and management of the associations.²¹⁴ Socialists' calls for female emancipation and equality were something that Mill found very attractive.

Justice and Equality

All of Mill's endorsements of socialist schemes on the grounds of justice have evident links to his assertion in *Principles* that it is not a "salutary" state of things when any one class does not labour,²¹⁵ and also to his assertion in the *Autobiography* that he "looked forward to a time when society will no longer be divided into the idle and the industrious; when the rule that they who do not work shall not eat, will be applied not to paupers only, but impartially to all; when the division of the produce of labour, instead of depending, as in so great a degree it now does, on the accident of birth, will be made by concert, on an acknowledged principle of justice."²¹⁶

Mill was concerned about the tradeoff between equality and the scope for individuality, "repudiat[ing] with the greatest energy that tyranny of society over the individual which most Socialistic systems are supposed to involve," and thought it would be wrong to exchange liberty for equality.²¹⁷ This remained a particular concern for him regarding communism, with its emphasis on equal shares. But Mill thought other forms of socialism might preserve both justice and individuality – for instance, something approximating equality would "practically result" from Fourierism's arrangements of labour and distribution, "not, (as in Communism) from the compression, but on the contrary, from the largest possible development, of the various natural superiorities residing in each individual." The "higher" principles of justice endorsed by socialism, then – in particular the way in which socialist experiments would make them more widely expedient – was something Mill found attractive in socialism.

It is worth mentioning here a further related question on which Mill changed his mind during the late 1840s and early 1850s. Communism aimed to secure at least subsistence for all its members – and as noted,

Mill thought we had a duty to secure the survival of our fellow citizens if we could (and that we in fact could, he thought the Poor Law Commission had proved without a doubt).[218] This was something attractive, then, about communism, but it was not something that *only* communism could achieve. Still, it was an important gain, and one about whose importance Mill changed his mind in the late 1840s and early 1850s.

In the manuscript and 1848 editions, Mill considered the desirability of communism based on its ability to increase utility through securing subsistence exaggerated: "Those who have never known freedom from anxiety as to the means of subsistence, are apt to overrate what is gained for positive enjoyment by the mere absence of that uncertainty."[219] When "the necessaries of life" "have always been secure for the whole of life," they "are scarcely more a subject of consciousness or a source of happiness than the elements."[220]

In 1849, Harriet Taylor (whose input into *Principles* was "conspicuous"[221]) changed her mind about whether this "positive enjoyment" was, in fact, "overrate[d]."[222] Mill pointed out that the position taken in the earilier editions, to which she now objected "strongly & totally" had been "inserted on your proposition & very nearly in your words." It was, he said, "what has always seemed to me the strongest part of the argument ... against Communism," noting that even Proudhon admitted it. "[O]mitting" this line "once ... printed would imply a change of opinion," and before doing that it was required, first, to ascertain whether they both really *had* changed their opinion, and second, to consider whether it would be better to write a treatise on communism that acknowledged this change before amending *Principles*.[223]

In the 1849 edition of *Principles*, the passage in question was replaced with "on the Communistic scheme, supposing it to be successful, there would be an end to all anxiety concerning the means of subsistence; and this would be much gained for human happiness."[224] Mill immediately followed this with a caveat, regarding not whether this really *would* be something gained for happiness, but whether communism was *necessary* for such a gain (which is reminiscent of his position in the 1820s): "But it is perfectly possible to realise this same advantage in a society grounded on private property."

This question is not referred to directly in later editions of *Principles*, though Mill did note that assurance as to "the means of subsistence" was a primary "personal want of human beings."[225] This perhaps reveals another change of mind (on Mill's part, or Taylor's, or both). It perhaps reflects that Mill edited *Principles* to align it with the social climate, which was much less open to socialism after the events of 1848 and "the success of an unprincipled usurper in December 1851," which "put an end, as it seemed, to all present hope for freedom or social improvement in France and the Continent,"[226] though I do not think this is persuasive. It perhaps reflects a change of focus regarding the real problems with communism in the wake of experiments in France in 1848–49. Clearly, Mill always thought that security of subsistence would be *some* gain for human happiness, though he was unsure how desirable this feature made communism (both in terms of whether it made communism *necessary* and in terms of whether communists would give it the appropriate weight in a utilitarian calculus).

Improvements to the Social Ethos

Mill put the desirability of socialism on this ground most plainly when he wrote that "the moral objection to competition, as arming one human being against another, making the good of each depend on evil to others, making all who have anything to gain or lose, live as in the midst of enemies, by no means deserves the disdain with which it is treated by some of the adversaries of socialism ... Socialism, as long as it attacks the existing individualism, is easily triumphant."[227]

One aim of contemporary socialism was to radically transform antagonistic class relations, which Mill abhorred; the mediation of all interactions through a "cash nexus"; and the "elbowing, trampling and crushing" of one another that constituted public relationships.[228] This endeavour to improve social morality and the social ethos, to make these more "organic" and harmonious (without losing the benefits of a critical age in terms of independence of thought), was something Mill both desired himself and found attractive in the ideas of contemporary socialists.

Mill had taken the idea of an "organic" age from the Saint-Simonians. He recognized that organic periods of history are held together by a generally agreed upon "moral influence" or religion.[229] He was keen to establish such another "general agreement" and "confidence in received opinions" without sacrificing what was good about the free-thinking element of a "critical" age.[230] In part, this would be done through a modern "clerisy" of intellectuals, poets, artists, and scientists.[231]

Mill disagreed somewhat with the Saint-Simonians' semi-religious elevation of the "industrials," which extended them the power to direct society. In his view, industrialists were very likely to be motivated only by selfish ambition, which would lead to what he saw as the general societal ill of worship of "production."[232] But though he did not view "the industrials" with religious fervour, he adopted with zeal the Saint-Simonian idea of a "Religion of Humanity" (though he did not adopt the *content* of their "New Christianity"[233]), saying this could perform all the good functions of religion with none of the bad ones.[234] Moreover, he endorsed the view held by Comte (who Mill first came to know of as a Saint-Simonian) that "the true moral and social idea of labour [worked] for the benefit of others as a good in itself." This presupposed a less competitive and self-interested social ethos.[235]

Mill spoke warmly of the "harmony and unanimity which Communists hope would be found among the members of their association," and he worried not that communists wanted to exorcise "individualism" and "selfish ambition" from their communities, but that they would find it difficult to do so, given the imperfection of people in that day.[236] There would still be "rivalry for reputation and for personal power," neither of which were particularly laudable.[237] Still, even if "Communist association would frequently fail to exhibit ... mutual love and unity of will and feeling," Mill called communism an "attractive picture," and its aims seemed desirable, even if there was no certainty it would achieve them.[238] Indeed, in *Considerations* he goes so far as to say that "whenever it ceases to be true that mankind, as a rule, prefer themselves to others, and those nearest to them to those more remote, from that moment Communism is not only practicable, but the only defensible form of society; and will, when that time arrives, be assuredly carried into effect."[239]

We should remember that Mill did not think such a change in preferences impossible, and particularly note that he thought them desirable.

CONCLUSION

As others have noted, Mill had several concerns about contemporary forms of socialism. None of those concerns, though, was strong enough to prevent him from considering himself a socialist. Moreover, there was much in socialism that Mill found attractive. That is, there were negatives to capitalism that "pushed" him away from it, while socialism offered "positive" attractions that drew him closer to it, and eventually, into a position that was "under the general designation of Socialist."[240]

We see this very clearly in the praise Mill heaped on cooperative socialism. After lauding the co-operators' "elevated sentiment" and "capacity for exertion and self-denial" "in the name of some great idea," he sketched how cooperation was a means of changing industrial relations.[241] No longer would it be the case that the poor viewed themselves, and were viewed, as "instruments of production, worked for the benefit of the possessors of capital." Rather, they would be seen, and see themselves, as equals.

Mill praised the "admirable qualities by which associations were carried through their early struggles" (including self-sacrifice in the name of emancipation), as well as the self-discipline that workers imposed on themselves, which was much more salutary than anything imposed on them by capitalist employers.[242] He endorsed the principles of justice the associations adopted – not the "higher" principle of equal shares, but a mixture of securing "to every one a fixed minimum, sufficient for subsistence," "apportion[ing] all further remuneration according to the work done," which accorded with Mill's own view of expediency in the current state of human improvement. He spoke warmly of how cooperation "increase[d] the productiveness of labour" through "the vast stimulus given to productive energies, by placing the labourers, as a mass, in a relation to their work which would make it their principle and their interest ... to do the utmost, instead of the least possible, in exchange for their remuneration" – a "material benefit" that, he said, "it is scarcely possible to rate too highly."[243] Yet even this was "as nothing compared with the moral revolution in society" that would accompany a wider spread of cooperation: "the healing of the standing feud between capital and labour; the transformation of human life, from a conflict of classes struggling for opposite interests, to a friendly rivalry[244] in the pursuit of a good common to all; the elevation of the dignity of labour; a new sense of security and independence in the labouring class; and the conversion of each human being's daily occupation into a school of the social sympathies and the practical intelligence."[245]

Moreover, as society developed, we might transcend cooperative socialism (or those elements of it that still represented a "compromise" with selfishness), leading to even greater gains for liberty, equality, justice, efficiency, and the social ethos, thus transforming society step by step ever closer to "the ideal standard" of society, with every stage being a "positive improvement" upon the last.[246]

In the next chapter, I lay out Mill's core principles, the achievement of which would evidence this "positive improvement"; then in Chapter 5 I will explore the institutions of Mill's preferred "ideal" socialism in more detail. But even without this further detail, Mill's praise of cooperative socialism shows how deep his socialist commitments went and how plausible it was for him to consider himself "under the general designation of Socialist,"[247] even when writing *On Liberty*.

CHAPTER FOUR

Mill's Socialist Principles

It is wretched to see the cause of legitimate Socialism thrown so far back by the spirit of reaction ... Still it makes one better pleased with Humanity in its present state than I ever hoped to be, to see that there are ... so many men ... who have sincerely every noble feeling and purpose with respect to mankind ... and ... who ... most purely and disinterestedly desired (and still seek to realize) all of "liberty, equality and fraternity," which is capable of being realized now, and to prepare the way for all which can be realized hereafter. I feel an entireness of sympathy with them which I never expected to have with any political party.[1]

In the previous chapter, I considered Mill's view of existing socialist plans for regeneration, outlining his criticisms and also what attracted him to socialism and specific socialist schemes. In the next chapter, I will map Mill's own "utopia." First, however, we need to understand "the *reasons* [Mill] offers for various reforms, and whether his reasons would lead in a more socialist direction."[2] Those reasons are the focus of this chapter, in which I explore Mill's fundamental theoretical commitments. Once we understand those, we can see what any future institutional arrangement would have to achieve to be "a good place" in Mill's view – and we can also see that, to really encapsulate all of his core commitments, this would have to be a broadly socialist set of arrangements. It is Mill's core principles, as much as if not more than any blueprint he found attractive for future society, that put him "under the general designation of Socialist."[3]

As both Piers Norris Turner and Joseph Persky recognize, these reasons "are not captured simply by a direct appeal to the principle of utility," for Mill himself tells us, "I do not mean to assert that the promotion of happiness should be itself the end of all actions, or even of all rules of action. It is the justification, and ought to be the controller, of all ends, but is not itself the sole end."[4] That is, reform may legitimately be guided toward other "ends," so long as the pursuit of those ends can be justified by utility. For example, we may legitimately pursue "health" (which is the "end" of medical science) via personal actions and reforms to public health provision. "Happiness" is not the "end" of medical science – but happiness legitimates the pursuit of health.

Mill's life gives other examples. The philosophic-radical reforms he championed in his youth were all justified by Jeremy Bentham's utility principle, but none of them were *directly* aimed at the "end" of happiness. Instead, these reforms aimed at other important "ends" (all justified, ultimately, by utility), such as security, proper representation of interests (which makes exploitation and oppression less likely), efficiency and increased production, better exchange of knowledge, and reduction in inequality.

Importantly, following his mental "crisis" and first introduction to Saint-Simonian thought, Mill came to see *any* set of reforms and institutions as "merely provisional" rather than "absolute principle[s]." "In Politics ... I ceased to consider representative government as an absolute principle, and regarded it as a question of time, place and circumstance ... I looked upon the choice of political institutions as a moral and educational question more than one of material interests, thinking that it ought to be decided mainly by the consideration, what great improvement in life and culture stands next in order for the people concerned, as the condition of their further progress, and what institutions are most likely to promote that[?]"[5]

Mill acknowledged that just before the July Revolution of 1830, this made no difference to his "practical political creed as to the requirements of my own time and country. I was as much as ever a radical and democrat, for Europe, and especially for England." But this was because he felt that these "radical" and "democratic" reforms were the "great improvement in life and culture" that stood "next in order" for England, emerging as it was into the system we would now call capitalism, not because they represented the end point of possible human progress.

Even at this stage, Mill's reasons, he emphasized, were not about "material interests" but rather about "improvement in life and culture." We see this very strongly in the reasons he provided for opposing "the predominance of the aristocratic classes, the noble and the rich, in the English Constitution." Indeed, after his "crisis," he saw that predominance as "an evil worth any struggle to get rid of." It was, he wrote, "the great demoralizing agency in the country." It made "the conduct of the government an example of gross public immorality, through the predominance of private over public interests in the State, and the abuse of the powers of legislation for the advantage of classes." It made "riches, hereditary or acquired ... the almost exclusive source of political importance," and "riches, and the signs of riches ... almost the only things really respected, and the life of the people ... mainly devoted to the pursuit of them." It allowed the self-interest of aristocrats, combined with their political power, to prevent "the instruction and improvement of the mass of the people." Democracy would make it in "the interest of the opulent classes to promote" the education of the masses, "in order to ward off really mischievous errors, and especially those which would lead to unjust violations of property." Thus, prior to 1830, he supported the spread of Owenite and Saint-Simonian ideas, in order to frighten the aristocracy into instituting democratic and educational reforms.

Mill's ideas about reform changed substantially between 1830 and 1850, in particular because of events in France in 1848.[6] But even in this early sketch of his views, and his reasons for those views, we get a clear sense of his approach to reform after his crisis. The merits of reforms were to be judged not solely in terms of "material interests," but also in terms of the historical content of that country ("what great improvement in life and culture stands next in order for the people concerned[?]"). This view owed much to the Saint-Simonian and

Comtean idea of an "order" of "stages" in human progress through which all societies must pass. Were proposed reforms or institutions likely to promote "further progress"?

Persky, then, is right to emphasize *progress* in his consideration of Mill's political economy. Similarly, Oskar Kurer is right to emphasize progress as a key element of Mill's politics.[7] And John Rawls rightly emphasizes the importance of progress in Mill's idea of "the permanent interests of man as a progressive being,"[8] arguing that Mill thought we had an interest in "the social conditions that are necessary for the continual progress or advance of civilisation until the practically best state of society (morally speaking) is reached."[9] Mill was committed to progress both normatively and as inherent in humans and human societies. Persky, Kurer, and Turner rightly all see Mill's commitment to progress as leading him toward socialism.[10] Shortly after his "crisis," Mill stopped seeing his current "age," and philosophic-radical reforms, as the final "improvement in life and culture" for all people at all times (and, particularly, for English people at the current time), and engagement with the Saint-Simonians opened up possibilities for much greater progress and far "great[er] improvement in life and culture." Many of these improvements could be achieved via reform to the existing regime of individual property and through some of the schemes being championed by contemporary socialists. However, there were still significant problems regarding the achievement of important things such as liberty, justice, efficiency, and the social ethos.

Other scholars have suggested some of these "secondary principles" already – particularly regarding progress, justice, and liberty.[11] (Not to mention the vast literature on Mill's concept of utility, which must ultimately justify these secondary principles.) Still other scholars have explored the institutions of Mill's "utopia."[12] Here, I want particularly to further recent debate regarding the nature of Mill's egalitarianism,[13] especially regarding his attitude toward Louis Blanc's concept of distributive justice. I also want to emphasize something that is missing from existing accounts: Mill's commitment to social harmony, to "fraternity," and to a particular social ethos that is not just tolerant and open, but communal, and concerned with the common good.

Mill was, and remained, a utilitarian. Though most agree that his utilitarianism differed from Bentham's, debate rages as to exactly what "type" of utilitarian Mill was and whether his utilitarianism was either internally consistent or consistent with other of his key commitments. It is not necessary to get drawn in, here, to the question of whether Mill was, fundamentally, an act or a rule utilitarian (or neither). I only suggest that for Mill, there were "ends" worth pursuing that, though subordinate to and justified by happiness, were not in themselves happiness; and that there were rules of conduct that he thought, generally, we should adopt as guides to individual and collective action that are separate to (though ultimately justified by) the general happiness principle.[14] As Mill said, his approach was to provide not universal prescriptions but rather "principles from which the institutions suitable to any given circumstance might be deduced."[15] I hope this position is general enough neither to take a particular stand in the act/rule debate, nor to make everything I say next entirely unpersuasive to a holder of either of these positions on Mill.

I am particularly concerned with five "secondary principles"[16] that are at the core of Mill's political philosophy, the ever-increasing realization of which he equated with achieving the "great improvement in life and culture which stands next in order for the people concerned."[17] That is, movement toward achieving these principles would indicate that society was moving in a desirable direction. Along with maximization of utility (or, rather, as underpinning the realization of that overarching principle), Mill's five secondary principles are progress[18], security, liberty, equality, and fraternity.[19] I dealt with progress earlier. In the remainder of this chapter, I take each of the remaining four in turn.

SECURITY

As others have argued, security was a key element of Mill's understanding of utility, something he drew from Bentham. Mill counted security as "the most vital of all interests" and the "most indispensable of all necessaries, after physical nutriment."[20] Indeed, Mill's idea owed much not just to Bentham but to Thomas Hobbes as well. This is one reason why Mill did not support "revolutionary Socialism."[21] The "chaos" that would follow any revolution such as described by "revolutionary socialists" would be "the very most unfavourable position for setting out in the construction of a Kosmos," and we would be plunged into the kind of state of nature characterized by insecurity as described by Hobbes.[22]

Thus "security," for Mill, concerned not just personal security (of life and limb) but also stability: an assurance that things would go on as they were, that the rules would not suddenly be changed overnight. This was one reason why Mill thought we should not take the radical step of – for instance – abolishing property immediately, even though laws of property were human constructions that society could change if it saw fit. One contemporary example of this view related to slavery. Mill was an ardent abolitionist, yet he thought that slave-owners had just grounds for compensation following compulsory emancipation, given that at the time they purchased enslaved people they were doing nothing illegal.[23] This is a very controversial view today, but other practices based on the same principle still pertain, such as compulsory purchase orders and eminent domain. Similarly, Mill thought that if land was to be "nationalized," then landowners should be compensated (and his concern about whether the finances of this would stack up was one reason he did not support calls for immediate land nationalization, but instead a land value tax).[24]

Likewise, Mill saw stability of political institutions as – in general – a good thing, even when those political institutions were less than perfect. But this in itself did not rule out *all* revolutionary action (i.e., extralegal, violent, immediate radical political change).[25] For instance, in the immediate aftermath of the February Revolution, Mill rejected John Austin's criticisms of the events in France based on their negative impact on individual interests: "The monetary crisis in London last October produced quite as much suffering to individuals as has arisen, or … is likely to arise, from an event which has broken the fetters of all Europe."[26] That is, sometimes revolutionary political reform was justified, and the insecurity (and other pains) it caused were counterbalanced by the great gains in utility that would be achieved by the change.[27]

Again, the importance of security, stability, and predictability to utility explains why general rules of conduct, backed up by the force of law, public opinion, or individual conscience, are a core part of utility: "Rules are necessary, because mankind would have no security for any of the things which they value, for anything which gives them pleasure or shields them from pain, unless they could rely on one another for doing, and in particular for abstaining from, certain acts."[28] This suggests why Mill related our fundamental sense of justice to a desire that "a rule of conduct," universally applicable to humanity, be followed in relation to us, so that harm or injury not be done (or not be done without legitimate warrant) to ourselves and to those with whom we have sympathy.[29] Some of the necessary rules, then, involve respect for rights (though, on Mill's account, many of these rights – for instance, to £300 if you have invested £10,000 at 3% – are social constructs that will change over time).

Lastly, security of subsistence was a key element of Mill's utility. He supported recognition of a "right to relief" for people facing privation where empirical evidence showed (as he thought it had in England) that respecting this right would not "fatally relax the springs of industry and the restraints of prudence" and thus do greater overall harm to "the permanent interest of the labouring class and posterity":[30]

> [I]t may be regarded as irrevocably established, that the fate of no member of the community needs be abandoned to chance; that society can and therefore ought to insure every individual belonging to it against the extreme of want; that the condition even of those who are unable to find their own support, needs not be one of physical suffering, or the dread of it, but only of restricted indulgence and enforced rigidity of discipline. This is surely something gained for humanity, important in itself, and still more so as a step to something beyond; and humanity has

no worse enemies than those who lend themselves ... to bring odium on this law, or on the principles in which it originated.[31]

Whatever we think of Mill's opinion of the reformed Poor Law, what is important is the emphasis he placed on security of subsistence: he felt that, it having been proved that *at least* a less eligible form of poor relief was feasible, then this was a right that could no longer be denied or violated: society could and therefore not only should but must secure this for all its members.[32] He added that "an end to all anxiety concerning the means of subsistence ... would be much gained for human happiness"[33] and that "the means of subsistence" being "assured" is a primary "personal want of human beings."[34] This was the bare minimum that any "improved" society would have to provide – and in fact, when we move on to consider Mill's view of distributive justice we will see that he thought society should provide quite a lot more, once this was feasible and therefore expedient.

Thus, one important test, for Mill, of the desirability of a proposed reform, or test of whether a proposed utopia was, in fact, a "good place," was whether it provided people with security – in particular, whether it provided people with more security than contemporary social arrangements. This might be in terms of the effective, impartial rule of law; or of the predictability and durability of institutions, social mores, and/or actions by government officials; or of protection of fundamental rights, one of which was to security of subsistence. This commitment did not preclude change – it did not even preclude violent, immediate, sudden, extralegal change of a revolutionary nature. For Mill, security, like all other goods, had to be weighed in a utilitarian balance. This did not make security any less of a vital secondary principle, the securing of which was, *ceteris paribus*, likely to maximize utility.

This may seem a relatively conservative principle, but Mill's commitment to security of existence and subsistence coupled with his belief that distribution was at least partly a matter of human will made it a much more radical one. Societies with stable sets of rules and institutions were better than unstable ones, and societies that ensured no one was starving or needed to fear privation were better than societies that did not. It was – to at least some extent – a matter of human choice whether we lived in a society that did secure subsistence, or one that did not. Moreover, although stability was important regarding property rules, this did not render those rules unchangeable. Nor was the importance of security enough to entirely preclude revolutionary action (as, for example, in Paris in February 1848), when the gains for utility were evidently great, and when people were retaliating against injury done, or threatened to be done, to themselves. More secure societies were certainly better than more insecure ones – but societies that secured more for their citizens in terms of fundamental rights and interests were better than those that secured less.

LIBERTY

In response to the events of February 1848, Mill wrote: "I believe that the principle members of the Provisional Government, and many of the party who adhere to them, most purely and disinterestedly desired (and still seek to realise) all of 'liberty, equality and fraternity,' which is capable of being realised now, and to prepare the way of all which can be realised hereafter. I feel an entireness of sympathy with them which I never expected to have with any political party."[35]

I open with this quote for two reasons. First, because it indicates the progressive nature of Mill's commitment to *all* of the secondary principles I am concerned with here. The revolution of 1848 was not good "because it made people free" (or equal, for that matter) but because it was led by men who were sincerely committed to realizing "all of 'liberty, equality and fraternity' which was capable of being realised, as well as preparing the way of all which can be realised in the future." That is, "liberty" (and equality, and fraternity) are concepts that we can realize *some of* now but that we may not achieve fully as yet. So instead, we should look to achieve as much as we can, and to have institutions that will allow us to progress toward achieving more. When we think about Mill, liberty, and socialism, it is important for us realize that liberty is like this. What is protected and described in *On Liberty* may not be Mill's idea of "full" liberty, but it is the best we can hope to achieve right now, and that will allow us to progress toward more. Similarly, the "liberty" of *laissez-faire* may also be a progressive, transitional, freedom liable to transform into something else in the future.

Second, I open with this quote because it emphasizes what is *not* emphasized enough in Mill scholarship: that Mill saw these principles as ones that went together. "Liberty, Equality, Fraternity!" had been the slogan of the French Revolution, and Mill was evidently referring to it in 1848 to link the two revolutionary movements together. But this was a rallying cry with real resonance for Mill. Indeed, it had resonated with him right back when he first read about the French Revolution (as a teenager) and realized that there had been a democracy in Europe only a few years before he was born.[36] That is, democracy *was* achievable in "the old world," and not only in the "new," and thus there was real hope for the British democratic reform movement. He continued to be greatly interested in French politics and was deeply affected by the events of 1848, which paired democratic political with socialist economic reform. This is one reason why, as others have emphasised, we should consider the impact of Mill's commitment to liberty, independence, and "the free development of individuality" on the economy, and see his commitment to worker cooperation as fundamental, not just peripheral, to his thought.[37] Mill's commitment to liberty caused him to move away from the view he is traditionally seen as endorsing – that of *laissez-faire* capitalism and a solely "negative" understanding of freedom – toward a kind of liberty that was not only compatible with socialism but required socialism for its realization.

For Mill, liberty was fundamental to the achievement of happiness. He believed that a society in which a principle of liberty was respected was the only one in which the greatest happiness of the greatest number could be achieved.[38] In particular, liberty allows us to freely develop individuality, which is of intrinsic value to happiness.[39] But a number of other freedom-related concepts played an important, and connected, role in his understanding of liberty, including sovereignty, (freedom from) oppression, autonomy, and independence. In considering Mill's principle of liberty, it is important to bear all this in mind, for it helps explain the differences between what Mill *means* by liberty, how he *justifies* liberty, and how he thought society could (and should) best *secure* liberty.

When speaking of Mill's concept of liberty, most commentators refer to his "harm principle" (or, as it is sometimes called, his "liberty principle" or "principle of liberty").[40] That is, his assertion in *On Liberty* that "the sole end for which mankind are warranted, individually or collectively, in interfering with the liberty ... of any of their number, is self-protection" and "the only purpose for which power can be rightfully exercised over any member of a civilised community, against his will, is to prevent harm to others."[41]

However, Mill's harm principle did not constitute his definition of liberty, but rather a mechanism for achieving it.[42] By liberty, Mill meant what he called "sovereignty" – that is, being unhindered in our ability to authentically plan, pursue and choose our actions in accordance with our own standards of excellence and unique character, which is what he meant by our "individuality."[43] As Bruce Baum rightly argues, social, government, and individual adherence to the harm principle creates a space in which people, being exempt from coercion, can exercise sovereignty.[44]

Mill's belief that such space needs to be as large as possible in order to maintain "active" people – that is, those who do develop their own individuality, rather than passively being moulded by society around them – means that his circle of exemption was very wide. It extended up to the point at which actions caused harm to others.[45] Mill adds that this principle is underpinned by utility "in the largest sense," that is, "grounded on the permanent interests of man as a progressive being," which interests "authorize the subjection of individual spontaneity to external control, only in respect to those actions of which concern the interest of other people." So "harm" involves a negative impact on interests, and underlying our account of "interests" (and thus harm) must be the idea of "permanent interests ... as a progressive being," or utility.

As others have noted, Mill does not provide a comprehensive list of these "permanent interests," but *contra* John Gray, in itself this is not a fatal weakness in his argument.[46] Gray's view that Mill means by these interests only security and autonomy is too narrow (apart from an unhelpfully wide understanding of both "security" and "autonomy"). Better accounts are given by Alan Ryan, John Rawls, Wendy Donner, and Jonathan Riley.

Ryan and Donner link our "permanent interests" with securing "the circumstances of individuality,"[47] or those that allow self-development, which include security of person, provision of the basic necessities of life, education, and a system of equal rights and liberties.[48] Riley gives another comprehensive account and is right to emphasize security, though the weight he places on *stability* is perhaps too heavy (given Mill's endorsement of *some* social instability as beneficial, in certain circumstances – not only in individual cases of violent revolution, but also more generally, in terms of the beneficial outcomes of critical ages, which are not characterized by great social stability).[49]

Rawls rightly includes among our permanent interests freedom of thought, opinion, conscience, speech, feeling, tastes, and pursuits; the capacity to frame our own mode of life; the discovery of the truth; progress; and social conditions and institutions that guarantee justice and equality. He is not entirely correct, though, regarding what *kind* of justice and equality that will be.[50] This approach is useful because it emphasizes that the rights we can claim, grounded in our permanent interests, may change as society progresses. For instance, we *always* have a "permanent interest" in subsistence and prevention of privation, but we cannot claim these as *rights* (on Mill's view of rights as things we can legitimately claim society *ought* to protect our possession of) until society can, in fact, provide everyone with subsistence (because, for Mill, *ought* implies *can*). As soon as society can provide subsistence, though, it both *ought to* and *must* do so.

That said, the idea of "social conditions" invokes much more Rawlsian language than Millian. Rawls is right to include "the free development of individuality," "education," and freedom of thought and conscience in his account of our "permanent interests," but it seems somewhat convoluted to call these "social conditions." Mill was not *just* concerned with a version of Rawls's "primary goods," or solely with institutional arrangements, when considering our "permanent interests." Perhaps it would be better to say we have an interest in such social conditions, rather than that they are, in themselves, constitutive of our permanent interests.

Similarly, one concern with Rawls's formulation is that it appears to lend weight to Gray's criticism that Mill thought we might reach a morally perfect society in which neither progress nor individuality would be necessary, and change would be as ardently opposed as in the Kallipolis of Plato's *Republic*.[51] Mill did not think we would ever exhaust the possibilities of human progress, and though he did not see *all* change as good (drawing a distinction between "changeable" and "progressive"), openness to improvement is a key element of good institutions on his account.[52]

Both Donner and John C. Rees are right to link harm with rights, as harm involves some negative impact on our interests.[53] But this does not necessarily mean that *all* harms are rights-violating, as some of our interests may not be weighty enough to ground a right, and – as Mill noted – sometimes we may be legitimately harmed, for instance, in a competitive job market.[54]

When harm is threatened, people become liable for coercion, either to prevent them from causing harm or to force them to act when inaction would cause harm.[55] Whether we *should*, in fact, coerce people in these situations, and what mechanism should be used (the law, public opinion, friendly remonstrance, individual conscience, etc.), is to be determined by whether coercion itself would cause greater harm than the action we are seeking to coercively interfere with. Coercive action, although *a priori* allowable in all cases of harm, is actually only justified when interfering would cause less harm than the action we seek to prevent/cause.[56]

Mill asserted that "over himself, over his own body and mind, the individual is sovereign," and it is this sovereignty he is concerned to secure in *On Liberty* by limiting legitimate interference in people's self-directed actions.[57] Sovereignty implies notions of self-government, of planning one's own life, of reflectively deciding on goals and making plans for achieving them, and of doing what Mill wanted us to do – reflectively construct our own moral code, and live by it. That is, sovereignty implies our ability to determine what we believe to be the good life, and the principles it embodies, and to live it to the best of our abilities, rather than passively allowing society to dictate our moral code. Thus, sovereignty includes the ability freely to develop our individuality and to actively choose as we see best among a range of options, the width, depth, and quality of which are also important criteria for individuality, sovereignty, and – ultimately – utility.

Thus, to exercise sovereignty, we need to be able to develop ourselves. To develop ourselves we need to be able to propose goals for ourselves; to make plans for how we can achieve steps in our own development; to reflect on options and make choices between them; to have the capacity to realize the goals we determine on; and to develop rules by which we think we ought to live, which will help us define goals and make choices. In short, we need to be sovereign over ourselves. Sovereignty is, therefore, not the same as individuality, but it is a precondition for the free development of individuality and is, therefore, more than simply a means to achieving individuality.[58] So sovereignty, as Mill used the term, is conceptually akin to autonomy.[59]

Sovereignty is what Mill meant when he spoke of liberty in the modern world.[60] For Mill, in an age where people are capable of it, to be free is to be autonomous, and merely being free from constraints is no longer enough.[61] That this is the case is clear from other of Mill's writings on liberty, and understanding his concept of liberty in this way makes sense of how Mill, in works from almost thirty years before *On Liberty*, and a decade beyond, talked of liberty as freedom from oppression.[62]

Mill saw oppression as coming in many different guises, but all of them – from the oppression of working-class people by middle-class people through their monopoly over positions that demand a certain level of education,[63] to the oppression of women through the warping of their very natures and ideas of womanhood through what modern feminists would define as the patriarchy – are linked to our ability to freely develop our individuality.[64] (Thus, we see that all these different elements of Mill's view of liberty are connected.) Oppression exploits people by ignoring their interests and indeed using those interests as means to further the oppressors' interests; it limits the opportunities open to people; it prevents them from pursuing some of the options that are open to them; it renders them passive rather than active (especially by making them believe they need protection and demanding their deference); and it limits (especially through the denial of educational opportunities, but also through refusing to treat people as equals) their ability to enjoy higher-quality pursuits.[65] Oppression thus limits our opportunities for developing our individuality and renders any development we do achieve unfree, because some agency other than our own, authentic, reflectively chosen standards of excellence is guiding that development. (This is one reason why paternalism is also bad, on Mill's account.)

Mill's concern with sovereignty and his anti-paternalism caused him to speak at times about rendering people "independent." For example, he wrote that over what concerns only himself, an individual's "independence is, of right, absolute."[66] Moreover, he wrote that his ideal society would be populated by "self-governing ... human being[s]."[67] Similarly, he talked about a growing desire for independence among the working classes, who had "come out of leading-strings and cannot any longer be governed or treated like children."[68] "To their own qualities must now be commended the care of their destiny," he added, and "modern nations will have to learn ... that the well-being of a people must exist by means of the justice and self-government ... of the individual citizens." Labourers were in need of "the virtues of independence," and "whatever advice, exhortation, or guidance is held out to the[m] ... must henceforth be tendered to them as equals, and accepted by them with their eyes open."

These terms – sovereign, independent, self-governing, free from oppression – are synonymous for Mill and describe his concept of liberty. Mill wrote that "the only freedom which deserves the name is that of pursuing our own good in our own way." That is exactly what sovereignty ensures – it allows us to formulate our own conception of the good, and it allows us to pursue it in the way we think best; that is, it allows us freely and authentically to develop our individuality.[69]

Evidently, this is a reading of Mill as endorsing a "positive" view of liberty. Mill is often hailed as giving us the quintessential defence of negative liberty, yet some scholars contend that this is a misreading of his view.[70] Nadia Urbinati offers instead the label "freedom from subjection."[71] Similarly, Eugenio Biagini links Mill to a "classical republican" tradition that sees freedom as non-oppression,[72] and Fred R. Berger sees Mill as anxious that people be "not subjected to the arbitrary will of another."[73]

These are useful insights into Mill's position. But it would be a mistake to identify oppression (on Mill's understanding) completely with subjection understood as submission to the arbitrary will of another.[74] Mill thought it was oppressive to have one's options unreasonably curtailed, and this applied to democratically determined rules as much as to dictates by authoritarian rulers. Similarly, Urbinati is right that Mill admired ancient Athens because all its citizens participated in government, and deliberately elected experts as leaders where suitable.[75] But Mill also admired Athens because it respected diversity and individuality in a private sphere (though this Athenian idea was not identical to Mill's concept of a self-regarding sphere). Participation in democracy was undoubtedly important to Mill, not solely as a means to ensure that people were not subject to the arbitrary will of another, but also as a means of self-development and the cultivation of democratic virtues. But protection of a private sphere from "democratic" interference was also important. Thus, Mill's commitment to democratic participation, and the aspect of his thought that is akin to the republican idea of living according to a non-arbitrary will, have been emphasized at a cost to his fundamental commitment to a self-regarding sphere and the protection this affords for self-development and individuality.[76]

Rather than adopt this terminology, therefore, I suggest the term "freedom as independence."[77] Mill's idea of independence, although not going so far as to embrace an idea of self-realization, or to identify a "higher" or "better" self that ought to rule, demands the active development of authentic, self-imposed standards of excellence and a life lived in the pursuit of or in accordance with them.[78] In a similar vein, Baum suggests that "Mill's conception of freedom is best understood in terms of the power of persons for self-determination,"[79] and it is this power that is summarized by Mill's understanding of "independence" and "sovereignty."

The harm principle was one method by which Mill believed this independence could be protected.[80] Both society (through its representative, the state) and individuals could act in self-defence, and to that extent state institutions were somewhat involved in Mill's "harm principle." It was not, however, primarily a principle about state action; it was more a principle about the legitimate coercive scope of public opinion (which can move state apparatus when it has the power to do so).[81] Mill believed that, because of the power of public opinion, contemporary individuals were tending toward the same kind of character.[82] This was not an exaggerated fear: Mill recognized that if the natural human tendencies to want people to think as we think, believe what we believe, and act as we think people should act were successful, then people would end up having the same experiences, and thus (according to his associationism), have the same opinions, which would render them identical, unless they could be rescued by a reflective self-developing self that had not been coerced into conformity.[83] Individuality depends on some people (at least) having different characters, and on *everyone* having an authentically and reflectively developed character, not one that has been imposed by the majority of their neighbours. Thus, public opinion, when it becomes the tyranny of the majority, threatens individuality, and through it, happiness.[84]

The problem of the "tyranny of the majority" had particular bite for Mill because he believed that his contemporary critical age was about to solidify into a new organic age, and such ages are characterized by social stability predicated on everyone accepting the underlying social ideology. Mill was concerned that the ideology of this new society might be what he saw around him. This combined a stultifying anti-intellectualism, which rejected expertise as soon as it went beyond the comprehension of someone with only a very basic education and insisted that people were the best judges of their own interests on every issue, with a repressive insistence that everyone "keep up with the Joneses" or emulate their "betters," and thus act in exactly the same way.[85] Mill believed such an ideology to be antithetical to individuality and thus to happiness. Indeed, he placed so much emphasis on achieving a proper balance between free-thinking and respect for authority within his preferred ideology because he believed that reflection on one's own ideas was integral to developing individuality.

In *On Liberty*, Mill's greatest concern was the coercive power of public opinion as it emanated from contemporary ideology. Mill was not opposed to *all* exercises of power over the individual – he was concerned about *unjustified* ones, and the harm principle was intended to indicate which coercive actions were justified and which were not.[86] Thus, the harm principle was one mechanism by which Mill thought we could protect liberty – it is not what he *meant* by liberty itself.

But while the harm principle was a key mechanism for protecting liberty, it was not the *only* one, in that it was concerned mainly with social (and to some extent political) freedom. Mill recognized that freedom is greatly violated in the economic sphere as well, and he sought to liberate this sphere of human life just as much as the social one.

Baum writes that "in contrast to many other 'classical liberals,' Mill rejects the view that the freedom of individuals in the economic sphere is maximised to the extent that state power is restricted to protecting property and maintaining security ... His conception of economic freedom strongly challenges the now common understandings of economic freedom in terms of capitalism, 'free markets,' 'free trade,' private property and 'freedom of production and exchange.'"[87]

For Mill, such institutions had "a tenuous relationship to the economic freedom of individuals," and thus other commentators are wrong to contend "that Mill regards capitalism as 'the system of economic freedom.'"[88] I showed earlier how, for Mill, this relationship was "tenuous" (i.e., historically contingent). It is sometimes true that capitalism makes people more free (i.e., than under feudalism), and it is also true that some capitalist arrangements make people more free than others (e.g., people are less free when being treated paternalistically by their employers than when in profit-sharing schemes). However, Baum is right to argue that "Mill's view of economic freedom is a direct extension of his broader conception of freedom" and that this concept involves "not merely the absence of burdensome constraints on economic activity, but also the power of individuals to direct the course of their lives with respect to their economic activities and relationships."[89]

Baum also rightly argues that Mill incorporated sovereignty or autonomy, which he saw as necessary for people to develop "their own characters, preferences and tastes," and the idea that people need a wide range of opportunities and resources in order to pursue their own lives in their own way, into an idea of economic freedom. Or, as I would put it, these things remained central to Mill's concept of freedom as expanded into the economic sphere, the upshot being that to be free, we needed the opportunity to exercise "self-government within … economic enterprises."[90] Thus, for Mill, individual independence when applied to the economic sphere led not to a proliferation of individual workers working on their own account, but to "practices of collective government" in worker-cooperatives.

Similarly, Claeys argues that "cooperation was the economic means by which the majority could begin to share in the vision of the individual development and richly varied self-forming character which would be described in *On Liberty*, and was in this sense an essential component in Mill's 'positive' notion of liberty."[91] However, he adds: "where liberty is defined in terms of society helping to provide the preconditions for individual self-development, not either forcing all to develop in a particular way, or allowing only the wealthy and powerful an opportunity to achieve independence." This seems to conflate liberty with the conditions necessary for liberty. I agree that Mill wanted to expand the set of people who enjoyed the conditions of liberty to include everyone (or, at least, every adult "in the full maturity of their faculties"[92] in modern societies), but there is a difference between Mill's concept of liberty itself, and those conditions. This is in part because the conditions might be subject to questions of expediency and historical contingency, whereas the meaning of freedom, for Mill, was not.

Mill also applied his commitment to democratic *practice* to the economy. His critiques of contemporary capitalism as they concern freedom revolve around workers' lack of independence in their working lives. They have little control over what work they do, when, for how long, or in what conditions.[93] They have relatively little freedom of movement and are dependent on the will of another. (A Marxist would add that, as their employer owns the product of their labour, workers also have no control over what happens to what they produce, and that the wage economy makes them dependent on the very products they have made – but Mill does not go that far.[94]) Besides that, half the population lives in domestic subjugation – which, as we know from *Subjection of Women*, is also characterized by conditions of dependence.[95]

In worker cooperatives, however, workers would have (democratic) control over their work, working conditions, and working hours and would be governed by a democratically determined "will" in which they had an equal voice (and, importantly, the ability to exit if they felt they were being illegitimately overruled, and form a permanent minority).[96] It is because of this that Mill said, always supposing they accorded women equal rights, that worker cooperatives would be "the nearest approach to social justice, and the most beneficial ordering of industrial affairs for the universal good which it is possible at present to foresee."[97]

Baum encourages us to see that for Mill, "democracy" was not just about government institutions and "democratic" life was about more than participating in elections for representative government.[98] Mill had a much more radical view than this: all of the fundamental institutions of society needed to be democratized, from the government down to interpersonal relationships – the state, the workplace, and the family. In this, of course, we also see how "liberty, equality, and fraternity" go hand in hand. Even when we elect as our representatives those whom we recognize as our superiors in relevant ways, democracy is fundamentally about equality as well as freedom. Fraternal feelings too are importantly grounded in equality (unlike, say, paternal feelings), but democracy also needs a certain sense of the common good for it to work (on Mill's account), something also strongly linked to fraternity. Worker cooperatives give people a sense of the common good, as well as experience with working and making decisions on and for the common account. All of this is vital for democracy to flourish.

Moreover, as Baum notes, cooperation is an extension of another fundamental freedom – that of association.[99] Supporters of free trade often interpret this as the freedom of buyers and sellers to "associate" with one another via market relations, or of workers to freely "associate" with employers via working for them. (As Baum rightly notes, for Mill it also involves the workers' right to join unions and go on strike in a market economy.) But Mill's concept of "associations of the labourers among themselves" moves away from this free market view.[100]

Mill describes the birth of such associations after the February Revolution in 1848 as follows: "For the first time it then seemed to the intelligent and generous of the working classes of a great nation that they had obtained a government who sincerely desired the freedom and dignity of the many, and who did not look upon it as their natural and legitimate state to be instruments of production, worked for the benefit of the possessors of capital."[101] "The ideas sown by Socialist writers" in this environment regarding "emancipation of labour to be effected by means of association, throve and fructified," and "many working people came to the resolution, not only that they would work for one another, instead of working for a master tradesman or manufacturer, but that they would also free themselves, at whatever cost of labour or privation, from the necessity of paying, out of the produce of their industry, a heavy tribute for the use of capital; that they would extinguish this tax, not by robbing the capitalist of what they or their predecessors had acquired by labour and preserved by economy, but by honestly acquiring capital for themselves."

Here we see the extreme of Mill's view regarding the unfreedom of workers, who not only were under the yoke of "a heavy tribute" and "tax" and in need of "emancipation," and directed by another (the "master") rather than by themselves, but also had been reduced and objectified into "instruments of production" and were being "worked for the benefit of the possessors of capital." (It is significant that Mill here uses "worked," not "working" – "worked" emphasizes how workers are used, and exploited, as instruments by employers, whereas "working" would have implied some self-directed activity on the part of the workers.) And we see, therefore, what worker cooperation freed workers from, making them independent.

Baum reads Mill as committed to "two distinct but interrelated forms of individual economic freedom ... *political freedom* – i.e. the freedom of citizens to share in determining the laws and public policies governing them – [and] *individual freedom*," which Baum parses as "pursuing our own good in our own way."[102] Baum rightly argues that cooperation realizes freedom in the economic sphere. But we do not need to see Mill as endorsing two distinct (even if interrelated) conceptions of freedom: "freedom as independence" covers both "pursuing our own good in our own way" *and* collective democratic decision-making, because this is the only way in which free (and equal) people can legitimately make, and freely obey, decisions.

Baum takes Mill's passage "the only freedom which deserves the name, is that of pursuing our own good in our own way so long as we not attempt to deprive others of theirs, or impede their efforts to obtain it," as something solely individualistic.[103] But this wording also justifies democracy, as well as all that Baum wants to include in "economic freedom." Non-democratic, non-representative institutions stop us from pursuing our own good in our own way (or, at least, they give us no security of being able to do so, and generally – at the very least – they demand taxes from us that limit our ability to do that). Only in democracies can we be assured of the maximal and *equal* liberty that Mill defended (though mere formal democratic institutions are no *guarantee* of such freedom). In many ways, capitalism does the same thing. That is, many innovations of capitalism (compared to feudalism) allow people to pursue their own good in their own way, but capitalism also impedes many people's (notably, workers') ability to do this. Worker cooperation, on the other hand, is a mechanism by which we can maximize this kind of freedom, each of us pursuing – in combination with others – our own good in our own way, while not impeding others in doing the same. The "good" may be rather different – an economic good rather than, say, a spiritual one – but the gist of the matter is still the same. And while "our" may have taken on a more communal meaning, "my" interest is still represented, and the "good" is meaningfully "mine," particularly because cooperatives are both voluntary and collectively owned.

Thus, we do not need the term "economic freedom": Mill did not have a different concept of freedom in the economy – rather, his commitment to independence led him to envisage radical changes in the economy. However, Baum is right to say that, while Mill was concerned with maximizing utility, he was not concerned with maximizing freedom. Rather, he sought "substantial freedom for all."[104] Baum is also right that this application of freedom to the economy, for Mill, shows how deeply equality and freedom were intertwined for him.

Overall, Mill's commitment to individual liberty as a necessary element of utility meant that he supported radical change in the political, social, and economic spheres. In his view, these were tightly linked: to be properly independent, one could not be in dependent relationships, be it at work, in politics, or in the home. The economy, for him, was not separate from politics or from a "sphere" in which individual liberty needed to be protected.

Thus, for Mill, as society progressed it needed to ensure more and more freedom – not "in sum," as Baum rightly notes, but for more and more people. This had to involve female emancipation (including fairer and freer access to the workplace, including democratic workplaces[105]) and worker emancipation more generally. As society progressed, its economic institutions needed to progress in tandem, away from relations of dependency toward independence (combined with the cooperation of labour, which capitalism had brought to full fruition).[106] Realization of this kind of liberty, for all, was an important step in terms of maximizing utility, and it was both an important goal for reformers and an important yardstick by which to judge actual societies, proposed reforms, and utopian schemes. Note that when Mill wrote that the final judgment regarding whether we moved to communism or remained with a reformed system of individual property would come down to which best preserved and promoted individuality, this had an economic as well as a political element.

Mill's concept of freedom remained central, not just "even when" he moved toward socialism, but "as part of" his move toward socialism. He realized that independence could not be attained without significant economic reform: the "formal" freedoms (and equality) of, for instance, the Reform Act were not actually setting working people free, because of the "heavy tribute" they still had to pay to capital for the freedom to work at all (and the way in which their labour was directed by, and thus they were subject to, someone else's will). This could not be wholly eradicated by profit-sharing; it would have to be by (at least) worker cooperatives and the socialist aim of organizing production on the common account.

EQUALITY (AND DISTRIBUTIVE JUSTICE)

Mill praised the Provisional Government for sincerely trying to achieve "all of 'liberty, equality and fraternity,' which is capable of being realised now" and for "prepar[ing] the way of all which can be realised hereafter."[107] His commitment to liberty has been much discussed in the academic literature, but far less has been said about his commitment to equality and his concept of distributive justice.[108] This has left a gap in our understanding, for equality was one of Mill's core principles. Increasing achievement of equality was a sign of progress and a means by which utility could be maximized.

Mill examined several questions pertaining to equality in a nuanced and sophisticated way, though often rather briefly. Here I suggest that, as argued by both Berger and Turner, Mill had "a strong commitment to substantive 'base-line' equality," including a sufficientarian idea combined with a need to justify all inequalities of wealth, education, and power (which are *"prima facie* wrong") in terms of the general interest, and a belief that "inequalities must not undermine the status of persons as equals."[109] However, I go further and argue that Mill's belief that inequalities in, for example, remuneration could be earned through voluntary effort or desert was limited to a particular historical moment – one that he thought humanity might transcend. In the same vein, I suggest that though Mill was keen to eradicate the illegitimate impact of brute luck on people's lives (as recently suggested by Persky[110]), this was only one step on the way to achieving a much "higher" concept of equality, one that would ultimately see us treating one another as equals in such a way that we could sustainably implement the distributive principle "from each according to his capacities, to each according to his wants" (or needs).

There has recently been an excellent debate between Turner and Persky on Mill's egalitarianism. Persky reads Mill as a relational egalitarian whose progressive political economy moves away from relational equality toward luck-egalitarianism. That is, he reads Mill as endorsing, finally, distributive principles in which inequalities due to what luck-egalitarians call "brute luck" are eradicated, and the only justification for those inequalities that remain is that they are the outcome of individual choices (which luck-egalitarians sometimes call "option luck"). People ought not to be disbenefited by disability (on this view), and also ought not to benefit – on this view unfairly – from natural advantages such as talent. But people also ought to be responsible for their choices: those who saved are entitled to have more in their retirement than those who did not.[111] Turner reads Mill's egalitarianism as always relational and situates his concern with luck in that context.[112] That is, he sees Mill as *always* being concerned with equal relationships, and he recognizes that questions of "brute" and "option" luck have a bearing on our ability to interact as equals at different stages in human progress.

My reading accords more with Turner (and Berger) than with Persky: Mill was committed to meaningful relational equality between persons. As part of that, he was also committed to the Blancian idea "that all should work according to their capacity, and receive according to their wants" as a "still higher standard of justice" than equal shares, or proportioning to effort.[113] This needs weaving into existing accounts of Mill's egalitarianism.

Mill's egalitarianism was progressive, in that he saw humanity as capable of achieving more and more equal relations and institutions as we progressed, and that what was expedient in terms of egalitarianism would change over time. Similarly, greater equality was for him a sign of greater progress. Yet this did not undermine his core commitment:

> In my estimation the art of living with others consists first & chiefly in treating and being treated by them as equals … As I look upon inequality as in itself always an evil, I do not agree with any one who would use the machinery of society for the purpose of promoting it. As much inequality as necessarily arises from protecting all persons in the free use of their faculties of body & mind & in the enjoyment of what these can obtain for them, must be submitted to for the sake of a greater good: but I certainly see no necessity for artificially adding to it, while I see much for tempering it, impressing both on the laws & on the usages of mankind as far as possible the contrary tendency.[114]

Likewise, in *Utilitarianism*, he wrote that "[t]he equal claim of everybody to happiness in the estimation of the moralist and the legislator, involves an equal claim to all the means of happiness, except in so far as the inevitable conditions of human life, and the general interest, in which that of every individual is included, set limits to the maxim ... All persons are deemed to have a *right* to equality of treatment, except when some recognised social expediency requires the reverse."[115]

That is, Mill had a strong commitment to equality, but he also saw how much of it we can practically attain to be a question both of the development of human character and institutions, and of a utilitarian calculation regarding tradeoffs with freedom. Inequality, then, was for him always an evil, albeit sometimes a necessary one.

These passages go a good way toward showing that Mill had a relational concept of equality. Relational equality too may require (and permit) inequalities of distribution in a way that sits well with other of Mill's pronouncements on equality.

There are a number of core elements to Mill's egalitarianism. As with the wider question of "a good society," Mill was more concerned with these principles and with evaluating how well a proposal would meet or achieve them than with laying out prescriptive rules or designing equal institutions. For example, he was committed to the idea that marriage should be "an association of equals," but beyond that he had no prescriptions for what individual marriages should look like. He has recommendations for what laws, economic arrangements, political rights, and social mores and customs we would need (and need to change) in order to create the right social conditions for equal marriages, but he was not prescriptive, for instance, regarding whether both partners should work equally long (or, as some feminists have critically noted, demanding that men do an equal share of the housework).[116] That might be what "an association of equals" looked like for some – it might not be for others. The same goes for his writings on cooperative associations: so long as merely being given power did not equate to higher wages, Mill wanted them to democratically determine their own rules, terms of membership, working conditions, and distribution of the surplus of combined labour, leading to a plurality of associations that could all meaningfully be called "equal."[117] In terms of social arrangements, and some secondary principles, too, Mill was not prescriptive. So long as people recognized, adhered to, or tried to achieve some specific principles of equality, the kind of society they built was open to experiment, discussion, and debate.

Berger argues that Mill's "strong commitment to substantive 'baseline' equality [w]as defined by these propositions": one, that "inequalities of wealth, education, and power are *prima facie* wrong and require justification"; two, that "inequalities must not permit any to 'go to the wall'" – "subsistence must be guaranteed"; three, that "inequalities must not undermine the status of persons *as equals*," in particular, "inequalities must not result in some gaining power over others that undermines their autonomy or that degrades them"; and four, that "certain grounds *can* justify inequalities" – including where the inequality makes no one worse off, where it rewards according to desire, where advantages have been earned through voluntary effort, or where inequalities are somehow "justified by desert."[118]

Turner offers a different account, though in a somewhat similar vein.[119] He notes that Mill's egalitarianism contains "three secondary principles – impartiality, sufficiency, and merit – that he believes should guide public discussion and reform."[120] Overall, he sees Mill as a relational egalitarian. "Impartiality," or "equal consideration," Turner argues, is "the most important of these, because it fundamentally shapes his account of what justice requires in any advanced state of society."[121] He rightly adds that "the question is: what does equal consideration require?," a fundamental question with which Mill engages in interesting ways.

Ultimately, I read Mill as seeing contributing according to your capacity, and receiving according to your wants, as "what equal consideration requires." That is, when we treat one another as equals, and when an impartial observer considers treating us equally, with an eye to retaining equality between us (and our status as equals), we are giving what we can to help meet the burden of individual and social existence, and being given what we need for the equal opportunity to have as flourishing a life as possible. The latter part of the maxim mitigates the heaviness of the burdens that ought to be imposed by the first part, and the rule also applies to everyone: there should be no free-riders, but also no exploited "strong" characters like Boxer, in Mill's "higher" and more just state of the world.[122]

This principle, of course, would involve much inequality. The strong, the talented, the "quick," would take on a far greater share of the burdens than the weak, the less talented, the "slow" (though with a recognition that these burdens are not *proportionally* so much heavier, if heavier at all, for the stronger to bear). And the weak, the old, the young, the ill, the disabled, and so on might get a much larger share of resources so that they could meet their needs. Such a principle of justified inequalities (but "real" equality) can only come into being in a society with substantive relational equality between people who recognize not only that other people are equals, but also that other people's needs must be met (with no special claims to beneficial inequalities for those with unequal strengths and talents). In this sense, luck-egalitarian, relational, and more "socialist" egalitarian concerns are bound together in Mill's view.

Equal Treatment

A commitment to "equal treatment" arises from Mill's utilitarianism, which demands "perfect impartiality between persons."[123] Although this is logically consistent with inegalitarian societies, Mill added that the "highest standard of social and distributive justice" implied by impartiality meant that "society should treat all equally well who have deserved equally well of it." "Equal treatment," then, as a way of parsing "impartiality", becomes something that Mill thought utilitarianism required both of individuals concerning individual actions or choices and of individuals acting collectively in society.[124] The question then arises as to what this would entail – a question whose answer is historically contingent.

The case for equal treatment is predicated on Mill's fundamental commitment to the equal moral standing of persons. Every individual is capable of experiencing pleasure and pain and has a right to have his or her happiness considered.[125] *One* should not count for *more than one* – or *less than one*. That is, the principle of "equal treatment" applies when we are considering equals. That Mill made this commitment is clear in his championing of women's equality, racial equality, and religious equality as well as in his belief that all classes were inherently equal, notwithstanding contemporary inequalities in wealth and status.[126] It is the basis of his critique of the "aristocracies of colour, race, and sex."[127] This means that all people have an equal claim to have their happiness considered (though in itself, this does not commit Mill to egalitarian outcomes). More than this, it is one of the core commitments that underpinned Mill's view that "all inequality is *in itself* an evil" and that inequalities need justifying specifically as regards the general good.

It was a radical step on Mill's part to insist that "treating equals as equals" applied to *all* adults in the possession of their mature faculties in developed countries – even though, to the modern ear, all the caveats there (and particularly the last one!) can seem deeply conservative. But Mill was writing at a time when slavery was still legal in the United States (*Utilitarianism* was published the year the American Civil War started); when women had no claims to being viewed as "persons," never mind as equals (to men); and when people really believed in morally significant differences between rich and poor, "noble" and "common." Moreover, although Mill had caveats for "equal treatment" for children and people in non-modern countries, these included a commitment to the innate potential in everyone (or, on a wider scale, in every society) to progress to a stage where they attained equal status.[128]

From this, it might be thought that Mill was committed to equality of welfare and that welfare was his particular conception of happiness. But though Mill believed that everyone was fundamentally to be accorded a claim of equal weight to happiness, this was not the same as saying that everyone had a claim to an equal amount of happiness. For one thing, Mill recognized that such an outcome would be impossible to achieve – "happiness" was not something that could simply be doled out, and what made one person happy might not make someone else happy at all, because tastes (and people) differ. Instead, he was concerned with maximizing equal opportunities to pursue one's own happiness in one's own way. Society could influence a great many of these opportunities (but not all of them), and this, in turn, involved some distribution of resources (and opportunities) and benefits of social cooperation, as well as fair distribution of the burdens. That is, Mill's idea of "equal treatment" did not lead to an outcome of "equal welfare," but to a commitment that people would be treated equally as regards opportunities for happiness.

With regard to capitalist societies, as part of his utilitarian principle of impartiality Mill endorsed equal political rights to protect our interests and foster individual development through participation in democratic government.[129] Besides political rights, people needed equal civil rights (to divorce, to own property, to access the professions, and so on). Similarly, people needed equal rights to receive basic education and the equal right to access further and higher education (and specialist training), depending on their capacities and desires.[130]

In a similar vein, Mill was anxious to secure for each person the maximum amount of freedom consistent with an equal amount of freedom for all.[131] In some respects this is guaranteed by the political, civil, and educational rights just mentioned, but it is also something more, because it relies on the institution of Mill's proposals concerning not only state power (which controls and accords political and civil rights) but also the power of public opinion. We all have an equal right to a sphere in our affairs in which neither public opinion nor the law can coerce our actions nor intrusively inquire into them. (And we all have an equal responsibility to respect that for others.)

Impartiality, therefore, committed Mill to much more than "equal treatment before the law." Indeed, from these considerations we can already see that Mill was committed – by "equal treatment" – to an idea of "equal (opportunity for) independence." Mill makes this explicit in his correspondence with Arthur Helps quoted above: in Mill's view, dependency and inequality are intrinsically linked. Taking marriage as a specific example of a more general issue, Mill said he could not "think that relation will ever be other than a comparative failure while instead of being an association between equals, it is grounded on 'sway' on one side, dependence on the other, & the dependent is systematically educated for feebleness of mind. The 'petting' of which you speak is a wretched substitute for reason & justice."[132]

That is, he associated "dependence" with inequality and independence with equality. In this, we see how Mill's concepts of liberty and equality are intimately linked – some people can enjoy liberty in unequal societies, but Mill saw no justification for unequal protection of liberty once people achieve adulthood (in modern societies) unless people have somehow merited a restriction on their liberty (e.g., people imprisoned). Moreover, independence is only really possible in relations of equality.

That people's rights can legitimately be violated because they have been forfeited (through rights-violating actions) is what Mill meant when he said that "society should treat all equally well who have deserved equally well of it."[133] That is, society should proceed on a *prima facie* basis of equal treatment, recognizing some inequalities where people do not "deserve ... equally well of it" through their own actions, not – importantly – through some inherited demerit (or merit). At core, we all deserve equally well of society, and should be treated equally by merit of our status as humans. There are some exceptions, where we forfeit this right, but this is the rule.

Thus, on Mill's account of impartiality, people deserve equally well; we should be impartial between them; this means they should get equal treatment (i.e., equal rights, liberties, and opportunities). The specific outcomes (e.g., equal access to education and the professions) are related to Mill's commitment to liberty and also to the idea of people interacting as equals (a core element of relational equality). It is hard to do this if there are unequal political and civil rights; if there is unequal access to education based on arbitrary distinctions (rather than inclination or capacity); if there is a general sense that, without any rights-violating action on their part, some people deserve worse of society than others. (That is, it does not undermine relational equality if we all agree that murderers deserve "less well" of society than non-murderers, and have no grounds for complaint if they are imprisoned; but it does undermine relational equality if we think racial minorities deserve fewer rights.)

In terms of distributive justice, the idea of impartiality is at play in Mill's nuanced considerations of this problem – considerations on which his progressive view of justice had an impact. This ends with him endorsing "a transition to a still higher standard of justice" (than "absolute equality in the distribution of the physical means of life and enjoyment"), "that all should work according to their capacity, and receive according to their wants."[134]

It is true that in *Principles* – and elsewhere – Mill emphasized "the principle that economic rewards should be proportioned to one's labour or exertions."[135] Indeed, this was the basis for one of his harshest criticisms of contemporary capitalism. However, Berger rightly notes: "I know of no argument by Mill to support the principle." Berger rightly emphasizes that though Mill did refer to this principle as "an 'acknowledged' principle of justice," he meant by this "recognised by contemporaries" (both capitalists and socialists), which was not – in itself – a justification.

Berger notes that this principle does not quite fall under what he calls Mill's "dictum of 'good for good,'" "since useful productive exertion or effort need not be a case of 'doing good.'" Thus, proportionality might be expedient, but it does not meet Mill's basic criteria for justice. Berger may be mistaken here. Mill wrote that "society receives more from the more efficient labourer" and thus "society owes him a larger return for" his services, which is a species of "good for good" and also of impartiality.[136] That said, I agree with Berger, and Turner, that Mill's support for a proportionality principle, and with it private property, is only contingent on certain social arrangements.[137]

After all, "good for good" does not *only* support a private property principle underpinned by the idea of securing to the labourer the fruits of his or her own labour. For Mill also entertains the idea that "whoever does the best he can, deserves equally well," which is also predicated on the idea of "good for good." This is one reason he takes the idea of equal shares seriously as a concept of justice: If we all do what we can, don't we all deserve the same in return? If we are being impartial, oughtn't we equally distribute the product of our communal labour?

Mill's reason for rejecting equal shares as the "highest" standard of justice arose from his realization that this principle, though ostensibly treating people as equals, does not result in them being treated equally. Mill noted that "whoever does the best he can ... ought not in justice to be put in a position of inferiority for no fault of his own ... superior abilities have already advantages more than enough ... and ... society is bound in justice rather to make compensation to the less favoured, for this unmerited inequality of advantages, than to aggravate it."[138] But equal shares *may* put us "in a position of inferiority for no fault of [our] own": the talented, the strong, and the "quick" enjoy "advantages" over and above what they receive, and can do more with what they get through an accident of birth. That is, if we give equal shares to the handsome, the strong, the intelligent, the healthy, and/or the charming, they start from a better position, and will end up with better outcomes, than the plain, the disabled, the ill, the averagely intelligent, and/or the socially inept.

Mill sometimes invoked the idea of "everyone starting fair in the race," and he noticed that people do *not* start fair in the race, not only because of inherited wealth and bad political and economic institutions that privilege some at the expense of others based on class, race, and sex, but also because talent is arbitrary in distribution.[139] Even in an "ideal" system of private property, this would entail unequal initial holdings.[140] Once we transcend private property, it requires unequal distributions of property.

As noted, Mill said that society is "bound in justice" to "compensate" for these inequalities. This compensation, however, is not for having inferior abilities,[141] but for the fact that inequality in abilities results in inequalities of advantages, and thus in inequalities of opportunities and outcomes. As Turner rightly notes, "impartiality, understood to imply equal treatment, thus calls for the elimination of differences due to accidents of birth that lead to some enjoying greater opportunities or other goods."[142] This, he adds, led Mill to argue for "a fair start – as equal as possible – for all." I argue that it goes further, requiring consideration of the distribution not only of the benefits, but also of the burdens, of cooperation, and of cooperative labour. Mill was not concerned *solely* about our "start," particularly as society progressed away from individual property; he was also concerned about equality of treatment regarding what work we are required to contribute and what return we get for that work. Impartiality demands that, if we all give equally in terms of "doing the best we can," we all deserve equally well of society – which involves unequal rewards – in order that we can enjoy equal chances of good outcomes and "be" equal, no matter our initial holdings of talent, strength, and aptitude. From the idea of "good for good" and equal treatment, then, evolves the Blancian idea of "from each according to his capacities, to each according to his needs."[143] This is why Mill called it a "still higher" principle of justice even than equal shares (and certainly than proportionality), though this would only be expedient in a much-improved future in which no compromise is necessary between selfishness and justice.

Sufficiency

Turner argues, very plausibly, that a second principle in Mill's egalitarianism was a sufficiency principle. Similarly, Berger argues that Mill's concept of equality meant that no one could legitimately be allowed to "go to the wall."[144] Mill wrote that "if there be any who suffer physical privation or moral degradation, whose bodily necessities are either not satisfied or satisfied in a manner which only brutish creatures can be content with, this, though not necessarily the crime of society, is *pro tanto* a failure of the social arrangements."[145] Importantly, once it was *possible* to ensure that people need not "suffer physical privation or moral degradation" in society, then it *was* a crime (or at least a wrong) to permit this to happen. That is, it *was* a crime in Mill's contemporary society, just as it would be in all future "civilised" (i.e., sufficiently developed) countries. Mill was emphatic that people had a *right* to subsistence, and when we had a right, we were justified in calling on society to protect it. Rights violations, for Mill, *were* "crimes." Mill thought they counted as "wrong" actions, even if they were not *formally* illegal.[146]

Thus, Mill was concerned that everyone be given the means of subsistence if they had been rendered incapable of working (either through sickness or age) and that they be guaranteed work if they were capable of working.[147] He went so far as to say that recognition of the "droit au travail" (right to work) "is the most manifest of moral truths, the most imperative of political obligations."[148] That is, people had a right to work (and receive at least subsistence wages) if they were able, as well as a duty to work if they were able. This was the "right" being claimed by workers who found themselves unemployed during the financial crisis and recessions of the "the Hungry Forties" (and was thus something rather different from modern conceptions of unemployment benefits). Thus, although Mill did not think we all have an equal claim to bring children into the world (we should not, for example, do so if we cannot be sure how we will feed them, without reliance on some form of state support), once born, everyone had an equal right to be supported in the necessities of life by the rest of society, though in return we ought to work for them when we can.[149]

Society, then, owes it to people to keep them from starvation. This is not merely because starvation is not good for happiness; it is also because we owe it to people to ensure their existence, simply because they are other human beings, and we ought to treat them in certain ways because of that fact. How we ought to treat them is as equals. That is why we read Mill best as a relational egalitarian.

I will take up this idea in more detail later on, but let me first deal with what Turner calls "the merit principle" in Mill's egalitarianism (which Berger also refers to, as "desert"), which is at the root of Persky's delineation of Mill as (ultimately) a luck-egalitarian.[150]

Merit and Desert

Turner sees Mill as justifying inequalities (where he does justify them) on the grounds of merit.[151] He sees Mill as separating "merit" into three elements: "exertion (effort, earnings), relevant talent (intelligence, skill), and virtue (roughly, public-spiritedness)."[152] He takes up only exertion and talent.

Difference in talent, he argues, "Mill generally attributes ... to differences in opportunity (especially educational opportunities) and previous exertion, rather than to natural endowments," though he notes that Mill did not deny that some people have "greater natural endowments."[153] Like Turner, I believe we read Mill most correctly when we see that he defended unequal remuneration justified by talent only as an expedient principle in non-ideal circumstances (which included contemporary society), but that he was very uneasy about the *real* justice of rewarding talent, which was only giving more to those who already had most.[154]

For instance, when Mill pondered the question in *Utilitarianism*, he wrote:

> On the negative side of the question it is argued, that whoever does the best he can, deserves equally well, and ought not in justice to be put in a position of inferiority for no fault of his own; that superior abilities have already advantages more than enough ... and that society is bound in justice rather to make compensation to the less favoured, for this unmerited inequality of advantages, than to aggravate it. On the contrary side it is contended, that society receives more from the more efficient labourer; that his services being more useful, society owes him a larger return for them ... that if he is only to receive as much as others, he can only be justly required to produce as much, and to

give a smaller amount of time and exertion, proportioned to his superior efficiency. Who shall decide between these appeals to conflicting principles of justice? ... Social utility alone can decide the preference.[155]

Similarly, in *Principles* Mill wrote:

The proportioning of remuneration to work done, is really just, only in so far as the more or less of the work is a matter of choice: when it depends on natural difference of strength or capacity, this principle of remuneration is in itself an injustice: it is giving to those who have; assigning most to those who are already most favoured by nature. Considered, however, as a compromise with the selfish type of character formed by the present standard of morality, and fostered by the existing social institutions, it is highly expedient; and until education shall have been entirely regenerated, is far more likely to prove immediately successful, than an attempt at a higher ideal.[156]

As Turner aptly puts it, "the first sentence seems to express a 'higher ideal' for a distant state of society, in which rewarding differences in talent ... would be an injustice. The second sentence, by contrast, expresses the thought that rewarding differences in talent in the current state of society is ... justified (if not just)."[157]

Turner is also right that, in Mill's ideal world, "the more talented would *themselves* reject receiving higher remuneration than others who have exerted themselves equally." I would add the proviso, though, that "exertion" would have to mean something like "comparable effort" (rather than *actual* effort, or amount of labour), for as we have seen, Mill was very aware that different kinds and amounts of labour present different burdens to different people. *Making an effort* is, to some extent, a talent – some people find it easier than others to be motivated for certain tasks, or to work hard at them, or for long periods of time, all things that might be imagined to form part of "exertion." Turner links "exertion" with "industry, work, or effort, as well as 'abstinence' in the sense of accepting some immediate personal cost or inconvenience for some long term or overall benefit." Mill's concern about equality of burdens of labour should make us cautious as to whether *all* of these elements would be legitimate grounds for inequalities. "Industry," for instance, may come much easier to the young, hale, and hearty than to the old, sick, or disabled. But if we could – and Mill's words cited above mean he thought we *could* – somehow determine equality of burdens, then any *inequality* of burden would legitimate unequal remuneration.

Mill also justified some unequal treatment and granting of benefits to the talented when everyone benefited from this – for example (as Turner notes), he thought that competence should help determine who holds political offices, "because promoting the general happiness requires skilled government." This was both for reasons of expediency and for "real" justice.

Turner therefore suggests that we understand Mill's "merit principle" as being "encapsulated by the claim that, given impartiality and sufficiency, there should be 'proportionality ... between success and exertion.'"[158] This is true, but only for "non-ideal" societies (even if it will remain true in much-reformed societies). Mill endorses not only equal shares as a just outcome (concerned as he is not about the injustice of equal remuneration, but about the injustice of unequal *burdens* if labour is *also* apportioned equally), but also the Blancian principle "from each according to his capacities, to each according to their needs." Under such a principle of distributive justice, though equal treatment is being properly realized, there is no proportionality between exertion and success.

Mill deliberately tied the need to link exertion with unequal outcomes to a certain kind of non-ideal "selfish" character, and ultimately he saw all demand for proportionality between exertion and reward as something that would slowly be erased from human nature as we progressed to better institutions and developed better characters.

This leaves us with a final consideration regarding "virtue." It is true that Mill wrote that "the very idea of distributive justice, or of any proportionality between success and merit, or between success and exertion, is in the present state of society so manifestly chimerical as to be relegated to the regions of romance. It is true that the lot of individuals is not wholly independent of their virtue and intelligence; these do really tell in their favour, but far less than many other things in which there is no merit at all. The most powerful of all the determining circumstances is birth."[159] Here, then, he mentions "virtue and intelligence" as something that apparently legitimately *should* affect reward (and in a limited sense, *does*). "Intelligence," for Mill, was a talent cultivated by exertion and open to pretty much everyone to develop given the right educational opportunities. I suspect that "virtue" here refers to "abstinence," that is, to saving, prudence, delaying consumption, and imposing self-discipline to control the size of one's family. In some respects, then, "virtue" is also covered by "effort" (as sacrifice and self-discipline all involve effort). It may also be covered by one of the corollaries of Mill's principle of impartiality – that of equal sacrifice. This is a core principle in Mill's view of legitimate taxation, but it may also be the case that, where people are making unequal (i.e., larger) sacrifices, they are entitled to greater compensation.

Thus, at core, Mill saw "proportionality between success and merit" as justifying inequalities in our current state of human progress, as well as some justification for inequalities on the grounds of talent. He thought we would eventually come to see both of these as unjust (and no longer expedient) as human society, human nature, and human institutions progressed. That is, once we were at a stage of human progress where the "still higher" principle of "from each according to his capacities, to each according to his needs" would be expedient (which means it would also have to be feasible and "available as a present resource"), then unequal rewards based on effort and talent would no longer be justified (though unequal *contributions*, based on effort and talent, would be).

Importantly, such a world would not be one that could plausibly be called luck-egalitarian: Blanc's distributive principle was not a luck-egalitarian one, though obviously it paid some attention to matters of brute luck regarding capacity and needs. Turner's work goes a long way toward showing that it is a mistake to link Mill to luck-egalitarianism except as short-term means of moving toward something better. It is certainly true that Mill, in many places, points out the unjust effects of brute luck, both good and bad. His defence of "proportionality … between success and exertion," however, does not commit him to a luck-egalitarian position except in the short term, and his commitment to Blancian distributive principles as "higher" even than equal shares shows him adopting a position that was not luck-egalitarian for an "ideal" society toward which humanity was progressing.

Rather than see Mill as a luck-egalitarian, then, I agree with Turner, Berger, Maria Morales, and Elizabeth Anderson that we should read Mill as a relational egalitarian.

Relational Equality

My basic claim is that Mill wanted us to live in (and to know we live in) a society of equals. Our recognition of others as equals, and our own knowledge that others consider us to be equals and treat us as such, was a key part of happiness as he understood it, and it was this that allowed us to be meaningfully independent. If we no longer believe that we ought to be subservient to others, nor others to us, then we can be independent, and we will not attempt to prevent anyone else from so being. Independence was, for Mill, key to happiness because it was about autonomy, self-respect, decision-making, and the free development and exercise of our individuality. Moreover, relational equality allows us to feel that we are an equal part of a joint project. This links to Mill's principle of social harmony and fraternity, which I discuss at more length below. This concept of equality sits best within the school of "relational egalitarianism."

Berger rightly notes that among Mill's substantive principles was the belief that "inequalities must not undermine the status of persons *as equals*. In more concrete terms, this means that inequalities must not result in some gaining power over others that undermines their autonomy or that degrades them."[160] Morales, too, rightly notes that Mill's "principle of perfect equality is an inclusive and substantive moral idea of human relations 'admitting no power of privilege on the one side, nor disability on the other.'"[161]

Put simply, relational egalitarians "are motivated by the conviction that we should … aim for a relational conception of equality, whereby emphasis is put on reaching egalitarian social relations rather than the equal distribution of something."[162] They see justice as more than a question of what people are *owed*, and instead think it is importantly about how people are *treated*, both by institutions and by one another. They believe that unequal *relationships* are not only bad, but a problem for *justice*, and are particularly concerned with questions relating to power inequalities; powerlessness; oppression; marginalization; and structural, systematic violence. Relational egalitarians "demand democratic equality, according to which all individuals have to be rendered capable of participating on equal terms in society's most important activities, such as relations of production, and collective decision-making."[163] In addition, "they seek to identify a distinctive set of inegalitarian relationships as primary injustices, seizing especially on domination as the core unjust relation to be ruled out."

As Anderson puts it, in the foundational work of this school of modern egalitarianism: "The proper negative aim of egalitarian justice is not to eliminate the impact of brute luck from human affairs, but to end oppression, which by definition is socially imposed. Its proper positive aim is not to ensure that everyone gets what they morally deserve, but to create a community in which people stand in relations of equality to others."[164]

"In seeking the construction of a community of equals," her theory of "democratic equality integrates principles of distribution with the expressive demands of equal respect." Moreover:

> Democratic equality guarantees all law-abiding citizens effective access to the social conditions of their freedom at all times. It

justifies the distributions required to secure this guarantee by appealing to the obligations of citizens in a democratic state. In such a state, citizens make claims on one another in virtue of their equality, not their inferiority, to others. Because the fundamental aim of citizens in constructing a state is to secure everyone's freedom, democratic equality's principles of distribution neither presume to tell people how to use their opportunities nor attempt to judge how responsible people are for choices that lead to unfortunate outcomes. Instead, it avoids bankruptcy at the hands of the imprudent by limiting the range of goods provided collectively and expecting individuals to take personal responsibility for the other goods in their possession.

She adds that relational egalitarians "claim that inequality is unjust when it disadvantages people: when it reflects, embodies, or causes inequality of authority, status, or standing" (which allows them to adopt some Pareto-efficient inequalities).[165] They "identify justice with a virtue of agents (including institutions)," that is, they take justice to be "a disposition to treat individuals in accordance with principles that express, embody, and sustain relations of social equality," thus seeing distributions as just if they are the outcome of actions made by agents acting in the right kind of ways (or with the right motivations). Moreover, "most relational egalitarians follow a second-person or interpersonal conception of justification," adopting a "contractualist" approach, which sees "the principles of justice" as being "whatever principles free, equal, and reasonable people would adopt to regulate the claims they make on each other."

Mill broadly fits this description. His emphasis was much more on the equality of relationships than on any specific pattern of distribution of goods (or welfare, or utility). He moved away from questions of what we are *owed* (i.e., desert) and had a deep concern for how we are treated (i.e., as equals). He believed that unequal relationships were a problem for justice, and he was very concerned with oppression, marginalization, and powerlessness. He spent much of his life identifying, and trying to improve, inegalitarian relationships, and trying to eradicate domination. The idea that everyone has to be made capable of participating in collective decision-making and the relations of production almost perfectly sums up his view and justification for unequal distributions.

Mill sought to do more than eradicate the effects of brute bad luck on people's lives (even if it was an outcome of his preferred principle of justice); he also sought to end oppression. He was fundamentally concerned with building a society in which people stood in relations of equality to one another, and he saw justice not in specific patterns of distribution but in individual dispositions to treat individuals in ways that would express, embody, and sustain relationships of equality. This would involve guaranteeing law-abiding citizens effective access to the social conditions of their freedom at all times, as well as bringing people to recognize that they should make claims on one another (and perform duties toward one another) "in virtue of their equality ... to others." For Mill, the recognition of inequality on the basis of need was not about people making claims based on their inferiority to others, but on their fundamental equality (as persons) and their right to equal opportunities for well-being. Like other relational egalitarians, Mill was keen not to tell people what to do with their opportunities. He was also interested in striking a balance between collective provision (which might prevent any one individual from privation) and personal responsibility (including, in the future, a sense of an obligation to contribute to the costs of social living).

That said, there might be some judgment to be passed on people's responsibilities for their bad option-luck, even in ideal circumstances (where Mill thought public opinion – which involves judgment – would help people not to free-ride, or to be so impecunious that the whole community would suffer). And Anderson might find judgments of "needs" to be too intrusive, though it is not clear that such assessments would necessarily undermine relational equality: acknowledging different needs does not necessarily mean acknowledging inferiority, when the recognition that we ought to distribute according to need is founded in a recognition that meaningful equality necessitates unequal distribution of resources. Mill did not say that compensation is owed *for personal inferiority*; rather, he was saying that individual differences can lead, unfairly, to different outcomes because of the advantages some differences provide. The distinction here is nice but significant. As a small example, it is the difference between saying I should get free glasses if I can prove my eyesight is "inferior," and saying "something approximating 20:20 vision is important for living a flourishing human life, and the community will do what it can – including giving people glasses – to ensure that as many people as possible enjoy good vision." An optometrist's exam would therefore not be a test of inferiority, but a means of determining need.

Lastly, and perhaps most importantly, Mill was not a contractualist. He certainly thought it was good for groups of people to adopt their own principles of justice (i.e., in cooperatives, political communities, and families[166]), and he recognized that the expedient principles of justice are those which people can agree to and live together under. In this sense, then, he adopted a second-person view of justice. Mill saw these contractualist principles as important in fostering the right kind of society, social ethos, and interpersonal relationships for equality, and he saw the power of some of these claims regarding not only what is important about equality but also how we can meaningfully achieve it. But his principle of impartiality demanded equal treatment, which can be determined from a third-person standpoint: equal treatment may well mean that everyone needs an equal say in formulating the laws, institutions, and principles of justice under which they live as free individuals, but this is not simply *because they were formulated in this way*. That is, Mill remained opposed to Kantianism at a metaphysical level, even though endorsing elements of contractualism in considerations of expediency. That principles of justice be determined democratically is important for ensuring one key element of justice (that no one is being exploited, or their interests ignored); it is also an outcome of equal relationships and an important marker of independence – but the principles so determined can also be ranked in terms of their justice from an external perspective.

Christian Schemmel further notes a split between two broad schools of relational egalitarianism: those that are "pluralist" about justice and equality (i.e., they do not see all of equality as encapsulated in justice), and those that are not.[167] Given Mill's utilitarianism, he was *always* going to balance equality with other claims (such as to liberty, and fraternity, and security, and progress), with the principle of utility (which relates, also, to questions of expediency) as the "principle" at the level of which such competing claims were to be balanced. Thus, he *had* to be a pluralist (in this sense).

If this position is compatible with relational egalitarianism – and I believe it is – then Mill was a relational egalitarian. If one *has* to be a thoroughgoing Kantian and/or contractualist and relativist about principles of justice, and if there is no room at all for third-person or consequentialist thinking, then he was not. More importantly than a label, though, we can see from this discussion what was important to him regarding equality, and why it led him to endorse particular equalities and particular distributive principles.

Overall, then, Mill's position is best understood as a form of pluralist social egalitarianism, based – in contrast to most post-Rawlsian thought – on utilitarianism. He was fundamentally committed to "perfect equality" between people. What this entailed in substantive principles – as was the case with all his principles – was subject to questions of expediency and historical progress, but it led him to endorse the idea of treating people as equals (and being treated by others as an equal), which in turn led him to endorse the distributive principle of from each according to his capacities, to each according to his needs (mitigated – as necessary – by his commitment to independence). This distributive principle seeks to eradicate the impact of "bad" brute luck (by unequally allocating resources in order to meet "needs," and by tailoring demands to capacity) while disallowing at least some benefits based on unequal "good" brute luck, because those with greater capacity are expected to contribute more. But it is not concerned with otherwise justifying resulting inequalities (as luck-egalitarianism is), and it provides more of a security net for those with bad option-luck than traditional luck-egalitarianism (at least), for needs are met without inquiring into how one came to be "needy." Moreover, the *aim* of this principle is not to apportion distribution according only to individual choices (though doubtless diversity due to individual choices was important to Mill); instead, the principle itself is the eventual outcome of treating people as equals.

This egalitarianism is only possible in a certain kind of society – radically different from our own, and from Mill's – characterized by a very different way of seeing one another, and interacting with ine another, generated by "fraternity."

FRATERNITY

Mill praised the Provisional Government for its desire to achieve "all of 'liberty, equality and fraternity' which is capable of being realised now, and … [to] prepare the way for all which can be realised hereafter."[168] His commitment to "fraternity" has been mostly ignored in Mill scholarship. Notable exceptions are Mill's early critic, James Fitzjames Stephen; Morales's communitarian reading of Mill's egalitarianism; Kurer's recognition of "the doctrine of the improvement of man" as being "at the heart of Mill's concept of progress"; and Biagini's identification of the link between Mill and the republican liberalism associated with William Gladstone and Giuseppe Mazzini.[169]

Stephen identifies Mill's commitment to fraternity in *Utilitarianism* and uses *Subjection* as the target for his critique of Mill's egalitarianism.[170] Morales, on the other hand, uses Mill's feminist works, most notably *Subjection*, as the basis for her communitarian reading of Mill.[171] Biagini links Mill's concern with public virtue and the right kind of social ethos with his liberalism.[172] Kurer links similar concerns directly to Mill's social philosophy, and to his socialism.[173] I argue that Mill's commitment to fraternity is visible in many of his works – not least *Utilitarianism* and *Subjection*. He shared some core "communitarian" beliefs regarding the contextuality of values and expedient reforms and the key role society played in the making of the individual[174] (while also preserving a "third-person," objective standpoint that sits less well with communitarianism[175]). He valued "community" and "fraternity" or communal feeling as valuable for human beings both in itself and as a guarantor of good government and the securing of justice, equality, security, and progress (and thus, ultimately, utility). He was famously wary of "tradition" and "custom" as having normative weight merely by virtue of *being* traditional or customary, and emphasized the need to protect individuality from the tyranny of social oppression,[176] which put him at odds with some communitarians.[177] "Communitarianism" as a modern political theory is a direct response to Rawls, so reading it back into Mill's work is somewhat anachronistic. Indeed, Mill was not involved in a debate over types of liberalism: his commitment to fraternity was one of the things that made him a socialist.

So instead of adopting the label "communitarian," I suggest we focus on "fraternity,"[178] and recognize that there is a strong commitment to this in Mill – that is, to cooperation, "association," and the idea of a common good as important and normatively valuable things. Despite what one might intuitively think, these do not contradict his commitment to the "free development of individuality," for he sees this as something we can achieve in a social setting (perhaps only there), and he separates it out from "individualism," which he opposes.

Kurer is right to identify Mill's fraternalism with his commitment to progress: Mill saw human society as progressing toward a more and more harmonious, fraternal state in which people, ultimately, would be capable of being motivated by the common good and not merely by their own selfish interests. This is a somewhat overlooked element of his description of his socialism, which, while emphasizing individual freedom (as independence), looked forward to a time of equality and justice, when "it will no longer either be, or by thought to be, impossible for human beings to exert themselves strenuously in procuring benefits which are not to be exclusively their own, but to be shared with the society they belong to."¹⁷⁹ He saw "the social problem of the future" as being "how to unite the greatest individual liberty of action, with common ownership in the raw material of the globe, and equal participation of all in the benefits of combined labour," and he "saw clearly that to render any such social transformation either possible or desirable, an equivalent chance of character must take place both in the uncultivated herd who now compose the labouring masses, and in the immense majority of their employers. Both these classes must learn by practice to labour and combine for generous, or at all events for public and social purposes, and not, as hitherto, solely for narrowly interested ones."

Fraternity was thus both necessary and desirable. Without it, we would not achieve the right kind of liberty and equality, nor progress, security, and – ultimately – utility: it was instrumentally vital. Without it, what liberty, equality, progress, security, and utility we *did* achieve would be suboptimal. Fraternity was also normatively valuable in its own right as a secondary principle through which we maximize utility.

Fraternity is a sense of fellowship with other people. It has its roots in a sense of brotherhood – that is, close family relations – but is used more expansively to mean having this sort of feeling about people outside one's immediate family. What links it to a sense of family is both the element of meaningful care and concern and a willingness, and capacity, to treat other people's interests as at least as important as, perhaps more important than, our own. That is, when we feel a sense of "fraternity" for (and with) other people, we feel a sense of "oneness" or that there is something important we have in common, and we are motivated to act in the interests of our common good, even where this might conflict with our "narrow" interests. Fraternity, then, is the feeling that allows us to expand our sympathies outside of a narrow sphere and act for the common good of all our fellow citizens (perhaps even all fellow humans).

We see this desire for fraternity in Mill's writings even before he was publicly endorsing socialist schemes – for instance, in his desire to end the "widening breach" between employees and employers and to create a sense of "partnership" between them.[180] Or even earlier, when he criticized those who were incapable of seeing society as a shared project "to do each other most good."[181] As Stephen rightly noted, we see Mill's commitment to fraternity very plainly in *Utilitarianism*, where he wrote that utilitarian philosophy would not be able to take root in society until "by the improvement of education, the feeling of unity with our fellow creatures shall be ... as deeply rooted in our character, and to our own consciousness as completely a part of our nature as the horror of crime is in an ordinarily well-brought up young person."[182] He added that it was possible for this "feeling of unity" to become "deeply rooted," and not eroded by our powers of analysis, only because of a "basis of powerful natural sentiment ... which, when once the general happiness is recognised as the ethical standard, will constitute the strength of utilitarian morality."[183] That is, Mill believed that we had a basic desire for unity with our fellow creatures and that this could be developed into a deep and powerful motivation for acting in the common good. When speaking of "fraternity," then, I mean this sense of "unity," of "sympathy," and of "oneness."

"Unity" is compatible with liberty and individuality in exactly the same way that law-abidingness and a moral conscience are compatible. Many people have a "deeply rooted" "horror" of crime and would not pursue their own good in their own way if it involved doing something "criminal" or immoral, be that stealing, having an affair, committing fraud, acting violently when not in self-defence, or lying under oath. Some people, no doubt, avoid "criminal" activity only out of "horror" of the punishment that might befall them if they were to be caught, but fear of punishment is not the only thing that makes people have a horror of "criminal" or immoral behaviour. Instead, our own consciences, "deeply rooted" in our nature (even if instilled via artificial means of education from birth) give us this "horror." But it seems odd to argue that we are not "free," or "freely developing our individuality," when we refrain from behaviour for which we feel such a "deep-rooted" "horror" – particularly when we can say that our own reflection on moral matters has made these feelings authentically our own such that they are "living truths" with us, and not merely "dead dogmas" we pay lip service to once they have been instilled in us through inauthentic associations.

On Mill's view, then, people who refrain from theft (even if their interests might have been advanced by stealing) owing to a deep-rooted "horror" of thieving are still free because this "deep-rooted" "horror" is, in itself, a key part of their individuality. In the future, this "horror" will – Mill hoped – be extended beyond "criminal" activity to include anything that impairs a feeling of "unity" of sympathy and interests. In other words, people will recoil in horror from doing something unfraternal. Dominating, instrumentalizing, and exploitative relationships will be impossible, as will the "trampling, crushing, elbowing, and treading on each other's heels, which form[ed] the existing type of social life."[184] So, too, will much of capitalism, which is predicated on profit-seeking behaviour that relies on "buying cheap and selling dear" and a fundamental opposition of class interests. Impossible, also, will be the kind of state domination of people's lives so often associated with "socialism" in the twentieth century – fraternity, on Mill's account, is incompatible with totalitarianism and, indeed, with authoritarian attempts to enforce unity by imposing artificially unified interests upon people. Mill's account of fraternity is not state-imposed, and our interests are not dictated by the state. Instead, unity is achieved through harmonization of individual consciences so that people desire a feeling of unity with their fellow humans: the urge toward unity comes from within; it is not externally imposed.

That said, there is a key role to be played by external institutions, including the state, in achieving this "internal," deep-rooted "horror" regarding non-fraternal behaviours. Mill sees our characters (and thus our motivations) as being formed by a range of institutions, from early-years education in the family, through formal schooling, to our political institutions, our workplaces, our religious societies, and our relations with lovers, friends, colleagues, and fellow citizens. Still, we ought not to conflate this role for "external" forces with totalitarianism, in particular as so many of these formative relationships are self-chosen (particularly under socialism).

As Mill saw it, contemporary life led people to have "narrow interests" – that is, they were concerned with their own well-being, pleasure, security and social advancement, and that of their immediate family (husband/wife, children, and favoured relatives). They found it much more difficult to be interested in anything "broader" or more "general." Such relationships were also often dominating. Yet as Morales rightly argues, "Mill endorsed forms of community that promote all its members' well-being, and advance their permanent interests ... From Mill's perspective, no well-constituted community is possible where the hostile, antagonistic, and selfish feelings that power engenders infiltrate human life. Well-constituted communities are founded on sympathetic, cooperative, and egalitarian values."[185] They are also founded on valuing individuality (and its free development).

Mill also noted: "it is only by slow degrees, and a system of culture prolonged through successive generations, that men in general can be brought up to th[e] point" of being motivated by the general good.[186] He added:

> But the hindrance is not in the essential constitution of human nature. Interest in the common good is at present so weak a motive in the generality, not because it can never be otherwise, but because the mind is not accustomed to dwell on it as it dwells from morning till night on things which tend only to personal advantage. When called into activity as only self interest now is, by the daily course of life, and spurred from behind by the love of distinction and the fear of shame, it is capable of producing, even in common men, the most strenuous exertions as well as the most heroic sacrifices. The deep rooted selfishness which forms the general character of the existing state of society, is so deeply rooted, only because the whole course of existing institutions tends to foster it.

It would take fundamental and transformational change to the family and gender relations, the economy and class relations, and politics and inter-citizen relations to really achieve "unity of interests." Fraternity would be both the outcome of these changes and an important virtue making current progress sustainable and further progress possible.

Cooperatives were a key institution for this social transformation. Mill explained that he "welcomed with the greatest pleasure and interest all socialistic experiments ... (such as the Cooperative Societies), which, whether they succeeded or failed, could not but operate as a most useful education of those who took part in them, by cultivating their capacity of acting upon motives pointing directly to the general good, or making them aware of the defects which render them and others incapable of doing so."

Experiments in profit-sharing that helped make both capitalists and workers better prepared for cooperation, and that in themselves would go some way toward healing the "widening breach between those who toil and those who live on the produce of former toil," were also important.[187] So were democratic reforms, including but not limited to universal suffrage, paired with institutions for promoting the common good.

Reform to the family and to gender relations was also key. Morales offers an excellent account of the transition Mill envisioned toward "well-constituted" family, and sexual, relations,[188] whereby a "command and obedience" relationship would be replaced with one of "reciprocity and friendship."[189] Mill's socialism went hand-in-hand with his feminism, and it is no coincidence that his initial interest in socialism was motivated by his feminism.

Similarly, reform to religion was vital – indeed, not merely reform but the actual founding of a new "Religion of Humanity."[190] This new secular "religion" would create a new "clerisy," consisting of scientists and poets (broadly conceived), who would help guide social progress and foster social harmony.[191] Mill thought there were several "inducements for cultivating a religious devotion to the welfare of our fellow-creatures as an obligatory limit to every selfish aim."[192] He thought it was not irrational to believe in a benevolent but not omnipotent "Being" and that there was value in feeling that, in pursuing the general welfare, "we may be co-operative with the unseen Being to whom we owe all that is enjoyable in life" in an ongoing "battle … between the powers of good and evil." However, his preference was for "religion" that had no supernatural element, and he thought the idea of Humanity, as an ever-existing and endlessly improving entity, could take the place of an idea of Heaven and God.

This "religious devotion to the welfare of our fellow-creatures" was a strong normative good, and goal, for Mill, which perhaps is why Stephen identified him as an acolyte of the "religion" of "Liberty, Equality, Fraternity!"[193] When we do not take it seriously as one of his core secondary principles, we misread Mill's political, social, and ethical project. Indeed, so important is it to his view of the future that he wrote an even lengthier account of how slow social progress would achieve this "utopia" than he did of how it would happen in the economy in *Principles*.[194]

Mill argued that "the social feelings of mankind; the desire to be in unity with our fellow creatures," was a "leading department of our nature." He did not base this on some "fact" of human psychology, because he disliked those kinds of arguments; rather, he traced the long social history of the creation, "nourishment," and growth of this feeling, which had charted the same course as human history itself. Thus, in order to live together, humans have to have this "social feeling"; and *because* we do, and must, live together – and indeed, as human society progresses – we start to conceive of ourselves as social creatures, and everything that can be done by society (and in the individuals within it) to foster this "social feeling" is done. "[A]dvancing civilisation," which creates greater and greater equality and more and more cooperation among equal citizens, makes this feeling ever stronger, slowly but surely, "removing the sources of opposition of interest, and levelling those inequalities of legal privilege between individuals or classes, owing to which there are large portions of mankind whose happiness it is still practicable to disregard." "In an improving state [of humanity], the influences are constantly on the increase, which tend to generate in each individual a feeling of unity with all the rest; which feeling, if perfect, would make him never think of, or desire, any beneficial condition for himself, in the benefits of which they are not included." A "society of equals can only exist on the understanding that the interests of all are to be regarded equally," and the history of human progress is toward this equality, as well as the individual feelings it requires.

Such a "feeling of unity" would be particularly strengthened if it were "taught as a religion, and the whole force of education, of institutions, and of opinion, directed ... to make every person grow up from infancy surrounded on all sides by both the profession and by the practice of it." Mill wrote: "I think no one, who can realise this conception, will feel any misgiving about the sufficiency of the ultimate sanction for the Happiness morality." That is, we should not fear – as some did – that in a secular, utilitarian society, nothing would prevent people from acting in an "anti-social" (i.e., criminal or immoral) way. Socialism would be the perfection of this "society of equals"; we would find within its bounds the required character-forming religion, education, institutions, and public opinion, with all individuals professing the importance of unity of interests and practising that unity. Thus, socialism was necessary in order to maximize utility, and the "social feelings" that human society requires to even be sustainable in the first place lead inexorably to utilitarianism and thus to socialism.

Given this, it is no wonder Mill welcomed the events of 1848; they furthered radical democratic aims (such as universal suffrage, republicanism, education, and state seizure of church property), and the revolutionaries meant to achieve not just liberty and equality but "fraternity" as well. Thus his enthusiasm for the possibilities of "association" as developed by Blanc and others in discussions at the Palais de Luxembourg. This was an opportunity to take important strides in human progress.

This notion of fraternity, and of moulding people's characters through institutional change – in particular, by creating a new religion – may sit uncomfortably with some liberals. On the one hand, perhaps this only goes to show that Mill was *not* a liberal, but a socialist. Socialists, after all, have always been more comfortable with the idea of shaping human nature via institutional means, and they recognize the corrupting influence on human character of apparently "free" institutions such as the market, individual employment contracts, and other "bourgeois" liberties. On the other hand, it is worth emphasizing how Mill saw this alignment of sympathies as compatible with and indeed complementing "the free development of individuality": alignment of sympathies would prevent people from even *wanting* to cause harm to others (or render them sanguine about inadvertently causing it) as they pursued their own good in their own way; it would also prevent people from wanting to prevent others from developing as they best saw fit (this being a fundamental interest) and thus protect everyone in the development of their individuality. That is, Mill saw his "liberal" commitments to individuality and freedom as compatible with this widening of sympathies – liberty was achievable with (and full liberty *only* with) equality and fraternity.

We might worry that fraternity, as Mill saw it, is incompatible with diversity. Evidently, he did not think so. Instead, he saw fraternity as properly incompatible only with social tyranny and selfish individualism. Societies do not need to be homogenous for them to be fraternal or for there to be a sense of "unity of interests" between people. Having "unity of interests" with others does not mean we all have to be identical. Our "interests as progressive beings" are, for Mill, sufficiently broad and universal that they can sustain a great deal of diversity. Those interests include security (including of subsistence), liberty as independence, and equality. Fraternity is not compatible with fascism, totalitarianism, racism, misogyny, and other dominating views – and thus *some* contemporary social diversity would be lessened – but it is compatible with a wide range of religious, political, and ethical beliefs.

Let us take a common example – religious belief. A deep-rooted desire for unity of interests with others – even with people who do not believe the same thing – is not incompatible with religious belief. Almost all deeply religious people may wish more people held their views (for those other people's own good), but they don't try to forcibly convert others or otherwise harm them as punishment for their nonbelief. Even where we might harbour negative feelings toward someone's beliefs (scorn, disgust, horror, dismay, disapproval, incomprehension, etc.), these are not necessarily incompatible with fraternity – it depends on how we act based on those feelings: Do we try to impose our standards on others? Do we start to treat them as inferiors or social pariahs? Do we tolerantly let them get on with their own lives up to the point where they threaten harm to others? Or do we cherish them as diverse individuals and seek to support as well as understand their developing individuality? It seems clear from *On Liberty* that in Mill's preferred future, we might engage more in persuasion to get people to change their views than we are perhaps willing now to do, but this persuasion will be motivated by concern for one another, not by a desire to impose our will on others. This, really, is at the heart of fraternity: it is a kind of mutual sympathy that leads us to modify our own behaviour so that we impinge less on the interests of others, while others do the same for us. That is compatible with diversity – which Mill, after all, deeply cherished – and *not* compatible with the kind of social pressure so often destructive of diversity. This mixture of freedom and shared basic commitments epitomized for Mill the ideal synthesis of the best elements of a critical and an organic age: liberty is vital, but so is fraternity.

Kurer rightly notes that "at the heart of Mill's concept of progress is the doctrine of improvement of man towards more intellectual power and advanced moral standards"[195] – indeed, Mill is generally recognized as a "perfectionist" liberal rather than as endorsing liberal neutrality. Kurer also rightly notes that "the doctrine of improvement calls on the one hand for a large amount of liberty … [but] [o]n the other hand, it also calls for particular measures to change people's preferences."[196] Kurer is correct that "[t]his does not imply Mill … wanted to force the adult populace to act *against their will*. He did, however, [seek to] create institutions with a view of *changing their will*, either by constructing an appropriate structure of incentives, or by 'educating' them with the help of particular political and economic institutions."

This, Kurer argues, "is ... a form of paternalism." He adds that Mill believed in "the importance of the government as an agency for progress" and that the government had a responsibility "to promote an environment that stimulates progress," thus to become "the motor force in the evolutionary process." So whoever "controls it, has the means to impose stagnation, progress or retrogression."

It is not clear, however, that this *is* a form of paternalism, for the preferences are being changed not for the individual's own good (against their will) but for the *general* good – that is, for everyone *else*'s good (though no doubt Mill thought individuals would also benefit). Rather, as noted above, this is a kind of perfectionism. Mill clearly thought that humanity *ought to* progress toward this better state of things, where our sympathies would be in tune with one another and where "my" good would be intimately wrapped up in "your" good and the "common good." He recognized that governments (among other social and political institutions) had a powerful role to play in the formation of character and in people's capacity to achieve alignment in their sympathies. He also thought that as much as possible they should be judged by – and in particular, *praised* for – their efforts to forward these sentiments and this character progression. For instance, regarding the events in France in 1848, he wrote that the violent insurrection against the government of Louis Philippe was justified because it had shown itself to be "a government wholly without the spirit of improvement," and that no government can "now expect to be permanent, unless it guarantees progress as well as order: nor can it continue really to secure order, unless it promotes progress."[197]

To emphasize a "liberal" Mill, we would have to read passages in his work praising "fraternity" as an "inconsistency" in his thought. But if we take these passages seriously as being as integral to his philosophy as his love of individuality, then a consistent view is discernible – one that is committed to liberty, equality, *and* fraternity as core secondary principles necessary for the achievement of the general happiness. His vision of a much improved society was one in which we have a deeply rooted horror of not having "unity of interests" with our fellow citizens, and where we are so motivated by a sense of care for one another that we see our roles as citizens and as workers to be those of "public functionar[ies]," working freely for one another's good, and seeing that as a "good in itself" that we desire for its own sake.[198] In this, Mill was evidently not a libertarian; the view also goes beyond what we usually consider to be liberal and shows why Mill thought himself (rightly) to be "under the general designation of Socialist."[199]

CONCLUSION

As others have noted, it is important, when studying Mill, not only to look at the kinds of institutions he suggested or campaigned for, but also to understand the underlying principles to which he was committed and which he thought justified those institutions, or which he thought those institutions were likely to embody and sustain. Mill recognized that people's character is deeply affected and shaped by the institutions in which they are embedded and raised, so he saw it as important that those institutions be properly designed (not just left to chance and tradition) and that they be assigned a vital role in improving future society. Mill's principles were "abstract" in that he deduced them from a primary commitment to utility, but they were informed by a contextualized understanding of what furthers utility, and the institutions he supported based on these principles were always designed in an historically and socially nuanced way. This chapter has been concerned with developing a deeper understanding of Mill's core principles. In the next chapter I consider what we can say regarding Mill's preferred institutions – his "utopia."

As secondary principles that would help us achieve maximum utility for the most people, Mill was committed to progress, security, liberty, equality, and fraternity. Mill thought there would always be a need to balance each of these against the other(s) in order to achieve the greatest happiness for the greatest number. The ideal society, for him, was one in which all were balanced correctly and none were sacrificed at the expense of anything but increasing utility. This is one reason why his socialism remains attractive – it is fundamentally committed to individuality as well as to justice, equality, and fraternity. It does not look to achieve homogeneity or stagnation, and it will not allow individuals to be sacrificed on an altar of community or progress. At the same time, it *does* look to secure much more harmony, equality, and engagement with our fellow citizens in meaningful human relationships, and it asks us to value self-developed individuality without also worshipping selfish individualism.

Much attention has long been paid to Mill's concept of liberty. But when we understand his commitments – to the free development of individuality; to relational egalitarianism; to social progress; to security (including of subsistence); to fraternity; and to the principle of justice "from each according to their capacities, to each according to their needs" – we find him to be someone with a political program much more radical than is suggested by our usual picture of him as a classical, *laissez-faire* liberal. The society he looked forward to was radically different from our own (indeed, from *his* own) in the care we would take toward one another; the way we would share and produce resources; what we would cherish and value; how we would act in the public and private spheres; and how well *all* people's lives would actually go. In Mill's preferred future there would be no kings, no billionaires, and no real estate moguls, but there would also be no homelessness, no poverty, no labour exploitation, no cheating, no fraud, no scams, no domestic violence, no racism, no patriarchy, no homophobia, no xenophobia, no misogyny, no attempts to dominate, and no thoughtlessness regarding the impact of our actions on the life chances of others. I do not think we can even imagine the radical impact on the world of adherence to, and realization of, Mill's preferred principles. Which is why, perhaps, he left the working out of precise institutions for the people of the future to decide.

Mill did, though, have some firm ideas about what possible reforms we could institute here and now to realize these aims, and where these might lead us. It is to this "utopia" that I now turn.

CHAPTER FIVE

Mill's Socialist "Utopia"

If, on a subject on which almost every thinker has his Utopia, we might be permitted to have ours; if we might point to the principle on which, at some distant date, we place our chief hope for healing the widening breach between those who toil and those who live on the produce of former toil; it would be that of raising the labourer from a receiver of hire – a mere bought instrument in the work of production, having no residuary interest in the work itself – to the position of being ... a partner in ... a work of cooperation, not of mere hiring and service.[1]

In describing his hopes for the future of humanity, John Stuart Mill was willing to use the word "Utopia," but unlike many contemporary socialists (for instance, Robert Owen, William Thompson, Etienne Cabet, Charles Fourier, and Henri Saint-Simon), he was unwilling to draw detailed blueprints for a future society, prescribing exactly what institutions people ought to adopt in an ideal future. (This is one reason why "utopian socialist" is not the best label for Mill.) That said, he did engage in detail with a series of potential reforms and with the institutional designs put forward by a number of socialists. He also made suggestions regarding the kinds of institutions that he thought "would be the nearest approach to social justice, and the most beneficial ordering of industrial affairs for the universal good, which it is possible at present to foresee."[2]

Mill wished to see "liberty, equality, and fraternity," along with security, progress, and utility, embodied in the institutions of the new organic age. He also thought these institutions – in keeping with his commitment to progress – would act so as to continue the cultivation of these principles.³ An incomplete picture of these institutions can be found in *Claims of Labour*, in which Mill directly addresses the question of what institutions he would like to see created in order to form a better society, going so far as to describe them as his "Utopia."⁴ A fuller description of a more radical vision can be seen in *Principles of Political Economy*⁵ and in some of Mill's other writings (including *Auguste Comte*, the *Autobiography*, *Considerations on Representative Government*, *Three Essays on Religion*, and several of his letters and speeches).

"Utopia" may at first seem an unlikely word to use in reference to Mill, as he once wrote that he "had not the presumption to suppose he could already foresee, by what precise form of institutions ... [his] objects could most effectually be attained."⁶ We also tend to see Mill as an empiricist with his feet firmly grounded on the floor, and not indulging in flights of fancy (with which utopianism is often associated). However, Mill did have clear ideas about what kinds of institutions would be best for humanity, even if he did not want to be "precise" about them.

The scope of changes Mill envisaged even in his philosophic-radical period were called "utopian" by his antagonistic contemporaries, precisely on account of how much important social change they would require.⁷ For his part, however, Mill was critical of opponents who based their visions of the future on what he considered to be impossibilities. Thus, Mill was always concerned with what was feasible, as well as what was desirable, when considering reform. As he put it, regarding the Saint-Simonians, theirs was a "scheme, impracticable indeed – but differing ... from every other Utopia we ever read of, in this, that the impracticability is only in *degree*, not in kind, and that while most other visionary projects for reforming society are not only impossible, but if possible, would be bad, *this* plan, if it could be realised, would be good."⁸

Mill's "utopia" was also – currently – "impracticable" only in degree; once "practicable" (or "available as a present resource"), it would be something "desirable" toward which existing reform efforts could immediately be aimed in a series of steps, however small, that would make it ultimately achievable.

The difficulty of describing an entirely new, holistic society, in which part of what makes it good is the interaction between its institutions, is one reason utopians often turn to fiction instead of trying to use the tools of formal political philosophy. Mill eschewed that approach, so we have to use our own imaginations to envision his utopia.

In *Claims* he used the term "Utopia" to describe not a set of institutions so much as a "principle."[9] This "would be that of raising the labourer from a receiver of hire – a mere bought instrument in the work of production, having no residuary interest in the work itself – to the position of being, in some sort, a partner in it." He added that "in some form of this policy we see the only, or the most practicable, means of harmonizing the 'rights of industry' and those of property; of making the employers the real chiefs of the people, leading and guiding them in a work in which they also are interested – a work of co-operation, not of mere hiring and service; and justifying, by the superior capacity in which they contribute to the work, the higher remuneration which they receive for their share of it."

This "Utopia" evidently bears some strong resemblance to the "régime of individual property ... as it might be made" in the old world, explored in Chapter 2. That is, Mill looked to profit-sharing as the means of healing the contemporary antagonism between employers and employees. He echoed Saint-Simonism regarding the desire to make "the employers the real chiefs of the people, leading and guiding them in a work in which they are also interested," and he sought to justify unequal returns not on the basis of inherited privilege but on that of "superior capacity." He evidently had in mind a "Utopia" of small-scale employer-managers, working in managerial roles in companies they own, and entering into profit-sharing arrangements with their employees, much as – in fact – M. Leclaire did for his Parisian house-painting firm, which Mill mentions in *Claims* and describes in great detail in *Principles*.[10]

That said, Mill was already concerned about the social ethos and relational equality between employers and employees; he was already interested in labour being "a work of cooperation," an idea closely linked not only to equality and fraternity but also to liberty; and he was already concerned with justifying inequality, in this case via desert. These are some of Mill's core principles, but the "Utopia" sketched in *Claims* does not fully realize them.

In 1845, Mill evidently thought that even this "Utopia" was not "available as a present resource," though it was something we could meaningfully work toward.[11] He did not go much further than this in the 1848 edition of *Principles*. What Mill calls his "utopia" in *Claims* and *Principles* has been called "modest."[12] However, this underplays the radicalism of Mill's conception of "the régime of individual property ... as it might be made."

The expanded chapter "On the Probable Futurity of the Labouring Classes" in the 1852 edition (where "examples of the association of labourers among themselves" – that is, worker-cooperatives – are included for the first time) reveals more concerning Mill's Utopia. It also indicates that he believed more reform was feasible and immediately available than he had previously thought (because of the events of 1848). His socialist utopia, as expressed in *Principles* (and supplemented elsewhere), is even more radical than that in *Claims*.

Mill gave a relatively lengthy account of both the future and our transition to it in the closing pages of the section on these associations.[13] Cooperatives would multiply as the best workers moved into, or formed, them. So in order to compete for good workers, private employers would have to adopt profit-sharing. This might evolve, "in perhaps a less remote future than may be supposed," into a universal expansion of cooperation (as employers might follow Leclaire's example of leaving their profit-sharing company to the workers as a cooperative, or go out of business as their workers joined cooperatives). Those remaining workers who had "too little understanding, or too little virtue, to be capable of learning to act on any other system than that of narrow selfishness," and thus could not join cooperatives, would become increasingly rare, and their employment increasingly unprofitable. (They were unlikely, in Mill's view, to be particularly good workers, which would result in costly disciplinary measures, but they would also be able to demand relatively high wages, given the "competition" from cooperatives, which they could at least threaten to join if they were not well remunerated, especially if we also suppose some form of poor relief.) Thus, capitalists "would gradually find it to their advantage" (i.e., more profitable and secure) to invest in cooperatives, "to do this at diminishing rates of interests, and at last, perhaps, even to exchange their capital for terminable annuities." Over time, cooperative associations, being "a course of education in those moral and active qualities by which alone success can be either deserved or attained," generate their own sustainability. He concluded: "In this or some such mode, the existing accumulations of capital might honestly, and by a kind of spontaneous process, become in the end the joint property of all who participate in their productive employment: a transformation which, thus effected, (and assuming of course that both sexes participate equally in the rights and in the government of the association) would be the nearest approach to social justice, and the most beneficial ordering of industrial affairs for the universal good, which it is possible at present to foresee."

This change "would combine the freedom and independence of the individual, with the moral, intellectual, and economical advantages of aggregate production; and ... without violence or spoliation, or even any sudden disturbance of existing habits and expectations, would realize, at least in the industrial department, the best aspirations of the democratic spirit, by putting an end to the division of society into the industrious and the idle, and effacing all social distinctions but those fairly earned by personal services and exertions."

In the *Autobiography* he summarized this as follows:

While we repudiated with the greatest energy that tyranny of society over the individual which most Socialistic systems are supposed to involve, we yet looked forward to a time when society will no longer be divided into the idle and the industrious; when the rule that they who do not work shall not eat, will be applied not to paupers only, but impartially to all; when the division of the produce of labour, instead of depending, as in so great a degree it now does, on the accident of birth, will be made by concert, on an acknowledged principle of justice; and when it will no longer either be, or be thought to be, impossible for human beings to exert themselves strenuously in procuring benefits which are not to be exclusively their own, but to be shared with the society they belong to. The social problem of the future we considered to be, how to unite the greatest individual liberty of action, with a common ownership in the raw material of the globe, and an equal participation of all in the benefits of combined labour.[14]

In both these works we see Mill's core commitments to progress, liberty, equality, fraternity, and security (especially via the organic, peaceful, voluntary transition to socialism). We also see him advocating radical reforms to social, political, and economic institutions. In the rest of this chapter, I explore these in more detail. I separate out economic from political elements for ease of navigation, but the whole also needs to be appreciated (and is more than a sum of its parts), and all the elements interact, supporting and being sustained by one another. That is, democracy in the workplace supports and sustains democracy at the local and national levels in politics, and vice versa. Similarly, egalitarian relationships in the family are the basis for egalitarian relationships both at work and with our fellow citizens in political life. Likewise, a religion of humanity motivates us at work, in our political decision-making, and in our personal relationships and ethics.

THE ECONOMY

Mill sought to "unite the greatest individual liberty of action, with a common ownership in the raw material of the globe, and an equal participation of all in the benefits of combined labour."[15] His solution to this was cooperation and further socialist experimentation – for example, with Fourierist phalanxes.[16] Cooperation secures liberty: cooperators are self-governing and independent, working as equals within a democratic enterprise; they live under under rules determined by themselves, and elect their own managers; and they receive a share of the product of their combined labour that they see as just. Mill thought Fourierism was a feasible scheme that could preserve individuality while ensuring equality and fraternity, and he called for a fair trial by those who wished to make it work.

In both schemes, property in the means of production was to be communally owned by the community (or cooperative). Mill did envisage some ownership of property (especially land) by the state, which would either provide it to cooperatives or intentional communities on long leases,[17] or preserve it from development for the enjoyment of all.[18] Similarly, small communities and cooperatives might communally own the land they occupied – this would depend on the actual process of transition from "here" to "there."

Articles of consumption would be divided among people according to an acknowledged principle of justice (i.e., acknowledged as just by every member of the affected community, be that at a state level or within a cooperative), and once distributed, individuals would have most of the rights over it that we currently associate with property. That is, people could consume it, trade it, save it, or bequeath it (or destroy it).

Mill did not provide details as to exactly what this division would be *of*, but several options were open. The distribution might be of money, it might be in kind, or it might be a mix of the two. For instance, one might receive a share of the money for which goods and services had been sold to another community, in addition to some in-kind contributions such as accommodation within a community, and/or food supplied by a communal canteen. As a worker in a consumer cooperative, you might get wages, which you could then spend in that cooperative, or you might simply take the value in goods. Cooperation is designed to work within a market system that uses money, but it does not rely on money (as a means of exchange) to work. Intentional communities might use money to fund their own creation, and in this regard, Fourier saw a role for money within the community (otherwise there could be no return on capital as part of his tripartite division). Mill envisaged a future in which the rate of profit was zero. This encouraged capitalists to invest in cooperatives. Thus, many elements of banking as we know it would disappear, for cooperation would destroy the need for much of the financial industry and the stock market (though it is possible that pension schemes and the like would still exist, and invest in cooperatives and/or government bonds). (Mill does not give details regarding the future of banking, but it is not implausible to think that banking, if it went on at all, could also be cooperative.)

Mill advocated, as an ideal, a reformed system of individual property in which people could inherit only a "moderate independence." Under cooperative socialism, there would be even less to bequeath (only articles of consumption). It is worth reiterating that Mill was emphatic that "I do not recognise as either just or salutary, a state of society in which there is any 'class' which is not labouring; any human beings, exempt from bearing their share of the necessary labours of human life, except those unable to labour, or who have fairly earned rest by previous toil."[19]

In an ideal world, then, everyone would work,[20] and they would do so not because the government forced them to but because they recognized it was their *duty* to work in order to help meet the costs of their existence in society. As Mill put it "[t]here is a portion of work rendered necessary by the fact of each person's existence: no one could exist unless work, to a certain amount, were done either by or for him. Of this, each person is bound, in justice, to perform his share."[21] In particular, no one could be born with no duty to work, or having had that duty "paid off" for them by inherited wealth. (On the other hand, it might be that they *could* not work, and in that case, as ought implies can, this duty would not fall on them – instead, a different duty would fall on the rest of society to provide the necessary care and support.)

Mill envisaged cooperatives determining their own principles of distribution. People would work in the cooperatives for which they were most fit, and all of us would choose cooperatives where the principles of justice were most expedient. That is, we would all choose to work in a more just place than not, but our views of what is "just" are clouded by what justice we, ourselves, are capable of. He insisted that power should not automatically result in more remuneration within cooperatives, and given the limits imposed by equality, fraternity, and the inability to purchase private property, it is plausible to say that greater remuneration could not, in Mill's utopia, mean greater power.[22]

Mill saw cooperatives as trading with one another. Consumer cooperatives, for instance, would source their goods from producer cooperatives or cooperative wholesalers; and producer cooperatives would sell their goods either to consumer cooperatives or cooperative wholesalers, or to other producer cooperatives (depending on the type, or quantity, of the goods – that is, cooperative farms might sell both to consumer cooperatives providing food for individual consumers, and to cooperative restaurants).[23] He insisted that competition was good for workers because it lowered the prices of goods, thus increasing the real value of their wages.

That said, Mill thought that an ideal society would contain far fewer "middle-men"; he writes about competition being a "friendly rivalry" (i.e., "Who can do most for the common good[?]"[24]), and that it is not impossible that we would work out how to trade at cost price between cooperatives, thus preserving the advantages of specialization while eradicating a profit motive (which, when it involves the desire to unfairly benefit from the needs of others, is not in line with fraternity or relational equality). Moreover, in a cooperative future, cooperatives might compete with one another for the best labour, but there would not be the same sense of workers competing with one another for *any* work, at *any* price, as there is under capitalism (which eradicates many of the socialist concerns with competition for which Mill had sympathy).

Lastly, there would be some state provision of goods and services, especially those that tended to monopoly. For Mill, these included utilities, street lighting, sewers, public baths, public health initiatives, communication networks (e.g., – in modern times – telephone and internet), means of communication (such as roads, canals, and railways),[25] the coining and printing of money,[26] the provision of schools (though not a monopoly on education) combined with mandating that all be educated,[27] local and national provision of parks and wildernesses,[28] and the funding of endeavours of public benefit such as geographical exploration and research in the arts and sciences, including "endowments" for "the learned class."[29]

This may seem like a short list, in part because in the contemporary imagination, socialism is generally linked with a "big" state – one that provides welfare support, education, housing, health services, utilities, transport infrastructure and services, and sometimes even employment, besides owning key industries (e.g., resource extraction and large manufacturing concerns). Left-wing people may be dismayed, for instance, not to see Mill advocate a welfare state that includes something like a National Health Service (though his category "public health" might have encompassed much more than the efforts to address pollution and basic sanitation in his own day). In Mill's day, some socialists advocated similar schemes, but not the socialists with whom Mill was most in sympathy. (That said, Mill was not as opposed to state provision as might be supposed by those who see Mill as a classical *laissez-faire* economist, for he distinguished between "authoritative" and "non-authoritative" state interferences, and some of these proposals would have been "non-authoritative."[30])

It was not Mill's view that state provision should encompass the entire economy. Rather, it should provide that which was less efficient, or less expedient, to provide via individual initiative. Industries that did not tend toward monopoly in a competitive market would be populated by competing worker cooperatives. But where industry *did* tend to monopoly, Mill argued that everyone in society should benefit from the monopoly profits rather than some lucky few. Moreover, some vital functions of society and politics, as well as the economy, that were important for well-being (health and education being two obvious candidates) should be provided by the state (at the local or national level, whichever was most expedient). Exactly what state provision would look like, then – as with all of Mill's proposals – came down to expediency and to what people in the future would be "ready" for or think most just. But in the main, Mill remained a decentralized socialist who preferred local, small-scale, communal arrangements to state provision, for such arrangements encouraged independence (as well as equality and fraternity) rather than dependence on the state.

For this reason, I have my doubts that Mill would have supported Scandinavian-style social democracy.[31] I agree with Persky when he argues that

> [I]t is less clear what [Mill's] attitude would be to the type of social democratic/welfare states that emerged in northern Europe after the Second World War. The promise of cooperatives was precisely that the national government would not be required to engage in substantial direct redistribution. Mill was very cautious as to the use of taxation to achieve greater income equality. He hoped workers could reach both prosperity and security without requiring the coercive force of the central government. Thus, Mill was, on the one hand, more radical than the social democrats, since he looked forward to a genuinely new mode of production. Indeed, it is his commitment to worker cooperatives that makes Mill's reform agenda a coherent whole.[32]

But at the same time, I appreciate the point that Mill was an empiricist, and a social scientist, and perhaps if he had seen how such schemes generated utility (coupled with an egalitarian and fraternal social ethos) without necessarily eroding independence, he would have supported them. Moreover, Turner does an excellent job of carefully appraising Mill's view of taxation, showing it was compatible with the kinds of progressive taxation regimes that support today's northern European social democracies (and goes much further than any existing government policy on inheritance).[33] I just think declarations like that are hard to make, because we can't speak for Mill and can't *really* know what he would have made of developments beyond his knowledge or imagination.

That said, I do not think such social democratic schemes are necessarily anti-Millian (or un-Millian), for they encapsulate his secondary principles of security, progress, liberty, equality, and fraternity (though the grass may, perhaps, appear somewhat greener to American eyes on this question). Perhaps more obviously in line with Mill's commitments, however, would be the idea of "community wealth building" that is currently (it seems) gaining traction in both the US and the UK. This is "a local economic development strategy focused on building collaborative, inclusive, sustainable, and democratically controlled local economies" that eschews "traditional economic development through locational tax incentives and public-private partnerships" in favour of "democratic collective ownership of the economy through a range of models. These include worker cooperatives, community land trusts, community development financial institutions, so-called 'anchor' procurement strategies, municipal and local enterprise, and ... public and community banking."[34] In short, and what brings it closer to Mill's ideas than Scandinavian social democracy, "community wealth-building is economic system change, but starting at the local level."

One might think that community wealth-building is not in itself a form of socialism – indeed, one might not think that social democracy is a form of socialism either. My point is only to emphasize that – whatever else he might have come to see as positive – we can most firmly see Mill as having in mind "utopian" or ideal institutions, which would be started at the local, community level, and which would be decentralized, diffusing power as well as ownership of the means of production, and embracing plurality not only of character but of principles of distributive justice.[35]

POLITICAL INSTITUTIONS

Much of the focus of this book has been on economic institutions. In part this is because where Mill talks about socialism and "utopia" he is generally talking about the economy and reforms to industrial relations and property ownership. However, Mill also had strong beliefs about "ideal" political and social institutions, including Parliament, religion, marriage, and the family. These are linked: reform to our industrial organizations would bring about change in people's characters (they would become more "social"); "social" people were necessary for important reforms of political life and institutions (from Parliament through to the family). Similarly, people who experienced equality in the family (and who grew up with equal parents as role models) would be better prepared to labour as equals in the workplace and live as equals in society.

Political Foundations

Mill retained a commitment to universal suffrage and representative government from his earliest years, extending this from national political institutions into worker democracies and the economy itself. He had many worries about the actual workings of modern democracies, particularly their negative impact on individuality – as we see in *On Liberty* and in his reviews of Alexis de Tocqueville's *Democracy in America*[36] – and about the potential for class domination rather than rule in the common interest – as we see, in particular, in *Considerations*.[37] He was concerned to protect individual liberties and an inviolable sphere within which people might freely develop their individuality, but he was *also* very concerned to cultivate a social ethos and individual type of character whereby we would not *want* to prevent others from developing that individuality, and we would be able to direct our vote (and other public-affecting actions) towards the common good.

Mill advocated a wide range of liberties, some aimed at "everyone," some specifically aimed at women, that would help us progress toward an improved state of humanity in which we could both cherish individuality and cherish one another as fellow citizens with whose interests we wished to be in unity – that is, a society in which we could fully experience, and enjoy, "liberty, equality, and fraternity."[38] He identified the movement toward equality between the sexes as a litmus test for social progress, and he recognized that without undermining the fundamental notion of inequality that was at the root of women's subordination to men, relational egalitarianism would never be achieved, nor would meaningful fraternity between the sexes.[39] Thus, achievement of "utopia" involved radical reform of the family, marriage, and all the elements of education (beginning in the earliest years) that gave men an apparently unassailable sense of superiority to one half the human race.[40]

Mill recognized that some steps toward this radical transformation could be taken in his own day by extending political rights to women as well as other rights that at the time were extended only to men. He also also insisted that it was "of course" only if "both sexes participate equally in the rights and in the government of the association" that cooperation could bring about a state of affairs that would be "the nearest approach to social justice, and the most beneficial ordering of industrial affairs for the common good."[41] To truly achieve his "utopia," then, we would need to ensure that there were no "glass ceilings" or other patriarchal structures in cooperatives that prevented women from participating equally in the benefits of combined labour or from freely developing their individuality through their work. Moreover, he recognized the vital importance of women's economic independence and of preventing marriage from being women's only option for respect, security, and self-respect. Thus, put briefly though by no means simply, we would have to dismantle the patriarchy in order to achieve Mill's utopia – and Mill was very aware of that, even if he could not have foreseen exactly what it would entail or how such a transformed society would look (as, perhaps, neither can we, it still being very far distant).

Family life, then, as well as working life, would be radically different in Mill's "utopia" – though he was, as usual, scant on details, preferring not to be prescriptive and perhaps not thinking we could as yet imagine what such relationships would really be like. But in order to be "utopian" and to sustain his "utopia," the family would have to be a "school of genuine moral sentiment" based on a relationship between two equals – that is, a "school of sympathy in equality, of living together in love, without power on one side or obedience on the other," that would forge the characters of citizens who would be fit for equality, and who could freely develop their individuality while also developing "deeply-rooted" aversions to living out of sympathy and unity with their fellow citizens (an extension, in many ways of "living together in love" to social and even economic relations).

In *On Marriage*, Mill outlined a world in which equality and respect meant that people would come together to form partnerships and families based on mutual attraction, and these relationships would be dissolved as soon as one person desired it (with a "cooling off" period, to check that they really meant it before a divorce was granted).[42] Divorce would be "no fault" – it would be enough that at least one partner no longer wished to continue in the partnership. Men would no longer view women as their dependents, inferiors, or property, and women would no longer rely entirely on men for respect, self-respect, and financial security (or on men's continued good favour for access to their children). Mill seems to have thought there might be fewer acrimonious break-ups and perhaps even less jealousy. He sketched a very brief idea of a harmonious future "melded" family or "regulated community of living," in which separated parents lived in the same house, along with their new partners and all their children. Indeed, our very ideas of sexual morality ("chastity" and "promiscuity") would be fundamentally changed, and we would make judgments no longer based on people's marital status, but rather on the quality of their relationships (i.e., whether or not there was "affection").

Governmental Institutions

Regarding governmental institutions, Mill identified his movement toward "Socialism" with a movement away from "Democracy."[43] Although he had more in mind concerning this shift than just political institutions, his movement away from his earlier ideas (echoing, aside from female suffrage, his father's *Essay on Government*) are most evident in *Thoughts on Parliamentary Reform* and *Considerations*, in which Mill advocates what may seem to be anti-democratic institutions such as public, and plural, voting. But this move was not away from a commitment to democracy *per se* (or from the fundamentally democratic concepts of liberty, equality, and fraternity) – it was a movement away from the philosophic-radical beliefs of his youth.

As ideal democratic institutions, Mill envisaged a unicameral legislature with a separate executive, headed by an individual appointed by the legislature (but not necessarily a member of it), who would then appoint his or her own cabinet (also not necessarily from the legislature) and oversee a bureaucracy of skilled experts appointed by competitive examination.[44] The legislature would debate policy, demand that the bureaucracy draft bills, vote on (but not amend) the bills so drafted, and monitor the bureaucracy and executive (whom it would have the power to impeach).[45] At the same time, the executive would monitor the legislature and have the power to dissolve it.[46] There would also be representative local government, as well as workplace democracy, both of which would be important in their own right and provide an important education for participation in national politics.

The specifics of legislative institutions are best understood as Mill's best estimation as to what would best ensure the goals of representative government (i.e., good government). Mill was much more interested in outcomes than in dogmatically sticking to design blueprints in the face of empirical evidence. Local and workplace democracy were more fundamental than his specifics for national institutions (e.g., unicameral legislatures), because the very diffusion of democratic practice, and the educational opportunities it would provide to everyone, were in themselves central elements of good government. He did not offer detailed plans for democratic institutions in the workplace (though he did offer examples of democratically run associations in *Principles*), and he was open to empirical evidence about how best to run industrial enterprises democratically, weighing competing claims of equality, efficiency, democratic education, independence, expertise, and so on.

This brings me to two further – and notorious – elements of Mill's ideal theory of democracy: the public ballot and plural voting. Both, Mill admitted, were "ideal" institutions that might often have to be rejected on the grounds of expediency – we should have secret ballots when there is a likelihood of voter intimidation; we should have "one person, one vote" where it does not seem likely that people will accept good grounds for plural voting[47] (and we should vehemently oppose all plural voting schemes based on *bad* grounds – for instance, property ownership, for these will not achieve the outcomes that justify plural voting in the first place). That said, they *are* fundamental elements of his "ideal" view,[48] and though this has mystified many commentators (because such practices do not easily fit with our views of liberal democracy), they are explainable through proper understanding of Mill's commitments to utility, progress, security, liberty, relational equality, and fraternity.

The Ballot

We tend to view the secret ballot (which Mill refers to as "the Ballot") as a fundamental democratic institution. Yet voting by secret ballot, which was one of the six demands of the Chartists, was not introduced into the UK until 1872 (the year before Mill's death). Mill recognized the expedient claims for the secret ballot in certain circumstances but felt (rightly or wrongly) that such circumstances had already passed in England (even by 1859).[49] His discussions of the ballot show him balancing concerns about individual freedom with those about the common good (and, relatedly, equality and fraternity). Whether or not we agree with his characterization of the need for the secret ballot in his own time (or ours), we can see why Mill would think it unnecessary, and perhaps dangerous, in a socialist future.

"The operation of the Ballot," Mill said, "is, that it enables the voter to give full effect to his own private preferences, whether selfish or disinterested, under no inducement to defer to the opinions or wishes of others, except as these may influence his own."[50] When outside influence is likely to "mislead" the voter, "while, if left to his own preferences, he would vote as he ought," then we ought to have a secret ballot; conversely, "when the voter's own preferences are apt to lead him wrong, but the feeling of responsibility to others may keep him right, not secrecy, but publicity, should be the rule." His argument, then, relies on his idea regarding how we "ought" to vote, and as this is rather different from how many think we "ought" to vote today, we can see how his ideas diverge from modern ones regarding the ballot.

Mill viewed voting as a "public trust." Our vote is not a "right" – on Mill's view of rights – but a "power." This is because a vote is not self-regarding, but other-regarding: what I do with my vote affects everyone in society (myself included). For Mill, rights are things I can rightfully claim from society – for instance, a right to subsistence means I can justifiably claim support from society if I cannot support myself. Once society has legally created a democratic system in which certain classes of people (e.g., all adult citizens) are to have a vote, then, as Mill acknowledged, everyone in that class *does* have "a right ... in the purely legal sense" to vote – that is, this is something we can claim as "ours."[51] But he denied that *anyone* has a *moral right* to the vote. This is not an anti-democratic argument saying we should never have voting or universal suffrage; instead, it is a specific understanding of a "right" as something that belongs to you and can be claimed from society. Mill thinks we do not have that "right," morally speaking, because "no person can have a right ... to power over others: every such power, which he is allowed to posses[s], is morally, in the fullest force of the term, a trust" – that is, it does not "belong" to him, but is something that must be exercised for the common good, just as, when one is a "trustee" for money, one cannot use it to one's own advantage, but must use it only for the advantage of the person whose "trust" it is (be that an individual, a charity, or a fund). And as "the exercise of any political function, either as an elector or as a representative, is a power over others," the vote is a trust. Thus we do not have a "right" to use our power over others; rather, we ought to have immunities from certain kinds of exercises of power over us. Non-democratic regimes almost always illegitimately exercise power over people, and their unrepresentative nature makes it almost impossible to ensure they will use their power in a legitimate way (i.e., as a trust); but democratic regimes can do this, too, unless voters treat their power as a trust. This affects how we ought to use our vote (or exercise this power) and, by extension, the design of voting institutions, which ought not to undermine our ability to use our vote properly.

Mill's example is the contrast between what use I make of my own house (no one's business but my own, and something I could ask society's protection for – e.g., against burglary, invasion, squatters, trespassers) and the decision of a jury.[52] Jurors are supposed to consider not their *own* interests but the guilt or innocence of the accused. It might suit their self-interest to return a swift guilty verdict rather than carefully considering the evidence, so that they can get back to their work, families, hobbies, and so on, but if they were asked why they thought a defendant guilty and they said, "I wanted to be home in time for dinner," we would think they had been derelict in their duty. Voters ought to act like jurors and give their "best and most conscientious opinion of the public good," after paying due attention to the "evidence" given in public debate (and their own private study/knowledge) when they vote.

Electoral politics, for Mill, is not each individual's chance to vote in accordance with his or her interests and preferences, regardless of any other's; and politics is not a struggle between self-interested preferences for power, wielded by a majority whose self-interest coalesces (or by an elite that can persuade enough of a majority that they will accurately represent those interests). Instead, it is each individual's opportunity to express his or her considered opinion as to what would be the public good, and for all individuals to add their small amount of power to one side of the debate, the outcome of which will affect everyone. There can be reasonable disagreement about what *is* in the public good, and this is what political discussion ought to be about. To take one example: there can be reasonable disagreement about expedient tax regimes and how these affect the common good. Arguments that concern fairness of burdens; the efficiency of taxing certain groups more or less than others; the expediency of direct or indirect taxation; where government resources should be focused regarding tax avoiders; and what amount of money governments need to levy by tax in order to meet their spending commitments (and, by extension, what those ought to be), are all the kinds of considerations Mill thought we would be justified in entertaining when determining which party's tax policies we think would best achieve the common good, because our reasoning is concerned with the eventual impact of such policies on the common good. If we choose which candidate or party to support based merely on the idea that we ourselves would like to pay less tax (or, alternatively, that we ourselves would like the government to spend more on things that benefit us, and we're happy to support its tax policies if that's what they achieve), then we are not thinking about the issue in the right kind of way.

Mill linked this ability to use our vote in the right way with "publicity" in two ways. First, if we have to vote publicly, we are more likely to be swayed by a good form of public pressure. This is because, if we have to openly declare our vote (and give reasons for it to interested parties), then we are more likely to vote in the right kind of way (even if we vote for policies or candidates with which others disagree) because of the internal pressure we feel to avoid a difficult discussion regarding a course of action we know we cannot justify with the right kind of reasons (i.e., public-oriented ones). It is also because we would want or feel compelled to copy good examples of voting in the right kind of way. Mill ardently defended people from the pressure of public opinion regarding their self-regarding acts, yet he was happy for public pressure to be brought to bear on our *other*-regarding acts. His thought here seems to have been that it would be harder for me to vote for (for instance) a tax cut for purely self-interested reasons if I had to publicly articulate my choice, and perhaps (as a result) be asked by interested persons (friends, family, loved ones, those who would suffer by my choice through reduced public spending, etc.) to defend my view (and suffer their opprobrium when they realized I had voted for purely selfish reasons). Indeed, this would be a good thing. Again, this has to do not with the *content* of the policy I support, or oppose, but with the *reasons* I have to support it: Mill was not saying there is only one right policy, and all must vote for it, but that there is only one right way of approaching the question of good policy, and all must adopt it. Thus, if I can articulate reasons for supporting a tax cut that are articulated with regard to the public good, others may disagree with my understanding of economics, but they ought not to disapprove of my approach to the general question.

Second, Mill thought we owe reasons to all those people who do not have the same power as we do. Even under conditions of universal suffrage, some will be unable to vote – children, people lacking the necessary mental capacities, non-citizens, people who have the right but are unable to exercise it on the day (perhaps because of illness or absence).[53] When we vote, then, we exercise power over *all* the other people within the same political jurisdiction (and, arguably, far beyond), and we ought to be able to explain our exercise of power over them (even if we cannot adequately justify it, in their eyes). Moreover, the people we exercise power over have a right to know how we have exercised it (or tried to).

The secret ballot "perverts" voters and, by extension, politics and political institutions. It allows them to act like despots. Just as the publicity of their voting record in the legislature keeps legislators honest, and working in the common interest (even where there is reasonable disagreement about what that would be), so the publicity of voting by individual voters keeps them honest, and allows us to live in a democracy and not a tyranny of the majority.

"Publicity" of voting, then, contrary to what we might intuitively think, on Mill's argument, preserves liberty. It prevents power being exercised arbitrarily over us (whether we have the vote or not). Thus, it supports independence (besides requiring some strength of character and independence of mind on the part of voters, particularly those voting for what might not be popular policies, even when approached from the right kind of perspective). It is also connected to fraternity – not only is fraternity concerned with furthering the common good (i.e., everyone's good), but publicity of voting allows us to show that, and know whether, our interests and actions are in harmony with everyone else's. That is, in a properly fraternal future society we should *want* people to know how we voted and that we take their interests into due account (and that we have a "deep-rooted" desire to do just that).

Moreover, publicity of voting has links to relational equality. It helps ensure that we treat people properly (as equals, deserving of equal treatment and consideration, rather than as people of little worth whose interests – even vital interests – we can ride roughshod over in order to achieve even very small personal gains); it also helps us recognize what inequalities exist among us (of citizenship, of expertise, of power), hold those with more power to account, and give us a due sense of the responsibilities of power when we have it to wield.

Given the importance of acting in the common interest both for Mill's view of what an ideal society would be like, and for our chances of progressing toward such an ideal, we can also see that public voting is key for progress. Secret ballots allow for selfish voting and thus for actions that might retard progress. Of course, if men had to publicly justify to their female relations why they did *not* vote for female emancipation, then many (as we see from the contemporary debate) would probably not bat an eyelid, being able to offer what they thought of as arguments against women's suffrage very much rooted in the common good (that women are bad at politics and would make bad decisions, or that women being kept out of politics was good for society in some other way). Publicity, then, was not the *only* guarantee of progressive voting. But Mill thought it was an important step, particularly in the education of voters regarding the right kind of attitude toward their vote.

Lastly, given all these other considerations, we can see why Mill supported publicity of voting on the grounds of maximizing utility – most notably because good government (maximizing utility) necessitates policy aimed at the common good, and this is more likely to be achieved if voters cast their votes with this goal in mind.

On Mill's account, publicity of voting would be even more necessary if we also adopted plural voting. He thought that when some people had even more power than others (e.g., four votes compared to one), it would be even more important that they be able to justify their voting decisions.

Plural Voting

Mill was fundamentally committed to the idea that every adult ought to have a vote: "There ought to be no pariahs in a full-grown and civilized nation; no persons disqualified, except through their own default. Every one is degraded, whether aware of it or not, when other people, without consulting him, take upon themselves unlimited power to regulate his destiny."[54] Again, the language of "pariahs" and being "degraded" speaks volumes to his relational egalitarianism. However, Mill also said that "though every one ought to have a voice, that every one should have an equal voice is a totally different proposition."[55] If two people have "a joint interest" and differ in opinion, justice does not demand that their opinions be treated as equally valuable. Superior virtue, or superior knowledge and intelligence, make an opinion "worth more than that of the inferior," "and if the institutions of the country virtually assert that they are of the same value, they assert a thing which is not."

Because of this, those whose opinions are "worth more" ought to have "more" of a say in decision-making, and thus Mill endorsed, as "ideal," plural voting:

> I do not propose the plurality as a thing in itself undesirable, which, like the exclusion of part of the community from the suffrage, may be temporarily tolerated while necessary to prevent greater evils. I do not look upon equal voting as among the things which are good in themselves, provided they can be guarded against inconveniences. I look upon it as only a relative good; less objectionable than inequality of privilege grounded on irrelevant or adventitious circumstances, but in principle wrong, because recognising a wrong standard, and exercising a bad influence on the voter's mind. It is not useful, but hurtful, that the constitution of the country should declare ignorance to be entitled to as much political power as knowledge.[56]

Mill did not think this was in tension with democracy or with his core aims of security, progress, liberty, equality, or fraternity – or, ultimately, utility. Plural votes were not "necessarily invidious to those assign[ed] the lower degrees of influence."[57] Plural votes do not exclude anyone from collective decision-making; they merely give greater power to those with greater capacity. Being denied a voice would rightly leave us feeling "insulted" and "being made a nobody." But only "a fool ... feels offended by the acknowledgment that there are others whose opinion ... is entitled to a greater amount of consideration than his." What is important is that this "superior influence should be assigned on grounds" that those with less influence "can comprehend" and of which they can "perceive the justice."

Sarvasy argues that plural voting is part of Mill's concept of democratic institutions in, and as, "transition" from modern capitalism to socialism.[58] She rightly notes that Mill's emphasis on the need for a literate (and numerate) electorate – and his adoption of the idea of plural voting – arises from his disappointment following the first elections by universal suffrage in France after 1848, which created the presidency of Louis Napoleon (and, shortly afterwards, the end of republicanism in France).[59] That is, he realized there was a tension between his desire for progress and the mechanism he had previously advocated for achieving it – universal suffrage.

Sarvasy is also right to note that Mill thought a "revolution" in the character of the middle *and* working classes would need to occur before progress (and socialism) could be achieved – a need he identified from events after 1848 in France, as well experience from England.[60] Mill realized that class antagonism would endure (and with it the "bad" characters of the working and middle classes) until "a peaceful overturn of the wage labour system" had been achieved (via profit-sharing and cooperation). And "until that process is well under way, class antagonism between labourers and employers will continue to undermine the ability of democratic political institutions to articulate and safeguard a truly collective interest." Hence plural votes, which are intended to at the very least ensure there will be a compromise in discussions within the legislature (and thus enacted laws) between a dominant class interest and the common good. As Sarvasy correctly identifies, balancing of class interests (and a means of amplifying that shared, common interest, which exists between the classes, on Mill's view) would be unnecessary in a socialist future, which Mill defined as a classless one.⁶¹ On her reading, then, plural voting would no longer be necessary to overcome the problem of antagonistic class interests and the fear of the tyranny of a majority class. So it was not part of Mill's "ideal."

Several other authors agree with Sarvasy's reading that plural voting is a "transitional" mechanism, though without situating that "transition" as firmly within a transition between capitalism and socialism.⁶² Yet this is belied by Mill's own words. Apparently alone in Mill scholarship, Dale Miller argues that plural voting is a much more permanent element of Mill's "ideal" view of democracy (and representative government).⁶³ The textual evidence of *Considerations* and *Parliamentary Reform* supports Miller's argument, though Sarvasy is correct that under socialism, there would no longer be class antagonism. Miller argues that Mill has three reasons for supporting plural voting,⁶⁴ in addition to the one about balancing class interests in Parliament and thereby creating a greater chance of achieving the common good. At least two of these other three would still be salient in a classless society.

First, "government will be more effective, or in other words … its decisions will better promote the public interest, if those with more education are given more political power." Second, plural voting "would make a valuable contribution to 'national education,'" teaching people not to think that "ignorance [should] … be entitled to as much political power as knowledge," a view that is encouraged by equal votes.⁶⁵ Third, equal voting is unjust, and plural voting is just.⁶⁶

Miller agrees with his opponents that, when we have transitioned to a society in which labourers "receive a decent education," "whether plural voting is employed or not will make increasingly little difference to political decision-making." In such a society, increasing numbers of workers would, themselves, have plural votes, so plurality would not serve to amplify any particular group of more knowledgeable voices: instead of one-person-one-vote, we might have one-person-four-votes, and plurality itself would not guarantee better decisions.

We might add that, as society transitioned toward Mill's "utopia" of cooperative socialism, more workers would qualify for plural votes through proxies for competence other than formal education. Mill suggested granting one extra vote to "skilled labourers" because their work "requires an exercise of mind and knowledge of some of the laws of external nature"; and three to foremen and superintendents (so long as they had done their jobs competently for at least three years), "whose occupation requires something more of a general culture, and some moral as well as intellectual qualities."[67] Farmers, manufacturers, and traders, whose work "requires a still larger range of ideas and knowledge, and the power of guiding and attending to a great number of various operations at once, should have three or four." Members of professions (such as lawyers, doctors, clergymen, artists, and public functionaries) "ought to have five or six." (There is here, in some of the categories Mill included, a strong connection to the Saint-Simonian idea – and idealizing – of "the industriels" which links back to *Claims* and his ideal regime of individual property.) Under cooperative socialism, more and more people might be able to claim plural votes based on the competencies associated with skill, management, "exercise of mind," and "knowledge of external nature," because of the democratic nature of decision-making. Even if, under socialism, there were only the same number of professionals (and university graduates, and "members of learned societies," who also merit plural votes on Mill's scheme), the opportunity to access such professions would be much more equal, because of the eradication of a middle-class stranglehold on such positions and the education needed to attain them.

It is also worth noting that Mill did not think his suggestions were an exhaustive list, so even if cooperatives did not have "foremen" in the traditional sense, or were not solely concerns set up by "skilled" labourers, there might be other roles that would stand as a proxy for competency. After all, working in a producer cooperative involves some competency in democracy, and in identifying and working toward the common interest, which is what Mill thought warranted more "say" in issues at a national political level. (Indeed, one might read the proxies in *Considerations* – even without considering a transition to socialism – as being meant to award plural votes to professionals, manufacturers, artisans, and other skilled labourers, but not the illiterate peasants who had delivered electoral victory to Louis Napoleon.)

Mill predicted a transition to worker cooperatives (and the eradication of class) and thought this would go hand-in-hand with improved education (formal and moral) among labourers. Given this, Miller writes that "there is good reason to believe that Mill anticipates that both the 'greater competence' and 'class-balancing' arguments for plural voting will eventually lose much of their force – though not necessarily all, since so long as some are more educated than others the greater-competence argument will still have some teeth."[68] Miller adds, however, that the "education" and "justice" arguments did not dissipate under socialism.

I agree with Miller's characterization of the issue, though I emphasize that Mill thought plural votes were warranted not just by (formal) education but also by "superior knowledge and cultivation," which is something rather broader.[69] True, Mill said that "what is important to ascertain is education," and he proposed a system whereby all individuals could present themselves for examinations for the awarding of plural votes. But other proxies were also important, particularly the competencies that could be learned and evidenced in the workplace.[70]

Miller emphasizes that even when a high level of education had been attained by a broad swathe of the population (in both the narrow sense and the wider), there would be a need for ongoing public education of the kind provided by plural voting (not least to educate voters who had recently reached the age threshold for getting any votes at all).[71] That society endorsed plural voting would be an important element of educating children that "everyone is entitled to some influence, but the better and wiser to more than others."[72] Moreover, it would remind citizens with votes (of whatever number) of their duty in regard to casting those votes: the *only* reason people got more than one vote would be that they were deemed "better and wiser" when it came to determining, and voting in accordance with, the common good (i.e., of properly exercising their functions as citizens, whose vote ought to be seen as a trust held for society as a whole).[73]

Under socialism, we might still need this educative element of plural voting, because socialist societies need to educate their members so that they can act in the common good, and plural voting is an important reminder of that. On the other hand, in a really ideal future, *everyone* would have the right character: their sympathies would be "in unity," and they would be motivated to work and act in the common interest, so everyone would have the right kind of "knowledge and cultivation" that warrants plural votes. This is another reason for thinking that, in a socialist future, almost everyone (perhaps only excluding those who have immediately attained their majority and have yet to prove their voting competency) could conceivably have plural votes. However, the institution would still serve an important educational function: it would remind people why competency is important and what justice demands when it comes to voting (always presuming it does not become a "dead dogma," in which case socialist society more generally might be under threat).

This educative purpose might be performed not just by plural votes for members of a representative government (at both local and national level). Given that Mill expected workers, in a socialist future, to elect their own management (and being a manager is a role that would bring with it plural votes in external elections), we might also think that plural votes would form an important part of worker democracy. Indeed, the kind of justice-based claim that Mill made might be easier to comprehend in a worker cooperative, where it would be much clearer that our interests were mutually concerned, than in democratic elections, where electorates are so large it is hard to feel a sense of "unity" with all of one's fellow citizens. Mill was clear that people ought to be able to see the justice of the claim that those with more knowledge and cultivation should have a greater say, and it is plausible to think that this does, in fact, play out in (at least some) workplaces, and might play out in more workplaces that were democratic, where workers trusted in the greater competency and skill of management and thus went along with their decisions. (This is not to say that I think this is how most workers *currently* view management, and where workers *do* so view management in contemporary capitalism, this may be based much more on deference to wealth and existing power than on recognition of competency – a justification Mill would not accept for obedience.[74] But it does not seem impossible to think that worker democracies would elect management based on assessment of competence and would acknowledge that one of the purposes of management is to make decisions in which the "voice" of management has much more weight than the "voice" of workers.)

It is interesting here to note Fourier's ideas regarding peer review of performance and ability. Mill came to greatly admire Fourier's ideas around the time of his transition from "Democracy" as usually understood to something "far beyond Democracy," that is, socialism.[75] On Fourier's view, we would be happy – in a socialist future – to accord greater rewards based on competency, and would fairly judge one another's competencies (and thus remuneration), not feeling ourselves hard done by if our share was smaller than someone else's whom we acknowledged was more competent (or more talented, or had put in more hours). Though Fourier did not think about plural voting, I mention this because it shows how a sense of fairly judging competency, and not seeing inequality grounded on competency as unjust, played a role in Mill's favoured forms of socialism. It is not, therefore, such a stretch to think that he might have envisaged unequal "voice" in worker cooperatives as also being acknowledged by workers themselves as just. And this, in itself, would be an important part of their education, on Mill's view, regarding democratic practice and justice.

This brings me to the question of justice, which is even more solid ground for the idea that Mill retained a notion of plural voting even in his "ideal" understanding of representative government and democracy. Mill was insistent both that justice requires everyone to have a say and that it does *not* require that everyone have an equal say.[76]

The idea that relational egalitarianism demands universal suffrage is hardly controversial. The question is how – given his commitment to a relational form of egalitarianism – Mill could defend plural votes on the grounds of justice. One might think that Mill merely thought the justice that defends plural voting is something other than egalitarianism. His offering of instrumental reasons for plural votes (regarding protection of interests and promotion of the common good) might suggest that Mill saw two principles that were in tension and that he resolved them through appeal to the Utility Principle: equality is affirmed in that everyone gets a vote, but some other principle of justice or expediency (perhaps utility itself) is also affirmed (or achieved) when some people get more votes.

I suggest, however, that this acknowledgment of superiority in certain fields is in fact a central element of Mill's relational egalitarianism. That is, for Mill, the demand that we treat one another as equals, and see one another fundamentally as equals, also entails a demand that we acknowledge where we are not, in fact, equals. Though there is something fundamentally disrespectful (and wrong) in not recognizing someone's claim to be seen as an equal citizen (that is, it involves not recognizing that person, fundamentally, as a human being), there is *also* (for Mill) something fundamentally disrespectful in not recognizing superiority, be it moral or in some other form.

Mill wrote that "[i]f it is asserted that all persons ought to be equal in every description of right recognised by society, I answer, not until all are equal in worth as human beings. It is the fact, that one person is *not* as good as another; and it is reversing all the rules of rational conduct, to attempt to raise a political fabric on the supposition which is at variance with fact."[77]

Mill had in mind both "moral" qualities and more "technical" ones such as literacy and numeracy, as well as scientific, geographical, historical, political, economic, philosophical, theological, and cultural knowledge, so long as this had really been "digested" and the individual had "exercised his own mind, or derived an original thought from his own observation, experience or reasoning." He concluded: "There is no one who, in any matter which concerns himself, would not rather have his affairs managed by a person of greater knowledge and intelligence, than by one of less. There is no one who, if he was obliged to confide his interest jointly to both, would not desire to give a more potential voice to the more educated and more cultivated of the two."

Where Mill said that some people are morally superior to others, he did not mean that this made them "more" of a person than other people or that their interests should have greater weight in a utility calculus (though his language of "rights" can make the modern reader think he does – we should remember, though, the specific meaning of "right" for Mill). Instead he meant what we do indeed recognize in other people – that some are more virtuous than others (and than us); that some are kinder, braver, more generous, more conscientious, more competent, more intelligent, more capable, more practical, more loyal, more steadfast, more honest. That someone is less honest (or brave, or kind, or true, etc.) than another does not mean (on Mill's view) that we would thereby be justified in riding roughshod over their interests. Similarly, we do recognize expertise in certain fields, and often (if not always) do prefer to place our interests in the hands of those whom we see as having greater knowledge (doctors, nurses, financial advisers, lawyers, teachers, counsellors, mechanics, plumbers, electricians, chefs, train drivers, taxi drivers, bus drivers, estate agents, booking agents, travel agents, restaurant reviewers, theatre and film critics, the writers of *Which?* Magazine, etc.). His claim was that we acknowledge, in our daily lives (and, on his view, rightly so) that sometimes people are "worth" more than we are (or are more "worthy" of respect, reward, recognition, etc., than we are), and in certain situations – particularly where our joint interests are concerned – we do, and should, listen to their opinion and treat it as more weighty than our own. To not do so is to disrespect them as persons, and to not have "unity of interests" but instead wrongly try to impose on them.

As an example, imagine a case from Mill's own work – that of working people clubbing together to found a workers' cooperative. Everyone saves up some of their earnings, and eventually – let us imagine – there is enough capital to pay the rent on a suitable building and buy the necessary equipment. All of the founding partners should have a say in how the money is spent (which premises, what equipment), but it is not impossible to think that, as members of this initial committee, we might defer to people with better knowledge and understanding and give their opinions greater weight. This might be knowledge based on research into the success (or otherwise) of other businesses in the surrounding area, the proximity of competitors, and so on – that is, I might trust someone who I thought generally did good research and understood the relevant issues when they said one location would be better than another. Similarly, it might be more situated knowledge – I might defer to the opinion of someone who has experience with using the kinds of machines we are considering buying regarding their quality, usefulness, and whether we are being offered a good price. The decision would have to at least involve a majority, but in the decision-making some voices might well have more weight than others – a weight that Mill's idea about plural voting institutionalizes. But the underlying idea is already there – that some people's opinions, on certain topics, are worth more than others. (It is important to note, of course, that one person's opinion might be more weighty in some areas and much less weighty in others: one person, for instance, might be very trustworthy on good places to dine out in their home city but not at all trustworthy on where to invest money.)

Mill's view was that this should be extended to politics – or at least to voting – because when we vote, we are exercising power over other people, and people who are better qualified to do that should have more power than those who are less qualified. (And where everyone is qualified to wield *at least some* power by virtue of being an adult human being who is a member of this society.) Plural voting does not give people more weight regarding consideration of their interests, but it does give them (fractionally) more power. We might have concerns about inequalities of power, but power inequalities are not necessarily bad, and Mill thought that competency justified (some) inequalities. Moreover, he thought it was important that we recognize that as a society, in order to actually make collective decisions aimed at the common good (and not just what ill-informed mass opinion has been tricked into thinking is the common good).

I am not arguing that Mill was right in this. Perhaps politics is just a different kind of "shared interest" to family life, friendship, or joint business endeavours. Perhaps the fact that I would listen to my doctor's advice and often treat it as more "weighty" than my own inclinations does not mean I should accede more "weight" to an expert in – say – foreign policy or economics when it comes to voting. Or perhaps the issue is with translating the role of "adviser" into plural *votes* so that their voice becomes two, three, four, five, even six times "louder" than mine in public decision-making.

Many of the qualms we have about plural votes are based on concerns about abuse (and particularly disenfranchisement). Mill was aware of this problem,[78] and we ought not to ascribe to him a simplistic view that would be easily manipulated by a powerful (usually propertied, but perhaps also racial or gendered) elite. He was very clear that plural voting was not an experiment for which the world was ready.[79] Also, it is worth remembering that plural voting has to be grounded in reasons that those with *fewer* votes (or only one vote) "can comprehend, and ... [are] able to perceive the justice" of.[80] Again, this is an important element of Mill's relational egalitarianism, where we need to give one another justifications that others can accept. Though certainly "elitist," Mill's view of plural voting is not vulnerable to many of the egalitarian critiques made of elitism.

Some concerns are more fundamental. A different view of equality would see this kind of unequal voting power as fundamentally problematic. This might be because of another disagreement with Mill – specifically, his view that voting is not a right but a trust, as well as an exercise of power over other people (from which at least the instrumental concerns about competence grow). Or of a disagreement that politics should be directed toward a common good and ought not to be merely a fight between different vested interests, leading to majority rule.

Urbinati argues that contrary to what Mill believed, the mere existence of plural voting would undermine self-respect and cause resentment, being a humiliation for those who did not get the maximum number of plural votes.[81] It would signal, she feels, a lack of due consideration. Baccarini and Ivanković add that though it might not lead to a loss of self-respect, it would lead to mass disengagement with politics on the part of those deemed less competent.[82] In this way, they argue, Mill would be defeating his own educational purpose.

These points raise very fundamental questions about the nature of equality, the purpose of voting, and the nature of democracy. My goal is not to show that Mill was right, but only to reconstruct his view (his socialism) as accurately as possible. Reading Mill's writing on the "ideal" form of representative government, we have to acknowledge that he thought it was a fundamental requirement of justice that we have "universal, but graduated suffrage."[83] I am suggesting that he saw recognition of other people's competencies (inferior and superior) as well as our own as an important element of "living together as equals,"[84] and of relational equality and fraternity. His argument is that, in an ideal world, we would see it as dominating others if we insisted on an equal say (so long as we had *some* say) when it was evident that other people knew better than us what ought to be done. We would, on Mill's view, be "a particular kind of fool" to insist on this – more specifically, we would be unable to acknowledge our own lack of expertise in the face of experts, insisting as we do that our opinion weighs as heavily, and is just as valid, as that of those experts. We would be motivated by a desire to dominate, arrogance, or a sense of wounded *amore propre*, none of which are desirable in public life. Our social role instead requires trust (in experts and in other people generally) and a combination of humility and proper pride when it comes to our own competencies.

Mill's view is not in tension with his egalitarian commitments, because he does not see it as fundamentally undermining relational equality, but rather bolstering it. Indeed, plural voting may be a specific example of "from each according to their capacities, to each according to their needs," because Mill does not think you are "given" a vote; rather, you are asked to take up the burden, to the best of your capacities, of responsibly exercising power over others. It is also not in tension with his commitment to "the free development of individuality" in that he would argue that oppression of individuality is much more likely in a society with equal votes (where everyone's opinion is treated as equally good – even when those opinions are oppressive – and where decisions are not as likely to be taken in the common interest, which, for Mill, *always* involves people's ability to freely develop their individuality). Moreover, for Mill, voting is decidedly *not* a self-regarding act, but an other-regarding one (and thus people's use of their vote is within the purview of the harm principle, while individual liberties have not been curtailed, so long as everyone gets at least one vote). Similarly, for Mill, plural voting ensures both security and progress and is not in tension with his understanding of fraternity. Fraternal relations might well involve the recognition of higher competencies. Moreover, if we really did have a deeply rooted horror of acting in a way that was not in unity with other people's interest, we could not want to insist on our voice carrying equal weight with theirs on matters of joint interest where we recognize that they might know more than us about the issue, and make a better decision.

The Religion of Humanity

Mill believed that religion was an important element of social order and cohesion.[85] It helped sustain the belief system of an organic age, and it also played a vital role in creating individual character. However, he could not put his faith in Christianity (or, indeed, any other established religion), "never having believed in God, even as a child," and having been brought up in an intensely anti-religious atmosphere by his father and Bentham, who shared the Enlightenment anti-clericalism of the French Revolution.[86] He had deep respect for the character of Jesus as recorded in the Gospels and for the Christian ideal of "doing unto others as you would have done to you";[87] but at the same time, he had a deep respect for non-Christian figures (for instance, Socrates and Marcus Aurelius).[88] His ideas about a new religion, of humanity, were influenced by his contact with the Saint-Simonians.

Mill was attracted by the Saint-Simonians' recognition of religion as a "necessity ... for the maintenance of the social order,"[89] even while they rejected contemporary religion and sought to replace it with something based, not on propitiation of an all-powerful deity, or hope for reward (and life) after death, but instead "on purely human principles," with "the ideas of good and evil, or virtue and vice" being "establish[ed] in an earthly manner" on the principle "seek the conduct which can bring the greatest happiness on earth."[90] It is obvious how this *Nouvelle Christianitie* chimed with Mill's utilitarianism, and thus unsurprising that from Mill's earliest contact with the Saint-Simonians, he revealed a commitment to what he called "The Religion of Humanity," which he felt could perform all the good functions of religion without the negative ones.[91]

Toward the end of his life, Mill conceived of a theist religion that would allow a belief in a Being who had created the world but that posited (as the world around us proved) that this Being, although entirely good, was not all-powerful (and previously, Mill may not even have had room in his beliefs for such a circumscribed deity).[92] Religion, then, was about helping this Being to achieve good on earth (which was beyond the Being's power), in the face of evil; and, as people were not to rely on the aid of this Being, nor on a reward from it in some eternal afterlife, this was, as Mill puts it, a "purely human religion ... the Religion of Humanity."

Mill described the function of this religion as being to add "[t]o the other inducements for cultivating a religious devotion to the welfare of our fellow creatures as an obligatory limit to every selfish aim, and an end for the direct promotion of which no sacrifice can be too great," by giving us a "feeling that in making this the rule of our life, we may be co-operating with the unseen Being to whom we owe all that is enjoyable in life." It is important to note that Mill thought there were "other inducements," but he recognized the significant "animating and invigorating" value of seeing oneself as participating – in however small a way – in a ongoing (perhaps eternal) battle between good and evil. That such a Religion of Humanity "is destined ... to be the religion of the Future" he could not "entertain a doubt."

This is not to say that he thought there would be churches (as in August Comte's Positivist religion). Nor would such a "religion" be Established (like the Church of England), and Mill could presumably endorse a variety of different sects, so long as the basic purpose of these secular "religions" was the same, and the benefits they created for society similar. Similarly, there need not be religious services, festivals, or rites. We might observe here that many religious festivals (like Christmas) have already been adopted by secular people (and not just by commercial business) as a "religious" time in Mill's terminology: a time for reflection, and thankfulness, and family, and a commitment to – broadly speaking – aiding the good in the world rather than the bad. To this we might add other national holidays (Independence Days, Thanksgiving, Bank Holidays, May Day, and so on) that have served something of the same purpose, never mind other events that bring large swaths of the nation together – the Olympics, the FA Cup Final, the Derby, the Super Bowl, the final episode (or so the story goes) of *The Fugitive*. Certainly, Mill flagged an important element in creating the social "glue" that "sticks society together" and that enables us to feel a sense of community with our fellow citizens.

Mill's clerisy, then, would be a learned and poetic class intended to help people pursue the Religion of Humanity – that is, intended to help them serve Humanity through feeling a duty to ensure the welfare of our fellow humans; to help them through example (if nothing else) in their own free development of their individuality; to further social progress (of "good" against "evil"); and to help us all have that deep-rooted horror of not having unity of interests – a unity that was, for Mill, at the root of fraternal social relations. The institution of such a clerisy, and such a religious ethic, would, Mill felt, be conducive to the achievement of human happiness, and, indeed, one might say, was necessary to it.

CONCLUSION: MILL'S UTOPIA

Mill's utopia, as evidenced in *Principles, Considerations, Subjection, Autobiography*, and *Three Essays on Religion* (among other works) is a vision of a society transformed by a gradual, organic process into one in which as much of security, progress, liberty, equality, fraternity, and utility as can ever be achieved, would be. This involves a mix of state and cooperative ownership of the means of production, as well as provision of goods and services (perhaps with some other socialist experiments alongside, such as Fourierist phalanxes). Property is communally owned, and production done on the common account. This impacts what we make (only what we need and want, not what we think we can push onto the market), how we view our labour (as contributing to the social costs of our own existence, and as working for others, which we see as a good in itself), and how long we work for (when we make less, having abandoned the endless pursuit of profit and growth, we have more leisure time). Distribution is simplified, and middlemen are cut out, through consumer cooperation. There is no "leisured class" save those who have retired after having done their share of labour. Society provides for those who are unable to work. We do not see work as something bad, which we want to try and finish as soon as possible, but as a positive element in our lives that, even when disagreeable, allows us to discharge our social duties.

New modes of production (cooperation) allow us to be free, and to freely develop our individuality, at work as well as in our leisure time. Cooperatives are democratically organized; there is no contrariety of interests between employer and employee; no exploited labour; and no incomprehensible edicts from "management" that exercise power over our daily lives, into which we have no input and over which we have no say. The division of the product of our joint labour is determined by principles of justice we all acknowledge. These may vary among cooperatives depending on people's view of justice (and the progress of their character toward eradicating selfishness). As we approach an "ideal," both cooperatives and the state will adopt the principle of "from each according to their capacities, to each according to their needs." Cooperatives (and people within them) interact in a spirit of "friendly rivalry," spurring one another on to do the most for the common good. The eradication of a labour market and a profit motive means that the bad elements of competition have been eradicated as well.

There is meaningful equality between the sexes, and fraternity among all people in the home, in the workplace, and in society more broadly. Our ideas of "good" relationships, sexual morality, and the bases of individual worth have been transformed. We do not work just for ourselves and our immediate families, but for everyone, and we would not accept benefits that significantly disadvantaged anyone. A combination of reforms to property and to personal relationships means we have eradicated inequalities of wealth as well as patriarchy, racism, and other forms of structural oppression. The family has been be transformed from a site of oppression and school of inequality into a school of virtue for parents and children alike.

We value our own ability to freely develop our individuality, and we cherish it in others. Out of our respect for liberty, our egalitarianism, and our fraternity, we do not try to prevent others from exercising their individuality (unless they are causing harm to others), and we celebrate difference, genius, and human excellence as part of a Religion of Humanity. We see our lives as playing a part in a general struggle between good and evil, and we endeavour to do our part on the side of good, aiming to improve (and preserve) the world for future generations.

Political decision-making is done in the common interest. Voting is recognized as a trust, as an exercise of power over others, and though we all recognize our right to contribute to decision-making, we acknowledge that the superior skill, knowledge, or capacity of others may mean they deserve a weightier say than us. We are willing, and able, to give reasons that are publicly acceptable for how we voted, including via voting publicly (and those reasons have to do with the public good, about which there may be reasonable disagreement).

Most fundamentally, our institutions are designed to secure and promote security, progress, liberty, equality, fraternity, and – ultimately – utility.

I agree with Joseph Persky when he writes that Mill's "radical writings" are coherent and that "Mill's radicalism is made of whole cloth."[93] In this chapter I have tried to show how broad this cloth is and that Mill's "radicalism" goes well beyond his economics (which are the focus of Persky's book). Mill's "Socialism" is not an aberration but the organic result of his basic radical principles.

Persky suggests that in many ways, "Mill's Vision" is more attractive for the modern reader (and superior in some other ways) than Marx's,

Keynes's, and Rawls's. Mill avoids the "images of repressive discipline" "conjured" by Marx (or at least Marxists); the paternalistic elitism of Keynes; and the inability to grapple with the material conditions of history of Rawls. Mill was aware of the "vast opportunities opened by the industrial revolution," and his "agenda [was] sensitive to the working classes' widening demand for independence."

I agree with this summary of why "Mill's Vision" might be attractive to radicals today, though I would add – which should also increase the attractiveness of Mill's utopia – that Mill was also very aware of the environmental and social perils associated with the Industrial Revolution and the relentless pursuit of "growth" (which he saw as being understood simply as increasing production in order to keep the rate of profit from falling). Mill did not see "Utopia" in the domination of nature by humanity – rather, he saw the preservation of nature and the eradication of poverty and want as compatible goals to be strived for via better systems of economic, political, and social organization and distribution. He was also far more deeply, and radically, committed to gender equality and the reconstruction of the family than any of the other "Fathers" of modern radicalism named by Persky, and he did not have a view of an egalitarian future that, when one scratches the surface, was indeed only committed to the equality and brotherhood of men. He also took more seriously than some more "liberal" radicals the question of fraternity, which he saw as necessary for sustainable egalitarianism. This is intimately linked to his emphasis (also noted by Persky) not only on fairly *remunerated* work, but also on *meaningful* work, which would involve democratizing the economy and giving workers much more control over their working lives, their conditions of labour, and the products they produced.

As Persky also rightly notes, Mill (as with other radicals) exposed how *laissez-faire* capitalism "is a transitional mode, useful for laying a foundation but unattractive for any number of reasons" as "the last word" in social transformation[94] or "the ultimate result of human progress."[95] His entire "utopia" was a serious attempt to grapple with the facts of capitalism (and particularly the falling rate of profit), which our own generation today also needs earnestly and immediately to grapple with. Indeed, the pursuit of postponing the arrival of "the stationary state" is behind much of the existing globalization of the market, with the attendant production of carbon emissions, and climate change caused by human activity. Mill's utopian vision of an essentially *local* economy, democratically organized by worker citizens who are nonetheless cosmopolitan in their outlook and in their sense of moral obligations, has much to offer modern radicals who want to alleviate the consequences of climate change and prevent further global temperature rises but who also want to retain some of the positive elements of globalization rather than return to nationalism and even parochialism. Mill's ideal of a "unity of interests" among all of humanity might seem an impossible goal, but something at least approximating it is necessary to eradicate contemporary crises such as labour exploitation, sexual exploitation, modern slavery, human trafficking, gender-based violence, homelessness, poverty, pandemics, and climate change.

Persky is also correct to say that a key element of Mill's favoured mode of reform is cooperation, along with reform to inheritance in order to democratize and diffuse property ownership.[96] I noted how what Mill calls "the régime of individual property ... as it might be made" in the old world was akin to modern ideas regarding "property-owning democracy." Mill's ideas for such a regime, then, may be a useful resource for more modern theorists of this form of left-liberalism. But Mill's utopia offers many other resources, not only to left-liberals (particularly in his relational egalitarianism) but also to people interested in what Rawls terms "liberal socialism."[97] I think there are fewer resources in Mill for proponents of social democracy, but there could be many resources in his work for proponents of "community wealth-building" and other attempts to liberate and democratize the economy.

Mill's utopia, then is remarkably salient for modern times – indeed, in many respects it is remarkably modern. As Persky also rightly notes "[t]he claim is not that Mill had the full answer either for his time or for ours."[98] Instead, the claim – aimed perhaps most squarely at

Mill scholars, and at other academics and activists likely to dismiss the idea of Mill's socialism – is that Mill's socialism is coherent and is an organic outcome of his core commitments to happiness, security, progress, liberty, equality, and fraternity. A separate claim – aimed at modern activists – is that many of Mill's proposals are still worth considering seriously. He is more radical not only than many people suspect, but also than many "radicals." Importantly, he focuses on the individual, not only in terms of ensuring that people are not oppressed under a socialist "tyranny of society" (a concern I think many people still have with the term, and, which, as Mill puts it, "most Socialists systems are supposed to involve"[99]), but also in terms of it being individuals who will have to make change, and make it sustainable. This means that Mill rightly eschews dramatic seizures of power and the transformation of the whole fabric of society in an instant by the state in a revolution, and also that he rightly emphasizes that liberty and equality are not enough to sustain themselves – or progress, security, and (ultimately) happiness – without fraternity, and without a radical transformation of human character, which in itself is not impossible, but which will take perhaps generations to achieve.

This does not mean that Mill's utopia is irrelevant, or so far distant as to be meaningless. Instead, Mill uses the metaphor of the "North Star": we ought to *use* the ideal, or our sense of what society *ought* to be progressing towards, to inform our everyday policy changes and even our own individual choices regarding the extent to which we have control over our own characters and circumstances. (Not least, how we educate our children.) This is a view criticized by some non-ideal theorists such as Gerald Gaus, who think the "ideal" is not useful – is indeed harmful – for determining immediate policy actions.[100] But this view of "utopia" is not necessarily correct, as David Estlund rightly points out.[101] If we do not take utopia seriously, then there is a significant risk that we will never progress at all, and there is a real need, in our particular climate, for radical answers to contemporary questions. In this regard, Mill's utopia has much to offer.

CONCLUSION

[T]he moral objection to competition, as arming one human being against another, making the good of each depend on evil to others, making all who have anything to gain or lose, live as in the midst of enemies, by no means deserves the disdain with which it is treated by some of the adversaries of socialism ... Socialism, as long as it attacks the existing individualism, is easily triumphant.[1]

In Chapter 1, I acknowledged that many people find it hard to take Mill's socialism seriously because we often read him as having been raised by Utilitarians with a radical political agenda that overlapped with many of the core commitments of classical liberals (including free trade, representative government elected by universal suffrage, and freedom of speech), and ending up as a Liberal MP and author of *On Liberty*. As I noted at the start, there seems to have been very little room, or opportunity, for Mill to become a socialist. In that chapter, I explored how his "crisis" led him not so much to reject the basic tenets of the political program for which he had practically been bred as the standard-bearer, as to no longer see them as anything more than "merely provisional," necessary reforms – vital steps, it is true, but steps nonetheless on the road to something better.[2] In his own words, he saw them as no longer the "*dernier mot*" (last word) in social reform, but only as one further step in human progress.[3] In his developing sense of what was possible (and desirable) for future human progress, Mill – again in his own words – became "much less a Democrat" and, instead, "under the general designation of Socialist."[4]

Mill's relationship with a variety of forms of socialism helped him shape and grow his views regarding the "ultimate result of human progress"[5] (interactions with Samuel Taylor Coleridge, Thomas Carlyle, William Thornton, and Arthur Helps also played a role in that they introduced him to a kind of paternalism that he later rejected). In Chapter 2, I detailed Mill's criticisms of *laissez-faire* and contemporary capitalism and laid out his plans for a "reformed" system of individual property – the best that "the régime of individual property ... might be made."[6] In Mill's very brief sketch of this "régime" as it might be made in previously uninhabited lands, we see something akin to left-libertarian ideas regarding ensuring that everyone "starts fair" (including via unequal divisions of the original resources to compensate for disability); a principle of distributive justice based in desert (and potentially entailing strict limits on inheritance to ensure that earned inequalities would not be illegitimately passed on to later generations); and an emphasis on freedom, independence, and reliance on one's own efforts.[7]

Mill spends more time discussing the "régime of individual property ... as it might be made" in the "old world" – that is, from the very non-ideal circumstances in which he and his contemporaries currently found themselves, where property was based almost entirely on conquest and the rule of force, and almost every good thing in life was available only, or mostly, to those with property, while the propertyless worked long hours in poor conditions for remuneration that was apportioned almost directly in an inverse ratio to labour.[8] In contrast, Mill's proposed improvements to "the régime of individual property" involved profit-sharing; limits on inheritance; the break-up of large landholdings via a land tax that might lead to state ownership and much more diffused tenanting of land on long leases, or to much more diffused ownership of land by small landowners; a fairer distribution of the produce of labour, still based on a proportional link between effort and remuneration, with a safety net for the unemployed, old, ill, or infirm; and an improved social ethos in which class antagonisms have been replaced by a sense of partnership. This view has more in common with forms of left-liberalism than with left-libertarianism and might be classed broadly under the idea of "property-owning democracy."[9] There is diffusion of property-owning; much more equality of wealth-holding, and therefore of liberties and opportunities; and a broad range of rights and liberties guaranteed to all. Even here, though, we see Mill's emphasis on social harmony and on "partnership" between employers and employees, as well as his admission that the motivation that justifies proportioning remuneration to labour is a "compromise" between contemporary human selfishness and something more ideal. (This echoes some of G.A. Cohen's concerns regarding the justice and equality of John Rawls's ideal property-owning democracy.[10]) It is for this reason that Mill's "ideal" is not left-liberalism but rather a species of socialism.

In Chapter 3, I explored Mill's knowledge of, engagement with, and criticisms of contemporary socialism in order to get at the root of what he found attractive in socialism as well as where he thought his ideas differed from those of contemporary socialists. There are many more similarities between Mill's views and those of utopian socialists, and cooperative socialists (and even "revolutionary socialists"), than is often supposed. That said, as noted, Mill is neither a Marxist nor, I argue, a utopian socialist (he did not write the right *kind* of "utopia"), and is better thought of as a cooperative socialist (a grouping that is not usefully included under the heading of "utopian").

In Chapter 4, I laid out Mill's key secondary principles and laid out the institutions he favoured as "ideal" or "utopia." I charted his commitment to security, progress, liberty, independence, and "the free development of individuality"; his relational egalitarianism; and his desire for "fraternity" and for people to have a sense of unity between their interests and those of others, all of which formed key secondary principles by which we might achieve maximum utility. In Chapter 5, I extracted from several of Mill's works a sketch of his ideal institutions, including cooperatives, representative government, state provision of some goods and services, a radically restructured and equal family, and a Religion of Humanity. It is this "utopia" that Mill thought of as "best," though he denied he was predicting it *would* come to pass and acknowledged that in the end, these institutions might not be what the "people of the future" would certainly choose. But this does not undermine his own commitment to these principles and institutions as a "North Star" by which we ought to navigate our social reforms. This is what Mill's socialism entailed: a commitment to a socialist "ideal" as a desirable goal for human progress and a commitment to reforming society in light of that ideal, even if progress would necessarily be slow (and involve a variety of reforms that were also attractive to liberals).

Mill himself felt that his core commitments and his preferred institutions put him under "the general designation of Socialist."[11] There is some hesitancy around following Mill in this – and not only among those who deny he had any "real" commitment to socialism. Even Joseph Persky accords Mill's "socialism" only a short "note" in a book entirely dedicated to Mill's "progressive" political economy.[12] As Mill is so famous as a "liberal," there can be some difficulty in conceptualizing even his most radical proposals as "socialist," because the two ideologies are generally seen as being antithetical to each other. (William Stafford expressed the problem well when he asked, "How can a paradigmatic liberal call himself a socialist?"[13]) There is a sense that Mill might have *called* himself a socialist but was not *really* one.

This book has endeavoured to show that Mill was right to think that his mature political theory was "under the general designation of Socialist." The qualifiers "general" – and, elsewhere, "qualified" – are not to be seen as Mill's attempt to show that his commitment was only tentative; rather, they are an acknowledgment that he (or, rather, he and Harriet Taylor) embraced an individual and original form of socialism that differed in significant ways from other existing forms, particularly as regards individuality and competition, but that nonetheless was very much within that school. That is, Mill was qualifying not his socialism but his fit with any of the existing *socialisms*.

Mill was not a Marxist, but one does not have to be a Marxist to be a socialist. Viewing socialism and Marxism as identical does a disservice both to history and to the potential future of socialism – that is, Marxism may be a *form* of socialism, but not all socialisms (or socialists) are Marxist. As we move away from the Cold War and the domination of a particular Leninist/Stalinist reading of Marx in world politics, with luck we are also moving away from that view. But it may also be the case that we are moving away from thinking that there is *any* valid, interesting, or useful content to "socialism," whereas the history of socialism is a rich and varied one, and many forms combine the kind of emphasis on individuality modern readers may find essential in any legitimate or desirable political theory, with a strong emphasis on egalitarianism and fraternity that may also be what many are seeking. That is, Mill's "utopia" may provide an attractive vision to contemporary readers: his nuanced and sophisticated considerations of questions of liberty, equality, fraternity, progress, utility, and the meaning of "good government" may contribute useful ideas to existing contemporary debates in political theory and politics more widely. We may not want to adopt *all* of Mill's preferred institutions, but he paints some attractive pictures of an improved future and raises challenging questions about our existing practices, which ought to give rise to fruitful discussion, and action, in modern times.

Three concerns raised by previous discussion of Mill's socialism remain, and ought to be put to bed as a conclusion to this book. First, the argument that Mill's commitment to socialism, though real, was short-lived – in particular, that though he was a socialist in 1852, he was not one by 1859. Second, the assertion that it was not *Mill* who was the socialist, but Taylor. Again, this leads to the argument that he was not a socialist by 1859 – Taylor died in 1858. And why this emphasis on 1859? Because – of course – it is the year of the publication of *On Liberty*. This leads to the third concern: people resist the idea of Mill's socialism largely because they either cannot believe or do not want to credit that a socialist could have written the foundational textbook of liberalism.

Clearly, these arguments are linked. What is more, they cut to the heart of the debate about Mill's socialism, and – more broadly – the general understanding of what liberalism, and socialism, can be. If these arguments have any weight, then we may not need to take Mill's socialism seriously and can just read him as a liberal, the author of *On*

Liberty and champion of a standard, negative conception of freedom (both personal and economic) or, if we adopt a more Rawlsian view, of some kind of left-liberalism. Similarly, liberals themselves can carry on as usual, founding their philosophy in these readings of Mill, and also need not reconsider their positions in light of his socialist commitments. But if, as I argue, it is *not* right, then not only Mill scholars but also both liberals and socialists ought to re-evaluate how they see Mill, and socialism.

THE LONGEVITY OF MILL'S COMMITMENT TO SOCIALISM

Rather than deny that Mill possibly could have been a socialist, some commentators merely strive to show that though he was *interested* in socialism, his socialism waned after 1852, and he was not a socialist at the important times of his life (such as when he wrote *On Liberty*).[14] Two purported pieces of evidence are generally offered for this view: first, the later changes to the Preface of *Principles*, which omitted the endorsement of socialism Mill made in the 1852 edition; and second, what he wrote in *Chapters on Socialism*.

In *Chapters* Mill appeared to praise socialism in less warm terms than in previous works; indeed, some people have read *Chapters* as plainly antipatheic to socialism, for there Mill wrote: "it seemed desirable to begin the discussion of the Socialist question by these remarks in the abatement of Socialists exaggerations ... The present system is not, as many Socialists believe, hurrying us into a state of general indigence and slavery from which only Socialism can save us."[15] It has been said that *Chapters* presents Mill's "mature" ideas on the subject of socialism – where mature equates to less than warm.[16] Further support for the liberal–socialist–liberal narrative of his philosophy is supposedly found in Mill's caution about the impact of communism on individuality in *Chapters*.[17]

Negative comments about communism, however, have no bearing on the question of Mill's socialism. That Mill was critical of communism, then, provides about as much proof that he was critical of socialism in general, as a dislike of Wagner proves a general dislike of opera.

Despite claims to the contrary,[18] the argument of *Chapters* echoes in many respects that of *Principles*. Mill showed that socialists make out a frightful case against contemporary economic arrangements, although some of what socialists attack, or think they could solve, is due to basic errors in economic understanding of the laws of nature.[19] However, Mill endorsed their attack on the unjust and dreadful nature of contemporary arrangements concerning the laws of distribution.[20] Indeed, Mill was even more eloquent on this subject than in *Principles*, likening the current economic system to a race declared by an evil Roman Emperor in which those "who came hindermost" would be put to death. "[I]t would not be any diminution of the injustice," Mill insisted, "that the strongest or nimblest would ... be certain to escape. The misery and the crime would be that any were put to death at all." It was a "failure of the social arrangements" when there were people who suffered physical privation or moral degradation, or whose needs were not satisfied above a level with "which only brutish creatures can be content." Mill asked for a fair trial of socialism, just as he did in *Principles*.[21]

In what it attacks, then, *Chapters* comes to the same conclusions as *Principles*. What *Chapters* lacks is the positive assessment present in *Principles*. However, *Chapters* also lacks the means to provide us with such an account. It was unfinished at Mill's death, and although it has chapters corresponding to the analysis of socialism offered in *Principles*, it has no chapter corresponding to, for example, "On the Probable Futurity of the Labouring Classes."[22] This chapter was one of the most famous parts of the *Principles* (indeed, in 1853 the Christian Socialist Frederick J. Furnivall was interested in reprinting just that part as a pamphlet for working people, to which Mill agreed); indeed, it forms an important part of Mill's analysis of and commitment to cooperative socialism.[23] It is not unlikely that the finished version of *Chapters* would have contained a similar chapter, though this is speculation.

Mill also insisted in *Chapters* that there would be "no ground for complaint against society if everyone who was willing to undergo a fair share of labour and abstinence could attain a fair share of the fruits."[24] This might be achievable in a much-reformed regime of individual property: but much hangs on what is meant by "fair," and Mill had a transitional view of justice, in which socialist principles were "higher" than capitalist ones (though their expediency was historically contingent). In his *Autobiography*, he sketches a view of what would be "fair" that is definitely socialist.[25]

Moreover, Mill's final edition of *Principles*, published in 1871, contains all the pro-socialist comments of the 1852 edition, apart from in the Preface. Mill was continually revising *Principles*, and if his ideas had changed radically, he could easily have said so. Similarly, Mill revised his *Autobiography* throughout his life but did not take out the declaration of his socialism, nor did he recant it further on in the book. The *Autobiography* and the final edition of *Principles*, both firmly under Mill's editorial aegis, were published shortly before the posthumous, and incomplete, *Chapters*. The weight of the commitment to socialism in the completed *Autobiography* and *Principles* surely outweighs any negative comments to be found in the unfinished *Chapters*, especially when one considers that these negative comments are very similar to ones made in *Principles* that nevertheless did not prevent Mill from considering himself to be some kind of socialist (just not one who misunderstood the fundamental laws of economics).

What, then, should be made of the fact that Mill deleted the socialist commitment he made in the 1852 Preface? First, it will have been noted that I took the assertion that Mill did make a commitment beyond the usual in this Preface for granted when assessing the arguments put forward for Mill's supposed later withdrawal from socialism. Now, however, it is time to look at it more carefully. In the 1852 Preface Mill wrote that he "was far from intending" in previous editions to write anything that could be "understood as a condemnation of Socialism, regarded as an ultimate result of human progress," and went on to say that it appeared to him that "the great end of social improvement should be to fit mankind by cultivation, for a state of society combining the greatest personal freedom with that just distribution of the fruits of labour, which the present laws of property do not profess to aim at."[26] He went on to declare that "the time is ripe for a larger and more rapid extension of association among labourers, than could have been successfully attempted before."

This is an expansion of the 1849 Preface, with the same message. There, Mill had written that "the increased importance which the Socialist controversy has assumed since this work was written [i.e. the events of 1848] has made it desirable to enlarge the chapter which treats of it; the more so, as the objections therein stated to the specific schemes propounded by some Socialists, have been erroneously understood as a general condemnation of all that is commonly included under that name."[27] By which he meant that he was *not* opposed to socialism *per se*, but that he did have some concerns with specific elements of some contemporary socialist schemes. Or, as he put it in 1852, what he wrote in the chapter "On Property" should not be read "as a condemnation of Socialism, regarded as an ultimate result of human progress," but rather as a critique of specific socialist ideas for contemporary reform.

Mill added that a "full appreciation of Socialism, and of the questions which it raises, can only be advantageously attempted in a separate work," something he also alluded to in private correspondence with Taylor, and which – it would seem – they planned to write. (The unfinished *Chapters* is all we have of that separate book.)

Neither Preface says anything different from what Mill declares in the main text of *Principles*. What Mill asserted both in 1849 and (perhaps more explicitly) in 1852 was, first, that there is nothing intrinsically impossible about socialism, but without either better education or very coercive power structures, it may prove impossible to maintain for long periods of time. Second, that what society ought to be aiming at is fairer division of the burdens and benefits of society, where no one may be idle except for those who have earned rest by previous toil, but where no one ought to face the situation, so prevalent in contemporary society, where even the longest and hardest of toil cannot secure the basic necessities of life. Finally, that practical experiments of socialism ought to be made; and that in particular, society is ready for workers' associations to be given a fair trial. This is what Mill continually has to say about socialism. Although he deleted the 1852 (and 1849) Preface from later editions of his *Principles*, he did not delete similar passages from the main text. The content of his Prefaces, then, has little to contribute to a discussion of whether he withdrew from socialism in later life. Perhaps he merely felt that the sections on socialism in the main text of *Principles* were no longer misread as they had been, so these assertions were no longer necessary.

It is true that Mill added to *Principles* in 1852 a line regarding how not being able to exactly foresee how the problems of communism would be solved "does not prove that it may not be the best and the ultimate form of human society." This is deleted from subsequent editions.[28] However, given Mill's differentiation between communism and socialism, this in itself does not show a "falling away" from socialism on his part. Indeed, this deletion may not show much of a change of mind regarding communism at all, for almost a decade later Mill would write that "whenever it ceases to be true that mankind, as a rule, prefer themselves to others, and those nearest to them to those more remote, from that moment Communism is not only practicable, but the only defensible form of society; and will, when that time arrives be assuredly carried into effect. For my own part, not believing in universal selfishness, I have no difficulty in admitting that Communism would even now be practicable among the *elite* of mankind, and may become so among the rest."[29]

Overall, then, although *Chapters* is mainly concerned with laying out socialist critiques of contemporary capitalism, and critiquing socialist ideas, and thus seems at least less pro-socialist than *Principles* (perhaps even anti-socialist at times), we should read that book with Mill's Prefaces to *Principles* in mind, in which criticisms of specific socialist ideas are not meant to be read as opposition to socialism *per se* as the "ultimate" end of human progress. Nor should the deletion of these Prefaces in itself make us think that Mill stopped being a socialist after 1852 (even if he may have become less sanguine about the hopes for socialism after events in France, about which he said "it is terrible to see the cause of legitimate socialism thrown back"[30]). Instead, we should trust Mill's assertion that by the mid- to late 1840s his political views were "under the general designation of Socialist" and be confident that they remained so for the rest of his life – including, of course, when he wrote *On Liberty*.

THE ROLE OF TAYLOR IN MILL'S SOCIALISM

This brings me neatly to the question of the role of Taylor in Mill's socialism, and in the content and development of his ideas more generally (including the authorship of *On Liberty*). Several commentators have laid Mill's interest in socialism squarely at Taylor's feet and consider it to have been solely the product of her influence over him (which is seen as malign).[31] They take seriously Mill's claim that Taylor co-authored at least sections of *Principles* (perhaps even solo-authored them), in particular "On the Probable Futurity," in which cooperative socialism is discussed and endorsed.[32] Yet they do *not* take seriously Mill's claim that Taylor *also* co-authored *On Liberty*.[33] Instead, they see her death as allowing Mill to reassert, or move back to, his original (and true) liberalism. Taylor has thus become a convenient scapegoat for Mill's socialism, whose marriage to Mill (in 1851) coincided with the "height" (as it is seen) of his socialism in the 1852 edition of *Principles*, and whose death (in 1858) leaves *On Liberty* free of socialist taint.

As may be already evident, I do not find this argument persuasive. It relies on a misreading of Mill's socialism; on a misunderstanding of Taylor's own ideas; and on a misinterpretation of their co-authoring relationship.

To echo Mill's Preface to *Principles*: properly exploring, understanding, and explaining their co-authoring relationship would take a separate work. But some things ought to be said to tackle head-on this pervasive "Harriet Taylor myth."[34] It is clear that Mill and his future wife discussed *Principles* a great deal and that they jointly wrote and edited both this and many other of his famous works.[35] It is equally clear, however, that Mill's socialism was not entirely due to Taylor and that it neither immediately nor completely waned at her death.[36] Mill's socialism was an organic product of his commitment to security, progress, liberty, equality, fraternity, and – ultimately – happiness; it is at the very heart of his political philosophy, not an inorganic add-on to one or two chapters of one of his works. It began in the late 1820s (even before he met Taylor, via his connections to Robert Owen, William Thompson, and the Saint-Simonians) and endured long after her death, as shown by his ongoing links with cooperative socialism (including heralding the "Millennium" of cooperation in 1864 in a relatively rare public appearance at a "Great Cooperative Soiree"[37]), land tenure reform, and support for radical changes to, for instance, taxation and inheritance.

Similarly, we should take with a pinch of salt the idea that Taylor was "more" of a socialist than Mill. There is no evidence in Taylor's single-authored texts to suggest she was "more" of a socialist than Mill, and the only evidence for this view relies on a particular reading of their correspondence regarding changes to *Principles* for the second edition, which should be challenged.[38]

Certainly, it seems plausible – from this correspondence – to say that at least in 1849, Taylor thought communism was more feasible, and more immediately available (particularly in France), than it was for Mill; that she thought security of subsistence more likely to make a significant impact on utility than he did; and that she had fewer concerns than him regarding whether communism would make life a "dead-level."[39] Perhaps this makes her more "left-wing" than Mill.

However, three things should be noted. First, it is not clear whether these comments were Taylor's reflective position on communism or ideas she was still working through (with Mill) – if *Principles* represents their *joint* position, then certainly it does not reflect the opinions she seems to have held at the time of this correspondence, and it may well represent her considered opinion on the issue as much as Mill's.

Second, the issues at stake are more empirical than normative: that, for instance, Mill thought communism less *feasible* than Taylor (if true) does not affect his *normative* commitment to socialism. The issue is not that life being a "dead level" might not be a normative problem, it is whether it is likely to become so under communism. Similarly, the issue is not whether communism *if feasible* would be desirable, but the speed at which it might become a feasible option. That is, the differences in opinion are much more about the *means* of instituting social change and do not cast doubt on Mill's commitment to the *ends* (of non-communist socialism).

Third, even if Taylor *was* more left-wing than Mill (endorsing a different end – communism – than him), this does not in itself undermine his own socialism. People can be authentically socialist without that being the fault of their communist partners. Mill differentiates between socialism and communism and states outright that the potential problems of communism do not provide good grounds either for refusing to reform current capitalism, or for taking socialist ideas seriously. (Moreover, Mill was not wholly opposed to communism, particularly as a desirable mode of organizing a future, less-selfish society.)

Further attempts to deny Mill's own commitment to socialism (and view of communism as potentially the "ultimate" end of humanity) are rooted in another assertion founded on this correspondence – that whatever Taylor said went as law for Mill, and her "influence" over him (and his work) in fact amounted to complete control. A few excerpted letters from Mill's side of their lengthy correspondence are flimsy grounds for this assertion (as they are for Taylor being "more" of a socialist), and a closer examination of the evidence that Mill's letters do give offers further reason to doubt this narrative.

In what has been called a "notorious"[40] phrase in this correspondence, Mill said he was sure his opinion would change, for "by thinking sufficiently I should probably come to think the same [as you] – as is almost always the case, I believe *always* when we think long enough."[41] He also expressed "the certainty I feel that I should never long continue of an opinion different from yours on a subject which you have fully considered."[42]

It is undoubtedly true that Mill admired his wife's intellectual capacities, thinking them vastly superior to his own.[43] It is also evident that they discussed ideas, and works, in great depth. Neither of these things, nor what he says in this correspondence, however, are enough to show that his socialism was entirely due to slavish adherence to her will. Most obviously, *Principles* in 1849 – indeed, every edition of that work – contains several objections to communism.[44] Even where the specific point regarding utility and subsistence is admitted in the 1849 edition, Mill immediately adds: "But it is perfectly possible to realise this same advantage in a society grounded on private property; and to this point the tendencies of political speculation are rapidly converging."[45] Moreover, the system of private property has the distinct advantage of securing greater individual freedom and individuality. There is even less evidence that the other concerns raised in the 1849 correspondence had a significant impact on *Principles*. We should, then, treat cautiously the idea that Taylor somehow forced Mill to adopt her own ideas or positions, or that (with or without her desire) he slavishly changed his own position to be in complete harmony with hers.

Lastly, the idea that Mill's socialism was inauthentic relies on a particular reading of the trajectory of his thought, which permits some interest in socialism in the 1840s and 1850s (and, particularly, during his marriage to Taylor), but sees her death as marking a "return" to liberalism, such that Mill was free of her nefarious influence to write *On Liberty*. But this argument reasons backwards: given that *On Liberty* can't have been written by a socialist, and given that Mill wrote *On Liberty*, then Mill can't have been a socialist. As Taylor was dead when *On Liberty* was published, and as she is credited with at least some of the socialist elements of *Principles*, she must have been the socialist, and Mill the liberal.

A much more accurate understanding of their political philosophy, and of their writing relationship, poses an interesting challenge to scholars and also to politicians and citizens: Mill and Taylor were *both* socialists – and they *both* wrote *On Liberty*.

Mill gave a lengthy account of the writing of *On Liberty* in the *Autobiography*, and in the dedication to the essay itself, he credited Taylor with an important role in writing it:[46]

The *Liberty* was more directly and literally our joint production than anything else which bears my name, for there was not a sentence of it that was not several times gone through by us together, turned over in many ways, and carefully weeded of any faults, either in thought or expression, that we detected in it ... With regard to the thoughts, it is difficult to identify any particular part or element as being more hers than all the rest. The whole mode of thinking of which the book was the expression, was emphatically hers. But I also was so thoroughly imbued with it that the same thoughts naturally occurred to us both.[47]

That is, *On Liberty* was jointly written; jointly edited (until Taylor's death); and represented their joint position, developed over a period of many years.

Of course, that is denied by some, who think that if Taylor had managed to give it a final edit, then it would have turned into a piece of socialism, rather than being *the* classic defence of liberty. But that reasoning, again, relies on a misunderstanding of Taylor's role and political philosophy. We find, for instance, in a jointly written manuscript the thought that desirable political reforms should include "complete freedom of speech, printing, public meetings and associations, locomotion, and industry in all its branches,"[48] and from some of her earliest single-authored writings, a principle not unlike the harm principle: "every human being has a right to all *personal* freedom which does not interfere with the happiness of some other."[49] Plus, if we take seriously the idea of Taylor as co-author of *Principles*, then the stirring defences of individuality found there are *also* legitimately to be seen as *her* work (along with Mill's).[50]

These facts, I know, will not convince those with an entrenched conviction that Mill *couldn't* have been a socialist and written *On Liberty*, and that, therefore, if there is anything at all in his claim to be a socialist, it is all due to his wife. But as Mill (and Taylor) put it in *On Liberty*, it is not "pretend[ed]" that "the freedom of enunciating all possible opinions would put an end to the evils of ... philosophical sectarianism. Every truth which men ... are earnest about, is sure to be asserted, inculcated, and in many ways even acted on, as if no other truth existed in the world, or at all events none that could limit or qualify the first ... But it is not the impassioned partisan, it is on the calmer and more disinterested bystander, that this collision of opinions works its salutary effect."[51]

All I hope is that you – the reader – are such a "disinterested bystander" and can accept it as plausible that Taylor's co-authoring with Mill did *not* entail her forcing him to adopt positions that were not organically and authentically *also* his own, and that it is not impossible that *both* could have writen *On Liberty*, despite *both* being socialists.

I know that that is the real challenge, conditioned as we are to see *On Liberty* as the foundational text of liberalism and to see liberalism and socialism not merely as entirely distinct ideologies but as opposites, such that no one who held any "liberal" positions could possibly be a socialist. (Perhaps, in American political language, this is now changing: "liberal" has become synonymous with "socialist" and "communist" and both are equally despised by those on the right; perhaps, too, more Rawlsian left-liberalism has opened up academic scope for a zone of similarity between the two.) I realize that one exciting challenge of recognizing Mill's socialism is to somehow square our own understanding and interpretation of *On Liberty*, liberalism, and socialism with this new knowledge. But in this, I think, lies one of the great opportunities for understanding Mill's socialism. For his view (and Taylor's) denied the need to choose *either* liberty *or* equality, *either* liberty *or* fraternity; it also denied the idea that socialism must go hand-in-hand with oppression, lack of individuality, propaganda, limited opportunities for those who do not toe the Party line, and the forced "re-education" of any whose "eccentricity" and demand for free expression is seen as a challenge to state power. That is quite an old-fashioned view of socialism (though not necessarily any the less prevalent for its age). On a more positive note, Mill's (and Taylor's) socialism encourages us to imagine a society in which not just personal liberties but *all* human interactions, from the economic through the political to the intimate, are reconstituted so as to fully allow for the free development of *everyone*'s individuality. That this is a much more radical program, involving what are still very radical reforms, than Mill's nineteenth-century image might suggest needs recognzing and embracing as we face the challenges of our own future, which will include climate change, pandemics, globalization, and a surge in authoritarian politics around the globe, all of which will make the free development of individuality almost impossible for *anyone* (save, perhaps – predominantly – white men who own large amounts of easily transferable capital).

OUR "PERMANENT INTEREST" IN SOCIALISM AS "PROGRESSIVE BEING[S]"

Attempts to deny Mill's socialism, or to show that his commitment was never long-lived or particularly deep, can be disproved on many grounds, but in the end, they all fail because they mistake the very nature of Mill's political philosophy. His socialism cannot be shown to conflict with any of his core commitments; it cannot be chipped away at, or ignored, as though it were peripheral to his "real" political philosophy; nor can it be blamed on his affection for (or, as some seem to see it, intellectual thrall to) his wife.

Moreover, although Mill evidently had strong liberal credentials, and shared his commitment to liberty with all liberals, and his commitment to equality with liberal-egalitarians, his liberal commitments ought not to be seen as conflicting with his socialism, for Mill's commitment to liberty informed and shaped his commitments to equality and fraternity (and to security, progress, and utility), just as those commitments shaped and informed his concept of liberty. Indeed, we might conceptually regard Mill as a "liberal socialist" in Rawls's terminology.[52]

This becomes particularly apparent when we consider Mill's liberal commitments as they actually were, and do not understand him to have endorsed a sort of shorthand for classical liberalism, including a deontological commitment to rights; *laissez-faire*, free-market economics and a "nightwatchman" state; formal equality only understood as equality before the law, and a very limited kind of equality of opportunity that in practice mainly only means no legal barriers on entry to education and the professions (but takes, for instance, individual poverty to be an acceptable barrier); and a commitment to representative government elected by universal suffrage.

Instead, Mill has in mind a much more radical program of reforms – and utopian vision – where "the free development of individuality" is vital; where this certainly entails many liberties of speech, thought, conscience, and action; but where it *also* entails self-governance in the workplace (via cooperation), reimagination of intepersonal relationships between intimate partners, colleagues, and fellow citizens, redistribution of property, equalization of wealth, and a complex system of democracy founded on equality of respect and recognition of expertise. Certainly, in Mill's preferred future, a young working-class woman of colour could plausibly dream of, and achieve her dream of, becoming a doctor with the help of state funding for her education – something most liberals would also endorse (even if few liberal states can deliver on that promise). But no one would be born expecting to inherit their parents' privately owned multimillion-pound business (or their parents' shares in any such business), entailing no need to work at all. And no one would have to fear precarity, overwork, the need to hold down two or three jobs merely to make ends meet, in-work poverty, or insecurity over their welfare in old age. These are all common features of "liberal" economies (though, of course, many liberals as well as socialists criticize them on the grounds of liberty [and equality]).

Mill goes much further than most liberals: in his ideal there would be no class monopoly on the professions, because there would be no "working class" at all – that is, there would be no class that did not labour, no "class" inherently born to inequality and fewer opportunities than a richer "class" (be that "middle" or "upper"), no "class" bias in quality education in the first place. Moreover, in Mill's ideal, we would have transformed our relationships with one another: it would become as horrific to exploit, dominate, or succeed at the expense of someone else as it currently would be to murder them. No more class warfare between employers seeking to increase "productivity" without increasing payment while workers seek every imaginable means of resisting; no more desire (especially among men) to dominate, lead, order, or control one's sexual partner, no sense that women "owe" men sex, or sexual and emotional services, no in-built belief that males, by virtue of their biology, are inherently better (at everything bar childbearing, childrearing, and domestic work) than females; and any remaining urge to out-perform others channelled into socially beneficial competitions.

This would be a world in which there could be no people sleeping rough on the streets (because of a robust social safety net and the eradication of many of the causes of homelessness, including low wages and high rents) and it would be as impossible to walk by a homeless person (as we all – I am sure – currently do, possibly every time we leave the house) as it would currently be to walk past someone bleeding to death. A world in which domestic violence would be almost unimaginable – much rarer now than murder, and where murder would be nigh-on impossible. Assuredly a world where no one could kneel on another person's neck for nine whole minutes. Where there would be no "contrariety of interests" between managers or employers and workers; no one earning hundreds of times as much as other people in the same organization; no billionaires (or millionaires), and no one living in poverty. A world in which we would have managed to eradicate sexism, racism, xenophobia, homophobia, and even our inner desire to make other people more like us. Instead, we would celebrate and embrace diversity, all the while staunchly denying people the power to harm others (if we could even have that desire in a properly fraternal future), yet also have drawn together through a shared sense of purpose and common interests to endorse, and hold as deep-rootedly as most people hold the proscription against murder, theft, assault or treachery, many shared commitments on matters of fundamental interest and importance which even when trying to achieve our own good in our own way we would be wary of transgressing (and yet remain free).

Mill wrote:

> The *Liberty* is likely to survive longer than anything else that I have written ... because ... it [was] a kind of philosophical text book of a single truth, which the changes progressively taking place in modern society tend to bring out into ever stronger relief: the importance, to man and society, of a large variety in types of character, and of giving full freedom to human nature.[53]

Even in a time of "transition," as Mill described it, during which "the development of new opinions" was generally encouraged, and those opinions received "a much more unprejudiced hearing than they previously met with," the book made a "great impression" and was not everywhere favourably received. But as society moved toward a new "organic" age, it would become more and more salient. In particular, he and Taylor were motivated to speak "lest the inevitable growth of social equality and of the government of public opinion should impose on mankind an oppressive yoke of uniformity in opinion and practice."

I do not want to underplay the "fear" they felt that socialism might – if done wrongly – crush individuality and thereby destroy a key element of utility. I only want to emphasize that they thought that "the free development of individuality" and socialism were compatible and that there were socialist institutions (which real people might really adopt) that made them compatible, including cooperation.

What most people know from *On Liberty* is the "harm" or "liberty principle" (regarding freedom of action), as well as Mill's famous defence of freedom of speech. In Mill's "ideal" world we would not really need the harm principle as a principle governing coercive interference, not because coercive interference would suddenly be permissible, but because the motivations that might allow us – currently – to act in ways that harm people (and therefore necessitate coercive action against us) would be tempered, perhaps even eradicated, by fraternity. If we had fraternal feeling, and a kind of democratic, relational equality, then we would not seek to harm others (and would probably be much more aware of behaviours that currently might be said to unintentionally harm others) – which involves all the ways in which we currently try to curtail or limit the free development of other people's individuality.

In *On Marriage*, Mill sketches an "ideal" ethical character. "Beautiful" characters, he writes, are "the natural objection of admiration and love" and are "induced, by their qualities of mind and heart, to promote by their actions, by all that depends upon their will, the greatest possible happiness of all who are within the sphere of their influence."[54] "If all persons were like these ... morality ... would not exist at all as morality, since morality and inclination would coincide," as such, "it would be idle to prescribe rules for them." Following their own impulses and judgment, "they would find more happiness, and would confer more, than by obeying any moral principles or maxims whatever," as these "cannot possibly be adapted beforehand to every peculiarity of circumstance which can be taken into account by a sound a vigorous intellect worked by a strong will and graded by ... 'an open, loving heart.'" "Where there exists a genuine and strong desire to do that which is most for the happiness of all, general rules are merely aids to prudence, in the choice of means; not peremptory obligations. Let but the desires be right, and the 'imagination lofty and refined' and provided there be disdain of all false seeming, 'to the pure all things are pure.'"

That is, in a truly ideal future, we would not need the harm principle or any other secondary moral principles. By instinct and inclination we would guarantee the kinds of freedoms extolled in *On Liberty* and *Subjection of Women*, and we would treat one another in the kinds of ways praised in *Auguste Comte, Utilitarianism, Autobiography, Three Essays on Religion, Considerations on Representative Government*, and *Principles*.

We may think this vision entirely "utopian" – that people could never "instinctively" be moral but will always need laws, "peremptory" moral rules backed up by the force of something more than inner conscience. And it is not certain that Mill thought we would ever reach the day where this vision was actually reality across the entirety of humanity. But this desire is the natural outcome of Mill's view of the ideal character, and of ethics itself (as he writes in *Utilitarianism*). For such characters would be the result of "the improvement of education" such that "the feeling of unity with our fellow creatures" would be "as deeply rooted in [their] character, and to [their] own consciousness as completely a part of their] nature as the horror of crime is in an ordinarily well-brought up young person."[55] That is, they are the ideal toward which we ought to aim. We may never arrive there, but to the extent that *any* "peremptory" moral laws are a compromise between the contemporary, selfish kind of character and an "ideal," the "liberty principle" is as "merely provisional"[56] as the laws of property.

Mill was politically astute – he knew there would be continued tussles between "authority" and "liberty" and that these were merely being made more diffuse (but no less powerful) by democracy, as public opinion became the oppressive tyrant rather than, as in ancient times, a single man like Dionysus of Syracuse, or the Emperor Tiberius.[57] As he writes in the *Autobiography*, he and Taylor "repudiated with the greatest energy that tyranny of society over the individual which most Socialistic systems are supposed to involve" while also

> look[ing] forward to a time when society will no longer be divided into the idle and the industrious ... when the division of the produce of labour, instead of depending ... on the accident of birth, will be made in concert, on an acknowledged principle of justice; and when it will no longer either be, or by thought to be, impossible for human beings to exert themselves strenuously in procuring benefits which are not to be exclusively their own, but to be shared with the society they belong to. The social problem of the future we considered to be, how to unite the greatest individual liberty of action, with a common ownership

in the raw material of the globe, and an equal participation of all in the benefits of combined labour.[58]

In a socialist future, then, we would have to be alert to oppression and resist it. But Mill also thought that if humanity progressed in the right kind of way, our very desire to oppress others might be tempered, even eradicated. For him, a key element of exerting ourselves strenuously in procuring benefits that were not to be exclusively our own was *not* that this meant the community (or state) could oppress and exploit our goodwill, forcing us to work for others at almost no benefit to ourselves, but that we were motivated not by selfish interests but rather by a genuine sense of caring for others and seeking their happiness. As we freely developed our individuality, then, we would naturally do so in a way that did not oppress or harm those around us – to use Mill's favoured metaphor, humanity would grow like a forest in which the trees, forming their own beautiful and organic shapes, nevertheless never hindered the growth of other trees, and without the need for this to be enforced by pollarding or pruning.

This is not to say that there would not be some compromises: some life choices that are currently viable in our own day (being CEO of a huge company; being a property magnate; marrying an aristocrat; setting up a payday loans company; being a stockbroker; potentially even being self-employed; and certainly being the owner of a small business) would no longer be available. To borrow Robert Nozick's phrase, some capitalist acts between consenting adults would no longer be legal – just as some capitalist acts between consenting adults that were legal in the past would no longer be legal in our day (not least the sale of persons, but also the sale of some drugs that were freely available in Mill's day and are not in our own, or the sale, for instance, of some animal products such as elephant ivory and rhino horn). This would all come about – as Dale Miller rightly notes – via an organic, voluntary, and consensual set of exchanges to which libertarians ought not to be able to object,[59] though no doubt many will object to the idea of *any* capitalistic acts between consenting adults (including, of course, the holding of private property and the founding of private firms) becoming viewed – as on Mill's view they must do – in the same light as any properly brought up young person nowadays views crime.

Mill evidently believed that his preferred form of socialism was compatible with "the free development of individuality," including extensive freedoms of speech, thought, conscience, and action. In a future society made up of people with improved characters, we might not need "peremptory rules" like the harm principle to enforce respect for other people's interests (which include liberty) – not because we would not need liberty, but because we would so fundamentally understand that need that we would no longer try to limit it. Moreover, on Mill's understanding of what was necessary for "the free development of individuality" – which included respect for the need for progress via individuality; personal security and far greater equality of wealth; and the kind of interpersonal relationships generated by relational equality and a sense of fraternity – that development would be maximally aided under socialism. As Marx put it, in a socialist future "we shall have an association, in which the free development of each is the condition for the free development of all."[60] This was also true of Mill's vision of socialism and one of the reasons why he thought it was so desirable a state of affairs. One exciting thing about recognizing Mill's socialism is how it enables us to interpret Marx's adage in a new and much more "liberal" way, rather than seeing it as clouded by the history of state socialism, over the course of which such a promise came to ring hollow (or to sound like "doublethink").

There are several examples of potential "applications" in *On Liberty* that tend to imply that Mill was committed to more traditional "liberal" (i.e., not "socialist") views. He talks, for instance, about competitive job markets, capitalist forms of trade, and limits to government interference.[61] That said, two things ought to be emphasized. First, it is no surprise that Mill's "applications" might refer to existing forms of economic, social, and political institutions (rather than "ideal" forms), because *On Liberty* was intended to have an immediate impact – that is, to help secure an organic age, one that would not be dominated by the tyranny of the majority. Second, when we read what Mill has to say on these topics, we see a position that is not incompatible with his socialism.

Regarding competitive job markets, Mill wrote that people who "win" in these situations do not harm those who do not win.[62] This in itself, however, is not an endorsement of them. Though Mill thought such markets were more efficient than nepotistic appointments (here, he had in mind the civil service reforms and the contemporary battle to have civil servants appointed by merit rather than by their connections[63]), he had reservations about their overall utility. This is not to say that in a socialist future specialized worker cooperatives (for instance, law firms, engineering firms, or medical practices) might not have examinations for applicants to ensure their suitability as members of the cooperative.

Concerning trade, Mill clearly states that "trade is a social act" and thus legitimately subject to social control, and that "the so-called doctrine of Free Trade ... rests on grounds different from, though equally solid with, the principle of individual liberty asserted in this Essay."[64] That is, we might not have one and still have the other. Moreover, in Mill's preferred socialist future there would be no need to restrict trade between cooperatives except for the reasons he endorsed in *On Liberty*, such as to prevent fraud (particularly by adulteration) and to promote sanitation and workers' health and safety. (Though there would be a restriction on non-cooperatives setting up as traders: Mill evidently thought that in a socialist future there would be far fewer "traders" in the sense of middlemen and small shopkeepers, this being a current significant inefficiency of contemporary capitalism.)

Moreover, cooperation might well resolve several of these issues without the need for state-backed enforcement – consumer cooperatives, for instance, were often set up in order to counter adulteration and secure high-quality products (particularly food) for workers. As all members of a consumer co-op would also be the consumers (or purchasers), there would be no incentive to sell adulterated or poor-quality products (or otherwise defraud consumers), because the only people who might profit from such a fraud would also be those consuming those inferior products, who would suffer much more significantly. Similarly, worker management in cooperatives might well lead to higher safety standards, assuming that poor conditions were driven by owners' desire to derive as much profit as possible from their enterprise (i.e., by resisting the implementation of health and safety policies, which would add to their costs). The workers themselves would be conducting a cost–benefit analysis between better working conditions on the one hand, and potentially lower remuneration on the other, and the risks they therefore decided to take would at least be their own rather than imposed on them by employers who did not have to take such risks at all. Lastly, "sanitary precautions" – by which Mill is referring particularly to pollution – might be stronger in a cooperative socialist future, one with proper representative democracy, because the institutions Mill was promoting would seek to avoid the kinds of sinister interests (in Bentham's phrase) that in his time often stood in the way of improvement (interests such as high-pollution private industries like oil, gas, and chemicals). Of course, history shows that state-owned industries also pollute the environment. But Mill's "utopia" would be environmentally aware as well as robustly democratic in ways that would pressure government not to pollute and to take proper "sanitary precautions" in state-owned industries. After all, societies that truly are aimed at the common good and that have institutional mechanisms to ensure they will continue to be cannot really cause significant amounts of pollution (or, in the modern day, be significant carbon emitters), because this would only benefit a (generally rich) minority of the population.

Lastly, what Mill says about government provision of goods and services in *On Liberty* is entirely compatible with that he says in *Principles* about government "interference" and also with his socialism. Mill does think that government has some role to play in providing goods and services (particularly utilities) and that there are justice claims to be made for why industries that tend toward monopoly should be state-owned (so that everyone benefits from the monopoly profits rather than a mere few). But his endorsement of worker cooperatives rather than, for instance, Saint-Simonian or Cabetian forms of state socialism aligns precisely with his view (in *On Liberty* and *Principles*) that in general, people do things better for themselves, and that people's characters are more independent when they are encouraged to be self-reliant by a lack of state provision. Indeed, it is precisely for these reasons that Mill endorsed cooperation, for this would make workers even *more* self-reliant than they would have been under capitalism (and it follows, less reliant on private employers and thus less "passive").

In making his case for individual liberty, Mill noted: "I forego any advantage which could be derived to my argument from the idea of abstract right, as a thing independent of utility. I regard utility as the ultimate appeal on all ethical questions: but it must be utility in its largest sense, grounded on the permanent interests of man as a progressive being. Those interests, I content, authorise the subjection of individual spontaneity to external control, only in respect to those actions of each, which concern the interest of other people."[65]

As a final note on the compatibility of *On Liberty* with socialism, I want to emphasize this idea of "permanent interests ... as a progressive being" – interests that align with the secondary principles explored earlier in this book – that is, with security, progress, liberty, equality, and fraternity. Our permanent interests (as progressive beings) are those that are unchanging and universal. Mill thinks that we *always* have interests in security, progress, liberty, equality, and fraternity (because, ultimately, of how they bring about utility). At different times, some of these interests may have more weight than others. Thus, security might have been more important than liberty in an earlier age of human progress, when – as Mill argues in *On Liberty* – societies needed charismatic, authoritarian, "people-building" leaders like Akbar the Great (1556–1605, unifier and consolidator of the Mughal Empire) or Charlemagne (748–814, who united most of western and central Europe under the Carolingian Empire).[66] Widespread equality might not be feasible at some points in human progress – or at least, not compatible with security and progress. Liberty for everyone is impossible without equality but can also be threatened by it. Hierarchies based on physical might are sometimes necessary for security and progress but are incompatible with real equality and with fraternity. That not all of our interests are equally realizable at different times in human history, however, does not undermine their "permanence" for Mill. We *always* have an interest in having *as much of* these goods as possible and in living in a society that is progressing toward achieving more of them. This will be just as true in the future as it was in the past.

Mill saw human progress as being toward greater security, greater liberty, greater equality, greater fraternity, and therefore greater utility. He recognized that the people in the future will have to determine the exact balance among all of these permanent interests. He also recognized that this balance was not completely predictable from where he himself stood (nor is it today from where we stand). And finally, he recognized that people in the future might progress even beyond what is currently seemed desirable, never mind feasible.

We see this very clearly in Mill's description of his (and Taylor's) socialism:

> The social problem of the future we considered to be, how to unite the greatest individual liberty of action, with a common ownership in the raw material of the globe, and an equal participation of all in the benefits of combined labour. We had not the presumption to suppose that we could already foresee, by what precise form of institutions these objects could most effectually be attained, or at how near or how distant a period they would become practicable. We saw clearly that to render any such social transformation either possible or desirable, an equivalent change of character must take place both in the uncultivated herd who now compose the labouring masses, and in the immense majority of their employers. Both these classes must learn by practice to labour and combine for generous, or at all events

for public and social purposes, and not, as hitherto, solely for narrowly interested ones.[67]

Or, as this might be parsed:

The basic question of achieving maximal utility, we saw to be, how to unite the greatest possible individual liberty, with equality and fraternity and modern modes of production, which are themselves the outcome of progress, and help ensure security (of subsistence). We had not the presumption to suppose we could predict the exact outcome of organic human progress. But we saw clearly that to achieve this transformation, people's characters would need transforming to make them capable of perfect equality and fraternal living.

Or, more briefly,

In order to maximise happiness, we realised we needed to ensure the right kind of socialism. We saw that in order to achieve this, a revolution would have to happen not only in political, economic, and social institutions, but in people's characters.

This remains the great social problem of our own future. How can we achieve human well-being (which entails ensuring planetary well-being)? How can we maximize individual freedom to develop our own personalities, untrammelled by the tyranny of illegitimate social pressure (be that patriarchal, heteronormative, classist, racist, or anything else), while also ensuring that everyone receives a fair share of the burdens and benefits of social cooperation? How can we all be happy, where "all" really means all human beings, and where a central part of that happiness must be the knowledge that others are not paying for our happiness, our freedom, our welfare, our security, through their own suffering and oppression? (How can we really be happy, if we know that *is* what our happiness is predicated upon?)

The challenge Mill and Taylor realized, then, and spent a lifetime trying to help humanity overcome, remains a challenge today. Their preferred solution – gender equality; radical transformation of the family; cooperation and worker democracy; the organic transfer of private property in the means of production into communal ownership (through a mixture of cooperatives and state enterprises, at the local and national levels); an end to large intergenerational transfers of wealth through reform to inheritance; a fair, adequate and secure welfare system; environmental protections, and a cherishing of the environment beyond what it can produce in terms of profit or produce for humans; proportional representation that combines recognition of equal citizenship with similar recognition of unequal expertise; a new civil religion that inspires us to do one another the most good; celebration and cherishing of diversity in a really meaningful fashion right down to the individual level; and a transformation of people's characters such that we would seek unity, not contrariety, of interests with our fellow citizens (perhaps of the world, not just our own country) – is not one that anyone has yet trialled. It offers a different vision of the future, of utopia, and of socialism than any so far experimented with by governments, though some features appear, and reappear, in radical agendas.

FINAL WORDS

For Mill scholars, the aim of this book has been to challenge much of the received wisdom about Mill's commitments; the radical, revolutionary imagination of his utopia; and the plausibility of him calling himself a socialist. For those who might be thought of as more "disinterested bystanders," the idea has been to introduce you to a vision of the future that I think has much to recommend it but that has been forgotten and overlooked by generations of reformers since Mill's *Autobiography* was first published and his self-identification first dismissed. I am not the first, of course, to point out that socialism does not need to be state-centric; that it does not need to be totalitarian or authoritarian (if such systems can even really be called "socialist"); that it does not need to sacrifice individuals, and individuality, to the tyranny of the collective (too often merely an excuse for a new form of tyrannical oppression by an elite). But even among alternatives to the state socialism that dominated vast areas of the world, and of political discourse, in the twentieth century, Mill's socialism is distinctive and unique.

Both his utopia and his plan for reaching it put a lot of emphasis on individuals. Not just in terms of cherishing and championing individuality, but because only individuals working together and taking incremental steps often only made achievable by significant personal sacrifices to transform their political lives, work lives, home lives, and, in the end, personal characters (and those of their children) will achieve Millian socialism. But this is common knowledge among socialists, and indeed among most radical reformers. That we are the only people who can, in the end, save humanity and the world in and on which we live may be a difficult truth to swallow, but that does not make it less true. People make politics, and in the end people will have to make political change. Of course there are strong structures of power that prevent most individual actions from having a significant impact on a global scale, and there are very powerful vested interests that will push back against people-led, grassroots radical activity as hard today as they did in Mill's day.[68] But no extraterrestrial superhero is coming to our aid, and the state in and of itself will not do so either.

Obviously, as I have shown in the preceding chapters, Mill had a deep-rooted commitment to equality that he wanted to see permeate politics, the economy, the family, and even our own sense of self. More than contemporary left-liberals, however, he also understood the need for a radical transformation of interpersonal relationships and individual characters. It is too simplistic to say that exploitation happens because, at root, people do not care enough, because there are complicated power structures that render some people unable to avoid being complicit. (Can any family on the median wage in Europe, for instance, afford to feed itself without buying *some* products that, at some point in the production or supply chain, involve labour exploitation? Can the typical consumer even find out whether products have been made by exploited labour?) But a lack of empathy, a lack of "horror" at our interests not being in unity with others, a lack of fraternal feeling, does make the battle harder to win and the casualty toll higher. It is in Mill's view of transformed interpersonal relationships that I think there is most that is inspiring, radical, and truly transformative. And from that starting point, all his other preferred reforms flow.

Mill, then, recognized and set a formidable challenge for anyone concerned with improving human happiness and ensuring that the future will be better than both the present and the past. He also offers inspiration for the journey and a useful map for planning a campaign of reform. It has been more than one hundred fifty years since Mill decided that his political commitments put him "under the general designation of socialist." It is high time Mill scholars, and political philosophers, recognized the truth of this claim. It is also time to listen to and take inspiration from his vision.

NOTES

Introduction

1. Mill, *Autobiography*, 237–9.
2. Stafford, "Paradigmatic Liberal"; Megill, "Religion of Humanity," 612.
3. Mill, *Autobiography*, 239.
4. Mill, *Principles*, 203.
5. Himmelfarb invented, and remains the leading proponent of, the "two Mills" thesis. Leading "revisionist" scholars, who see Mill's work as cohesive and coherent, include C.L. Ten, Alan Ryan, Wendy Donner, and Jonathan Riley.
6. Winch, *Wealth and Life*, 50–4; Robbins: "Introduction," xxxix, and "The Classical Economics," 142; Flew, "Socialist or Libertarian?," 21; Légé, "Hayek's Reading of Mill," 199, 202; Von Mises, *Liberalism*, 195; Hayek, "Mill at Twenty-Five," xxx; Rees, *Mill's On Liberty*, 7; Schwartz, *New Political Economy*, 190–2; Levy, "Mill's Stationary State," 279; Ekelund and Tollison, "New Political Economy," 215. Although allowing that Mill had some independent interest in socialism, Reeves says it was radicalised and "sharpened" by Taylor. Reeves, *Victorian Firebrand*, 213. This view is also somewhat supported by Millgram's assertion that Taylor declared the outcomes, and Mill "made up" the arguments that would prove them: Millgram, *Meaning of Life*, 73–8, 132.
7. See Mill, *Autobiography*, 253–7.
8. Mill, "Fontana and Prati," 678. See also McCabe, "Navigating by the North Star," 291–309.
9. For more on Mill's logic of persuasion, and the political, persuasive nature of many of his texts, see McCabe, "Mill's Philosophy of Persuasion," 38–61.
10. This stricture mainly applies to non-democratic governments and to capitalists who tried, though strong-arm, cartel tactics, to drive producer cooperatives out of business. But it also applies to "elites" in the working class themselves, who benefited from cooperation but sought to restrict access to those benefits and insisted on employing other workers for wages. This said, Mill is not merely a "referee" in a boxing match

between capitalism and socialism when he makes these criticisms (as William Thomas [*Mill*, 190] argues): *both* groups are trying to stand in the way of progress to benefit their own narrow interests, so both are in the wrong.

11 Mill, *Principles*, 762–5.
12 Mill, *Autobiography*, 175, 239.
13 See Mill, *Principles*, 794.
14 Cf. some of the concerns Skinner raises with earlier exercises in the history of political thought in *Visions of Politics*.
15 Mill, *Autobiography*, 199.
16 Baum, "Liberal Socialism," 100.
17 For instance, Persky's recent book only has a short "Note on Mill's Socialism"; the 2016 *Companion to Mill* has no chapter on socialism; and the entry in the Stanford Encyclopedia on Mill does not mention socialism.
18 Baum, "Economic Freedom," 494–530; Capaldi, "Mill and Socialism," 125–44; Claeys, "Justice, Independence, and Industrial Democracy," 122–47; Davis, "Mill, Socialism, and the English Romantics," 345–58; Feuer, "Mill and Marxian Socialism," 297–304; Fredman and Gordon, "Mill and Socialism," 3–7; Hainds, "Mill and the Saint-Simonians," 103–12; Kurer, "Mill and Utopian Socialism," 222–32; Losman, "Alternative Economic Systems," 84–104; McCabe, "Navigating by the North Star," 291–309; "Mill's 'Modern' Radicalism Re-examined," 147–64; "Mill and Fourierism," 35–61; and "Mill and Socialism," 145–64; Medearis, "Labor, Democracy, Utility," 135–49; Miller, "Mill's 'Socialism,'" 213–38; Persky, "Mill's Socialism Re-examined"; Riley, "Capitalism versus Socialism," 39–71; Sarvasy: "Mill's Socialism," 312–33, and "Mill's Theory of Democracy," 567–87; Stafford, "Paradigmatic Liberal," 325–45; Schapiro, "Pioneer of Liberalism," 127–60.
19 Ashcraft, "Democratic Socialism"; Baum, "Liberal Socialism," 98–123; McCabe, "Mill's Analysis of Capitalism," 8–22; Flew, "Mill: Socialist or Libertarian?"
20 Claeys, *Mill and Paternalism*, 123–72; Duncan, *Marx and Mill*; Himmelfarb, *On Liberty*, 126–39; Hollander, *Economics*, 179; Kurer, *Politics of Progress*, esp. 33–59; Macpherson, *Life and Times*, 44–64; Pankhurst, *Saint-Simonians*; Reeves, *Victorian Firebrand*, 213; Robbins, "Classical Economics and Socialism," 142–68; Schwartz, *New Political Economy*, 165–92; Thomas, *Mill*, 190; and Winch, *Wealth and Life*, 49–53.
21 Sarvasy, "Mill's Socialism," 312.

22 Ibid. Sarvasy is referring in particular to Robbins, Macpherson, Schwartz, Himmelfarb, and Duncan.
23 Schapiro, "Pioneer of Liberalism," 142; Thomas, *Mill*, 190; Samuel Hollander, *Economics*, 179; Losman, "Alternative Economic Systems," 88–92.
24 Stafford, "Paradigmatic Liberal," 330; Baum, "Liberal Socialism," 99; Losman, "Alternative Economic Systems," 96–7.
25 Fredman and Gordon, "Mill and Socialism," 4.
26 Ibid.
27 Schapiro, "Pioneer of Liberalism," 137–8; Riley, "Capitalism versus Socialism," 48; Schwartz, *New Political Economy*, 187–8. For more on Mill's attitude toward revolution see McCabe: "Mill on 'Legitimate' Socialism," and "Mill and the French Revolution."
28 Schapiro, "Pioneer of Liberalism," 127–60; Hainds, "Mill and the Saint-Simonians," 103–12; Fredman and Gordon, "Mill and Socialism," 3–6; Losman, "Alternative Economic Systems," 84–104; Thomas, *Mill*, 190; Kurer, "Mill and Utopian Socialism," 222–32; Winch, *Wealth and Life*, 49–53.
29 Davis, "Mill, Socialism, and the English Romantics," 345–58.
30 Thomas, *Mill*, 190; Hainds, "Mill and the Saint-Simonians," 112; Reeves, *Victorian Firebrand*, 226.
31 Fredman and Gordon, "Mill and Socialism," 3; Riley, "Capitalism versus Socialism," 41; Kurer, "Mill and Utopian Socialism," 299–30; Losman, "Alternative Economic Systems," 99–102.
32 Riley, "Capitalism versus Socialism," 39–71.
33 Miller, "Mill's 'Socialism,'" 213–38.
34 Sarvasy, "Mill's Socialism," 312.
35 Persky, *Political Economy of Progress*, 199–200.
36 Mill, "Fontana and Prati," 678.
37 McCabe, "Navigating by the North Star," 291–309.
38 Mill, *Chapters*, 750. For more on desirability, feasibility, and availability as I am using them here, see McCabe, "Navigating by the North Star," 291–309. See also Persky's view (in "Mill's Socialism Re-examined," 165–80) that Mill's classical economics meant he thought socialism *would* arise naturally out of current economic institutions, and in a short space of time.
39 Skinner, *Visions of Politics*, 57–89.
40 For instance, Duncan, *Marx and Mill*.
41 For instance, see Halliday and McCabe, "Mill on Free Speech," 71–87.
42 Mill, *Autobiography*, 259.

43 Baum, "Liberal Socialism," 100.
44 Claeys, *Mill and Paternalism*, 123–72.
45 Sarvasy: "Mill's Socialism," 312–33, and "Mill's Theory of Democracy," 567–87.
46 Rawls: *Theory of Justice*, 280, and *Justice as Fairness*, 138–40.
47 Baum, "Liberal Socialism," 99–100.
48 Rawls, *Theory of Justice*, 53.
49 Baum, "Liberal Socialism," 99–100.
50 For instance, Nathanson, "Mill on Economic Justice," 161–76.
51 Maria Morales, *"Perfect Equality"*; Persky, *Political Economy of Progress*, 199–216; Turner: "Luck and Distributive Justice," 80–93, and "Evolutionary Theory of Justice," 131–46.
52 Persky, "Mill's Socialism Re-examined," 165–80; McCabe, "Mill's 'Modern' Radicalism Re-examined," 147–64; Turner, "Evolutionary Theory of Justice," 131–46.
53 See Mill, *On Liberty*, 257.
54 Indeed, the words "communist" and "socialist" were neologisms coined within Mill's own lifetime. "Socialist" was first used, in English, in 1827, and a little earlier in France; "communism" originated in the secret societies of France between 1830 and 1848 and was first recorded in English via Owenite periodicals in 1840. See Bestor, "Evolution of the Socialist Vocabulary," 277–8.
55 Marxists too might think Mill's "socialism" only interesting to historians, for without Marx's materialist conception of history, Mill's socialism remains "utopian" in the pejorative sense in which Marx (and Engels) used the word. Persky has recently argued that Mill has a theory of history similar to that of Marx and can be counted as a predecessor by modern Marxists. I think their theories are different in important ways (mainly because Mill's theory is not dialectic), but I agree there are more similarities in their views than many (including Marx) would generally accept. See Persky: *Political Economy of Progress*, 155–68, and "Mill's Socialism Re-examined," 176–9. See also McCabe, "Mill's 'Modern' Radicalism Re-examined," 149.
56 See, for instance, Guinan and O'Neill, *The Case for Community Wealth-Building*; Haagh, *Universal Basic Income*; and Kelly and Howard, *Making of a Democratic Economy*.
57 Berlin, "Two Concepts of Liberty," 118–72.
58 Mill, *Autobiography*, 259.
59 Marx, *German Ideology*, 225. Both Mill and Marx were heavily influenced by German Idealism, as we can see in their ideas of freedom.

60 Marx and Engels, *Communist Manifesto*, 506.
61 Mill, *Principles*, 201–12.
62 Mill, *On Liberty*, 224.

Chapter One

1 Mill, *Autobiography*, 199.
2 Ibid., 41–83.
3 Though a "modified" form, involving plural voting and proportional representation. Mill: *Autobiography*, 199, and *Considerations*, 473–9, 450–67, respectively.
4 Mill: *Subjection*, 270–1; *Considerations* 479–81. See also Mill's proposed amendment to the 1868 Reform Act (to replace "man" with "person"), which would have granted women the vote on the same terms as men.
5 Kinzer, "Introduction," x–xlii; Mill: "Jamaica Committee," 90, and "Disturbances in Jamaica" [1], [2], and [3], 93–5, 105–13, 123.
6 Mill, *Principles*, 936–71.
7 Mill, *Autobiography*, 137.
8 Ibid.
9 Ibid., 199.
10 Ibid., 107; see also Persky, *Political Economy of Progress* on Mill's early, and consistent, radicalism.
11 Which, for Mill and Bentham, though not James Mill, meant votes for women as well as men. Mill, *Autobiography*, 107.
12 Rosen: "Method of Reform," 125, and *Mill*, 50–2; Thompson, *Making of the English Working Class*, 507–8 and 660–1; Niesen, "Roots of Mill's Radicalism," 79–94.
13 I ignore here the debate surrounding whether a utilitarian can "really" be a liberal, and presume, for the sake of argument, that the positions are compatible.
14 Mill, *Autobiography*, 107. Fredman and Gordon, in "Mill and Socialism," 4, argue that Mill's "Malthusianism" prevented him from being a socialist. Malthus's population principle was certainly a bone of contention in the 1825 debates between Mill (as a philosophic-radical) and some Owenites. Mill, "Population: Reply to Thirlwall," 298. And Malthus opposed socialism because he felt that communal property would lead to overpopulation. Malthus, *Principle of Population*, 46–7. However, Mill was "Malthusian" only insofar as he adopted Malthus's population principle; he rejected Malthus's solutions to the problem (infamously, war, famine, and disease; or, alternatively, support for "delayed" marriage).

Malthus: *First Essay*, 139–40, and *Principle of Population*, II, 86. Moreover, though he shared some of Malthus's doubts about communal property and overpopulation, his mature position on this was that communal property might actually be the best way of guaranteeing a small population, for, as everyone would be able to see the difference any additional mouth to feed made to them, public opinion would be very much averse to large families. Mill, *Chapters*, 729. Furthermore, although some Owenites opposed Malthus's population principle (see Mill, "Population," 287–8, and "Population: Reply to Thirlwall," 297), this was not universally the case. Owen, for instance, did not deny that Malthus might be right in principle, but thought him wrong to think that increases in the comforts of the working classes *necessarily* led to an increase in population. Rather, Owen argued that a better-educated and better-organised workforce, especially if "double-digging" were used to improve the fecundity of land, would be able to produce more than enough to feed a larger population. Owen, *New View of Society*, 86. Mill's own solution was smaller families, achieved through contraception (Mill, "Question of Population" [3], 96) and the emancipation of women (Mill, "Co-operation: Closing Speech," 318), which is very similar to the position of Thompson, *Inquiry*, 538, 577; Neale, *Manual for Co-operators*, 150; and Blanc (see Mill, *Chapters*, 728), though Blanc preferred delayed marriage to contraception. More important than this, however, is the fact that Mill's disagreeing with the Owenites in the 1820s on this issue has little bearing on his socialism, for no one suggests Mill was a socialist in the 1820s, nor that he ever became an Owenite (though his own cooperative socialism was evidently influenced by the ideas of later Owenites, like Neale and Holyoake). Moreover, Mill's "Malthusianism" was consistent with the views of a number of Owenite, and other, socialists (including Blanc), and cannot plausibly be said to preclude him from socialism in the period he called himself a socialist (i.e., after c. 1845).

15 Mill, *Autobiography*, 67.
16 Mill, *Subjection*, 261.
17 Morales, "Perfect Equality," 21–48.
18 Mill, "Cooperation: Closing Speech," 314. Mill had probably also met Thompson, who stayed at Bentham's house (next door to the Mill family) on some of his visits to London (see Robson, "Introduction," CW XXVI, xxiin34).
19 Mill, Letter 501, 712–13.
20 James Mill, Letter 2256, 361; Owen, *Life*, 178–9.

21 James Mill, Letter 2256, 361. Bentham, Owen, Allen, and four others bought the mill.
22 "W.E.H.," *Co-operative Magazine*, 56; Mill, *Autobiography*, 127–9.
23 Mill, "Cooperation: Closing Speech," 322–4, 315.
24 Mill: "Co-operation: Intended Speech," 313; "Co-operation: Closing Speech," 319–20; *Principles*, 207.
25 Mill, "Co-operation: Closing Speech," 320–4.
26 Mill, *Autobiography*, 139.
27 See, for instance, Ashcraft, "Democratic Socialism," 170; Bain, *Mill*, 37–8; Carlisle, *Mill and the Writing of Character*, 49–76; Green, "Sympathy and Self-Interest," 259–60; Hamburger, *Intellectuals in Politics*, 100–12; Jones, *Victorian Political Thought*, 27; Millgram, "Mill's Incubus," 169–91, and *Meaning of Life*; Rees, *Mill's On Liberty*, 106; Ryan, *Mill*, 26–40; Stafford, *Mill*, 45; Reeves, *Victorian Firebrand*, 6; Stephen, *English Utilitarians*, 19–23; Thomas, *Philosophical Radicals*, 150–1.
28 Stafford, *Mill*, 45; Mill, *Autobiography*, 199.
29 For instance, Berlin, "Mill and the Ends of Life," 134; Rawls, *Lectures*, 254–5, 258–9; Donner, *Liberal Self*, 3, 8, 10–11; Eisenach, "Self-Reform," 249; Green, "Sympathy and Self-Interest," 259–77; Ryan, *Mill*, 54–5; Wollheim, "Mill and Berlin," 262–3; Riley, *Liberal Utilitarianism*, 3–4, and "Optimal Moral Rules," 119–20.
30 Mill, *Autobiography*, 175–7; Stafford, *Mill*, 31; Davis, "Mill, Socialism, and the English Romantics," 346.
31 Mill, *Autobiography*, 63.
32 Ibid., 171.
33 D'Eichthal's activities in Greece after the disbanding of the Saint-Simonians in 1832 meant he and Mill lost touch, but he recorded with delight how Mill came unannounced to see him in Paris in 1864, from which date, and until Mill's death, they resumed the close friendship of their youth. Mill, Letter 24, 26; Eugene d'Eichthal, "Introduction," 2–21.
34 Comte, at this time, counted himself as a Saint-Simonian. Mill, *Autobiography*, 171.
35 Eugene d'Eichthal, "Introduction," 2–21; Pankhurst, *Saint-Simonians*, 6–11.
36 Mill, *Autobiography*, 175.
37 Many commentators agree that Mill's philosophy of history changed at this period. Capaldi, *Mill*, 78–81; Halliday, *Mill*, 70; Hamburger, *Liberty and Control*, 37–8, 119–20; Ryan, *Mill*, 34–40; Lewisohn, "Mill and Comte," 316; Pankhurst, *Saint-Simonians*, 33; Raeder, *Religion of*

Humanity, 37; Williams, *Politics and Society*, 20–5. I do not disagree with their initial analysis, but rather with the conclusions they draw regarding how we should read Mill's later thought. See also Sarvasy, "Mill's Socialism," 312–33, for an excellent account of the impact of Mill's view regarding "transitional" ages on the development of his socialism through his changing views of wage-labour.

38 Capaldi, *Mill*, 78; Davis, "Mill, Socialism, and the English Romantics," 347; Reeves, *Victorian Firebrand*, 75; Ryan, *Mill*, 39.
39 Mill: *Autobiography*, 167; *Logic*, 915–17; Ryan, *Mill*, 39–40.
40 Mill: *Spirit of the Age* III [Part I], 255; Letter 28, 41.
41 Place, cited in Hamburger, *Intellectuals in Politics*, 107–8. Bain also found *Spirit of the Age* incomprehensible, especially the notion of society as being in a "transitional" phase. Bain, *Mill*, 40; Ryan, *Mill*, 41.
42 Reeves, *Victorian Firebrand*, 138.
43 D'Eichthal, *Rapports adressés*, 11; Saint-Simon, "Catechism," 187; Mill, *Autobiography*, 173; Ryan, *Mill*, 41; Raeder, *Religion of Humanity*, 47–8.
44 Mill, *Autobiography*, 173.
45 Mill acknowledges that these ideas had already been formulated by people other than the Saint-Simonians – "they were the general property of Europe" – but he insists that "they had never ... been so completely systematised as by these writers, nor the distinguishing characteristics of a critical period so powerfully set forth." Mill, *Autobiography*, 171–3.
46 Ibid., 170.
47 Mill, Letter 28, 42. This is also evident in his use of "transitional" and "natural" to describe the stages of history in *Spirit of the Age*.
48 Mill, *Autobiography*, 169; Capaldi, *Mill*, 78.
49 Mill: *French Affairs*, 1110; *Vindication*, 317–63. For more on Mill's commitment to "progress," see Persky, *Political Economy of Progress*.
50 See also McCabe, "Navigating by the North Star," 291–309.
51 Mill, *Autobiography*, 255–7.
52 James Mill not only encouraged David Ricardo to publish his economic treatise in 1819 (when Mill was 13), but also gave Mill daily perambulatory lectures on the key points, getting him to write notes of what he had learned – notes that formed the basis of James Mill's *Elements of Political Economy* (1821) – as well as marginal notes in the published version of *Elements*. Mill moved on to reading Ricardo for himself, as well as Adam Smith, Malthus, and Francis Place; stayed for three weeks with Jean-Baptiste Say in 1820; and studied political economy even further with a group of friends in the early 1820s. This led to his own first

publications on the topic. Mill, *Autobiography*, 31, 63–5, 107, 123, 171, 175; *Year in France*, 6–12, 54.
53 Mill, *Autobiography*, 71, 175.
54 Ibid., 255.
55 Ibid., 255–7.
56 Mill, "Miss Martineau," 227.
57 Smith, "Mill's Famous Distinction," 267–84; Marx, *Grundrisse*, 676; Cohen, *Marx's Theory of History*, 108–11. Most recently, Persky, in *Political Economy of Progress*, 157–60, has an excellent section on Marx's critique of this idea in Mill, offering the persuasive reason for Marx's extreme vituperation regarding Mill's ideas that Marx was most vicious about ideas most closely akin to his own.
58 Mill, *Autobiography*, 255–7.
59 Ibid.; Mill, *Logic*, 918.
60 Ryan, *Mill*, 164–5.
61 See, for instance, Mill, *Autobiography*, 239–41.
62 Mill, "The Corn Laws," 48–9.
63 Mill, "Fontana and Prati," 678.
64 See also McCabe, "Navigating by the North Star," 291–309.
65 Pickering, *Comte*, 606; Mill, *Logic*, 918. As Ryan, *Mill*, 37–41, notes, it is this desire for social harmony that led Himmelfarb to view Mill as a troubled conservative whose liberal pronouncements were due solely to the malign influence of his wife. Yet this ignores swathes of Mill's thought, and Himmelfarb's arguments are, as Ten, *Mill On Liberty*, 151–8, points out, inconsistent.
66 Mill, *Autobiography*, 173.
67 Ibid.
68 Mill, *Reform Party*, 487.
69 Mill, Letter 25, 29–30.
70 Mill: *Autobiography*, 143; Letter 29, 46.
71 Mill, Letter 25, 29.
72 Riley, *Liberal Utilitarianism*, 87; Mill, *Utilitarianism*, 231–3.
73 Riley, *Liberal Utilitarianism*, 87.
74 Ibid., 176, 193, 196–7.
75 Mill, *Considerations*, 547.
76 Mill, "Attack on Literature," 320–1.
77 Mill, Letter 72, 152.
78 Mill, *Bentham's Philosophy*, 9.
79 Mill, *Coleridge*, 134–8.

80 Mill, "The Gorgias," 149.
81 Mill, *Reform Party*, 487–8.
82 Mill, *Autobiography*, 239.
83 Mill: *Claims*, 383–9; *Principles*, 758–96.
84 Mill, *Considerations*, 547.
85 Mill, *Utilitarianism*, 232–3.
86 Mill, *Autobiography*, 239–41.

Chapter Two

1 Mill, *Autobiography*, 239.
2 Ibid., 199, 239.
3 Mill, *Chapters*, 750.
4 Mill, *Principles*, 207.
5 It is worth noting here that Mill never uses the term "capitalism," though later commentators have been happy to use it on his behalf in describing his views. Blanc is generally credited with the first use of the term in our modern meaning (in his *Pages de l'histoire de la révolution de 1848*, 1850), so Mill could have come across the term via his friendship with Blanc (and his reading of Blanc's work, though we have no evidence he read this particular one). Similarly, Ricardo had used the term "capitalist," and Mill was very familiar with his work. Where Mill uses "capitalist," it is in a similar sense – referring to a person who owns capital. His examples in *Principles* (56) are all of individual manufacturers who own factories, employ labourers, and are involved in the day-to-day running of their business, despite spending some of their income "in hiring grooms and valets, or maintaining hunters and hounds," which implies they also have a good deal of leisure. This is also similar to the way in which Coleridge (in 1823), Proudhon (in 1840), and Disraeli (in 1845) use the word. Even Marx only began using "capitalism" (rather than "the capitalistic system") in *Capital* (in 1867), and generally preferred "the capitalist mode of production."
6 Flew, "Mill: Socialist or Libertarian?," 21.
7 Mill, *Principles*, 936–74.
8 Baum, "Liberal Socialism," 104.
9 Mill, *On Liberty*, 293.
10 Mill, *Principles*, 944.
11 Mill, Letter 72, 152.
12 Mill, *Principles*, 800, 936–44.

13 Ibid., 800–2.
14 Ibid, 940.
15 Ibid, 938.
16 Ibid., 938–40.
17 Mill, *Attack on Literature*, 320–1.
18 Mill, *Comte*, 340–1.
19 Ibid.
20 Mill, *Principles*, 937.
21 Ibid., 950–2.
22 Ibid., 953–4.
23 Ibid., 947–50.
24 Ibid., 956–60.
25 Ibid., 956; Mill, Letter 377, 609.
26 Mill, *Principles*, 804. (Which is non-authoritative, for Mill, because one does not *have* to use money, but if you do want to engage in activities that are made easier by money, then a government-backed and -regulated currency may make this easier.)
27 Ibid., 955–6. In the case of railways, it seems Mill meant the state to own the railways but for private companies to provide the train services: at least, this is what he directly recommends for Australia. Mill, Letter 1428, 1598.
28 Mill, *Principles*, 955–6.
29 Ibid., 947–50.
30 Some have taken Mill's arguments to mean he would support a government-funded voucher scheme with all schools being privately run (Flew, "Socialist or Libertarian?," 25). I remain unconvinced that this fits Mill's position. It would certainly have to be within a very different social set-up of entrenched privilege than current private schooling in the UK. Moreover, state schools would not be there to "mop up" those who had failed to access private schools. Instead, Mill sees state-provided schools not merely as an efficient means of securing universal education, but also as exemplars of best practice. See also Gray, *Liberalism*, 4, for why the assertion that Mill was not a socialist but a libertarian who would have supported the proposals of the Selsdon group is misplaced.
31 Mill, *Principles*, 360.
32 Ibid., 968–70 – an idea that Mill endorsed, directly contrary to the supporters of *laissez-faire*, as early as 1831. See Mill, *Attack on Literature*, 320–1; and again in 1833. See Mill, *Writings of Junius Redivivus [II]*, 385.

33 Mill, *Coleridge*, 135.
34 Mill, *Principles*, 932.
35 It is true that Mill endorsed the right to strike as a temporary measure, aimed at bringing about a much-improved form of society; but unlike some socialists, who looked forward to a revolution instigated by a general strike, he did not view striking as a *necessary* route to improvement. Indeed, rather the opposite: he believed that the rise of profit-sharing and cooperative associations would mark the end of trades unions, for they would no longer be needed – an attitude shared by some employers, who adopted profit-sharing schemes (mentioned by Mill in *Principles*), though Mill felt this would be an organic process, and Henry Briggs and other profit-sharing employers (to the detriment of their schemes) felt they could force the issue (and sometimes introduced profit-sharing in a direct attempt to destroy unions). Mill: Letter 500, 735; Letter 1288, 1439–40; *Principles*, 754–5; Church, "Profit-Sharing," 6–10.
36 Mill, *Principles*, 214.
37 Mill, *Autobiography*, 239.
38 Mill, *Principles*, 207.
39 Mill: *Claims*, 365–82; *Principles*, 758–62.
40 See also McCabe, "Mill's Analysis of Capitalism," 8–22.
41 Mill, *Principles*, 204.
42 That is, "labour which does not terminate in the creation of material wealth; which ... does not render the community ... richer in material products, but poorer by all that is consumed by the labourers while so employed." Mill, *Principles*, 50–1. Mill's examples include actors, ballet teachers, opera singers, and mercenaries.
43 Mill, *Principles*, 54.
44 Ibid., 204, 791.
45 Ibid., 209.
46 Mill, *Newman*, 444. See also Miller on Mill's critique of capitalism as unjust in "Mill's 'Socialism,'" 217–18. Miller takes Mill's critique of the "crushing, elbowing and trampling" inherent in contemporary society as being, overall, outweighed by competition's invigorating effect on people's character, making them more "energetic." I agree that Mill does think competition beneficial; he also thinks a certain form of it is entirely compatible with socialism. But importantly, this is a form of competition that precludes the "race" from being one in which what we are competing with one another for is actually life itself. For more on this, see McCabe, "Mill and Fourierism," 35–61. Miller sees "the really

serious problems with 19th-century British capitalism," for Mill, not as stemming "from the institution of individual ownership of private property per se, but rather from the fact that legislators have failed to do what could be done consistent with this institution to ameliorate the inequalities that it produces by its very nature." Miller, "Mill's 'Socialism,'" 217. This certainly is *one* of Mill's critiques, but *even if* private property could be maximally reformed, it would still not result in principles of distributive justice as "high" (in Mill's terminology) as those proposed by Owen and Blanc. See Mill, *Principles*, 203. That is, it might be possible to reform individual property such that it was as just as was currently expedient: but this, as with *laissez-faire*, is only something true for *this* (critical) stage of human society, and Mill wanted us to progress to something more. For more on this, see McCabe, "Navigating by the North Star," 291–309.

47 Mill, *Autobiography*, 239.
48 Mill, *Principles*, 758.
49 Ibid., 207.
50 Ibid., 54.
51 Ibid., 207.
52 Mill, *Chapters*, 713.
53 Mill, *Principles*, 756.
54 Ibid., 207.
55 Ibid., 207–8.
56 Ibid., 213.
57 I say "proto-environmentalist" because Mill offers arguments in support of "green" initiatives such as protecting the diversity of species and habitats; protecting open space from development; and allowing access to undomesticated "wilderness" on anthropocentric, and utilitarian, bases, rather than as being goods in their own right.
58 Mill, *Principles*, 756.
59 Sarvasy, in "Mill's Socialism," 314, concentrates on Mill's criticism of class conflict and his account of workers' desire for independence. Kurer, in *Politics of Progress*, 35–6, also notes Mill's criticisms of capitalism on the grounds of "breeding egoism and class conflict"; inequality; and "because it did not allow for the full development of individuality." These accounts, though good in themselves, are incomplete.
60 Mill, *Principles*, 756.
61 Mill, Letter 501, 713.
62 Mill, *Principles*, 755.

63 The quote is from Thomas Carlyle's *Past and Present*.
64 Mill, *Claims*, 379–80.
65 Mill, *Principles*, 207.
66 See also McCabe, "Navigating by the North Star," 291–309, for more on Mill's view of "ideal" and "non-ideal" regimes, and his view of potential improvements of individual property.
67 Mill, *Principles*, 201.
68 Persky, *Political Economy of Progress*, 69, criticizes Mill's approach here as "not Mill at his best." But I feel that this method of a thought experiment, rather than what Persky seems to think Mill should have contributed – a detailed history of the institution of property – may be a radical means of making his point. The reader *might* imagine that if people went to "colonize" a previously uninhabited island, they would simply take with them – as naturally as taking their own bodies and talents – the institution of private property. Mill challenges this and makes us realize that, at least on (potentially mythical) *Terra Nova*, whether we had private property, or something more communal, would be a question of choice. Not because he *really* thought this was the choice facing colonists, but because this is *the choice facing us too*: the institution of private property *is* a choice, valid when it helps improve general utility, invalid when it doesn't. It is not one of the "fixed laws of production" but rather a question pertaining to distribution, and thus one of human decision, and liable to questions of justice. So I think this is a deliberate rhetorical strategy on Mill's part (though this says nothing as to its success).
69 Mill, *Principles*, 201.
70 Some feminist critics of Mill have charged him with not really allowing women equal access to the labour market, because in *Subjection*, 298, he says that "in an otherwise just state of things, it is not, therefore, I think, a desirable custom, that the wife should contribute by her labour to the income of the family." Okin: *Women in Western Political Thought*, 228, and *Justice, Gender and the Family*, 20; Hughes, "Reality versus the Ideal," 523–42. However, this misreads Mill's position – see McCabe: "Mill, Utility, and the Family," 225–35, and "'Good Housekeeping'?," 135–55.
71 Mill, *Principles*, 116–30.
72 Ibid., 210.
73 Ibid., 360 (i.e., people in receipt of state aid because they can't feed themselves and their families should not, on Mill's view, have more children).
74 Mill, *Claims*, 386–9; Mill, *Principles*, 227, 801.

75 Mill, *Principles*, 801. See also his similar wording in *Land Tenure Reform*, 690.
76 Mill, *Principles*, 227–8.
77 Ibid., 199–232, 227, 801.
78 Mill, *Land Tenure Reform*, 690.
79 Mill, *Principles*, 120–1, 325, 376, 921, 958–60, 966.
80 Mill, Letter 1690, 1848.
81 Mill, *Principles*, 201, 218–35.
82 Famously, Mill draws what may not be a wholly convincing distinction between the right of "bequest" (that of an owner to determine what happens to their property) and "inheritance" – the state cannot force people to *bequeath* (or not) in certain ways, but for reasons of the common good, it can step in and ensure that people do not *inherit* in line with the bequest. That is, someone could *bequeath* all their property to their eldest son; but the state could prevent him from inheriting it. Mill, *Principles*, 222–5.
83 Ibid., 225.
84 Ibid., 887.
85 Ibid., 225. In 1865, Mill added the thought that for the future good of the firm, the owners of privately owned companies might be permitted to leave the whole company to one (or some set) of their heirs whom they thought would run it best, even if this did mean leaving them more than a "comfortable independence." This implies that the inheritor would still be involved in the day-to-day management and work of the company: Mill is still ruling out allowing someone to inherit wealth arising from, or invested in, a company that allows them to live *without* labouring on the profits of someone else's labour and abstinence.
86 For a clear summary, see Claeys, *Mill and Paternalism*, 159n186. Ekelund and Tollison, in "Means to Social Justice," 218, rightly emphasize that, in the real world, Mill thought "government should optimise by raising the maximum amount of revenue consistent with precluding the incentive to evade payment (through *intervivos* gifts, etc.)." They emphasize that this inheritance-restricting policy "had the declared purpose of reducing the burden of the poor," but there were also fundamental questions of justice at stake.
87 Mill, *Principles*, 201–2.
88 Cf. ibid., 208, 222–5, 758, 887.
89 Ibid., 207–8.

90 It is also worth noting that Mill cites both de Tocqueville's view that "equality of conditions" in America has a "prodigious influence" on all of its institutions and "the whole course of society," which includes, of course, the "tyranny of the majority" and of public opinion, which Mill is so anxious to protect people from in *On Liberty*. Mill, "De Tocqueville on Democracy in America" (1), 49.
91 Mill, *Principles*, 207.
92 Ibid., 808–11.
93 Claeys, *Mill and Paternalism*, 75.
94 Mill, *Principles*, 812.
95 Interestingly, in the 1848 and 1849 editions of *Principles* (see 812, note n-n) Mill writes that "a just and wise legislation['s] … impartiality between competitors would consist in endeavouring that they should all start fair, and not that, whether they were swift or slow, all should reach the goal at once." In both cases, it is clear, Mill's idea of a "reformed" system of individual property would ensure meaningful equality of opportunity, but not equality of outcome.
96 Ibid., 807.
97 Mill, *Principles*, 820. This too is an idea with some modern salience.
98 Mill, *Principles*, 225, 887.
99 See Claeys, *Mill and Paternalism*, 70.
100 Mill and Taylor, *Complete Works of Harriet Taylor Mill*, 50. See also Mill, *Principles*, 235: "I see nothing objectionable in fixing a limit to what anyone may acquire by the mere favour of others, without any exercise of his faculties, and in requiring that if he desires any further accession of fortune, he shall work for it."
101 Mill, *Principles*, 221–2.
102 Mill, Letter 1690, 1848.
103 Claeys, *Mill and Paternalism*, 159.
104 Mill, Letter 1690, 1847–8.
105 Mill, *Principles*, 758.
106 Claeys, *Mill and Paternalism*, 71, 159.
107 Claeys goes into some detail regarding what this might have actually meant in monetary terms. Claeys, *Mill and Paternalism*, 76n61.
108 Mill, *Principles*, 207–8.
109 Ibid., 801. See also, Mill: *Land Question*, 672; *Land Tenure Reform*, 691.
110 Mill: *Claims*, 386–9; *Principles*, 227, 801; *Land Tenure Reform*, 691.
111 Mill: *Principles*, 227–9; *Land Question*, 675; *Land Tenure Reform*, 691.
112 Mill, *Principles*, 227–8.

113 Ibid., 230; Mill, *Land Question*, 672.
114 Mill, *Principles*, 801, 199–232.
115 Ibid., 227.
116 Mill, *Land Tenure Reform*, 690–2.
117 Mill, *Principles*, 793–4.
118 Claeys, citing Bain, *Mill and Paternalism*, 74.
119 Mill, *Land Tenure Reform*, 694–5.
120 Mill, *Principles*, 376–7.
121 Mill, *Land Tenure Reform*, 694–5. As well as forming part of Mill's preferred reforms for an ideal form of individual property, Claeys, in "Justice, Independence, and Industrial Democracy," 140–1, rightly explains how "correctly understood," these proposed reforms help "to reveal a number of aspects of [Mill's] conception of socialism." In particular, Mill saw "unearned increments" such as provided by landownership as unjust, because there was no connection between labour and reward (as Claeys also rightly notes) and, we might add, no justification to be found from other, "higher" principles of justice, either. Claeys also notes that Mill's "strategy for land reform was … intended to draw support away from those socialists who sought the immediate nationalisation of the land." As in other elements of his socialism, when it came to the practicalities of reform, Mill was a gradualist where possible, particularly where questions of basic security and rights were concerned.
122 Mill, *Principles*, 955–6.
123 Ibid., 937.
124 Ibid., 947–50.
125 Ibid., 783.
126 Ibid, 769.
127 Ibid., 769–75.
128 Ibid., 968–9.
129 Ibid., 752–7.
130 Ibid., 754.
131 Ibid., 210.
132 Ibid., 208.
133 Ibid., 207.
134 Ibid., 929–30.
135 Mill, *On Liberty*, 293.
136 Mill, *Principles*, 207.
137 Mill, *Principles*, 203. This quote is from Blanc. We would nowadays translate this as "needs" – as Mill did in *Utilitarianism* (244) from 1864

onwards, though he used "wants" in the first edition in 1861 (in *Fraser's Magazine*) and 1863 (as a book).

138 It seems Mill *did* think such principles would work in worker cooperatives, but only after the cooperators had undergone sufficient education in working for, and making decisions for, the common good. Mill, *Principles*, 781–2. That is, such principles would work when the social ethos had changed. Profit-sharing might be an important step toward achieving the necessary change to the social ethos; indeed, without that change, "higher" principles of justice would not be feasible.

139 Mill, *Principles*, 756.

140 For more on this, and on feminist critiques of Mill's attempts to free women from "domestic subjugation," see McCabe: "Mill, Utility, and the Family," 225–35; "'Good Housekeeping'?," 135–55.

141 Mill, *Principles*, 769–75.

142 Mill, "De Tocqueville on Democracy in America," 49.

143 On this, see also Ekelund and Tollison, "Means to Social Justice," 221.

144 Mill, *Principles*, 360.

145 Mill, *Claims*, 382.

146 Mill, *Principles*, 210.

147 Mill, *Autobiography*, 239.

148 On this, see also Jensen, "Mill's Theories of Wealth," 506–7. Mill, Jensen argued, "desired" a specific socialist outcome, but "warned himself against assuming that his proposals for reform might rapidly move society" in the right direction.

149 Claeys, "Justice, Independence, and Industrial Democracy," 123.

150 Mill, *Autobiography*, 214.

151 Riley, "Capitalism versus Socialism," 39–41.

152 Miller, "Mill's 'Socialism,'" 227.

153 Mill, *Principles*, 794.

154 Mill, *Autobiography*, 239.

155 Marx, "Afterword," 17.

156 Mill, *Principles*, 208–9.

157 Ibid., 794, 785; Mill, *Co-operation*, 8–9.

158 Mill, *Principles*, 763.

159 Ibid., 769–94.

160 Mill, *Parliamentary Reform*, 332–3.

161 Mill, *Autobiography*, 199. For more on this, see McCabe, "Navigating by the North Star," 291–309.

162 Mill, *Chapters*, 749–50; McCabe, "Navigating by the North Star," 291–309.

163 Mill, *Autobiography*, 239; McCabe, "Navigating by the North Star," 291–309.
164 Persky, "Mill's Socialism Re-Considered," 165–80.
165 Persky, *Political Economy of Progress*, 83–4.
166 Mill, *Principles*, 738, cited Persky, "Mill's Socialism Re-examined," 171.
167 Ibid.
168 See McCabe, "Mill's 'Modern' Radicalism Re-examined," 156, for further discussion of my disagreement with Persky regarding similarities between Mill and Marx, particularly on the question of "species-being."
169 Mill, *Autobiography*, 171.
170 Miller, "Mill's 'Socialism,'" 214.
171 Riley, "Capitalism versus Socialism," 39.
172 Mill, *Principles*, 794.

Chapter Three

1 Mill, "Fontana and Prati" (published February 1834, but probably written before 22 December 1833 – see editor's note, *CW* XXIII, 674).
2 See Fredman and Gordon, "Mill and Socialism," 4.
3 Mill, *Autobiography*, 239.
4 See Mill, *Principles*, 203–12.
5 Fredman and Gordon, "Mill and Socialism," 3; Schapiro, "Pioneer of Democratic Liberalism," 147. See also McCabe, "Navigating by the North Star," 291–309.
6 Mill, *Principles*, 793–4.
7 Kurer, "Mill and Utopian Socialism," 222–32; Claeys, "Justice, Independence, and Industrial Democracy," 122–47; Donner, *Liberal Self*, 7; Horowitz, "Review," 182; Mueller, *Mill and French Thought*, 170–224; Stephen, *English Utilitarians*, 224.
8 Mill, *Claims*, 382.
9 Marx, "Afterword," 17.
10 See Leopold, "Structure," 446–8.
11 Mill: *Autobiography*, 127–9; "Population," 289; "Population: Reply to Thirlwall," 296–307; "Co-operation: Closing Speech," 314–21.
12 Mill, *Autobiography*, 159–63.
13 With whom Mill helped pass the "Industrial and Provident Societies Act," which made it easier for people to pool capital and own it jointly, thus allowing them to more safely set up cooperatives (without the danger that the person who was legally nominated to "own" the funds – the only possibility under existing law – would abscond with them with

no possibility of redress). Neale was also the chair when Mill gave his speech "Cooperation" in 1864. Mill: *Co-operation*, 5–8; *Autobiography*, 133; Birchall, *Co-op*, 76.

14 On Mill's part at least, this relationship never quite blossomed into friendship: he was particularly angry when Holyoake republished Taylor's *Enfranchisement of Women* without seeking her permission, changing the first few paragraphs to talk of "Woman" rather than "women," a sentimentality both Mill and Taylor hated. Mill: Letter 667, 911; Letter 261, 509–10. Even so, Mill financially supported Holyoake and his newspaper *The Co-operator*; asked Holyoake's advice regarding printing a cheap edition of *Principles*; and, in 1870, when Holyoake was an MP, lent him his protection at a meeting of the Reform Society, for which Holyoake remained deeply grateful. Mill: Letter 575, 821; Letter 680, 924; Letter 667, 911; Letter 261, 509–10; Holyoake, *Sixty Years*, 1:105 and 2:42–3. Holyoake evidently continued to feel warmly about Mill: after Mill's death, he was concerned in the plans for his state funeral (which were dropped because of the scandal arising from Mill's being arrested when seventeen for distributing information about contraception) and wrote strenuous (though perhaps inaccurate) defences of Mill's beliefs about family planning. Holyoake, *Mill*, 1.

15 Mill, *Principles*, 786.
16 See Mill, *Year in France*, 7–24.
17 For d'Eichthal's activities in England see Pankhurst, *Saint-Simonians*, 6–11.
18 Mill, *Autobiography*, 173.
19 Mill, Letter 52, 108.
20 Mill, "Fontana and Prati," 674–80.
21 Mill, "Comparison" (printed in the *Globe*, 18 April 1832, and reprinted in *The Monthly Repository*, November 1833), 442–7.
22 Mill, Letter 39, 71.
23 Cf. Mill, Letter 52, 108.
24 Cf. *The Times*, 27 January 1832.
25 Mill: "French News [45]," 401–3; "Fontana and Prati," 674–80, where, though he does not defend Fontana and Prati themselves, he does defend Saint-Simonism. *The Times*, 8 November 1833 and 31 August 1832, for instance, called the Saint-Simonian missionaries in London "idiots in knaves' clothing" and thought they should be "ducked in a horsepond." The *Literary Gazette* called them "[s]windling, worthless, godless hypocrites and knaves, practising on dolts, weak enthusiasts and harlots

... beggars, charlatans and imposters," with views directed "to the indulgence of the most revolting profligacy" (773). *The Examiner* focused more on the comedy of the London meetings, poking fun at the Saint-Simonians' clothes and their mention of having "suffered grievously from the bowel complaint." It is easy to understand why Mill warned his friend d'Eichthal, "I expect that for a considerable time much obloquy will fall not only upon the St. Simonians, but even on all who venture to hint the possibility of their being other than madmen or rogues," and why he called his own attempts to defend them "un acte de courage." Mill, Letter 47, 96.

26 See many of Mill's letters to d'Eichthal, esp. Letters 28, 39, and 45.
27 Mill, "Fontana and Prati," 678.
28 Mill, Letter 64, 133; Pellarin, *Fourier*, 76.
29 Fourier's *Theory of the Four Movements* was published in 1808; his *Traité de l'association domestique-agricole* (later republished as *Theory of Universal Unity*) in 1822; and *Le Nouveau Monde Industriel et Sociétaire* in 1829.
30 Mill, Letter 64, 134.
31 Fourier, *Four Movements*, 50.
32 Mill, Letter 15, 1028. Mill refers to Considerant's 1848 work, *Le Socialisme devant le vieux monde, ou le vivant devant les morts* as "another volume" by Considerant. Mill, Letter 27, 1031. Exactly what he had previously read is hard to pin down: eight of Considerant's works had been published by this date. Claeys, "Justice, Independence, and Industrial Democracy," 131, dates Mill's more serious consideration to 1850, though the inclusion of Fourierism in the 1849 edition of *Principles*, as well as these letters, make 1849 a more plausible date.
33 Mill, *Principles*, 975–82.
34 Currently in the Somerville Collection, Somerville College, Oxford.
35 Mill: *Chapters*, 719–26;, Letter 15, 1027–8. Mill's two-volume copy of Fourier's *The Passions of the Human Soul*, translated by John Reynell Morrell (London, 1851), is preserved in the Somerville Collection. See also McCabe, "Mill and Fourierism," 35–61.
36 Cabet laid out his socialist utopia in an 1840 novel titled *Voyage en Icarie* – or, in English, *Voyage to Icaria* – and his followers were known as "Icarians," hence "Icarianism" rather than "Cabetism."
37 Mill, *Principles*, 203.
38 Mill: "French News [64]," 482; "French News [66]," 495; "French News [90]," 688.
39 Mill, "M. Cabet," 1144–6.

40 See, for instance, Mill, Letter 883, 1112, where Mill congratulates Blanc on his recent marriage and invites him and Madame Blanc to Blackheath, saying "it would be a great pleasure to see you both" (my translation).
41 This is preserved in the Somerville Collection. My thanks to Ruth Vorstman for her help translating the inscription.
42 Blanc, flyleaf of Mill's copy of *History of the French Revolution* (Paris, 1847) (in the Somerville Collection); Mill: Letter 523, 760; Letter 15, 1028; Moss, *Origins of the French Labour Movement*, 11, 20, 35, 38; Mill, Letter 56, 115.
43 Mill, Letter 531, 739. See also McCabe: "Mill on "Legitimate" Socialism"; "Mill and the French Revolution."
44 In contrast, of course, to how well Marx knew Mill's work. After moving to London he immersed himself in Mill's *Principles* to such an extent that Wilhelm Pieper told Engels, "Marx lives a very retired life, his only friends are John Stuart Mill and Lloyd, and when you visit him you are received with economic categories instead of with compliments." Pieper, cited Oakley, *Making of Marx's Critical Theory*, 45. This has on occasion been read literally as meaning Marx was friends with Mill, but the context shows that Pieper meant that Marx was spending all his time reading Mill (and William Forster Lloyd).
45 Mill learned German in his youth with Sarah Austin, but it is not clear he retained these language skills in later life, even if he could have got hold of a German copy (only 1,000 copies of the German edition were sold before 1873).
46 My thanks to David Leopold for information on this.
47 Schapiro, "Pioneer of Liberalism," 147.
48 Mill, Letter 1749, 1910–12. Mill also corresponded (though generally disagreed) with George Howell (a member of the council of the IWA in 1865) and William Randal Cremer (secretary of the British section of the IWA from 1871 until 1908). Mill was a friendlier correspondent of John Hales (active in the IWA from 1866, and secretary to its General Council in 1871). Through the Representative Reform Association, Mill also knew Thomas Mottershead (member of the General Council of the IWA from 1869–72), who later broke with Marx over his attitude toward revolution. He knew George Odger (first President of the IWA and pioneer trade unionist) well enough to write a letter of introduction to him for d'Eichthal. Mill also had a supporter in Harriet Law (the first female member of the General Council of the IWA), who asked a Reform meeting in 1867 to support a motion in favour of Mill's

proposition to give women the vote. This was passed, which greatly pleased Mill – he commented, "Is that not worth having worked for?" Mill's letter in reply to the Nottingham branch of the IWA in which he "warmly approved" of their program was published in the *Herald*, *Daily News*, *Daily Telegraph*, and *Beehive* that October and November. Mill: Letter 881A, 2011–12; Letter 1049, 1247–8; Letter 1667, 1821–2; Letter 1604, 1770; Letter 1658, 1816; Letter 1104, 1285; Letter 1749, 1910).

49 Claeys, "Justice, Independence, and Industrial Democracy," 144; Mill: Letter 1749, 1910–11; *Chapters*, 708, 737; Ryan, *Mill*, 183. Mill specifically referred to the Congresses of the General Council of the IWA held in Geneva in 1866 and Basle in 1869. Mill, *Chapters*, 708, 737. Marx wrote a very short preamble to the report on the Geneva Congress, which was published in England as part of a pamphlet titled *The International Working Men's Association: Resolutions of the Congress of Geneva, 1866, and the Congress of Brussels, 1868* in 1869. Marx, *Preamble*, 31. Furthermore, Marx wrote a report of the Basle Congress, which was published in England as *Report of the Fourth Annual Congress of the International Working Men's Association, held in Basle, in Switzerland* in 1869. Marx, *Report*, 68. Marx's report mentioned a "memorable strike on the part of the ribbon-weavers and silk-dyers" in Basle, which occurred shortly after the Congress met there, which may be what Mill was referring to when he wrote in *Chapters* (709) that revolutionary socialism had taken root "even in sober Switzerland." As Mill referred to the contributions made by the English delegates at these Congresses, he may have read the accounts of what occurred at them. However, there is no particular reason to suppose that Marx's name would have necessarily stood out from the rest of the contributors, and Mill does not mention Marx by name. Moreover, Mill says that in general, he thought it was only the English members of the IWA who were to be supported, as they were less willing to replace the entirety of society in one fell swoop without trying out some other form of social organization beforehand. Mill, Letter 1708, 1874–5.

50 Feuer, "Mill and Marxian Socialism," 297–304. Indeed, Sarvasy argues that Mill's support of land nationalization was a means of legitimizing the calls for it coming from the IWA. This, however, seems to overplay Mill's relationship with the IWA, and also overlooks his previous commitment to nationalization of land, an issue on which, however, Sarvasy is right to note the shared commitment of both Mill and contemporary Marxians. Sarvasy, "Mill's Socialism," 324; Reeves, *Victorian Firebrand*, 226.

51 This program called for "social and political revolution," the main aspects of which would be freedom of expression and education, abolition of classes and sex privileges, "emancipation of the land," national and racial equality, and "the protection of the rights of minorities by the principle of federalism and by decentralisation of power." Mill, Letter 1749, 1911. Mill particularly praised their commitment to the decentralization of power, and to minority representation through federalism, as well as their commitment to the equality of women, although he was concerned about the use of the term "the revolution" to mean the forthcoming social change, and not some specific revolution (as in, for example, the French Revolution). Mill, Letter 1749, 1911–12; see also Brady, "Introduction," lxvii. Mill later said he felt the English members of the IWA were reasonable men seeking to find practical ways of ameliorating the position of workers. Mill, Letter 1708, 1874–5. Many of these claims echoed Mill's own commitments. Indeed, Mill admitted as much, writing that "in the principles of the Association as set forth in the Program I find much that I warmly approve, and little, if anything from which I positively dissent," although he adds the warning that "the generality with which those principles are laid down" made it impossible to say to what extent he would agree with the practical measures the IWA might propose to bring these principles into operation. Mill, Letter 1749, 1911. And he was not enthusiastic about the practical proposals of "revolutionary" socialists. Mill: Letter 1708, 1874–75; *Chapters*, 708–9.

52 Mill, Letter 1749, 1910–11. This was a collection of letters that Smith had sent the *Daily Express* (Nottingham). Mill does not make much mention of the Paris Commune, though he evidently knew people involved in it and who held very strong views on the subject. See Mill, Letter 1666, 1820. His good friend Blanc, however, had recently returned from exile (in 1870), fought as a private in the National Guard, and was elected to the National Assembly in February 1871, voting for a continuation of the war. Blanc himself did not sympathize with the Commune and tried to exert his influence on the side of moderation. (This said, he introduced a proposal for amnesty for the Communards in 1879, which was carried.) Mill may have agreed with Blanc's view, but sadly we have no surviving correspondence between them from this period. Frederic Harrison (a celebrated jurist and fellow Positivist) recalled in his *Autobiographic Memoirs* that Mill "shared the indignation which I expressed in 1871 for the savage conduct of the Thiers Ministry in suppressing the Paris Insurrection," quoting Mill's letter to him in which Mill wrote that "the

crimes of the *parti de l'orde* are atrocious, even supposing that they are in revenge for those generally attributed to the Commune." Mill, Letter 1657, 1816. This is borne out by a letter from Mill to another socialist correspondent, Charles Dupont-White (whose *Essai sur les relations du travail avec le capital* (1846) earned him a seat with Blanc and Considerant – among others – in the Commission at the Palais de Luxembourg, established in 1848, which eventually led to the founding of the National Workshops). Dupont-White became a Prefect, and Secretary-General to the Ministry of Justice in 1848, and later made the first translations of *On Liberty* and *Considerations of Representative Government* into French (in 1859 and 1861, respectively). (Dupont-White's friend Sadi Carnot translated Mill's *Vindication of the Revolution of 1848* into French.) Mill wrote: "However dangerous the extremely crude ideas of the revolutionary socialists, what alarms me much more is the appalling abuse of the repression by the now victorious party, in whose eyes it is enough to have wanted the least of changes that appeared in the program of the commune to be an enemy of society, and who seem to want to massacre or deport *en masse*, if possible, the whole opposition party." Mill, Letter 1699, 1865 – my translation.

53 When "Working Men and the War" was published in the *Pall Mall Gazette*, it was signed by all thirty-two members of the Committee for the General Council of the IWA; Marx's appears in the second section of names, as the Corresponding Secretary for Germany. Marx, "Working Men and the War," 3–9.

54 "Working Men and the War," for instance, is not distinctively Marxist, but it does includes some important socialist ideas, most obviously an internationalism that believes that through working-class solidarity war between powerful classes can be prevented. It also heralds a future in which there will be peace because the world will be ruled by labour. Marx, "Working Men and the War," 3–9. Mill praised this idea in *Thornton on Labour and Its Claims* (668), and wrote to tell the IWA that "there was not one word in it [i.e., the pamphlet] that ought not to be there." Mill, Letter 1583A, 220. Although it is equally possible to believe that liberalism will bring world peace, the fact that this peace will come through the solidarity of working men, and the idea that, in the future, the world will be ruled by those who labour, is distinctively socialist.

55 Marx and Engels, *Communist Manifesto*, 505; Mill, *Chapters*, 737.
56 Mill, *Principles*, 203.
57 Mill, *Chapters*, 738.

58 Ibid.; Mill, *Principles*, 201–12.
59 Ibid., 203.
60 Ibid., *Principles*, 203; Mill, *Chapters*, 737.
61 Ibid., 737; Mill, *Principles*, 200–12, 793–4.
62 Mill, *Chapters*, 737–8, 747–8.
63 I use this as it handily connotes the kind of immediate, violent, extra-legal and total kind of "revolution" Mill had in mind when he thought of "revolutionary Socialism": obviously, though, in other ways *all* the forms of socialism he considered were "revolutionary" in that they all proposed solutions to contemporary problems that involved the transformation of the world into something radically different. Cf. Cohen on the meaning of "revolutionary" in *If You're An Egalitarian*, 104.
64 I list here only the ones that Mill engaged with in some detail in *Principles* and/or *Chapters*. Even here, Icarianism is a bit of a stretch, as Cabet is mentioned extremely briefly.
65 Mill, *Chapters*, 747–8.
66 Ibid., 737–8, 747–8; Mill, *Principles*, 201–12.
67 Mill, *Autobiography*, 199.
68 Mill, *Principles*, 203.
69 Cf. Mill, *Chapters*, 712–16.
70 Mill, *Autobiography*, 239.
71 Mill, *Chapters*, 716–27.
72 Stafford, "Paradigmatic Liberal," 330; Baum, "Liberal Socialism," 99; Losman, "Alternative Economic Systems," 96–7; Davis, "Mill, Socialism, and the English Romantics," 355. See also, most recently, Persky, "Mill's Socialism Re-Considered," 173–4.
73 Mill, *Principles*, 794–6.
74 Mill, *Chapters*, 727–33.
75 Blanc, translated Mill, *Chapters*, 716–19.
76 Mill, *Chapters*, 728–9.
77 Ibid., 730–1.
78 Ibid., 736.
79 Ibid., 731.
80 Mill, *Principles*, 791.
81 Mill, *Chapters*, 732–3.
82 Ibid., 731.
83 Mill, *Newman*, 444.
84 Mill, *Chapters*, 731–2.
85 Ibid., 733.
86 Neale, *Manual for Co-operators*, 37.

87 Holyoake, *History of Co-operation*, 674.
88 Moss, *French Labour Movement*, 36; Beecher, *Considerant*, 148.
89 Stafford, "Paradigmatic Liberal," 330.
90 Thompson, *Inquiry*, 156–7, 168–70, 274–80.
91 Moss, *French Labour Movement*, 36; Beecher, *Considerant*, 148; Fourier, "Series and Groups," 158–9; Fourier, "Attractive Labour," 164–5; Fourier, "Role of the Passions," 57–9; Considerant, *Exposition abrégée*, 36–7, and *Destineé Sociale*, 378. See also McCabe, "Mill and Fourierism," 35–61.
92 Mill, *Principles*, 205.
93 Ibid., 792.
94 Ibid., 758–69.
95 Ibid., 794.
96 Ibid., 736.
97 Mill, *Claims*, 382. See also Persky, "Mill's Socialism Re-examined," 168–70.
98 Mill, *Autobiography*, 199, 239.
99 Mill, *Chapters*, 737. Italics in the original.
100 Ibid., 748.
101 Mill: Letter 29, 47; "Fontana and Prati," 678; *Autobiography*, 175 (where he says he "neither believed in the practicability, nor in the beneficial operation of their social machinery").
102 Mill, *Principles*, 210–11, 981.
103 Mill, *Considerations*, 405.
104 Mill, "Co-operation: Intended Speech," 313.
105 Mill, "Co-operation: Closing Speech," 319–20.
106 Malthus, *Essay on the Principle of Population*, 46–7.
107 Mill, *Principles*, 975, 203.
108 Ibid., 975, 980, 206; Mill, *Chapters*, 738–9.
109 Mill, *Principles*, 206. See also Mill, *Chapters*, 729, where he says "there is much to be said for Socialism" regarding population control such that "what was long thought to be its weakest point will, perhaps, prove to be one of its strongest."
110 Mill, *Principles*, 975. Though this sounds like damning with faint praise, Mill immediately commented on what an improvement to existing conditions this would be for most people.
111 Ibid., 203. Mill did not mention this question at all in *Chapters*.
112 There are very interesting echoes, here, of Fourier's theories regarding human passions and particularly the "cabalistic" passion which excited people to "emulation." See McCabe, "Mill and Fourierism," 35–61.
113 Ibid., 204, 975–6. See also Mill, *Autobiography*, 239; and *Chapters*, 739.

114 Mill: *Principles*, 204, 979–80; *Chapters*, 742.
115 Mill, *Principles*, 204–5, 980.
116 Ibid., 205. See also Mill, *Chapters*, 742.
117 Mill: "Co-operation: Closing Speech," 320–1; *Chapters*, 739–42.
118 Mill, *Chapters*, 739–42.
119 Mill: *Principles*, 206–7, 976–7; *Chapters*, 743–4.
120 *Chapters* (744) has "People have unequal capacities of work, both mental and bodily, and what is a light task for one is an insupportable burthen to another."
121 Mill, *Principles*, 206–7.
122 The link to what Mill called Blanc's "still higher" principle of justice is clear (from each according to his capabilities, to each according to his wants), as is a link to the Saint-Simonian idea of "from each according to his capabilities; to each capacity according to its works."
123 Mill, *Chapters*, 744.
124 Mill, *Principles*, 213, 983–5. That said, in early editions, Mill did express concern that Fourierism's social machinery would not work if implemented by human beings as currently educated and constituted, who would not accept the differentiation of reward based on peer assessment of their relative merits (among other things). He was also concerned that each Fourierist community would be in competition with every other community unless they could be centrally managed, possibly on a global scale, and he did not think this would be possible for a very, very long time. It is not quite clear exactly why this latter point is a problem, as Mill saw it: he did not raise the problem of intra-association competition as a problem against cooperative socialism, for instance. But perhaps he meant only that this was a question to which the Fourierists had not yet worked out an answer, which would be needed before the scheme could be immediately available, and it would particularly be a very long time before a centralized scheme was immediately available. Moreover, he said these were "difficulties, not impossibilities," which suggests he saw Fourierism as feasible. Mill, *Principles*, 985. These concerns do not arise in the later editions, nor do they in *Chapters*. In the later editions of *Principles*, Mill concluded that "it must be evident that this system does no violence to any of the general laws by which human action, even in the present imperfect state of moral and intellectual cultivation, is influenced; and that it would be extremely rash to pronounce it incapable of success, or unfitted to realise a great part of the hopes founded on it by partisans." Ibid., 213.
125 Mill, *Chapters*, 738.

126 Mill, *Principles*, 211–12.
127 Mill, *Chapters*, 747.
128 Mill, *Principles*, 775–94.
129 Ibid., 793–4.
130 Ibid., 784–92.
131 Ibid., 784–5.
132 Ibid., 775–94.
133 Ibid., 210.
134 Ibid., 210, 783.
135 Ibid., 783.
136 Ibid., 208.
137 Ibid., 783.
138 Ibid.; Mill, *Comte*, 340–1.
139 Mill, *Autobiography*, 239.
140 Mill, *Claims*, 379–82.
141 Mill, *Principles*, 770–5.
142 Ibid., 210, 783; Mill, *Chapters*, 747–8.
143 For more on the meaning of "availability" as I use it in the sub-head here, see McCabe, "Navigating by the North Star," 291–309; Mill, *Chapters*, 750.
144 Mill, "Fontana and Prati," 678.
145 Mill, *Principles*, 211.
146 Ibid., 213. Mill's repeated insistence that Fourier's ideas be tried in practice led Fredman and Gordon to declare that Mill felt that "Fourierist communities can be tried within, and without hurt to, the wider, existing system," but that it was this system Mill was concerned to preserve, albeit with a little more cooperation. But this is to miss an important point about Mill's interest in Fourier, and his overall desire regarding the "system." Whether or not Fourier's phalanxes succeseded, or were even attempted, Mill desired changes that would do far more than merely maintain the current system, albeit with a few socialist experiments in the countryside: instead, socialist experiments held the potential for even *further* reform over and above Mill's highly radical and transformative plans. Fredman and Gordon, "Mill and Socialism," 6; Mill, *Principles*, 212–13.
147 Mill, Letter 24, 1030.
148 Mill: *Principles*, 213–14; *Chapters*, 738.
149 Ibid., 745–6. Fredman and Gordon, in "Mill and Socialism," 4, use Mill's concern about the speed at which people could be educated for communism as an argument for Mill never *really* being a socialist. However,

although Mill certainly thought it would take multiple generations for people to be educated enough to make socialism feasible (in terms of a radical character transformation on the part of both employers and employees), this does not undermine his commitment to that change as normative, desirable, and necessary, nor his belief that it was feasible. One does not have to think that full-blown socialism is immediately feasible to be a socialist.

150 Mill, *Chapters*, 745.
151 Mill, *Principles*, 746.
152 Mill, *Considerations*, 404–5. Given the argument that Taylor was the communist, not Mill, it is worth noting that *Considerations* was published two years after her death.
153 Ibid.; Mill, *Principles*, 748.
154 Mill's commitment to immediate reforms that could be scaled up as they were proved practicable may be one reason why he has been linked to Fabianism (both by Fabians themselves and by later commentators – Cole, *Short History*, 3:22; Fabian Society, *Economics of Direct Employment*, 245; Webb, "The Difficulties," 18; Crosland, *Future of Socialism*, 83–4, 88; Britton, *Mill*, 43). This perhaps applies more to his willingness to adopt *some* state-level reform and build toward a socialist future from there, than to his interest in small-scale, intentional communities. But this very interest is the reason why "Fabian" is not a good term for Mill's socialism. Crudely put, the Fabians favoured a method of reform whereby everyone adopted a very small amount of socialism, which would gradually increase until the whole of society was socialist. Mill preferred that a small group of volunteers adopt "all" of socialism; their good example would then encourage more and more people to adopt "all" of socialism, until the whole society was socialist. Moreover, the overall goal of Fabianism was a form of state-socialism, and Mill was not a state-socialist.
155 Mill, *Chapters*, 747–8.
156 Mill, *Principles*, 213–14.
157 Mill, "Co-operation: Closing Speech," 320.
158 Ibid., 323.
159 Mill, "M. Cabet," 1144–6.
160 Fredman and Gordon, "Mill and Socialism," 4; Riley, *Liberal Utilitarianism*, 218–19.
161 Mill, *On Liberty*, 261.
162 Mill, "Co-operation: Closing Speech," 321.
163 Mill, *Principles*, 207–9, 977–9 (including *f–f*).

164 Ibid., 209–10, 977–9.
165 The earliest editions have whether communism would lead "to the destruction of." Ibid., 978 *f–f*, 979, and 1852 had "would be favourable to." Ibid., 209. The sentiment is the same, but the change of phrasing (from more negative to somewhat more positive) is interesting.
166 Mill, *Principles*, 209. The 1849 edition reads identically apart from having "could" instead of "would." The 1848 and manuscript version is identical up to "points of view" but ends slightly differently, with "which by presenting to each innumerable notions that he could not have conceived of himself, are the great stimulus to intellect and the mainspring of mental and moral progression." Ibid., 207, 979, 978 *f–f*.
167 Mill, *Principles*, 208–10, 977–9.
168 Ibid., 209.
169 Ibid., 978 *f–f*. See also Mill, "Co-operation: Closing Speech," 320.
170 Mill, *Principles*, 977–9, 207–9.
171 Mill, *On Liberty*, 261.
172 Mill, *Principles*, 207.
173 Ibid., 209.
174 Mill, *Chapters*, 745–6.
175 Sarvasy, "Mill's Theory of Democracy," 570.
176 Mill, *Principles*, xcii.
177 Mill, Letter 30, 49–50.
178 Mill, *Principles*, 981.
179 Ibid. and 212–14; Mill, *Chapters*, 747–8.
180 Mill, *Principles*, 209. The link to Fourier's language about the natural "passions" and the importance of allowing them all their play is interesting.
181 Claeys, "Justice, Independence, and Industrial Democracy," 122; Baum, "Liberal Socialism," 104; Baum, "Economic Freedom," 501–2. This is another reason Riley's claim, in *Liberal Utilitarianism*, 218–19, that Mill was undecided which was better for individuality, socialism or a reformed system of capitalism, is misplaced: Mill was clear about the institutions that were best for individuality, and these were, as the previous discussion shows, socialist.
182 Mill, *Autobiography*, 241.
183 Mill, *Principles*, 208.
184 Persky, *Political Economy of Progress*, 207–8.
185 Mill, *Utilitarianism*, 244.
186 Mill, *On Liberty*, 287.

187 Ibid., 283. Here Mill seems to view individual contracts for work and wages as being within the self-regarding sphere, which is perhaps odd, given his assertion that "trade is a social act" and that "whoever undertakes to sell any description of goods to the public, does what affects the interest of other persons, and of society in general; and thus his conduct, in principle, comes within the jurisdiction of society." Mill, *On Liberty*, 293. Perhaps workers, on Mill's view, "sell" their labour not "to the public" but to individual employers, though this may be an overly nice distinction, given the range of possible employers even for quite skilled labour. If selling one's labour is *also* a social act, then workers might well have rights to exert pressure were harm being caused by certain labour contracts.

188 Mill, *Autobiography*, 239.

189 Ibid., 209–10.

190 Mill, *Autobiography*, 175.

191 Southey, "Doctrine de Saint Simon," 424–5.

192 Mill, "Fontana and Prati," 678. Interestingly, Mill uses almost exactly the same words in his *Autobiography* where he speaks of "the scheme gradually unfolded by the St. Simonians, under which the labour and capital of society would be managed for the general account of the community, every individual being required to take a share of labour, either as thinker, teacher, artist, or producer, all being classed according to their capacity, and remunerated according to their works," and saying it "appeared to me a far superior description of Socialism to Owen's." Mill, *Autobiography*, 175.

193 Mill, *Principles*, 210, 781–3.

194 Ibid., 980. This echo of Rawls gives plausibility to Rawls's assertion that Mill would have agreed with his two principles of justice (see Rawls, *Lectures*, 267), though Ryan is right to note there is no clear proof that Mill would have supported "maximin" (see Ryan, *Mill*, 124). Moreover, as Mill deletes this line in later editions of *Principles*, it is not clear whether he continued to hold as "just" anything approximating the difference principle.

195 Mill, *Chapters*, 743–4.

196 Mill, *Autobiography*, 175.

197 Mill, "Fontana and Prati," 678.

198 Mill, *Principles*, 203–5.

199 Ibid., 204, 791.

200 *The Examiner*, 3 November 1833.

201 For instance, Mill, "Co-operation: Closing Speech," 314, 321; Mill, *Marriage*, 37–48; Thompson and Wheeler, *Appeal*, 66–7, 86–8, 187–8. See also McCabe, "Taylor and Wheeler."
202 This is not directly addressed in the *Appeal* but was a common cause with other Owenites (and Owen himself). Cf. Owen, *The Charter of the Rights of Humanity*, in *Selected Works* vol. 2, 225–57; and Owen, *Lecture on the Marriages of the Priesthood of the Old Immoral World*, in *Selected Works* vol. 2, 263–5.
203 Which Mill takes directly from Owen (*Marriage*, 48–9n). See also Mill's opposition to "sensualists" (*Marriage*, 40), and Thompson and Wheeler on "sensualists" (*Appeal*, 194–5). That said, although Mill does advocate "regulated community of living, among persons intimately acquainted," as this would "prevent the necessity of total separation between parents even when they had ceased to be connected by any nearer tie than mutual good will and a common interest in their children" (*Marriage*, 47), he does not go as far as the Owenites at this stage in his feminist proposals regarding releasing women from what he later calls "domestic subjection" (*Principles*, 209), arguing point blank in *Marriage* (43–4) that "it does not follow that a woman should actually support herself because she should be capable of doing so: in the natural course of events she will not." The Owenites (including Thompson and Wheeler), however, went much further, with Owenite parallelograms involving children doing the housework, thus freeing women to contribute and develop in other ways, as well as deliberately involved communal living as a means of reducing the necessary domestic labour, which currently fell almost solely on women. See Taylor, *Eve and the New Jerusalem*, 245.
204 Moses, *French Feminism*, 42.
205 The Saint-Simonians, *The Doctrine*, 85. This historical account of women's position in society has clear echoes in Mill's *Marriage*; "Fontana and Prati," 680; and *Subjection of Women*, 266–82.
206 Enfantin, *Final Address*, 1258. Compare Mill, *Subjection*, 324–5, where Mill uses language almost identical to that of his much earlier translation, and also "Fontana and Prati," 680.
207 Mill, "Fontana and Prati," 678; Mill, *Marriage*, 40.
208 Mill, "Fontana and Prati," 679.
209 Moses, *French Feminism*, 46.
210 Being defended, after all, by two women at his trial in 1832 (who were evicted from the court). Pankhurst, *Saint-Simonians*, 90.

211 Mill, *Marriage*, 36–8. See Urbinati, "Mill on Androgeny and Ideal Marriage," 627; Pankhurst, *Saint-Simonians*, 96; and Moses, *French Feminism*, 49.
212 Mill, *Principles*, 209.
213 Mill, *Chapters*, 748n.
214 Mill, *Principles*, 793–4.
215 Ibid., 758.
216 Mill, *Autobiography*, 239.
217 Mill, *Principles*, 209.
218 Ibid, 360.
219 Ibid., 978n, *f–f*.
220 It is interesting that Mill did *not* think "the elements" were a source of happiness or a "subject of consciousness."
221 Mill, *Autobiography*, 257. Mill wanted to insert generally (and did put into some "presentation copies") a note that "to Mrs John Taylor ... this attempt to explain and diffuse ideas many of which were first learned from herself, is with the highest respect and regard, dedicated."
222 See Mill, Letter 15, 1027–8.
223 Claeys notes that, in this passage, Mill said if they do no longer think this regarding communism, "there is nothing to be said against Communism at all – one would only have to turn round & advocate it," and surmises that Mill wrote this "probably with a tone of suppressed irritation." Claeys, *Mill and Paternalism*, 151. This supposition is not warranted – tone, after all, being hard to read in letters, and given what changes are *actually* made to *Principles*. For more on this, see McCabe, "Harriet Taylor, and John Stuart Mill's Socialism," 197–234.
224 Mill, *Principles*, 978.
225 Ibid., 208.
226 Mill, *Autobiography*, 245.
227 Mill, *Newman*, 444.
228 Mill, *Claims*, 379; Mill, *Principles*, 754.
229 Mill, "Spirit of the Age Part IV," 291; "Spirit of the Age Part V (1)," 305. This thought is repeated in the much later *Utility of Religion* (407). For the Saint-Simonian view, see, for example, Saint-Simon, *Selected Writings*, 102.
230 Mill, "Spirit of the Age Part IV," 290; "Spirit of the Age Part II," 242; and *Autobiography*, 173.
231 Ryan, *Mill*, 36; Ryan, "Bureaucracy, Democracy, Liberty," 158–9.
232 Mill, Letter 26, 31–2; Mill, Letter 27, 37; Mill, *Autobiography*, 239.

233 Eugene d'Eichthal, in "Introduction," 212, recalls that "un point de dissidence entre nous a été sa négation do toute croyance religieuse." Mill was particularly worried about Saint-Simonian "religious" principles becoming dogmas, and the ensuing calcification of their radicalism (Mill, Letter 27, 37–8), and about the very notion of "organising" an "insensible influence of mind over mind" (Mill, Letter 28, 40–1; Mill, "Spirit of the Age Part IV," 291, and "Spirit of the Age Part V [II]," 312–13).
234 Mill, Letter 383, 560; Mill, *Autobiography*, 45; Mill, Letter 524, 734; Mill, *Theism*, 488–9.
235 Mill, *Comte*, 340–1.
236 Mill, *Chapters*, 744.
237 Ibid., 744–5. Mill's language of "rivalry" and "personal passions" is very reminiscent of Fourier and Considerant here. (See also McCabe, "Mill and Fourierism," 35–61.) It is possible that this account of communist associations being "torn apart" by dissent on these issues is based on Mill's knowledge of the actual demise of some Owenite experiments, though he does not cite any of them in the text.
238 Mill, *Chapters*, 745.
239 Mill, *Considerations*, 404–5.
240 Mill, *Autobiography*, 239.
241 Mill, *Principles*, 775.
242 Ibid., 780–2.
243 Ibid., 792.
244 For more on the Fourierist connections to this phrase, see McCabe, "Mill and Fourierism," 35–61.
245 Mill, *Principles*, 792.
246 Mill, *Autobiography*, 175.
247 Ibid., 239.

Chapter Four

1 Mill, Letter 531, 739.
2 Turner, "Evolutionary Theory of Justice," 134.
3 Mill, *Autobiography*, 239.
4 Mill, *Logic*, 952, quoted in Turner, "Evolutionary Theory of Justice," 134.
5 Mill, *Autobiography*, 177.
6 For more detail on Mill's reaction to 1848, see McCabe: "Mill on 'Legitimate Socialism,'" 335-53, and "Mill and the French Revolution of 1848," 119–62.

7 Kurer, *Politics of Progress*.
8 Mill, *On Liberty*, 224.
9 Rawls, *Lectures*, 292, 301–5.
10 Rawls identifies many of the same institutions but argues they amount to a form of property-owning democracy.
11 Notably, Persky, *Political Economy of Progress*; Turner, "Evolutionary Theory," 131–46; Kurer, *Politics of Progress*; Claeys, *Mill and Paternalism*; Baum, "Liberal Socialism," 98–123, "Freedom and Power," 187–216, and "Economic Freedom," 494–530; Sarvasy, "Mill's Socialism," 312–33, and "Mill's Theory of Democracy," 567–87.
12 Kurer, "Mill and Utopian Socialism," 222–32; Claeys, "Justice, Independence, and Industrial Democracy," 122–47; Stafford, "Paradigmatic Liberal," 325–45; Persky, *Political Economy of Progress*, 91–151.
13 Notably, Persky, *Political Economy of Progress*, 199–216; and Turner, "Evolutionary Theory of Justice," 131–46, and "Luck and Distributive Justice in Mill," 80–93.
14 See also Kurer, *Politics of Progress*, 5.
15 Mill, *Autobiography*, 169.
16 Cf. Mill, *Bentham's Philosophy*, 10.
17 Mill, *Autobiography*, 177.
18 One might think that "progress" is not a "secondary principle," but the means, and/or the measure, of the extent to which core principles are being realized. That is true, on one understanding of "progress." But given Mill's commitment to institutions *allowing for* the further progress of humanity, I retain "progress" here – Mill thought that a society closing off possibilities of reform was negative.
19 As Morales rightly notes, one of Mill's earliest critics, James FitzJames Stephen, identified "liberty, equality, and fraternity" as "the three central tenets of Mill's humanitarian creed." Morales, *Perfect Equality*, 22.
20 Mill, *Utilitarianism*, 251.
21 However, contrary to what some have argued – see Schapiro, "Pioneer of Liberalism," 137–8; Riley, "Capitalism versus Socialism," 48; Schwartz, *New Political Economy*, 187–8 – Mill's aversion to revolution (apart from in some specific circumstances) and to "revolutionary socialism" does not undermine his *own* socialism, as many forms of socialism are evolutionary rather than revolutionary in their preferred means, and speed, of enacting social transformation.
22 Mill, *Chapters*, 749.
23 Mill, *Principles*, 233.
24 Mill, Letter 1690, 1847–8.

25 Cf. Cohen, *If You're An Egalitarian*, 104.
26 Mill, Letter 525, 734.
27 For more on Mill's view of revolution, see McCabe, "Mill on 'Legitimate Socialism,'" 335–53, and "Mill and the French Revolution of 1848," 119–82.
28 Mill, *Whewell*, 192.
29 Mill, *Utilitarianism*, 249–51.
30 Mill, *Principles*, 360.
31 The emphasis on limiting "indulgence," on "conditions they do not like," and on "enforced rigidity of discipline" may well make modern leftists uncomfortable, though this rhetoric is still often heard regarding unemployment benefits (and not only from those on the right). In part, this is because people are often uncomfortable with Mill's views regarding people's right to have children, notwithstanding their ability to provide for them. For more on this, see Claeys, *Mill and Paternalism*, 173–210. As Ekelund and Tollison rightly note, however, "whether anyone today would defend Mill's means in this question is not important." Rather, we should recognize that this is an important attempt on Mill's part – and a significant break with earlier economists – to "design ... an 'optimum' system to alleviate (and ultimately eliminate) poverty" and trying to determine "the means for achieving three interrelated goals relating to poverty and distribution: aid [of] the destitute poor, provision of 'the right kind' of work incentives for the able-bodied poor, and use of poverty policy as a vehicle for (ultimately) altering income distribution." They link his ideas to modern proposals for a minimum income and conclude that "the goals he espoused, goals which, incidentally, are very close to those of contemporary assistance program proposals, represent a brilliant attempt to blend social justice with market economics." Ekelund and Tollison, "New Political Economy," 221. I agree that whether *this* solution is palatable to the modern reader is not particularly important, though I would also emphasize that any "attempt to blend social justice with market economics," if that involves private property and not just some markets in the trade of goods and services, was only Mill's goal for a specific period of history, not for all time, under Mill's progressive understanding of justice.
32 It is also worth noting that Mill endorsed workhouses because he thought people had a duty to contribute – where they could – to meeting the costs of their own existence (and working is the most obvious way of meeting that duty). Mill, *Negro Question*, 91. This also placed a duty on society to provide work for people: "the *droit au travail* is the most manifest of moral truths, the most imperative of political obligations,"

Mill wrote in defence of the actions of the Provisional Government in 1848. Mill, *Vindication*, 348–9. Again, it is also worth noting that Mill emphasized that workhouses should not be sources of shame, but only undesirable, and that in them "the bodily wants of the pauper [should] be amply cared for." Mill, "Poor Laws," 688. Although Mill was not a great supporter of government loans for producer cooperatives (thinking them more sustainable if they were founded from the joint capital of workers), this process on the part of the Provisional Government was, of course, a way of providing work without doing it via "indoor relief" in workhouses and thus (in the long run) probably with less government expenditure.

33 Mill, *Principles*, 978.
34 Ibid., 208.
35 Mill, Letter 531, 739.
36 Mill, *Autobiography*, 65.
37 See Baum, "Economic Freedom," 494–530; Sarvasy, "Mill's Socialism," 312–33.
38 Gray, *Liberalisms*, 220. Reeves (*Victorian Firebrand*, 6) is therefore correct to say that liberty was "necessary for" happiness, but not that liberty was "superior to" happiness. Mill remained a utilitarian, for whom happiness ought to be the final "end" of all human activity (though not always the immediate "end" or pursuit of individual action). Although one may think that Mill's faith that a society that was truly concerned with the greatest happiness of the greatest number would find it impossible to do other than respect liberty was misplaced (and also reject Riley's attempts to explicate this in terms of a liberal understanding of utility), it would be wrong to try and show that Mill grounded liberty in anything but utility (such as justice). Riley, *Liberal Utilitarianism*, 7, 69, 90, 164–207; Gray, *Liberalisms*, 218–21; Ryan, *Philosophy of Mill*, 223–30; Ten, *Mill On Liberty*, 5–6, 79–80; Rawls, *Lectures*, 267–308; Donner, *Liberal Self*, 129.
39 Mill, *On Liberty*, 260–75.
40 For example, Gray, *Liberalisms*, 223; Ten, *Mill On Liberty*, 52.
41 Mill, *On Liberty*, 260.
42 Baum, "Economic Freedom," 498.
43 Mill, *On Liberty*, 223–4.
44 Baum, "Liberal Socialism," 102.
45 Mill, *On Liberty*, 223–4.
46 Gray, *Liberalisms*, 222–3.
47 Ryan, *Philosophy of Mill*, 254, and "Open Society," 635.

48 Donner, *Liberal Self*, 160–97.
49 Riley, *Liberal Utilitarianism*, 177–80, 193–8.
50 Rawls, *Lectures*, 292 and 301–5.
51 Gray, *Liberalisms*, 223–4.
52 Mill, *On Liberty*, 273.
53 Donner, *Liberal Self*, 160–97; Rees, *Mill's On Liberty*, 3–4, 17–28, 46, 126–8, 139–52. Rees aligns rights with "the prevailing standards of what people can expect from others." On the one hand, this goes some way to encapsulating the *progressive* (and thus transitional) nature of rights for Mill. That is, as noted, we have a "permanent interest" in security of subsistence, but only in societies that have reached a certain level of coordination and technological and moral progress can this interest rightly be translated into a "right." On the other hand, Mill thought we *did have a right* even where people did not, as yet, generally respect that right – that is, people (in Britain, at least) *had a right to security of subsistence*, even though this view was not generally widespread, and it could not truthfully be said that guaranteeing subsistence was a "prevailing standard ... of what people can expect from others." So there is some merit in the critique of Rees on this point offered by Ten in *Mill On Liberty*, 11–16, 55–8, 74–5, and we should not see harm as *merely* contingent on the standard norms of behaviour, as this risks limiting liberty in the kinds of ways Mill is deliberately trying to prevent, particularly when it comes to "eccentric" behaviour. Furthermore, we should be cautious of trying to turn Mill into too much of a Kantian (or Rawlsian) liberal, allowing for *no* "impermanence" regarding rights. Against both Rees's and Ten's interpretations, I suggest that harm *always* means something detrimental to our permanent interests as progressive beings, and is only relative in the following sense: in a non-modern society it may not be that our permanent interests are best served by implementation of the harm principle (we need, for instance, a forcible Akbar or Charlemagne to weld the community together into a "people" who will obey laws and generally abide by rules of conduct in a peaceable fashion), but as soon as we are ready, as a people, for such a principle, it ought to be implemented.
54 Mill, *On Liberty*, 292.
55 Ibid., 223–5.
56 A position Ten rejects, but that I think is the most plausible reading of Mill. Ten, *Mill On Liberty*, 47. See also idem, "Mill on Self-Regarding Actions," 29–37.
57 Mill, *On Liberty*, 224.

58 Ryan, *Mill*, 133; Ten, *Mill On Liberty*, 18.
59 Baum, "Liberal Socialism," 102, and "Economic Freedom," 498; Donner, *Liberal Self*, 120–1. Mill did not use "autonomy" but did use "*autonomie*" in a (French) letter about *On Liberty*. Mill, Letter 1678, 1832. Skorupski also links autonomy and sovereignty in Mill's account of liberty, although he adds that autonomy and happiness must be separate ends (*Mill*, 21). This is not entirely true: autonomy and happiness are not the same thing, but autonomy only has value as a means to the end of happiness. Although autonomy may have worth to the individual as being in accordance with a self-imposed standard of excellence (and thus receive ends status), these standards of excellence are also ultimately justified in terms of happiness. Capaldi (*Mill*, 62) goes so far as to identify autonomy as Mill's *only* good, and to say he thought *any* action, so long as autonomous, was right. As Stafford, "Capaldi," 446, points out, this is clearly mistaken: Mill was a utilitarian (whose concept of utility was not adequately defined as autonomy), and not a disguised Kantian.
60 Mill, *On Liberty*, 226.
61 Ibid., 224–5. This adds weight to the many interpretations of Mill's concept of liberty as "positive" (*contra* Berlin and, more recently, Capaldi, who see Mill as having a purely "negative" concept of freedom). Capaldi, "Mill and Socialism," 125–44.
62 Mill, *Junius Redivivus [II]*, 383.
63 For more on this, see Jenson, "Mill's Theories," 499.
64 Mill: *Principles*, 207–8, 387–8, 977; *Marriage*, 41–3.
65 Mill: *Junius Redivivus [I]* and *[II]*, 374–5, 383; *Marriage*, 41–3; *Subjection*, 264, 271–2; *Claims*, 371–4, 379–82; *Principles*, 207–8, 387–8, 977.
66 Mill, *On Liberty*, 224.
67 Mill, *Claims*, 378.
68 Mill, *Principles*, 763.
69 Gray, "Introduction," xiv.
70 Urbinati, *Mill on Democracy*, 10–11; Baum, "Liberal Socialism," 102–3; Jones, *Victorian Political Thought*, 35–7.
71 Urbinati, *Mill on Democracy*, 10–11.
72 Biagini, "Liberalism and Direct Democracy," 21–2.
73 Berger, "Substantive Principles of Justice," 374.
74 Urbinati, *Mill on Democracy*, 10–11.
75 Ibid., 238–41.
76 Ibid., 156, 159–60; Riley, "Mill's Neo-Athenian Model," 237–8.

77 See also Claeys, "Justice, Independence, and Industrial Democracy," 134, where he writes that "the moral principle of independence ... was the basis of individuality of character and social diversity." Here, I think Claeys is separating out independence from individuality and freedom, whereas I feel the word well encapsulates what Mill took freedom to be. Claeys, 135–6, takes "independence" to mean something like contemporary co-operators meant by "self-help," or the ability of workers to stand on their own two feet and not be dependent on capitalists for work, wages, or the means of production. This was an important idea, both for co-operators like Holyoake, and for Mill (who, as Claeys quotes, said that cooperation achieves "freedom and independence"). It is an outcome of increasing worker's freedom, and a worthy goal in its own right, and not the same as freedom itself. So though we use the same word, Claeys and I have something slightly different in mind – and I only use the term "freedom as independence" as a way of highlighting important elements of what Mill *means* by freedom. However, I agree with Claeys that seeing the importance of independence to Mill (either as his concept of liberty, or as an important, but separate, moral principle) helps emphasize that his concept was more "positive" than "negative."

78 Thus Mill's conception is free from the charges usually levelled against positive ideas of liberty: Mill does not identify a ruling "self" that could be identified with any ruling group, or ideological construct that benefited such a group (that is, no one can know better than the individual agent what their "higher" self is like, as Mill has no concept of such a higher self, and is committed to the idea that adults are generally the best judges of their own interests). Moreover, for Mill we are only free if we are abiding by authentic, reflectively chosen, self-imposed standards of excellence: so our freedom cannot be corrupted into blind submission to any group, individual, or conception of a "general will." This also means that Mill can have no conception of being "forced to be free." One can be forced to do one's duty, and it is true that perfectly virtuous people will always do their duty. But Mill does not conflate those two ideas. If one is not perfectly virtuous, and one has to be forced to perform some duty, one is not thereby being rendered free. One is merely being forced to perform a right action, that one *ought* to have chosen to do in the first place. Ryan, *Idea of Freedom*, 5; Mill, *Liberty*, 299–300.

79 Baum, "Economic Freedom," 498.

80 For more on the harm principle "prescrib[ing] an area within which individuals ought to be free" rather than in any way itself defining what

freedom means, see Smith, "Mill on Freedom," 182–4, and "Social Liberty and Free Agency," 239. See also Baum, "Economic Freedom," 497–8, and "Freedom and Power," 187–216; and Ryan, "Property, Liberty, and *On Liberty*," 217–31.

81 As Ryan notes, Mill showed that this was the case, as he declared that his *On Liberty* was intended mainly for England, where social tolerance lagged behind political liberty. He writes that *On Liberty* was not "political," but was "a philosophic textbook of a single truth … the importance, to man and society, of a large variety in types of character, and of giving full freedom to human nature to expand itself in innumerable and conflicting directions" – that is, it is concerned with questions of giving scope to individuality, not with justifying a certain concept of the state or governmental power. *Contra* Himmelfarb, this assertion, however, does not show that this was Mill's *only* principle. Ryan, *Mill*, 134; Mill, Letter 339, 581, Letter 349, 589, and *Autobiography*, 259; Gray, "Introduction," xxii.
82 Mill, *On Liberty*, 271–2.
83 Ibid., 219, 264.
84 Ibid., 219–20; Baum, "Economic Freedom," 499.
85 Mill, *On Liberty*, 220–1, 264.
86 Mill is thus doing more than Gray imagines – he is not merely describing the only society in which people who had developed their individuality would consent to live, but the only society in which *all* people *could* live and maintain, or even begin freely to develop, their individuality. Because of the intimate connection between happiness and individuality, Mill is also describing an important attribute of the only society in which the greatest happiness of the greatest number can be achieved. Gray, *Liberalism*, 2.
87 Baum, "Economic Freedom," 494.
88 Baum, citing Schwartz, "Economic Freedom," 494–5.
89 Baum, "Economic Freedom," 495–6.
90 Ibid., 496.
91 Claeys, "Justice, Independence, and Industrial Democracy," 134–5.
92 Mill, *On Liberty*, 224.
93 Mill, *Principles*, 209.
94 This is one reason I disagree with Persky that Mill has a similar concept of "alienation" to that of Marx. See Persky, *Political Economy of Progress*, 157; and McCabe, "Mill's 'Modern' Radicalism Re-examined," 149.
95 Mill: *Principles*, 209, and *Subjection*, 259–340.

96 Miller, in "Mill's 'Socialism,'" 214, 228, suggests that, because Mill has a general presumption in favour of letting individuals decide for themselves, we should expect – on Millian grounds – that some workers will opt out of socialism, even in an "ideal" future. I agree that Mill does not *insist* that everyone *will* work in associations: there is scope in Mill's theory for "self-employed" workers, as well as civil servants and those working for government "pensions" including artists and scientists. In line with his view of individuality, there could not be a *compulsion* to work in an association: though there could be a compulsion to perform *some sort of work* that meets the costs of one's own existence. See Mill, *Autobiography*, 239. The important point, though, is motivation. In Mill's "ideal" future, lone geniuses ("mad scientists," "poets," "hermits" etc.) might well not work in associations for reasons to do with individuality and autonomy or control over their work, but the profit motive that might induce someone to leave a cooperative for greater personal *monetary* gain would be lacking. On Mill's view of progress, we will not need to make that illegal: people would simply cease to desire it (or allow themselves to be motivated by that desire, should they have it).

97 Mill, *Principles*, 794.
98 Baum, "Economic Freedom," 500.
99 Ibid., 502–3.
100 Mill, *Principles*, 769, 775–94.
101 Ibid., 775.
102 Baum, "Economic Freedom," 505n45.
103 Mill, *On Liberty*, 226.
104 Baum, "Economic Freedom," 506.
105 For more on Mill and feminist critiques of his account of women's role in the household, and external, economy, see McCabe, "'Good Housekeeping'?," 135–55.
106 Mill does not give a Marxist, or dialectical, account of this. Again, this makes me wary of Persky's claim that Mill has a materialist conception of history, or significant similarities to Marx (though perhaps we both mean something different by the term). But I do think Mill and Marx share this analysis of what capitalism has done in terms of changing the fundamental relations of production (via cooperation of labour on a mass scale, while ensuring economies of scale and expansion of business, and the change of production from small-scale industry to "manufactories," though of course these would seem pretty small-scale in comparison to modern-day industrial production lines, further revolutionised by,

for instance, Ford). And they both see the future as being one in which this combination of labour continues, only freed from capitalist control, rather than a reversion to smaller-scale production, and with it much less security of subsistence (never mind the promise of abundance). I think Mill gave a greater role to the superstructure than Marx seems to allow.

107 Mill, Letter 531, 739.
108 Berger and Morales are notable exceptions.
109 Berger, "Substantive Principles of Justice," 374; Turner, "Luck and Distributive Justice," 80–93, and "Evolutionary Theory of Justice."
110 Persky, *Political Economy of Progress*, 215, and "Mill's Socialism Re-examined," 177–9.
111 For the classic expression of luck-egalitarianism, see Dworkin, "What Is Equality? Part II," 283–345.
112 Turner, "Luck and Distributive Justice," 80–93, and "Evolutionary Theory of Justice." My thanks to Turner for clarification of his view here, and also for many discussions about Mill's egalitarianism over the past few years.
113 Mill, *Principles*, 203. For fear of begging the question, I will not deal with this in detail, but it is also worth considering that it has been argued that luck-egalitarianism is inconsistent with socialism. See, for instance, Miller, "Incoherence of Luck-Egalitarianism," 131–50.
114 Mill, Letter 495.
115 Mill, *Utilitarianism*, 257–8.
116 For more on this, see McCabe, "'Good Housekeeping'?," 135–55, and "Mill, Utility and the Family," 225–35.
117 See Mill, *Principles*, 775–94.
118 Berger, "Substantive Principles of Justice," 374.
119 Turner, "Luck and Distributive Justice," 80–93.
120 Ibid., 85.
121 In correspondence, Turner notes that he thinks Mill is committed to something stronger than abstract "equal consideration" – something more like "equal treatment, except where there is some strong positive reason for inequality."
122 See Orwell, *Animal Farm*, esp. 79–84.
123 Mill, *Utilitarianism*, 257.
124 Ibid., 218, cited in Clark and Elliott, "Mill's Theory of Justice," 473; Devigne, "Mill's Theory of Justice," 647.
125 See also, Clark and Elliot, "Mill's Theory of Justice," 475.

126 Mill: *Marriage*, 42; *Negro Question*, 92–3; Letter 24, 27–8; *Ireland*, 61–98; *Principles*, 767.
127 Mill, *Utilitarianism*, 259.
128 Mill took what is now a rightly criticized view that colonial activity – for instance, his own work at the East India Company – could kick-start, guide, and catalyse such progress. He also resisted the takeover of India by the Crown as unwarranted centralization, likely to retard progress and leave India open to exploitation. His support of colonial rule, though rightly hard to swallow by modern audiences, is not in contradistinction to his socialism, nor does it undermine it: Mill saw social progress as historical and contingent, and his argument is that some capitalist societies are ripe for beginning the transformation toward something better (i.e., socialism), a position more and more societies will find themselves in as they, too, progress along a broadly similar trajectory of economic, social, and political development. See Mill, *Memorandum*; *Constitutional View*; *Observations*; and *Moral of the India Debate*. For more on Mill and colonialism, see Tunick, "Tolerant Imperialism"; Jahn, "Barbarian Thoughts"; Sullivan, "Liberalism and Imperialism"; and Habibi, "Mill on Colonialism."
129 Mill, *Principles*, 784. Famously, this equality of rights is *to* vote, but not to an equal number of votes. Mill, *Considerations* 469–74. I discuss this in detail below.
130 Mill, *Principles*, 943. For more on this, see Turner, "Mill on Luck and Distributive Justice," 85–6.
131 Riley, *Liberal Utilitarianism*, 206.
132 Mill, Letter 495.
133 Mill, *Utilitarianism*, 257.
134 Mill, *Principles*, 203.
135 Berger, "Mill's Substantive Principles of Justice," 376. See, for instance, Mill, *Principles*, 208.
136 Mill, *Utilitarianism*, 245–55.
137 Berger, "Substantive Principles of Justice," 376. Berger (375) also says that "Mill held out as an ultimate ideal state of society one in which the product of labour would be commonly owned." Berger is correct here only if we parse this idea in a particular way. Even under a socialist scheme that permits the unequal division of articles of consumption, those are – in themselves – part of the product of labour, and that product is "owned" and divided by society (rather than individual workers or employers). Thus, we might say that the product of labour is owned communally,

until (part of) it is distributed, when people get rights usually associated with property over it (e.g., consumption, transfer, and saving).
138 Mill, *Utilitarianism*, 254.
139 The idea of "starting fair in the race" has been linked to luck-egalitarianism by those who read Mill's egalitarianism in this light. But Turner rightly notes that "the principle of impartiality is broader than the concern to eliminate inequalities due to bad brute luck. For example, it supplies Mill's core principle of taxation on earned income, the principle of equal sacrifice." Turner, "Luck and Distributive Justice," 85. See also, Mill, *The Income and Property Tax*, 472, and *Errors and Truths on a Property Tax*, 550. Thus, he argues, a principle of impartiality is a key element of relational egalitarianism rather than luck-egalitarianism. I agree, and also argue that the principle of impartiality is at play in Mill's endorsement of Blancian distributive principles.
140 Turner, "Luck and Distributive Justice," 85. See also Mill, *Principles*, 811.
141 This is also a connection between Mill and relational rather than luck-egalitarianism.
142 Turner, "Luck and Distributive Justice," 85.
143 For further discussion of Mill, justice, socialism, communism, and Blanc's principle, see McCabe, "Navigating by the North Star," 291–309.
144 Berger, "Substantive Principles of Justice," 374.
145 Mill, *Chapters*, 713.
146 Mill, *Utilitarianism*, 241–2.
147 Mill, *Principles*, 360; Riley, *Liberal Utilitarianism*, 216.
148 Mill, *Vindication*, 348–9. Ekelund and Tollison argue "there can be little doubt that Mill wished to implement a minimum income plan that utilised market forces to maintain work incentives." Ekelund and Tollison, "New Political Economy of Mill," 227. I feel there can be really quite a lot of doubt, though doubtless Mill was drawn to Fourier's provision of a minimum income as part of his complex system of remuneration (something Ekelund and Tollison do not engage with, but on which see McCabe, "Mill and Fourierism, 35–61). They see Mill as desiring to "utilis[e] ... a public assistance plan as a tool for social progress along market lines" and that he sought systems "which, once started, are able to keep themselves going without further help." Ekelund and Tollison, "New Political Economy of Mill," 227. "Publicly provided poor relief was one of those systems," they conclude – but this is not clearly true. Workhouses kept people in work (and in the habits of working), and made self-support more attractive than public support. But they did not

keep themselves going once initially set up by government – the aim was not that they be financially self-sufficient, but that they (instead) need continued government support. Moreover, if anything, Mill's hope was that they would eventually be unnecessary, as workers controlled population and also moved into cooperation. Similarly, Ekelund and Tollison (229) add that "Mill's commentary on public employment as a means of alleviating poverty actually constitutes a quite modern critique of the concept of government as an employer of last resort." But his support for workhouses means it is not clear he was critiquing the idea of "government as employer of last resort," though I acknowledge his concern over government funding for producer cooperatives in 1848. See Varouxakis, *Victorian Political Thought*, 75–6. Ekelund and Tollison see Mill as explaining the "futility of trying to help the non-able-bodied poor by offering them an above-market wage rate and making this opportunity available to all workers as a general right." But Mill does not speak of paying wages (for work) for the non-able-bodied poor at all (who were still eligible for "outdoor relief," and, thus, were not to be accommodated in workhouses). Nor was the "wage-rate" in workhouses to be above the normal rate – quite the opposite, in fact.

149 Mill, *Principles*, 360.
150 Turner, "Mill on Luck and Distributive Justice," 86–8; Berger, "Mill's Substantive Principles of Justice," 374; Persky, *Political Economy of Progress*, 200–6, and "Mill's Socialism Re-examined," 177–9.
151 Turner, "Mill on Luck and Distributive Justice," 186.
152 As Turner notes, concerning "effort" and "exertion," Mill is only interested in rewarding "good" exertion and "does not mean to reward talent or exertion in the service of vice." See Mill, *Chapters*, 714.
153 Turner, "Mill on Luck and Distributive Justice," 86.
154 Ibid., 87–8.
155 Mill, *Utilitarianism*, 245–55.
156 Mill, *Principles*, 210.
157 Turner, "Luck and Distributive Justice," 87.
158 Turner is citing Mill, *Chapters*, 714.
159 Mill, *Chapters*, 714–15.
160 Berger, "Substantive Principles of Justice," 374.
161 Morales, "Perfect Equality," 116, quoting Mill, *Subjection of Women*, 261.
162 Schemmel, "Distributive and Relational Equality," 124–25.
163 Schemmel, "Social Equality," 154.
164 Anderson, "What Is the Point of Equality?," 288–9.

165　Anderson, "Fundamental Disagreement," 2–3.
166　See McCabe, "Mill, Utility, and the Family," 225–35.
167　Schemmel, "Social Equality," 147–55.
168　Mill, Letter 531, 739.
169　Stephen, *Liberty, Equality, Fraternity*, 256–318; Morales, *"Perfect Equality"*; Biagini, "Liberalism and Direct Democracy," 21–42; Kurer, *Politics of Progress*, 5. Mill was an admirer of Gladstone, and admired by him, as well as often being associated in the popular imagination with him (for instance, their faces were featured together on banners). Mill was also friends with Mazzini. Undoubtedly, then, this "community" strand of Gladstonian liberalism and Mazzinian republicanism appealed to Mill and chimed with his own commitments to fraternity and equality. Biagini treats it entirely as an element of Mill's liberalism. However, this commitment was *also* a core element of his socialism.
170　Stephen, *Liberty, Equality, Fraternity*, 256–318.
171　Morales, *"Perfect Equality,"* 16.
172　Biagini, "Liberalism and Direct Democracy," 21–42.
173　Kurer, *Politics of Progress*, 5–7.
174　In this, though, Mill may still be "liberal," just not libertarian.
175　Mill is, in this sense, more of a "Rawlsian" than a communitarian like Taylor (e.g., *Philosophy and the Human Sciences*), MacIntyre (e.g., *Against the Self-Images of the Age* and *Whose Justice? Which Rationality?*), or Benhabib (e.g. *Situating the Self*, 23–38, 89n4).
176　Mill, *Autobiography*, 239.
177　Most obviously, Michael Walzer.
178　Pateman's *Sexual Contract* highlights the fact that "fraternity" really *does* mean – and *only* mean – "the universal brotherhood of man": that is, it deliberately excludes women in the formation of a new "social contract" between men as equals, creating a new patriarchy to replace the old one of paternal rule. We have no word for a really universal relationship of this sort. "Siblinghood" is not a word, "sisterhood" and "brotherhood" are both gendered; "community" is too weak; "solidarity" too unreflective. Because of this, and because Mill used it, I retain "fraternity" here, though conscious of its gendered nature. Mill, however, did not mean to exclude women from a new social construction.
179　Mill, *Autobiography*, 239.
180　Mill, *Claims*, 382.
181　Mill, "Attack on Literature," 320.
182　Mill, *Utilitarianism*, 227.

183 Ibid., 230–1.
184 Mill, *Principles*, 753.
185 Morales, "Perfect Equality," 18.
186 Mill, *Autobiography*, 241.
187 Mill, *Claims*, 382.
188 Morales, "Perfect Equality," 147–74; see also McCabe, "Mill, Utility, and the Family," 225–35.
189 Morales, "Perfect Equality," 166.
190 Mill: Letter 383, 560 (cited *Liberty and Control*, 108); *Autobiography*, 45; Letter 524, 734; *Theism*, 488; Megill, "Mill's Religion of Humanity," 616–17.
191 Ryan, *Mill*, 36; Ryan, "Bureaucracy, Democracy, Liberty," 158–9. As Ryan notes, the clerisy was not to be populated by "ideologues" who would feed the people some apparently socially useful ideology that had little or no connection to the truth: rather, the clerisy was to engage in free discussion among itself and encourage the people to do so too through, in particular, educating them. Moreover, Mill's view regarding the best way of treating clergy ought to be born in mind: he praised the Scottish system, where the fact that something was the opinion of a minister provided an *a priori* reason to heed it, but one that could be overridden by one's own considered thoughts. Ryan, *Mill*, 36, 56–7, 127–8.
192 Mill, *Theism*, 488–9. It has been suggested that in *On Liberty*, Mill rejected a Comtean Religion of Humanity, but as Hamburger notes, this "does not mean ... that he did not have one of his own," the kind of religion, indeed, that he later sketched in *Theism*, and that Raeder thinks he was instituting in his Principle of Utility. Though this is plausible, the further claim that "Mill's goal ... involved the divinization of humanity" and "the elevation of 'service to Humanity' to the *ultimate* end of religious aspiration" is not. Additionally, Megill emphasizes Mill's feeling that the potentially authoritarian power of such a religion would need to be carefully controlled. In itself, however, the fact that such a religion might tend to authoritarianism does not make Mill himself an authoritarian. Hamburger, *Liberty and Control*, 124; Raeder, *Religion of Humanity*, 321; Megill, "Mill's Religion of Humanity," 612–29.
193 Stephen, *Liberty, Equality, Fraternity*, 1–3.
194 Mill, *Utilitarianism*, 231–2.
195 Kurer, *Politics of Progress*, 5–6.
196 Kurer adds that it also involves "the control of the government by the elite, who have to assure that the appropriate policies are implemented."

This is true in the sense that Mill always supported representative, rather than direct, democracy; hoped people would elect those more competent than themselves; and believed any government would need support from an expert, and neutral, civil service. His idea of a "clerisy" was, in part, to create a *new* elite, rather than the old one based on aristocratic privileges and/or wealth. But as Sarvasy rightly notes, many elements of Mill's theory that are criticized as "elitist" are merely transitional as society transitions into socialism. See Sarvasy, "Mill's Theory of Democracy," 567–87.

197 Mill, *Vindication*, 334, 325.
198 Mill, *Comte*, 340–1.
199 Mill, *Autobiography*, 239.

Chapter Five

1 Mill, *Claims*, 382.
2 Mill, *Principles*, 794.
3 Rawls, *Lectures*, 252.
4 Mill, *Claims*, 382. Ekelund and Tollison see in *Claims* only a capitalist, anti-Romantic and anti-socialist desire to alleviate poverty by restructuring capitalism along the lines of a guaranteed minimum income. But this mistakes Mill's position (although he was in favour of a guaranteed minimum income for those who could not work, and favoured Fourier, who includes a similar view for workers, he never countenanced "negative" income taxes to boost wages); furthermore, it mistakes the breadth and depth of the reforms called for in *Claims* (which also does not cover Mill's complete utopia): Mill's reforms went much further than educating the poor with "a taste of capitalism," and in fact, he directly refuted the idea of turning workers into employers. Ekelund and Tollison, "New Political Economy," 221–25; Mill, *Co-operation*, 6.
5 Kurer, "Mill and Utopian Socialism," 229; Mill, *Principles*, 758–96. Kurer only thinks that this utopia can be seen in the 1852 edition, and that Mill later withdew from it.
6 Mill, *Autobiography*, 239.
7 Mill, "Spanish Government," 40.
8 Mill, "Fontana and Prati," 678.
9 Mill, *Claims*, 382.
10 Ibid.; Mill, *Principles*, 770–3.
11 Mill, *Claims*, 383–9.

12 Kurer, "Mill and Utopian Socialism," 223.
13 Mill, *Principles*, 793–4.
14 Mill, *Autobiography*, 239.
15 Several scholars argue that Mill cannot "really" have been a socialist because of his support for individual property. See, for example, Schapiro, "Pioneer of Liberalism," 142; Thomas, *Mill*, 190; Hollander, *Economics*, 179; and Losman, "Alternative Economic Systems," 88–92. However, Mill's commitment was (a) to security (rather than property *per se*) in that he did not think people's private property should be taken from them without compensation, or that a violent revolution leading to the state seizure of all private property on the behalf of the people was a good way of achieving sustainable progress; and (b) to a much reformed idea of individual property as a good "next step" in reform, with much to be gained from such reforms for liberty, equality, fraternity, and happiness. Crucially, Mill *also* saw even this much-reformed regime as "merely provisional," as people might move from it toward socialism (via cooperation), a transition he calls "the nearest approach to social justice" that it is currently possible to foresee. Mill, *Principles*, 794. Mill *did* have a commitment to individual property, then, but not as we currently understand it, and not as the "last word" in human progress.
16 Mill's embrace of cooperation, and his commitment to a transition that would involve, at least for some time, cooperatives competing alongside privately owned firms, leads Flew, in "Socialist or Libertarian?," 21, to claim that Mill was only ever converted to a "hesitant, deferred socialism," the hallmark of which is sympathetic interest in "co-operative enterprises [operating] without state subsidies and ... on equal terms against other competitors in a market." Yet there is more to Mill's socialism than a sympathy toward cooperative enterprises and a willingness to give them a free trial within existing institutions: such a free trial must be accorded by contemporary capitalists, but Mill firmly believed that, so long as cooperation stayed true to its fundamental proposals, it would triumph because of its superior economic efficiency and moral virtue. Furthermore, such a triumph was eminently desirable as a key part of transforming society into Mill's utopia.
17 Claeys ("Justice, Independence, and Industrial Democracy," 141) helpfully charts Mill's political strategy for land reform (including the expression "free trade in land," which sounds very far removed from socialism), and Mill's practical concerns about nationalization, which he said "at present I decidedly do not think ... expedient." He adds that Mill had a

"poor ... opinion of State management, or municipal management" and of general "public virtue and public intelligence." That said, Claeys also notes that Mill wrote, in private correspondence, that "the land ought to belong to the nation at large," though it would be "a generation or two before the progress of public intelligence and morality will permit so great a concern to be entrusted to public authorities without greater abuses than necessarily attach to private property in land." Claeys accuses Mill of "vacillating," but a clear view can be seen, distinguishing between what is "just" and what is currently "expedient." Indeed, the last line of this same letter (which Claeys does not quote) makes this plain: "Meanwhile [i.e., while the "progress of public intelligence and morality" occurs], we should try to go on limiting the power of individuals over land by imposing more and more conditions on behalf of the people at large." Mill, Letter 1533, 1702. The program of the Land Tenure Association (and the political strategy of trying to sway public opinion away from immediate nationalization) does not in itself show that Mill did not favour national ownership of land in an ideal future, when efficiency of state (or municipal) management, and public virtue and intelligence, had progressed to the necessary extent. That is, Mill felt that property in land was something that ought to be determined by expediency, and given his general commitment to communal ownership of land, and his opposition to nationalization as a matter of expediency, not of justice, we can plausibly say Mill supported some form of communal property in land as well as in other forms of capital, be that state ownership or more diffused, localized, communal ownership.

18 Mill: *Claims*, 384; *Principles*, 230–3, 756.
19 Mill, *Principles*, 758.
20 Mill has been read as saying that women should – in an ideally just world – work *only* inside the home: careful reading suggests this applied only to women with young families; only as a general rule to which there might be many exceptions; and only in non-ideal circumstances where men refused to do their fair share of household tasks. See McCabe, "'Good Housekeeping'?," 135–55. It also is worth noting that Mill did think housework constituted real work that contributed to the "work rendered necessary by the fact of each person's existence." In particular, we might associate traditionally "female" tasks with work of the kind such that "no one could exist unless [it] ... were done ... for him." This is, in itself, a radical step for Mill's time. Moreover, he overtly states that cooperation cannot be properly just unless women take an equal role

in the management of their affairs, and his idea of perfectly equal marriages would necessitate a just division of domestic (and other) labour (whether Mill tackles that issue head-on or not). See McCabe, "Mill, Utility, and the Family," 225–35.
21 Mill, *Negro Question*, 91.
22 Mill, *Principles*, 784.
23 Mill's commitment to competition has led to his being called a market socialist. See Stafford, "Paradigmatic Liberal," 332–4; Gray, *Liberalisms*, 6; Baum, "Liberal Socialism," 104; Ryan, "Bureaucracy, Democracy, Liberty," 164; Riley, "Capitalism versus Socialism," 39, 65; Medearis, "Labor, Democracy, Utility," 137. This is not, however, an illuminating label. Splitting socialism between centrally planned and "market" is not a very useful dichotomy, because it is impossible to fit in self-sufficient intentional communities. Some see worker cooperatives' socialism as *the* defining feature of market socialism. But even though Mill endorses such cooperatives, there are important ways in which he does not endorse "markets" in the way necessary for "market socialism." See McCabe, "John Stuart Mill: Market Socialist?"; Bergson, "Market Socialism Revisited," 655–7; Shleifer and Vishny, "Politics of Market Socialism," 165; Ghosh, "Capitalism," 3191; Miller, "Socialism and the Market," 473–90; Roosevelt, "Market Socialism," 3; Yunker, "Democracy under Market Socialism," 678–83; Yunker, "Market Socialist Forms," 131–62; Bardhan and Roemer, "Market Socialism," 101–16; Cohen, *Why Not Socialism?*, 66–72, and *Self-Ownership, Freedom and Equality*, 255–64. Though Mill talked about socialism as a form of "joint stock" organization to show his contemporaries that the idea was not as far-fetched as they might think, he endorsed communal ownership of property in cooperatives, not the maintenance of private property in a joint-stock operation. Thus Gray's description of Mill's "market socialism" as wanting to see an improvement in the capital market with a place for "an entrepreneurial class of industrial pioneers" (*Liberalisms*, 6) is mistaken.
24 Mill, *Principles*, 205.
25 Ibid., 955–6.
26 Ibid., 804.
27 Ibid., 947–50.
28 Mill, Letter 377, 609.
29 Mill, *Principles*, 968–70 – an idea that Mill endorsed as early as 1833. See Mill, *Junius Redivivus [II]*, 385.
30 Mill, *Principles*, 938–9.

31 See, for instance, Turner, "Mill's Evolutionary Theory."
32 Persky, *Political Economy of Progress*, 150–1.
33 Turner, "Mill's Evolutionary Theory."
34 Guinan and O'Neill, "From Community Wealth Building," 385.
35 For Mill thought that cooperatives could choose their own principles of distributive justice, and then workers could choose which cooperatives to work in, from a range of motives including their own sense of justice.
36 Mill, *De Tocqueville on Democracy*, 47–90, 153–204.
37 Mill, *Considerations*, 469–75.
38 Mill: *On Liberty*, 228–9, 281–2, 285–7, 298; *Marriage*, 39–43; *Subjection*, 274–5.
39 Mill: *Subjection*, 272; *Autobiography*, 253.
40 Mill's feminism has been criticized as not really "radical" enough. On this, among other things, see McCabe, "'Good Housekeeping'?," and "Mill, Utility, and the Family" regarding delineating between what Mill saw as expedient, given current non-ideal circumstances, and what we might be able to say about his "ideal" theory.
41 Mill, *Principles*, 794.
42 Mill, *Marriage*, 39–40.
43 Mill, *Autobiography*, 239.
44 Riley, "Mill's Neo-Athenian Model," 242; Mill, *Representative Government*, 513–33; Ryan, "Bureaucracy, Democracy, Liberty," 163.
45 Riley, "Mill's Neo-Athenian Model," 242; Mill, *Representative Government*, 422–34.
46 Ibid., 422–34.
47 Ibid., 476.
48 Ibid., 473–8; Mill, *Parliamentary Reform*, 322.
49 Ibid., 331.
50 Ibid.
51 Mill, *Considerations*, 488.
52 Ibid., 489.
53 Mill, *Parliamentary Reform*, 334, repeated in *Considerations*, 494.
54 Mill, *Considerations*, 470.
55 Ibid., 473.
56 Ibid., 478.
57 Ibid., 474.
58 Sarvasy, "Mill's Theory of Democracy," 567–87.
59 Ibid., 572–3. See also Baccarini and Ivanković, "Mill's Case for Plural Voting," 149.

60 Sarvasy, "Mill's Theory of Democracy," 574.
61 Ibid., 583. See Mill: *Principles*, 758; *Autobiography*, 239.
62 For instance, Morales, *"Perfect Equality,"* 86; Gutmann, *Liberal Equality*, 51; Donner and Fumerton, *Mill*, 104; Brink, *Mill's Progressive Principles*, 241; Baum, *Rereading Power and Freedom*, 243; Riley, "Mill's Neo-Athenian Model," 230.
63 Miller, "Plural Voting," 399–423. See also Baccarini and Ivanković, "Mill's Case for Plural Voting," 140–1.
64 Miller, "Plural Voting," 408–13.
65 Miller is quoting Mill, *Considerations*, 478.
66 Miller, "Plural Voting," 410.
67 Mill, *Considerations*, 475.
68 Miller, "Plural Voting," 413.
69 Mill, *Parliamentary Reform*, 324–5.
70 Baccarini and Ivanković, "Mill's Case for Plural Voting," 145, criticize the "classist" nature of this view of education, as it views "employers," via their employment, as more "educated" than workers. Careful reading of Mill, however, shows that many different kinds of labourers (and not just employers) were counted as "more educated," though it remains true that Mill saw managerial roles, in the main, as deserving more votes. This would benefit the bourgeoisie in Mill's own time, but not in his preferred socialist future, especially as in workplace democracies, workers would elect those they thought most competent at "political" skills such as leadership to be their managers. This connects to Urbinati's critique of Mill's plans; see Urbinati, *Mill on Democracy*, 98. Managerial skill or economic success, she argues, do not equate to moral probity or political competence: it is unlikely Mill would have given two votes to Silvio Berlusconi. However, it is quite likely Mill would have: plural votes are merely a mechanism for attempting to secure the most expert input into political life, and to recognize that some opinions are weightier than others: not everyone who gets a plural vote will necessarily be virtuous or competent to act in the public good. Moreover, in the grand scheme of things, two votes (or even five) have as little impact on electoral outcomes as one: individual incompetence even among plural voters need not outweigh the general benefits of the mechanism of plural voting, just as bribing one citizen, in a system of one-person-one-vote, would be unlikely to affect the final outcome of an election. Moreover, Mill thought these specific "private performances" are public in some important ways, and thus do give reason to suppose greater public competence:

he does not argue that good husbands (or wives) should get extra votes, nor that mere wealth in itself (i.e. ownership of property) should generate extra votes, but that exercise of certain politically relevant skills (as he sees them) in civil society ought to be.
71 Miller, "Plural Voting," 413–14.
72 Mill, *Considerations*, 478, cited in Miller, "Plural Voting," 414.
73 Miller, "Plural Voting," 414.
74 Cf. Mill, *Parliamentary Reform*, 325, and also his concern about paternalism in, among other places, *Claims*.
75 Mill, *Autobiography*, 239.
76 Mill: *Parliamentary Reform*, 322–3; *Considerations*, 473–4.
77 Mill, *Parliamentary Reform*, 323–4.
78 Ibid., 324.
79 Mill: *Considerations*, 476; *Parliamentary Reform*, 326.
80 We might still have some concerns regarding false consciousness (some minorities say it is just that they are oppressed, and seem to really believe it). But Mill would not acknowledge this "perception" as legitimating oppression.
81 Urbinati, *Mill on Democracy*, 98–9.
82 Baccarini and Ivanković, "Mill's Case for Plural Voting," 142.
83 Mill, *Considerations*, 474.
84 Mill, *Subjection*, 294.
85 Mill, *Utility of Religion*, 407.
86 Mill, Letter 383 (trans. Hamburger, *Liberty and Control*, 108). Doubt has been cast on this pronouncement by the fact that Mill was christened, but that has little bearing on the question: baptism was the only available means of legally recording a birth, with serious consequences for questions of age (and majority), inheritance, and legitimacy. Civil registration was not introduced in England until 1836.
87 Mill, *Utilitarianism*, 218. For an excellent account of Mill's relationship with Christianity, see Larsen, *John Stuart Mill: A Secular Life*. For a good review of some of Larsen's claims regarding Mill's belief in (a) God, see Miller, "Timothy Larsen, *John Stuart Mill: A Secular Life*," 289–94.
88 For example, Mill, *On Liberty*, 235–7.
89 Saint-Simon, *Selected Writings*, 102.
90 Ibid., 181.
91 Mill: Letter 383, 560 (*Liberty and Control*, 108); *Autobiography*, 45; Letter 524, 734.
92 Mill, *Theism*, 488–9.

93 Persky, *Political Economy of Progress*, 217–18.
94 Mill, *Autobiography*, 175.
95 Mill, *Principles*, xciii.
96 Persky, *Political Economy of Progress*, 218–19.
97 Rawls, *Justice as Fairness*, 136, 176; Baum, "Liberal Socialism," 101.
98 Persky, *Political Economy of Progress*, 219.
99 Mill, *Autobiography*, 239.
100 For instance, Gaus, *Tyranny of the Ideal*.
101 Estlund, *Utopophobia*.

Conclusion

1 Mill, *Newman*, 444.
2 Mill, *Autobiography*, 241.
3 Ibid., 175.
4 Ibid., 239.
5 Mill, *Principles*, xciii.
6 Ibid., 207.
7 Ibid., 201–2.
8 Ibid., 207.
9 Rawls, *Theory of Justice*, 280, and *Justice as Fairness*, 138–40.
10 Cohen, *Rescuing Justice and Equality*.
11 Mill, *Autobiography*, 239.
12 Persky, *Political Economy of Progress*, 148–51. Though see also Persky, "Mill's Socialism Re-examined."
13 Stafford, "Paradigmatic Liberal," 325–45.
14 Kurer, "Mill and Utopian Socialism," 299–30; Robbins, *Theory of Economic Policy*, 142ff; Losman, "Alternative Economic Systems," 85–104; Schwartz, *New Political Economy*, 190–2.
15 Mill, *Chapters*, 736.
16 Robbins, "Introduction," xxxix.
17 Mill, *Chapters*, 745.
18 Robbins, "Introduction," xl.
19 Mill, *Chapters*, 728.
20 Ibid., 713.
21 Ibid., 736.
22 Stafford, "Paradigmatic Liberal," 328.
23 Mill, Letter 477, 714.
24 Mill, *Chapters*, 714.

25 Mill, *Autobiography*, 239.
26 Mill, *Principles*, xciii.
27 Ibid., xcii.
28 Ibid., 207.
29 Mill, *Considerations*, 404–5.
30 Mill, Letter 531, 739.
31 Winch, *Wealth and Life*, 50–4; Robbins, "Introduction," xxxix; Robbins, *Economic Policy*, 142; Flew, "Socialist or Libertarian?," 21; Légé, "Hayek's Reading," 199, 202; Von Mises, *Liberalism*, 195; Hayek, "Mill at Twenty-Five," xxx; Rees, *Mill's On Liberty*, 7; Schwartz, *New Political Economy*, 190–2; Levy, "Mill's Stationary State," 279; Ekelund and Tollison, "New Political Economy," 215; Reeves, *Victorian Firebrand*, 213.
32 Mill, *Autobiography*, 253–5.
33 Ibid., 255–7.
34 Cf. how Pappe characterized the view of Taylor presented to posterity by Mill. Pappe, *Mill and the Taylor Myth*. For Mill's account of the co-authoring relationship, see *Autobiogaphy*, 251–61. For further discussions, see McCabe: "Harriet Taylor," 112–25, and "Taylor, and Mill's Socialism," 197–234; Philips, "Beloved and Deplored," 626–42; Rossi, "Sentiment and Intellect," 1–64.
35 Mill: Letters 15–27, to Taylor, 1027–31; *Autobiography*, 253–9.
36 Even if we think, as Winch argues in *Wealth and Life*, 50–3, that "On the Probable Futurity of the Labouring Classes" and "On Property" are *solely* the work of Taylor – which is in itself implausible – there are other socialist elements to Mill's work. The claim that the relative lack of endorsement of socialism in the 1848 edition of *Principles* is only because Taylor was insufficiently attentive to the manuscript, and that the relative warmth of the 1849 and 1852 editions is due to her insistence that he make these changes, seems to accord Taylor both an implausible amount of power over Mill and a psychologically implausible lack of attention on her behalf if she was, indeed, this kind of tyrannical and domineering mistress (never mind ignoring her actual role in the production of the first edition). Winch's claim that Mill did not retract the pro-socialist elements of *Principles* because he left it an untouched monument to her memory is also implausible.
37 Mill, "Co-operation," 8–9.
38 Winch, *Wealth and Life*, 137; Stafford, "Paradigmatic Liberal," 325–45, 327; Packe, *Life*, 313–14; Borchard, *Mill, the Man*, 99; Himmelfarb, *On Liberty*, 130–1.

39 Mill: Letter 15, 1027–8; Letter 16, 1028.
40 Winch, *Wealth and Life*, 137; Stafford, "Paradigmatic Liberal," 327.
41 Mill, Letter 15, 1027.
42 Mill, Letter 16, 1029.
43 Millgram, in *Meaning of Life*, 73–8, 132, suggests that Mill needed "authority figures" who he believed were his intellectual superiors, to whom he could look to set his intellectual agenda. This may or may not be true (the necessary evidence to decide either way would be hard to come by). Though Mill certainly admired many people as his intellectual superiors (where we might, or might not, agree), and had a relatively humble sense of his own abilities (firmly instilled by his father), we ought not to think that Mill was in any way a slavish adherent to anyone's views or agenda, as we can see quite clearly when we consider his attitude regarding Bentham, James Mill, Carlyle, Coleridge, Comte, and the Austins, to name a few.
44 Mill: *Principles*, 203–9; *Chapters*, 737–49.
45 Mill, *Principles*, 978.
46 Mill: *Autobiography*, 257–9; *On Liberty*, 216.
47 Mill, *Autobiography*, 257–9.
48 Mill and Taylor, "Papers on Women's Rights," 392.
49 Taylor, *Complete Works*, 19.
50 Mill, *Principles*, 209.
51 Mill, *On Liberty*, 257.
52 Rawls, *Justice as Fairness*, 136, 176.
53 Mill, *Autobiography*, 259.
54 Mill, *Marriage*, 39.
55 Mill, *Utilitarianism*, 227.
56 Mill, *Autobiography*, 241.
57 Mill, *On Liberty*, 217–18.
58 Mill, *Autobiography*, 239.
59 Miller, "Mill's 'Socialism,'" 213–38.
60 Marx and Engels, *Communist Manifesto*, 506.
61 Mill, *On Liberty*, 292–310.
62 Ibid., 292–3.
63 Northcote and Trevelyan published a damning report on the British Civil Service (and how civil servants were appointed) in 1854. Their proposed reforms (including appointment by competitive examination) were supported by Gladstone and finally put into practice in 1870.
64 Mill, *On Liberty*, 293.

65 Ibid., 224.
66 Ibid.
67 Mill, *Autobiography*, 239.
68 The challenges faced by the Wolverhampton Platelock workers is a historical example from Mill's experience that is probably exemplary of the kind of pushback likely also to be faced in modern times.

BIBLIOGRAPHY

John Stuart Mill

All references are to the *Collected Works of John Stuart Mill*, edited J.M. Robson and others, 33 volumes. Toronto: University of Toronto Press, 1962–91.

WRITINGS

"Attack on Literature." 22 (1986).
Auguste Comte and Positivism. 10 (1969).
Autobiography. 1 (1981).
Chapters on Socialism. 5 (1963).
The Claims of Labour. 4 (1967).
Coleridge. 10 (1969).
"Comparison of the Tendencies of French and English Intellect." 22 (1986).
Considerations on Representative Government. 19 (1977).
A Constitutional View of the India Question. 30 (1990).
"Co-operation: Closing Speech." 26 (1988).
"Co-operation: Intended Speech." 26 (1988).
Co-operation. 28 (1988).
"The Corn Laws." 4 (1967).
"The Disturbances in Jamaica" [1], [2], and [3]. 28 (1988).
"Errors and Truths on a Property Tax." 23 (1986).
"Errors of the Spanish Government." 22 (1986).
"Fontana and Prati's St. Simonism in London." 23 (1986).
French Affairs. 25 (1986).
"French News [45]." 23 (1962).
"French News [64]." 23 (1962).
"French News [90]." 23 (1962).
"The Gorgias." 11 (1978).
The Income and Property Tax. 5 (1967).
Ireland. 6 (1982).
"The Jamaica Committee." 28 (1988).
Journal of a Year in France. 26 (1991).

Land Tenure Reform. 5 (1967).
Leslie on the Land Question. 5 (1967).
"M. Cabet." 25 (1986).
Memorandum on the Improvement in the Administration of India During the Last Thirty Years. 30 (1990).
"Miss Martineau's Summary of Political Economy." 4 (1967).
The Moral of the India Debate. 30 (1990).
Newman's Political Economy. 5 (1967).
Observations on the Proposed Council of India. 30 (1990).
On Liberty, 18 (1977).
On Marriage. 21 (1984).
On the Negro Question. 21 (1984).
"Population." 26 (1988).
"Population: Reply to Thirlwall." 26 (1988).
"The Poor Laws." 23 (1986).
Principles of Political Economy. 2–3 (1965).
"Question of Population" [1,] [2], and [3]. 22 (1986).
Remarks on Bentham's Philosophy. 10 (1969).
Re-organisation of the Reform Party. 6 (1982).
"The Spirit of the Age." 22 (1986).
The Subjection of Women. 21 (1984).
A System of Logic. 7–8 (1973).
Theism. 10 (1969).
"De Tocqueville on Democracy in America" [1]. 17 (1977).
Thornton on Labour and Its Claims. 5 (1967).
Thoughts on Parliamentary Reform. 19 (1977).
Utilitarianism. 10 (1969).
Utility of Religion. 10 (1969).
Vindication of the French Revolution of February 1848. 20 (1985).
Whewell on Moral Philosophy. 10 (1969).
The Writings of Junius Redivivus, 1 and 2. 1 (1981).
Mill, John Stuart, and Harriet Taylor. "Papers on Women's Rights." 21 (1984).

LETTERS

15–27, to Harriet Taylor, 19 February 1849–31 March 1849. 3 (1965).
24, to Gustave d'Eichthal, 11 March 1829. 12 (1963).
25, to John Sterling, 15 April 1829. 12 (1963).
26, to Gustave d'Eichthal, 15 May 1829. 12 (1963).

27, to Gustave d'Eichthal, 8 October 1829. 12 (1963).
28, to Gustave d'Eichthal, 7 November 1829. 12 (1963).
29, to Gustave d'Eichthal, 9 February 1830. 12 (1963).
30, to Gustave d'Eicthal, 6 March 1830. 12 (1963).
39, to Gustave d'Eichthal, 1 March 1831. 12 (1963).
41, to Gustave d'Eichthal, 27 August 1831. 12 (1963).
45, to Gustave d'Eichthal, 6 December 1831. 12 (1963).
47, to Gustave d'Eichthal, 28 January 1832. 12 (1963).
52, to Gustave d'Eichthal and Charles Duveyrier, 30 May 1832. 12 (1963).
56, to John Taylor, 1 September 1832. 12 (1963).
64, to Thomas Carlyle, 27 December 1832. 12 (1963).
72, to Thomas Carlyle, 11 and 12 April 1833. 12 (1963).
261, to George Jacob Holyoake, 21 September 1856. 15 (1972).
339, to Theodore Gomperez, 4 December 1858. 15 (1972).
349, to Theodore Gomperez, 12 January 1859. 15 (1972).
377, to Herbert Spencer, 27 March 1859. 15 (1972).
383, to Auguste Comte, 15 December 1842. 13 (1963).
477, to Frederick J. Furnivall, 10 December 1853. 15 (1972).
495, to Arthur Helps, 1847[?]. 17 (1972).
500, to John Chapman, 4 August 1861. 15 (1972).
501, to John Austin, 13 April 1848. 13 (1963).
523, to William Thornton, "Thursday evening" [1862?]. 15 (1972).
524, to Sarah Austin, 7 March 1848. 13 (1963).
525, to Sarah Austin, March [?] 1848. 13 (1963).
531, to John Pringle Nichol, 30 September 1848. 13 (1963).
575, to Henry Pitman, 13 January 1863. 15 (1972).
667, to George Jacob Holyoake, 22 December 1863. 15 (1972).
680, to Thomas Bayley Potter, 14 March 1864. 15 (1972).
881A, to [George Howell?], 30 October 1865. 17 (1972).
883, to Louis Blanc, 4 November 1865. 16 (1972).
1049, to William Randal Cremer, 1 March 1867. 16 (1972).
1104, to John Elliot Cairnes, 30 June 1867. 16 (1972).
1288, to J.R. Ware, 13 September 1868. 16 (1972).
1428, to A.M. Francis, 8 May 1869. 17 (1972).
1533, to Alexander Campbell, 28 February 1870. 17 (1972).
1583a, to the General Council of the IWA, after 23 July 1870. 22 (1991).
1604, to Edwin Chadwick, 29 October 1870. 17 (1972).
1657, to Frederic Harrison, [May? 1871]. 17 (1972).
1658, to George Odger, 1 May 1871. 17 (1972).

1666, to Gustave d'Eichthal, 21 May 1871. 17 (1972).
1667, to John Hales, 28 May 1871. 17 (1972).
1678, to Emile Acollas, 20 September 1871. 17 (1972).
1690, to John Stapleton, 25 October, 1871. 17 (1972).
1699, to Charles Dupont-White, 6 December 1871. 17 (1972).
1708, to Georg Brandes, 4 March 1872. 17 (1972).
1749, to Thomas Smith, 4 October 1872. 17 (1972).

OTHER SOURCES

Anderson, Elizabeth. "The Fundamental Disagreement between Luck Egalitarians and Relational Egalitarians." *Canadian Journal of Philosophy* 40, supp. 1 (2010): 1–23.
– "What Is the Point of Equality?" *Ethics* 109, no. 2 (1999): 287–337.
Ashcraft, Richard. "John Stuart Mill and the Theoretical Foundations of Democratic Socialism." In *Mill and the Moral Character of Liberalism*, edited by Eldon J. Eisenach, 169–89. Pennsylvania: Pennsylvania State University Press, 1998.
Baccarini, Elvio, and Viktor Ivanković. "Mill's Case for Plural Voting and the Need for Balanced Public Decisions." *Prolegomena* 14, no. 2 (2015): 137–56.
Bain, Alexander. *John Stuart Mill: A Criticism*. London: Longmans, Green and Co., 1882.
Bardhan, Pranab, and John E. Roemer. "Market Socialism: A Case for Rejuvenation." *Journal of Economic Perspectives* 6, no. 3 (1992): 101–16.
Baum, Bruce. "J.S. Mill and Liberal Socialism." In *J.S. Mill's Political Thought: A Bicentennial Reassessment*, edited by Nadia Urbinati and Alex Zakaras, 98–123. Cambridge: Cambridge University Press, 2007.
– "J.S. Mill on Freedom and Power." *Polity* 31, no. 2 (1998): 187–216.
– "J.S. Mill's Conception of Economic Freedom." *History of Political Thought* 20, no. 3 (1999): 494–530.
– *Rereading Power and Freedom in J.S. Mill*. Toronto: University of Toronto Press, 2000.
Beecher, Jonathan. *Victor Considerant and the Rise and Fall of French Socialism*. Berkeley: University of California Press, 2001.
Benhabib, Seyla. *Situating the Self: Gender, Community, and Postmodernism in Contemporary Ethics*. Cambridge: Polity Press, 1992.
Berger, Fred R. "Mill's Substantive Principles of Justice: A Comparison with Nozick." *American Philosophical Quarterly* 19, no. 4 (1982): 373–80.

Bergson, Abram. "Market Socialism Revisited." *Journal of Political Economy* 75, no. 5 (1967): 655–73.
Berlin, Isaiah. "John Stuart Mill and the Ends of Life." In *J.S. Mill On Liberty in Focus*, edited by John Gray and G.W. Smith, 131–61. London: Routledge, 1991.
– "Two Concepts of Liberty." In *Four Essays On Liberty*, 118–72. Oxford: Oxford University Press, 1969.
Bestor, Arthur E., Jr. "The Evolution of the Socialist Vocabulary." *Journal of the History of Ideas* 9, no. 3 (1948): 259–302.
Biagini, Eugenio. "Liberalism and Direct Democracy: John Stuart Mill and the Model of Ancient Athens." In *Citizenship and Community: Liberals, Radicals, and Collective Identities in the British Isles, 1865–1931*, edited by Biagini, 21–41. Cambridge: Cambridge University Press, 1996.
Birchall, Johnston. *Co-op: The People's Business*. Manchester: Manchester University Press, 1994.
Blanc, Louis. *History of the French Revolution*. Paris: Langlois and Leclercq, 1847.
Borchard, Ruth. *John Stuart Mill, the Man*. London: Watts, 1957.
Brady, Alexander. "Introduction." In *Collected Works of John Stuart Mill*, vol. 18, edited by J.M. Robson, ix–lxx. Toronto: University of Toronto Press, 1977.
Brink, David. *Mill's Progressive Principles*. Oxford: Oxford University Press, 2013.
Britton, Karl. *John Stuart Mill*. London: Pelican, 1953.
Capaldi, Nicholas. *John Stuart Mill: A Biography*. Cambridge: Cambridge University Press, 2004.
– "Mill and Socialism." *Tocqueville Review* 33, no. 1 (2012): 125–44.
Carlisle, Janice. *John Stuart Mill and the Writing of Character*. Athens: University of Georgia Press, 1991.
Church, R.A. "Profit-Sharing and Labour Relations in England in the Nineteenth Century." *International Review of Social History* 16, no. 1 (1971): 2–16.
Claeys, Gregory. "Justice, Independence, and Industrial Democracy: The Development of John Stuart Mill's Views on Socialism." *Journal of Politics* 49, no. 1 (1987): 122–47.
– *Mill and Paternalism*. Cambridge: Cambridge University Press, 2013.
Clark, Barry S., and John E. Elliott. "John Stuart Mill's Theory of Justice." *Review of Social Economy* 59, no. 4 (2001): 467–90.
Cohen, G.A. *If You're an Egalitarian, How Come You're So Rich?* Cambridge, MA: Harvard University Press, 2000.

- *Karl Marx's Theory of History: A Defence*. Oxford: Clarendon Press, 1978.
- *Rescuing Justice and Equality*. Cambridge, MA: Harvard University Press, 2008.
- *Self-Ownership, Freedom, and Equality*. Cambridge: Cambridge University Press, 1995.
- *Why Not Socialism?* Princeton: Princeton University Press, 2009.

Cole, G.D.H. *A Short History of the British Working Class Movement*. London: Allen and Unwin, 1937.

Considerant, Victor. *Destinée Sociale*. Paris: Bureau de la Phalange, 1834–38.
- *Exposition abrégée du système phalanstérien de Fourier*. Paris: La Librairie Sociétaire, 1845.
- *Le Socialisme devant ou le vivant devant les morts*. Paris: Librairie Phalanstérienne, 1849.

Crosland, C.A.R. *The Future of Socialism*. London: Jonathon Cape, 1961.

Davis, Elynor G. "Mill, Socialism, and the English Romantics: An Interpretation." *Economica New Series* 52, no. 207 (1985): 345–58.

Devigne, Robert. "Building Bridges across the Channel: J.S. Mill's Theory of Justice." *History of Political Thought* 29, no. 4 (2008): 635–61.

Donner, Wendy. *The Liberal Self: John Stuart Mill's Moral and Political Philosophy*. Ithaca: Cornell University Press, 1991.

Donner, Wendy, and Richard Fumerton. *Mill*. Malden: Wiley-Blackwell, 2009.

Duncan, Graeme. *Marx and Mill*. Cambridge: Cambridge University Press, 1973.

Dworkin, Ronald. "What Is Equality? Part II: Equality of Resources." *Philosophy and Public Affairs* 10, no. 4 (1981): 283–345.

Eisenach, Eldon J. "Self-Reform as Political Reform in the Writings of John Stuart Mill." *Utilitas* 1, no. 2 (1989): 242–58.

Estlund, David. *Utopophobia*. Princeton: Princeton University Press, 2020.

d'Eichthal, Eugene. "Introduction to 'The Correspondence of John Stuart Mill.'" *Cosmopolis: An International Monthly Review* 6 (1897).

d'Eichthal, Gustave. *Rapports Adressés aux Pères Suprèmes sur la Situation et les Traveux de la Famille*. Paris: Au Bureau du Globe et de L'Organisateur, 1831.

Ekelund, Robert B., and Robert D. Tollison. "The New Political Economy of J.S. Mill: The Means to Social Justice." *Canadian Journal of Economics* 9, no. 2 (1976): 213–31.

Enfantin, Prosper. *Final Address*. Translated by Mill. *Collected Works of John Stuart Mill*, vol. 24. Toronto: University of Toronto Press, 1986.

Fabian Society. "The Economics of Direct Employment." In *Modern Socialism*, edited by R.C.K. Ensor, 241–63. London: Harper and Brothers, 1904.

Feuer, Lewis S. "J.S. Mill and Marxian Socialism." *Journal of the History of Ideas* 10, no. 2 (1946): 297–304.

Flew, Anthony. "J.S. Mill: Socialist or Libertarian?" In *Prophets of Freedom and Enterprise*, edited by Michael Ivans, 21–7. London: Kogan Page for Aims of Industry, 1975.

Fourier, Charles. "Attractive Labour." In *Selections from the Works of Fourier*, translated by Julia Franklin. London: Swan Sonnenschein & Co., 1901.

– *Fourier: The Theory of the Four Movements*, edited by Gareth Stedman Jones and Ian Patterson. Translated by Ian Patterson. Cambridge: Cambridge University Press, 1996.

– "Role of the Passions." In *Selections from the Works of Fourier*, translated by Franklin. London: Swan Sonnenschein & Co., 1901.

– "Series and Groups." In *Selections from the Works of Fourier*, translated by Franklin. London: Swan Sonnenschein & Co., 1901.

Fredman, L.E, and B.L.J. Gordon. "John Stuart Mill and Socialism." *Mill Newsletter* 3, no. 1 (1967), 3–7.

Gaus, Gerald F. *The Tyranny of the Ideal*. Princeton: Princeton University Press, 2016.

Ghosh, Arun. "Capitalism, Markets, Market Socialism, and Democracy." *Economic and Political Weekly* 30, no. 50 (1995): 3191–4.

Gray, John. "Introduction." In *On Liberty and Other Essays*, edited by Gray, vi–xxx. Oxford: Oxford University Press, 1991.

– *Liberalism*. Buckinghamshire: Open University Press, 1995.

– *Liberalisms: Essays in Political Philosophy*. London: Routledge, 1989.

Green, Michele. "Sympathy and Self-Interest: The Crisis in Mill's Mental History." *Utilitas* 1, no. 2 (1989): 259–77.

Guinan, Joe, and Martin O'Neill. *The Case for Community Wealth-Building*. Cambridge: Polity Press, 2020.

– "From Community Wealth Building to System Change." *IPPR Progressive Review* 25, no. 4 (2019): 383–92.

Gutman, Amy. *Liberal Equality*. Cambridge: Cambridge University Press, 1980.

Haagh, Louise. *The Case for Universal Basic Income*. Cambridge: Polity Press, 2019.

Habibi, Don. "Mill on Colonialism." In *A Companion to Mill*, edited by Christopher MacLeod and Dale E. Miller, 518–32. Oxford: Wiley-Blackwell, 2016.

Hainds, J.R. "John Stuart Mill and the Saint-Simonians." *Journal of the History of Ideas* 7, no. 1 (1946): 103–12.

Halliday, Daniel, and Helen McCabe. "John Stuart Mill on Free Speech." In *Routledge Handbook of Applied Epistemology*, edited by David Coady and James Chase, 71–87. London: Routledge, 2018.

Halliday, R.J. *John Stuart Mill*. London: Routledge, 2004.

Hamburger, Joseph. *Intellectuals in Politics*. New Haven: Yale University Press, 1965.

– *John Stuart Mill On Liberty and Control*. Princeton: Princeton University Press, 2001.

Hayek, Friedrich. "J.S. Mill at Twenty-Five." In *The Spirit of the Age*. Chicago: University of Chicago Press, 1942.

Himmelfarb, Gertrude. *On Liberty and Liberalism*. New York: A.A. Knopf, 1974.

Hollander, Samuel. *The Economics of John Stuart Mill*, vol. 2: *Political Economy*. Oxford: Blackwell, 1985.

Holyoake, George Jacob. *The History of Co-operation*. London: T. Fisher and Unwin, 1906.

– *John Stuart Mill as Some of the Working Classes Knew Him*. London: Trübner and Co., 1873.

– *Sixty Years of an Agitator's Life*. London: T. Fisher Unwin, 1893.

Horowitz, Irving Louis. "Review of *John Stuart Mill and French Thought* by Iris Wessel Mueller." *Philosophy* 35, no. 133 (1960): 181–3.

Hughes, Patricia. "The Reality versus the Ideal: J.S. Mill's Treatment of Women, Workers, and Private Property." *Canadian Journal of Political Science* 12, no. 3 (1979): 523–42.

Jahne, Beate. "Barbarian Thoughts: Imperialism in the Philosophy of John Stuart Mill." *Review of International Studies* 31, no. 3 (2005): 599–618.

Jensen, Hans E. "John Stuart Mill's Theories of Wealth and Income Distribution." *Review of Social Economy* 59, no. 4 (2001): 491–507.

Jones, H.S. *Victorian Political Thought*. Basingstoke: Macmillan, 2000.

Kelly, Marjorie, and Ted Howard. *The Making of a Democratic Economy*. Oakland: Berrett-Kochler, 2019.

Kinzer, Bruce L. "Introduction." In *Collected Works of John Stuart Mill*, vol. 28, edited by J.M. Robson, xii–lxi. Toronto: University of Toronto Press, 1988.

Kurer, Oskar. *The Politics of Progress*. London: Garland, 1991.

– "J.S. Mill and Utopian Socialism." *The Economic Record* 68, no. 202 (1992): 222–32.

Larsen, Timothy. *John Stuart Mill: A Secular Life*. Oxford: Oxford University Press, 2018.

Légé, Philippe. "Hayek's Reading of Mill." *Journal of the History of Economic Thought* 30, no. 2 (2008): 199–215.
Leopold, David. "The Structure of Marx and Engels' Considered Account of Utopian Socialism." *History of Political Thought* 36, no. 3 (2005): 443–66.
Levy, Michael B. "Mill's Stationary State and the Transcendence of Liberalism." *Polity* 14, no. 2 (1981): 273–93.
Lewisohn, David. "Mill and Comte on the Methods of Social Science." *Journal of the History of Ideas* 33, no. 2 (1972): 315–24.
Losman, Donald L. "J.S. Mill on Alternative Economic Systems." *American Journal of Economics and Sociology* 30, no. 1 (1971): 84–104.
Macintyre, Alasdair. *Against the Self-Images of the Age*. Notre Dame: University of Notre Dame Press, 1978.
− *Whose Justice? Which Rationality?* Notre Dame: University of Notre Dame Press, 1988.
Macpherson, C.B. *The Life and Times of Liberal Democracy*. Oxford: Oxford University Press, 1977.
Malthus, Thomas. *An Essay on the Principle of Population*. London: Routledge, 1996.
− *First Essay on Population*. London: Macmillan and Co., 1926.
Marx, Karl. "Afterword to the 2nd Edition." *Capital*, vol. 1. Translated by Samuel Moore and Edward Aveling, edited by Frederick Engels, 12–22. Moscow: Progress, 1887.
− *The German Ideology*. In *Collected Works of Marx and Engels*, vol. 5. Translated by Clemens Dutt, W. Lough, and C.P. Magill. New York: International, 1975.
− *Grundrisse*. Translated by Martin Nicolaus. Harmondsworth: Penguin, 1973.
− "Preamble to the Resolutions of the Geneva (1866) and Brussels (1868) Congresses of the International." *Collected Works*, vol. 21, 31. New York: International, 1985.
− *Report of the Fourth Annual Congress of the International Working Men's Association held in Basle, Switzerland*. Reproduced as two separate pieces in *Collected Works*, vol. 21, 65–82. New York: International, 1985.
− "Working Men and the War." Republished as "First Address to the General Council of the International Working Men's Association on the Franco-Prussian War." In *Collected Works*, vol. 22, 3–9. New York: International, 1986.
Marx, Karl, and Frederick Engels. *The Communist Manifesto*. Translated by Samuel Moore in cooperation with Engels. *Collected Works*, vol. 6, 477–519. New York: International, 1975.

McCabe, Helen. "'Good Housekeeping'? Re-Assessing John Stuart Mill's Position on the Gendered Division of Labour." *History of Political Thought* 39, no. 1 (2018): 135–55.
- "Harriet Taylor." In *A Companion to Mill*, edited by MacLeod and Miller, 112–25. Hoboken: Wiley, 2016.
- "Harriet Taylor, and John Stuart Mill's Socialism," *Nineteenth-Century Prose* 47 no. 1 (2020): 197–234.
- "Harriet Taylor Mill and Anna Doyle Wheeler on Marriage, Servitude, and Socialism." *British Journal of the History of Philosophy*, doi.org/10.1080/09608788.2020.1750348.
- "John Stuart Mill: Market Socialist?," *Review of Social Economy*, doi.org/10.1080/00346764.2020.1781923.
- "John Stuart Mill and Fourierism: 'Association,' 'Friendly Rivalry,' and Distributive Justice." *Global Intellectual History* 4, no. 1 (2018): 35–61.
- "John Stuart Mill on 'Legitimate Socialism' and the Revolutions of 1848." *Revue Philosophique de France et de l'Étranger*, no. 3 (2020): 335–53.
- "John Stuart Mill, Utility, and the Family: Attacking the Citadel of the Enemy." *Revue International de Philosophie / International Review of Philosophy* 272, no. 2 (2015): 225–35.
- "John Stuart Mill's Analysis of Capitalism and the Road to Socialism." In *A New Social Question: Capitalism, Socialism, and Utopia*, edited by Casey Harrison, 8–22. Cambridge: Cambridge Scholar, 2015.
- "John Stuart Mill's Philosophy of Persuasion." *Informal Logic* 34, no. 1 (2014): 38–61.
- "Mill and Socialism: A Reply to Capaldi." *Tocqueville Review* 30, no. 1 (2012): 145–64.
- "Mill's 'Modern' Radicalism Re-examined: Joseph Persky's *The Political Economy of Progress*." *Utilitas* 32, no. 2 (2020): 137–64.
- "Navigating by the North Star: The Role of the 'Ideal' in John Stuart Mill's View of 'Utopian' Schemes and the Possibilities of Social Transformation." *Utilitas* 31, no. 3 (2019): 291–309.
- "'There never was a time when so great a drama was being played out in one generation': John Stuart Mill and the French Revolution of 1848." *Revue d'études proudhoniennes*, no. 5 (2019): 119–62.

Medearis, John. "Labor, Democracy, Utility, and Mill's Critique of Private Property." *American Journal of Political Science* 49, no. 1 (2005): 135–49.

Megill, Alan D. "J.S. Mill's Religion of Humanity and the Second Justification for the Writing of *On Liberty*." *Journal of Politics* 34, no. 2 (1972): 612–29.

Mill, James. Letter 2256, to Jeremy Bentham, 3 December 1803. In *Correspondence of Jeremy Bentham*, vol. 8, edited by Stephen Conway, 361. Oxford: Oxford University Press, 1988.

Miller, Dale E. "Mill's 'Socialism.'" *Politics, Philosophy, and Economics* 2, no. 2 (2003): 213–38.

– "The Place of Plural Voting in Mill's Conception of Representative Government." *Review of Politics* 77, no. 3 (2015): 399–423.

– "Timothy Larsen, *John Stuart Mill: A Secular Life*." *Nineteenth-Century Prose* 57, no. 1 (2020): 289–94.

Miller, David. "The Incoherence of Luck-Egalitarianism." In *Distributive Justice and Access to Advantage: G.A. Cohen's Egalitarianism*, edited by Alexander Kaufman, 131–50. Cambridge: Cambridge University Press, 2014.

– "Socialism and the Market." *Political Theory* 5, no. 4 (1977): 473–90.

Millgram, Elijah. *John Stuart Mill and the Meaning of Life*. Oxford: Oxford University Press, 2019.

– "Mill's Incubus." In *John Stuart Mill and the Art of Life*, edited Ben Egglestone, Dale E. Miller, and David Weinstein, 169–91. Oxford: Oxford University Press, 2011.

Morales, Maria. *"Perfect Equality": John Stuart Mill on Well-Constituted Communities*. London: Rowman and Littlefield, 1996.

Moses, Clare Goldberg. *French Feminism in the Nineteenth Century*. Albany: SUNY Press, 1984.

Moss, Bernard H. *Origins of the French Labour Movement: The Socialism of Skilled Workers*. Berkeley: University of California Press, 1976.

Mueller, Iris Wessell. *John Stuart Mill and French Thought*. Freeport: Books for Libraries Press, 1968.

Nathanson, Stephen. "John Stuart Mill on Economic Justice and the Alleviation of Poverty." *Journal of Social Philosophy* 43, no. 2 (2012): 161–76.

Neale, Edward Vansittart. *Manual for Co-operators*. London: Macmillan, 1888.

Niesen, Peter. "Roots of Mill's Radicalism." In *A Companion to Mill*, edited by MacLeod and Miller, 79–94. Oxford: Wiley-Blackwell, 2017.

Oakley, Allen. *The Making of Marx's Critical Theory: A Bibliographical Analysis*. London: Routledge, 1983.

Okin, Susan Moller. *Justice, Gender and the Family*. New York: Basic Books, 1989.

– *Women in Western Political Thought*. Princeton: Princeton University Press, 1979.

Orwell, George. *Animal Farm*. Harmondsworth: Penguin, 1987.

Owen, Robert. *The Life of Robert Owen, By Himself*. London: G. Bell, 1920.
- *A New View of Society and Other Writings*, edited by G.D.H. Cole. New York: Dent and Sons, 1966.
- *Selected Works of Robert Owen*, edited Gregory Claeys, vols. 1–4. London: William Pickering, 1993.
Packe, Michael St. John. *The Life of John Stuart Mill*. London: Macmillan, 1954.
Pankhurst, Richard. *The Saint-Simonians, Mill, and Carlyle: A Preface to Modern Thought*. London: Sidgwick and Jackson, 1957.
Pappe, H.O. *John Stuart Mill and the Harriet Taylor Myth*. Cambridge: Cambridge University Press, 1960.
Patemen, Carole. *The Sexual Contract*. Cambridge: Polity Press, 1988.
Pellarin, Charles. *The Life of Charles Fourier*. Translated by Francis Shaw. New York: W.H. Graham, 1848.
Persky, Joseph. "Mill's Socialism Re-examined." *Utilitas* 32, no. 2 (2020): 165–80.
- *The Political Economy of Progress: John Stuart Mill and Modern Radicalism*. Oxford: Oxford University Press, 2016.
Philips, Menaka. "The 'Beloved and Deplored' Memory of Harriet Taylor Mill: Rethinking Gender and Intellectual Labor in the Canon." *Hypatia* 33, no. 4 (2018): 626–42.
Pickering, Mary. *Auguste Comte: An Intellectual Biography*, vol. 1. Cambridge: Cambridge University Press, 1993.
Raeder, Linda. *John Stuart Mill and the Religion of Humanity*. Columbia: University of Missouri Press, 2002.
Rawls, John. *Justice as Fairness: A Restatement*. Cambridge, MA: Harvard University Press, 2001.
- *Lectures in the History of Political Philosophy*, edited by Samuel Freeman. London: Belknap Press of Harvard University Press, 2007.
- *A Theory of Justice*. Oxford: Clarendon Press, 1972.
Rees, J.C. *John Stuart Mill's On Liberty*. Oxford: Clarendon Press, 1985.
Reeves, Richard. *John Stuart Mill: Victorian Firebrand*. London: Atlantic, 2007.
Riley, Jonathan. "J.S. Mill's Liberal Utilitarian Assessment of Capitalism versus Socialism." *Utilitas* 8, no. 1 (1996): 39–71.
- *Liberal Utilitarianism: Social Choice Theory and J.S. Mill's Philosophy*. Cambridge: Cambridge University Press, 1988.
- "Mill's Neo-Athenian Model of Liberal Democracy." In *J.S. Mill's Political Thought: A Bicentennial Reassessment*, edited by Urbinati and Zakaras, 221–49. Cambridge: Cambridge University Press, 2007.

- "Optimal Moral Rules and Supererogatory Acts." In *John Stuart Mill and the Art of Life*, edited by Egglestone, Miller, and Weinstein, 119–45. Oxford: Oxford University Press, 2011.
Robbins, Lionel. "The Classical Economics and Socialism: John Stuart Mill." In *The Theory of Economic Policy in English Classical Political Economy*, 142–68. London: Macmillan, 1961.
- "Introduction." In *Collected Works of John Stuart Mill*, vol. 4, edited by J.M. Robson, vii–xlii. Toronto: University of Toronto Press, 1967.
Robson, J.M. "Textual Introduction." In *Collected Works of John Stuart Mill*, vol. 27, edited by J.M. Robson, lvii–lxix. Toronto: University of Toronto Press, 1988.
Roosevelt, Frank. "Market Socialism: A Humane Economy?" *Journal of Economic Issues* 3, no. 4 (1969): 3–20.
Rosen, Frederick. "The Method of Reform: J.S. Mill's Encounter with Bentham and Coleridge" in *J.S. Mill's Political Thought: A Bicentennial Reassessment*, edited by Urbinati and Zakaris, 124–45. Cambridge: Cambridge University Press, 2007.
- *Mill*. Oxford: Oxford University Press, 2013.
Rossi, Alice S. "Sentiment and Intellect: The Story of John Stuart Mill and Harriet Taylor Mill." In *John Stuart Mill and Harriet Taylor Mill: Essays on Sex Equality*, edited by Rossi, 1–64. Chicago: University of Chicago Press, 1970.
Ryan, Alan. "Bureaucracy, Democracy, Liberty: Some Unanswered Questions in Mill's Politics," in *J.S. Mill's Political Thought: A Bicentennial Reassessment*, edited by Urbinati and Zakaras, 147–65. Cambridge: Cambridge University Press, 2007.
- *The Idea of Freedom*. Oxford: Oxford University Press, 1979.
- "John Stuart Mill and the Open Society." *The Listener* 89, no. 2303 (1973): 633–5.
- *J.S. Mill*. London: Routledge, 1974.
- *The Philosophy of John Stuart Mill*. London: Macmillan, 1970.
- "Property, Liberty, and *On Liberty*." *Royal Institute of Philosophy Lectures* 15 (1983): 217–31.
Saint-Simon, Henri comte de. "Catechism of the Industrialists." In *The Political Thought of Saint-Simon*, edited Ghita Ionescu, 182–203. Oxford: Oxford University Press, 1976.
- *Henri Saint-Simon (1780–1825): Selected Writings on Science, Industry, and Social Organisation*. Edited and translated by Keith Taylor. London: Croom Helm, 1975.

The Saint-Simonians. *The Doctrine of Saint-Simon: An Exposition, First Year, 1828–29*. Translated by Georg Iggers. Boston: Beacon Press, 1958.

Sarvasy, Wendy. "J.S. Mill's Theory of Democracy for a Period of Transition between Capitalism and Socialism." *Polity* 16, no. 4 (1984): 567–87.

– "A Reconsideration of the Development and Structure of John Stuart Mill's Socialism." *Western Political Quarterly* 38, no. 2 (1985): 312–33.

Schapiro, Salwyn J. "John Stuart Mill, Pioneer of Democratic Liberalism in England." *Journal of the History of Ideas* 4, no. 2 (1943): 127–60.

Schemmel, Christian. "Distributive and Relational Equality." *Politics, Philosophy, and Economics* 11, no. 2 (2011): 123–48.

– "Social Equality – or Just Justice?" In *Social Equality – on What It Means to Be Equals*, edited by Carina Fourie, Fabian Schuppert, and Ivo Wallimann-Helmer, 146–66. Oxford: Oxford University Press, 2015.

Schwartz, Pedro. *The New Political Economy of J.S. Mill*. Translated by Weidenfeld and Nicholson. London: London School of Economics, 1972.

Shleifer, Andrei, and Robert W. Vishny. "The Politics of Market Socialism." *Journal of Economic Perspectives* 8, no. 2 (1994): 165–76.

Skinner, Quentin. *Visions of Politics*, vol. 1: *Regarding Method*. Cambridge: Cambridge University Press, 2002.

Skorupski, John. *John Stuart Mill*. London: Routledge, 1988.

Smith, G.W. "J.S. Mill on Freedom." In *Conceptions of On Liberty in Political Philosophy*, edited by Z.A. Pelczynski and John Gray, 182–216. London: St. Martin's Press, 1984.

– "Social Liberty and Free Agency: Some Ambiguities in Mill's Conception of Freedom." In *J.S. Mill "On Liberty" in Focus*, edited by Gray and Smith, 239–59. Abingdon: Routledge, 1991.

Smith, Vardaman R. "John Stuart Mill's Famous Distinction between Production and Distribution." *Economics and Philosophy* 1 (1985): 267–84.

Southey, Robert. "Review of 'Doctrine de Saint Simon,' *Exposition*. Première Année 1828–1829, Seconde edition, Paris 1830." *Quarterly Review* 45 (July 1831): 407–50.

Stafford, William. "How Can a Paradigmatic Liberal Call Himself a Socialist? The Case of John Stuart Mill." *Journal of Political Ideologies* 3, no. 3 (1998): 325–45.

– *John Stuart Mill*. Basingstoke: Macmillan, 1998.

– "Nicholas Capaldi, *John Stuart Mill: A Biography*." *Utilitas* 18, no. 4 (2006): 445–7.

Stephen, James Fitzjames. *On Liberty, Equality, Fraternity*. New York: H. Holt and Company, 1882.

Stephen, Leslie. *The English Utilitarians*. London: London School of Economics and Political Science, 1950.
Sullivan, Eileen. "Liberalism and Imperialism: J.S. Mill's Defence of the British Empire." *Journal of the History of Ideas* 44, no. 4 (1983): 599–617.
Taylor, Barbara. *Eve and the New Jerusalem*. London: Virago Press, 1983.
Taylor, Charles. *Philosophy and the Human Sciences: Philosophical Papers* 2. Cambridge: Cambridge University Press, 1985.
Taylor Mill, Harriet. *Complete Works of Harriet Taylor Mill*. Edited by Jo Ellen Jacobs. Bloomington: Indiana University Press, 1998.
Ten, C.L. *Mill On Liberty*. Oxford: Clarendon Press, 1980.
– "Mill on Self-Regarding Actions." *Philosophy* 43, no. 163 (1968): 29–37.
Thomas, William. *Mill*. Oxford: Oxford University Press, 1985.
– *The Philosophical Radicals: Nine Studies in Theory and Practice, 1817–1841*. Oxford: Clarendon Press, 1979.
Thompson, E.P. *The Making of the English Working Class*. Harmondsworth: Penguin, 1968.
Thompson, William. *An Inquiry into the Distribution of Wealth Most Conducive to Human Happiness*. London: Longman, Hurst, Rees, Orme, Brown and Green, 1824.
Thompson, William, and Anna Doyle Wheeler. *Appeal of One Half the Human Race, Women, against the Pretensions of the Other Half, Men, to Retain Them in Political, and thence in Civil and Domestic, Slavery*. Bristol: Thoemmes Press, 1994.
Turner, Piers Norris. "Luck and Distributive Justice in Mill." In *The Routledge Handbook of the Philosophy and Psychology of Luck*, edited by Ian M. Church and Robert J. Hartman, 80–93. London: Routledge, 2019.
– "Mill's Evolutionary Theory of Justice: Reflections on Persky." *Utilitas* 32, no. 2 (2020): 131–46.
Tunick, Mark. "Tolerant Imperialism: John Stuart Mill's Defence of British Rule in India." *Review of Politics* 68, no. 4 (2006): 586–611.
Urbinati, Nadia. "John Stuart Mill on Androgyny and Ideal Marriage." *Political Theory* 19, no. 4 (1991): 626–48.
– *Mill on Democracy: From the Athenian Polis to Representative Government*. Chicago: University of Chicago Press, 2002.
Varouxakis, Georgios. *Victorian Political Thought on France and the French*. Basingstoke; Palgrave, 2002.
Von Mises, Ludwig. *Liberalism: A Socio-Economic Exposition*. Mission: Sheed Andrews and McMeel, 1978.
"W.E.H." *The Co-operative Magazine and Monthly Herald*. London, 1826.

Webb, Sydney. "The Difficulties of Individualism." In *Socialism and Individualism* by Sidney Webb, George Bernard Shaw, Sidney Ball, and Sir Oliver Lodge. The Fabian Socialist Series no. 3, 5–28. London: A.C. Fifield, 1908.

Williams, Geraint L. *John Stuart Mill On Politics and Society*. Hassocks: The Harvester Press, 1976.

Winch, Donald. *Wealth and Life: Essays on the Intellectual History of Political Economy in Britain, 1848–1914*. Cambridge: Cambridge University Press, 2009.

Wollheim, Richard. "John Stuart Mill and Isaiah Berlin: The Ends of Life and the Preliminaries of Liberty." In *J.S. Mill: On Liberty in Focus*, edited by Gray and Smith, 260–77. London: Routledge, 1991.

Yunker, James A. "A Survey of Market Socialist Forms." *Annals of Public and Cooperative Economy* 46 (1975): 131–62.

– "Would Democracy Survive under Market Socialism?" *Polity* 18, no. 4 (1996): 678–95.

PERIODICALS AND NEWSPAPERS

The Examiner, 3 November 1833–2 February 1834.
The Literary Gazette, 7 December 1833.
The Times, 31 August 1832–8 November 1833.

INDEX

1848, 14, 81, 97, 125, 133, 139, 146, 191, 194, 200, 220–1, 247; edition of *Principles of Political Economy*, 121, 132, 200, 286, 301, 328; February Revolution (in France), 97, 142, 145, 157, 163, 194; Provisional Government of France, 97, 145, 160, 183, 308

1868, Reform Act, 275

Anderson, Elizabeth, 177, 178–80

Appeal of One Half the Human Race, Women, Against the Pretensions of the other Half, Men, to Retain Them in Political, and thence in Civil and Domestic, Slavery, 95, 129

association, 74, 85, 87, 98, 99, 100, 101, 106, 107, 112–14, 115, 135, 157, 163, 184, 191, 200, 201, 210, 212, 247, 248, 313; communist types of, 99, 109, 111, 116, 128, 134, 305; of equals, marriage as, 163, 168; freedom of, 157, 253; Land Tenure Reform, 322; Marx's use of, 16, 262; and trade unions, 282; women's equal participation in, necessity of, 130–1, 201, 210. *See also* cooperation; profit-sharing

associationist psychology, 21, 24

L'Atelier, 106

Auguste Comte, 50, 198, 259

authoritative government actions, 48–50, 65, 77, 206

Autobiography, 16, 29, 41, 81, 83, 131, 198, 201, 233, 246, 252–3, 259, 260–1, 268, 302

autonomy, 147, 150, 155, 177, 310, 313; and equality, 164, 178; and happiness, 310; and Mill's use of *autonomie*, 310. *See also* liberty

Austin, John and Sarah, 142, 292, 329

Baccarini, Elvio, 229–30, 325

Baum, Bruce, 11–12, 45, 147, 156–60; on Mill's conception of freedom, 153–5, 158; on Mill's "liberal socialism," 12, 154–5

Bazard, Amand, 95

Bentham, Jeremy: early influence on Mill, 6, 19, 21, 44, 138, 231; link to Robert Owen, 22, 277; link to William Thompson, 276; Mill's critical appraisal of, 36–9, 42, 329; on women's suffrage, 275

Berger, Fred R., 152, 161–2, 164, 169, 171, 173, 177–8, 315–6

Biagini, Eugenio, 152, 183, 318

Blanc, Louis, 94, 96–7, 99–101, 191, 292, 294–5; and "capitalism," 280; on competition, 103–6; and delayed marriage, 276; principle of justice of, 99–100, 123, 125, 140, 162, 171, 175, 176–7, 287, 298

Briggs, Henry, 282

Buchez, Philippe, 97, 100, 106

Cabet, Etienne, 94, 96, 118, 197; and communism, 99–101; as form of state socialism, 265; and *Voyage en Icarie*, 291. *See also* Icarianism
Capaldi, Nicholas, 310
Carlyle, Thomas, 36–7, 40, 284; idea of a "cash nexus," Mill's use of, 80, 133; on Mill becoming a German mystic, 27; Mill's changing attitude toward, 34, 41, 240, 329
Carnot, Hippolyte, 106
Carnot, Sadi, 295
Chapters on Socialism, throughout; and communism, 116, 120–1; concerns about management in communist communities in, 110–11; consideration of socialist critiques of capitalism in, 103–8; and the longevity of Mill's socialism, 244–8; life as a "race" in, 64; and population control, 297
Chartists, 40, 213
Christian Socialism, 95, 245
Claeys, Gregory 81; on cooperation and liberty, 155–6, 311; on the development of Mill's socialism, 81; on Harriet Taylor and communism, 304; on Mill and having children if you cannot support them, 307; on Mill and inheritance, 67–71, 285; on Mill and land reform, 287, 321–2; on Mill and taxation, 66; on Mill's antipaternalism and his socialism, 12; on Mill's engagement with Fourier, 291
Claims of Labour, The, 65, 198, 199–200, 222, 320
class warfare, 36, 41, 56, 220, 240, 257, 283; eradicated in "ideal" reformed system of individual property, 64–5; healed by profit-sharing, 39–40, 41, 80, 220; Marx on, 16; Mill's hopes for a new Reform Party to help end, 39; and plural voting, 220–1; socialism as the way to end, 89, 133, 136, 223, 266, 295
Cohen, G.A., 241, 296
Coleridge, Samuel Taylor, 40, 41, 240, 280, 329
colonialism, 315; "home," 73; and India, 315; by Jesuits in Paraguay, 115; and landownership in Australia and New Zealand, 61; and population control, 39–40
colonists, as part of thought experiment, 57–65, 80, 284
Comte, Auguste, 329; idea of labour, 46–7, 114, 134; Positivist religion of, 232, 319; and the Saint-Simonians, 25, 134, 277; tripartite scheme of progress in history, 27, 34, 140
communism: changing assessment of, in *Principles of Political Economy*, 248, 301; in *Chapters on Socialism*, 244–5; different to socialism (for Mill), 83, 98–101, 121, 126–7, 251; and distributive justice, 123, 126; and efficiency, 128; etymology of, 98, 274; fate of Owenite experiments in, 305; feasibility of, 109–10, 115–16, 134–5, 248, 250–1, 299–300; Harriet Taylor's view of, 132–3, 250–1, 300, 304; if practicable, only defensible form of society, 117, 135, 248; impact of on utility, 131–3, 252; and individual property, 44, 54, 82–4, 91, 160; and liberty/individuality, 52, 84, 119–22, 127, 131, 244–5,

250–1, 301; meaning of, for Mill, 84, 99–101; Mill's criticisms of, 110–2, 119–20, 252; Mill's view of the availability of, 115–7, 135; and population control, 109; and social harmony, 134, 305; twentieth-century forms of, 14, 121

Communist Manifesto, The, 14, 98

communitarianism, 183–4, 318

community wealth-building, 14, 208, 237

competition, 104–8, 129, 205, 239, 282–3; Blanc's critique of, 104–5; from cooperatives, impact on the wage market of, 200–1; under cooperative socialism, 205, 234, 257; and Fourierism, 298; as "friendly rivalry," 106, 205, 234; Mill's assessment of socialist critiques of, 103–8, 126–7; Mill's commitment to makes him a market socialist, 323; possibilities for a reformed type of, 22, 51; reality of in contemporary society, 49; as reason Mill could not be a socialist, 8, 103, 107–8, 242; and the social ethos, 133, 239

Considerant, Victor, 96, 103, 105, 291, 295; on competition, 105; link to Mill's idea of "friendly rivalry," 305; Mill's use of as exemplar of socialism; 103; and Provisional Government, 97; and utopian socialism, 94; and women's suffrage, 275

Considerations on Representative Government, 12, 209, 259; discussion of communism in, 116, 135, 198, 300; and plural voting, 211, 218–31; and secret ballot, 211, 213–18

cooperation, 7, 101, 184, 202–8; "brilliant future reserved to principle of," 85; of labour, 160, 313–4; Mill's strictures on those who tried to selfishly limit benefits of, 271; movement of workers toward, 86–7; "new millennium" of, 85, 250; Owenite system of, 22–3, 276

cooperative socialism, 4, 11, 121, 127, 135–6, 204, 222, 241, 245, 250; and efficiency, 128; historical forms of, 97, 100; and liberty, 129; and social justice, 130

cooperatives: availability of, 115, 117; and communal property, 203, 234, 268; competition between, 106, 128, 205, 263, 298; consumer, 105–6, 112–13, 203, 205, 234, 263–4; and democracy, 156–7, 163, 220, 221–5, 234, 256; and distributive justice, 123, 181, 203–5, 234, 288, 324; farms, 73, 205; feasibility of, 112–13; and liberty, 121, 129, 155, 156–60, 202–4, 234, 258, 265, 311; and market socialism, 323; Mill's support for Wolverhampton Platelock, 330; Mill's view of state loans to support, 308, 318; Mill's work to change law to enable easier set-up of, 289–90; organic transformation of society by, 87–9, 91, 107, 114, 135–6, 189, 197, 199–201, 223, 321; preferred to state provision, 206–8, 263–5; producer, 106, 112–3, 205, 222; scope for work not in, under socialism, 313; and social justice, 83, 156, 201, 210, 321; and technological innovation, 87;

and trade unions, 282; and unity, 189–90; and welfare "relief," 308, 316–17; wholesale, 106, 128, 205; worker-owned, 39, 59, 72, 101, 135, 146, 155–8, 200–1, 241
Co-operator, The, 290
Cremer, William Randal, 292
critical ages, 20, 27–8, 33–42, 90, 134, 148, 153, 193, 278, 283

D'Eichthal, Gustave, 25, 95, 277, 291, 292, 305
democracy, 4, 12, 45, 146, 202, 212–13, 256, 320; achievable in the "old world," 146; and equality, 156–9; extension of, in the interest of the poorer classes, 139; and freedom, 157–9, 209, 260; importance of participation in, 152, 156–7; Mill's ideal institutions of, 212–31; and public health, 264; and worker-cooperatives, 11, 156–7, 268
Democracy in America, 79, 209, 286
democratic equality, 178–9. *See also* relational egalitarianism
desert, 161, 164, 165, 168, 173–7, 179, 200, 240. *See also* equality
Destinée Sociale, La, 96
Disraeli, Benjamin, 280
distributive justice, 12, 83, 99, 140, 160–83, 184, 202–5, 208, 234, 260; and capitalism, 53–4, 102, 113; Cohen's critiques of Rawls regarding, 241; as equal shares, 170, 175; equal shares and "higher" principles of, 77–8, 86, 99–100, 113, 114, 124, 125, 162, 170–1, 246, 283, 288, 298; as equality of welfare, 166–7; as "good for good," 169–70; and impartiality, 164, 165–71;

and inheritance, 68; and laws of distribution, 29–32, 284; and luck-egalitarianism, 161–83; and merit or desert, 173–77, 240; Mill's assessment of socialist principles of, 103 110, 113–14, 122–6, 131–3, 135–6; Mill's progressive view of, 123, 246, 307, 322; and monopoly profits, 49, 264–5; and piecework, 113; principles of adopted by worker-cooperatives, 288, 324; Rawls's, 302; in a reformed system of individual property, 57, 59–62, 65, 71, 75–8, 80–1, 91; and relational equality, 178–83; as reward proportioned to labour or exertion, 169, 173–5; and sufficientarianism, 161, 171–3, 245, 307; and taxation, 69, 72, 285, 287; understood as "from each according to his capacity, to each according to his needs," 140, 161–2, 164–5, 169, 171, 175, 182, 196, 230; and utility, 84–5, 143
divorce, 129–30, 167, 211
Donner, Wendy, 148–9, 271
"droit do travail," 172, 307–8
Dupont-White, Charles, 295
Duvreyier, Charles, 95

education, 78; as barrier to Mill being a socialist, 8; and change in character, 32, 34–5, 117, 138, 186–7, 191, 260; cooperation as, 114, 189, 201, 212, 288; democracy makes it in the interest of "opulent classes" to promote, 139; duty to provide by parents, 67–8; and equality, 161, 164, 167–8, 191, 210, 256; "moral," 116–17, 138, 174, 186; necessary for communism to be feasible, 113,

116, 247; and permanent interests, 148–9; and plural votes, 221–30, 325; and the population rate, 22–3, 87; and public voting, 218; radical reform needed, for achieving equality between the sexes, 210; state provision of, 49–50, 77, 205–6, 281; and talent, 173, 176

efficiency (and inefficiency), 29, 87, 138; of capitalism, 52, 103–5, 263; and justice, 173–4; of a reformed system of individual property; 63–5, 78; of socialism, 49, 128–9, 321; and state provision of goods and services, 73, 322

effort, 53–4, 63, 66, 74, 76, 100, 112, 114, 122, 124–5, 161–2, 164, 169, 173–6, 240, 317. *See also* desert; exertion

Ekelund, Robert B., 288, 307, 316–17, 320

emulation, 106, 109, 297

Enfantin, Barthélemy Prosper, 95, 130

Engels, Friedrich, 14, 16, 94, 274, 292

environmentalism, 14, 54, 62, 64, 79, 91, 236–7, 264, 268, 283

equality, 12, 16, 79, 131–3, 137, 160–83, 184–5, 202, 268–9, 294; advancing civilization creates greater, 190, 209; and capitalism, 52–4, 283; of electoral districts, 20; and equal justice, 40; as equal treatment, 164–77, 314; and exertion, 173–5; formal, 256; of happiness, 163; and impartiality, 164–6, 171, 181, 316; increasingly demanded by workers, 85, 151; and liberty, 84–5, 119, 121, 145–6, 157, 159, 160, 167, 262, 265–7; and luck-egalitarianism, 176–7, 182–3, 316; in marriage and the family, 163, 209–11, 234–5, 241; and merit, 164, 168, 170, 173–7 (*see also* desert); of opportunity, 23, 53, 75, 78, 286; and oppression, 151; patriarchal understanding of in social contract, 318; principle of perfect, 21, 26, 178, 182; and a reformed regime of individual property, 57–63, 65, 71, 76–7, 240–1; relational, 162–3, 177–83, 199–200, 205, 210–11, 217–18, 256 (*see also* relational egalitarianism); of rights, 21, 148, 167–9; of shares, 77–8, 84, 99, 113, 123–6, 131, 135, 162, 169–71, 175; social, 258, 286; society of, 191–2, 209, 230; and sufficiency, 161, 164, 171–3; and talent, 173–4; and taxation, 66–7, 176, 207, 316; and virtue, 173, 175–6, 179; of voice in decision-making, 156, 158, 225; of votes, 219–21, 226, 229–31, 315; of welfare, 166–7; of women, 19, 163, 129–31, 156, 201, 209–11, 234–5, 236, 284, 294, 322–3; of work, 110–11; between workers and employers, 135; of worth as human beings, 226. *See also* inequality

Enfranchisement of Women, 290

Essay on Coleridge, 37

Essay on Government, 26, 211

Estlund, David, 238

Examiner, The, 129, 291

exertion, 52–3, 61, 67–9, 72, 76, 102, 135, 169, 173–7, 201, 317. *See also* effort; desert

Fabianism, 300

family, 284, 324; radical change to needed, 189, 208–9, 210–11, 235, 241,

268; role of in character-creation, 187, 202, 209, 235; socialist treatment of, 26
feminism, 23, 151, 160, 163, 209–10, 284, 288, 313, 322–3, 324; and socialism, 21, 23, 129–31, 189, 303
Flew, Anthony, 281, 321
Fontana-Rava, Gregorio, 95, 290–1
Fourier, Charles, 94, 96, 100–1, 197, 203–4, 291, 301, 305; acceptance of limited individual property, 98, 203–4; on "attractive labour," 112; on competition, 106, 297, 298, 305; idea of minimum income, 316, 320; "peculiar opinions on marriage," 130; on peer review of performance and ability, 225
Fourierism, 94, 100–1, 121, 202–3, 234, 291, 299; availability of, 115–17, 298; and distributive justice, 123–6, 131; feasibility of, 108, 111–12, 298; and individuality, 121, 131. *See also* Fourier, Charles
fraternity, 140, 157, 183–95, 203, 205, 208, 217, 230–1, 234–6, 241, 243, 306; and "communitarian" liberalism, 318; patriarchal meaning of in social contract, 318; and permanent interests, 255–68
Fredman, L.E., 275, 299–300
freedom. *See* liberty
French Revolution (1789), 21, 38, 146, 231
friendly rivalry, 106, 136, 205, 234, 305. *See also* emulation
Furnivall, Frederick J., 245

Garnier-Pages, Louis, 106
Gaus, Gerald, 238
Girondins, 21

Gladstone, William, 183, 318; and reform of the civil service, 329
Gordon, B.L.J., 275, 299–300
Goudchaux, Michel, 106
Gray, John, 148, 149, 281, 308, 312, 323
growth, 54–5, 62, 64, 75, 78–9, 234, 236. *See also* stationary state

Hales, John, 292
Hamburger, Joseph, 319
happiness, 36, 138; "beautiful characters" promote without need for moral rules, 259; and the elements, 304; equal claim of all to, in the eyes of the legislator, 162–3, 165; and equality, 166–7, 177; general principle of, 141; indirect pursuit of, 24, 138, 141; and inequality, 175, 190; and liberty and individuality, 146–7, 153–4, 308, 310, 312; and religion of humanity, 232–3; and security of subsistence, 132–3, 144, 172; and social harmony, 36, 186, 191, 261; socialism will achieve greatest of greatest number, 18, 42, 194–6, 238, 266–7, 321. *See also* utility
harm, 143, 147–9, 192–3, 258–9, 261, 263, 302, 309
harm principle, 18, 147, 153–4, 231, 235, 257, 258–9, 262, 309, 311–12; Harriet Taylor's early version of, 253; and voting, 231. *See also* liberty; liberty principle
Harrison, Frederic, 294
Hartley, David, 21
Helps, Arthur, 167, 240
Himmelfarb, Gertrude, 279, 312; and "two Mills" thesis, 5, 271

history, Mill's philosophy of, 20, 24, 26–9, 34–5, 42, 81, 89–90, 191, 274, 277–8, 313
History of the French Revolution, 97, 292
Holyoake, George Jacob, 95, 100, 276, 290; on competition, 106; and independence, 311
Howell, George, 292

Icarianism, 94, 96, 101, 291; costliness of, 118, 127. *See also* Cabet, Etienne
incentives (for work), 74, 78, 110
independence, 147, 151, 160, 201, 241; and equality, 23, 84, 167–8, 182, 184; freedom as, 151–3, 155, 158, 159, 177, 192, 240, 311; and the harm principle, 153; and happiness, 177; and inheritance, 62–3, 65, 67, 69–70, 73, 204, 285; lack of in capitalism, 156; and public voting, 217; and a reformed regime of individual property, 240; and socialism, 118, 121, 136, 146, 155, 201–2, 206–7; of thought, a feature of critical ages, 134; of women, 129, 210; workers increasingly demanding, 85–7, 151, 236, 283. *See also* liberty
individualism, 16, 105, 133–5, 184, 192, 196
individuality, 52, 146–8, 150–4, 196, 209, 241, 243, 254–5, 256, 269, 312, 313; compatible with socialism, 203, 234–5, 242, 258, 262; and contemporary capitalism, 52, 153–4, 283; deciding factor in determining best form of future society, 84–5, 160; and fraternity, 184, 186–7, 192, 209, 259, 261; and happiness, 24, 241, 312; Harriet Taylor's defence of, 253; and independence, 177, 311; and plural voting, 230–1; and a reformed regime of individual property, 58–9, 79, 252; and the Religion of Humanity, 233; risks posed by socialism to, 82, 118–22, 131, 244, 258, 269; socialism necessary for, 146, 192, 262, 301, 312; socialism would improve, 129, 131, 188; and the tyranny of the majority, 46, 184, 209; and women, 210–11. *See also* liberty
inequality, 39, 52–4, 57–63, 66–7, 71, 76–7, 91, 124–5, 138, 161–6, 168, 170–1, 175–6, 226–7, 256, 298; and liberty, 84–5; and merit, 173, 199–200; permitted under socialism, 99, 114; and relational egalitarianism, 178–83; of votes, 228–31; of women, 209, 226; of worth as human beings, 226. *See also* equality
inheritance, 14, 29, 44, 62–3, 65–71, 73, 102, 204, 207, 237, 240, 250, 285; and generational inequality, 51, 64–5, 76, 268; Mill's distinction between right to bequeath and right to inherit, 285
International Workingmen's Association, 97, 293, 294
Inquiry into the Distribution of Wealth Most Conducive to Human Happiness, An, 95
Ivanković, Viktor, 229–30, 325

Jensen, Hans, 288
Jones, John "Gale," 95
July Revolution (1830), 95, 138

Keynes, John Maynard, 236
Kurer, Oskar, 140, 183, 184–5, 193–4, 283, 319–20, 320

laisser-faire, 44–5, 48–51, 80, 121, 146, 240; "the general rule," 41, 45, 48, 50–1
laissez-faire, 23, 30, 32, 36–9, 44–51, 80, 91, 146, 196, 206, 236–7, 255–6, 281, 283
Land Tenure Reform Association, 68–9, 250, 322
Larsen, Timothy, 326
Law, Harriet, 292
laws of production and distribution, difference between, 20, 24, 26, 29–32, 42, 81, 245, 284
Lechavalier, Jules, 96
Leclaire, Edme-Jean, 199, 200
left-libertarianism, 57–8, 240
lemonade (pink), sea to taste of after melting of polar icecaps, according to Fourier, 96
Letters on the Commune, 97
liberal socialism, 12, 15, 237
liberty, 21, 23, 34–5, 41, 52, 145–60, 193–4, 196, 235, 241, 243, 309; and authoritative government actions, 48; criticisms of capitalism on grounds of, 52, 120–1, 158; and economic freedom, 154–9; and equality, 84, 131, 163, 167–8, 178–80, 191–2, 266; and fraternity, 184–6, 191–3, 238; Harriet Taylor's view of, 253–4; and interests, 148, 262, 265; Mill's concept not to be confused with *laissez-faire*, 45; and plural voting, 219; "positive" and "negative" concepts of, 9, 15–16, 146, 152, 155, 244, 310, 311; of production and exchange, 29, 157; and progress, 266; and public voting, 217; and a reformed system of individual property, 58–9, 65, 76, 78–80, 84, 91; republican concept of, 152, 318; as self-government, 150–1, 155; and socialism, 11–12, 16, 22–3, 118–20, 129–31, 136, 155–60, 185, 201–3, 246–7, 250, 252, 254, 255, 259–62, 266–7, 294; and the tyranny of the majority, 258, 260; and utility, 140–1, 146–60, 265, 308, 310. *See also* independence; individuality; sovereignty
liberty principle, or principle of liberty, 147, 258, 260, 263. *See also* harm principle
Lloyd, William Forster, 292

Malthus, Thomas, 21, 109, 278; opposition to socialism, 275; "population principle" bone of contention between Mill and Owenites in 1820s, 275–6
Malthusianism, 8, 87, 275–6
Marie, Alexandre, 106
Marrast, Armand, 106
Marx, Karl, 10, 14, 16, 17, 31, 89, 97–8, 235–6, 243, 262, 274, 279, 289, 292, 293, 295, 312, 313–14; criticisms of "utopian" socialism, 84, 94; use of the term "capitalism," 280
Marxism, 4, 10, 14–17, 94, 97–8, 156, 242–3, 274, 293, 295, 313–14. *See also* revolutionary socialists
marriage, 49, 129, 130, 163, 167–8, 209–11, 303, 322–3; "delayed" as means to population control, 275–6
Martineau, Harriet, 30

Maurice, Frederick, 95
Mazzini, Giuseppe, 183, 318
Megill, Alan, D., 319
mental "crisis," 20, 23–5, 36, 40, 42, 43, 44, 138–40, 239
middle classes, 39–40, 55; need for revolution in character of, 220; oppression of working class by, 150–1, 222
Mill, James, 19, 21, 22, 26, 42, 231, 275, 278
Miller, Dale E.: on Mill's socialism, 9, 82–3, 86, 90, 261–2, 282–3, 313, 326; on Mill and plural voting, 221–3
Millgram, Elijah, 271, 329
Morales, Maria, 21, 177, 178, 183, 188, 189
Mottershead, Thomas, 292

Napoleon, III, Louis, 220, 223
national workshops, 97, 295
Neale, Edward Vansittart, 95, 100, 290; on competition, 106; on population control, 276
non-authoritative government actions, 48–50, 65, 206, 281

Odger, George, 292
On Liberty 15–16, 35, 45, 52, 146, 149–50, 154, 193, 209, 243–4, 249, 252, 258–9, 312, 319; compatible with Mill's socialism, 249, 254–5, 262–6; Harriet Taylor's role in writing, 5, 243, 249, 252–4
On Marriage, 130, 211, 259, 303
oppression, 100, 138, 150–2, 184, 235, 261, 267, 269, 326; freedom from, 147, 150–1; freedom as non-, 152; and relational egalitarianism, 178–80. *See also* liberty
organic ages, 10, 20, 27–8, 34–42, 84, 134, 153–4, 192–3, 231, 258, 263
Owen, Robert, 22, 94, 95, 99–101, 103, 105, 108, 197, 250; connection to James Mill and Jeremy Bentham, 22; distributive principles of, 283; Fourier "a sort of," 96; and population control, 109, 276
Owenism, 4, 95, 101, 117–18, 305; "costliness" of, 117–18; debates with supporters of in 1820s, 22, 93, 109–10, 117–19, 275–6; and distributive justice, 123, 283; and etymology of socialism, 274; feasibility of, 22, 33, 93, 108–11; and feminism, 130, 303; and liberty, 22, 118–19; and population control, 275–6; Saint-Simonism superior to, 25, 33, 302; spread of, good for frightening the aristocracy, 139

Palais de Luxembourg, 191, 295
Paris Commune, 294–5
Passions of the Human Soul, The, 96, 291
paternalism, 22, 151, 194, 240; anti-, 12, 23, 151, 326
patriarchy, 151, 196, 235, 318; need to dismantle, 210
perfection, 9, 28, 33, 37, 82, 93; perfectionism, 3, 37, 193–4
permanent interests of man as progressive being, 36, 143, 147–9, 188, 309; and socialism, 255–68. *See also* utility
Persky, Joseph, 9, 138, 235–7, 275, 284; on Marx's critique of Mill, 279;

on Mill's "luck-egalitarianism", 12, 161–2, 173–7; on Mill's materialist conception of history, 89–90, 274, 313; on Mill's progressive view of justice, 9, 123, 140, 236, 278; on Mill's socialism, 207, 242, 272; on similarities between Marx and Mill, 289, 312; on Mill's view of the likelihood of socialism arriving, 81, 86–90, 273

philosophic-radicalism, 20–5, 28, 32, 35, 39–40, 42, 138, 140, 198, 211–12, 275

Philippe, Louis I, 194

piecework, 113–14; opposition to by trade unions, 123–4

Pieper, Wilhelm, 292

Place, Francis, 27, 278

plural voting, 211, 212, 218–31, 275, 325–6

Poor Law, 50, 59–60, 79, 131–2, 143–4, 308

Prati, Giacchino, 95, 290–1

primogeniture, 44, 68

Principles of Political Economy, throughout; changes to the Prefaces of, 244–9; cheap editions of planned by socialists, 245, 290; Harriet Taylor's role in authoring, 5, 132–3, 249–53, 304, 328; Marx immersed himself in, 292

profit-sharing, 6, 59, 65, 74–80, 85, 91, 114, 155, 160, 189, 199–200, 240, 288; and trade unions, 282

progress, 27–8, 32, 33, 44, 51, 87, 89, 119, 123–4, 138–9, 140–1, 145–6, 148–9, 159–62, 176, 183–5, 189, 190–1, 193–4, 218, 220, 231, 233, 242, 261, 265–6, 272, 278, 306, 315; and equality between the sexes, 209–10; Mill's view of the "ultimate result of," 237, 239–40, 246, 247, 248

property: choice between individual and communal, 82–91, 116, 160; church, 191; communal, 20, 26, 31, 58, 88, 98–9, 201, 203, 322, 234, 323; compensation due for violations of rights in, 142, 321; current distribution of rooted in conquest and force, 65; diffusion of private, 78–9, 237; freedom and private, 52, 121, 154–5, 160, 252; just distributions of, 170–1; justice, and communal, 123, 126, 246, 283; justification of private, 52–4, 113–14, 122–3, 169–70, 246–7; in land, 54, 60–2, 71–3, 203, 240, 287 – problems with nationalization of, 68–70, 143, 321–2; Malthus's critique of communal, 275–6; men viewing women as, 211; Mill's commitment to private, a barrier to socialism, 8, 321; ownership of not good ground for plural votes, 213, 326; private not an "indefeasible fact," 29–34, 142, 145, 284, 321; private not necessarily fundamental to utility, 29; reform to regime of individual, 44, 51, 54, 56–81, 204, 235, 240, 286; rights, under socialism, 98–9, 315–16; "rights of industry" versus rights of, 199; security of subsistence and private, 252; socialism opposed to private, 98; socialism threatening "unjust violations of," 139

property-owning democracy, 12, 237, 240–1, 306

Proudhon, Pierre-Joseph, 132, 280

public voting, 211, 212–8. *See also* secret ballot

Raeder, Linda, 319
Rawls, John, 12, 15, 140, 148–9, 236–7, 241, 244, 254, 255, 302, 306, 309, 318
Rees, John C., 149, 309
Reeves, Richard, 271
relational egalitarianism, 161–5, 168–9, 172, 177–83, 196, 218–19, 225–6, 241, 316. *See also* equality
religion of humanity, 134, 189–90, 231–3, 235, 241, 319; clerisy of, 134, 189, 233, 319
representative government, 19–21, 25–6, 36, 85–6, 138, 156–7, 209, 212, 221, 224, 225, 230, 241, 256. *See also* democracy
Representative Reform Association, 292
revolution, 4, 18, 40, 100, 136, 142–3, 144, 145, 148, 220, 238, 267, 273, 287, 296, 307, 321; Mill's opposition to, a barrier to socialism, 8, 142–5, 273, 306
revolutionary socialists, 15, 93–4, 98, 100–1, 117, 127, 142, 241, 282, 292, 293, 294, 295, 296. *See also* Marx, Karl
Ricardo, David, 19, 21, 278, 280
rights, 21, 157, 163, 167–9, 172, 214, 227, 256, 294, 317; of bequest and inheritance, 65, 285; equal, 148, 167–8, 172, 180, 226; equal needed for women, 156, 201, 210, 294; fundamental, 133, 145, 148, 151, 163, 165–6; and harm, 149; Harriet Taylor on, 253; to have children, 284, 307; to individual liberty, 265; of industry and property, 199; to

personal freedom, of property, under socialism, 98–9, 203, 315–16; to "relief" irrevocably established, 143–4, 172; social construction, and non-absolute nature, of, 44–5, 72, 143, 148–9, 309; to strike, 282, 302; violations of, 172; to vote, 214, 217, 226, 229, 235, 315; to work, or "droit do travail," 172, 307–8
Riley, Jonathan, 8–9, 35–6, 82–91, 148, 271, 301, 306, 308, 323
Rochdale Pioneers, 100
Ryan, Alan, 5, 148, 271, 279, 302, 311, 312, 319, 323

Saint-Simon, Henri, 25, 95–6, 100, 125–6, 129–30, 197
Saint-Simonism, 4, 9, 20, 25–42, 43–4, 81, 89–90, 95–6, 101, 134, 138, 139–40, 199, 222, 250, 277, 278, 290–1, 302; availability of, 115–16; feasibility of, 108–9, 198; and feminism, 129–30, 303, 305; and freedom, 121, 265; might frighten aristocrats into supporting democratic reforms, 139; principles of justice of, 123, 125–6, 298; and religion, 134, 231–2, 304; superior to Owenism, 25, 33, 302
Sarvasy, Wendy, 8–10, 12, 120, 220–1, 278, 283, 293, 320
Say, Jean-Baptiste, 25, 278
Schemmel, Christian, 182
secondary principles, 140–1, 145, 194–6, 207–8, 241, 265; of equality, 163–4; moral, 259
secret ballot, 20, 212–18. *See also* public voting
security, 141–5, 154, 188, 207, 241, 262, 266, 321; economic independence

necessary for women's, 210–11; and justice, 143; and our permanent interests, 148, 192, 309; and revolutionary action, 141–2, 287; of subsistence, 133, 143–4, 183, 196, 250, 267, 309, 314
sexual morality, 130, 211
Skorupski, John, 310
slavery, 142, 166, 237; as metaphor for worker's unfreedom, 52, 105, 107, 244; voluntary, 49; and women's position in society, 95, 130
Smith, Adam, 19, 21, 278
Smith, Thomas, 97, 294
social ethos, 54–5, 62, 64–5, 75–6, 78, 79–80, 105, 133–5, 140, 183, 199, 209, 240, 288
social harmony, 36–40, 42, 140, 185–6, 241; in communist associations, 111, 134–5; contemporary capitalism incompatible with, 55–6; desire for made Mill a conservative, 279; improved by "ideal" regime of individual property, 64, 241; and the religion of humanity, 189. *See also* class warfare
social democracy, 207–8, 237
Socialisme devant le vieux monde, ou le vivant devant les morts, Le, 96, 291
sovereignty, 146–7, 149–53, 155, 310. *See also* liberty
Spirit of the Age, The, 27, 278, 304
Stafford, William, 242, 310, 323
state provision of goods and services, 4, 45–6, 49, 61, 65, 67, 72, 73–4, 77, 79, 104–5, 108, 203, 205–7, 232–3, 241, 264–5, 268, 281
stationary state, 54, 75, 78, 79, 80, 87–9, 90, 237

Stephen, James Fitzjames, 183, 186, 190, 306
Subjection of Women, The, 130, 156, 183–4, 233, 259, 284, 303
sympathy, 36–40, 56, 186–8, 193, 210–11. *See also* fraternity

taxation, 15, 66–71, 207, 250; and "equal sacrifice," 176, 316; "peculiar," on "Future Unearned Increase of the Rent of Land," 72, 240
Taylor, Harriet, 11, 13, 16, 29, 67, 242, 247, 260, 266–8, 290, 328; liberal, to Mill's conservative, 279; responsible for Mill's socialism, 5, 8, 243, 249–55, 271, 300, 328; role in writing *On Liberty*, 252–3; role in writing *Principles of Political Economy*, 304, 328; on utility and subsistence, 132–3, 250, 304
Ten, C.L., 271, 279, 309
Theory of the Four Movements, 96, 291
Thirlwall, Connop, 95
Thomas, William, 271
Thompson, William, 21, 22, 95, 100, 101, 106, 128, 197, 250, 276; and feminism, 21, 95, 129–30; 303
Thornton, William, 240
Thoughts on Parliamentary Reform, 211, 221
Three Essays on Religion, 198, 233, 259
Times, The, 290
Tocqueville, Alexis de, 79, 209, 286
Tollison, Robert D., 288, 307, 316–17, 320
trade unions, 50, 75, 123–4, 157, 282
Traité de Politique Positive, 25
Transon, Abel, 96

Turner, Piers Norris, 12, 138, 140, 161–4, 169, 171–7, 207, 314, 316, 317
tyranny, 100, 192, 267, 269; of custom, and social oppression, 184; of the majority, 46, 153–4, 217, 221, 263, 286; of society over the individual, 3, 131, 201, 238, 260

unity, 4, 35, 38, 39, 134, 186–94, 209, 211, 224, 227, 231, 233, 237, 260, 268, 270. *See also* fraternity
universal suffrage, 19, 21, 40, 189, 191, 209, 214, 217, 220, 225, 239, 256
Urbinati, Nadia, 152, 229, 325–6
utility, 17, 36, 49, 80–1, 84–5, 140, 159, 182, 195, 207, 267, 308; and competitive job markets, 263; and equality, 161, 174, 179; and fraternity, 185; and freedom, 159–60, 258, 310; indirect pursuit of, 24, 138, 140, 141, 184, 195, 235, 241, 265–6; in its "largest sense" related to "permanent interests," 36, 147–50, 255, 265; Mill's critique of Bentham's understanding of, 42; and plural voting, 219–20, 226–7; and property, 284; and public voting, 218; and the religion of humanity, 319; and security, 141–5; socialism necessary for maximization of, 191; and subsistence, 132, 143–4, 250–2. *See also* happiness

Utility of Religion, 304
utilitarianism, 3, 8, 35–6, 123, 141, 165–6, 182, 191, 232, 182
Utilitarianism, 15, 41, 162–3, 166, 173–4, 183, 184, 186, 259, 260, 287–8
utopia, 6–7, 33, 75, 80, 94, 106, 128, 190, 197–239, 241, 243, 256, 264, 268–9, 320, 321
utopian socialism, 6, 39, 84, 94, 160, 197, 241, 274

Voyage en Icarie, 291

wages, 30, 47, 50, 52, 58–9, 64, 65, 74, 75, 77, 80, 87–9, 91, 104–7, 114, 121, 123–4, 156, 163, 172, 200, 203, 205, 220, 257, 271, 278, 302, 311, 317, 320
Wheeler, Anna, 95, 129, 303
Winch, Donald, 328
working classes, 39–40, 50, 93, 98, 103, 117, 256, 271, 276; future in the hands of, for Mill, 85–6; increasing independence of, 85, 107, 151, 157, 236; oppression of, 150–1, 160; revolution in the character of, needed, 220; solidarity of, needed for world peace, 295; viewed as instruments of production, 135, 158
Workingmen and the War, 97